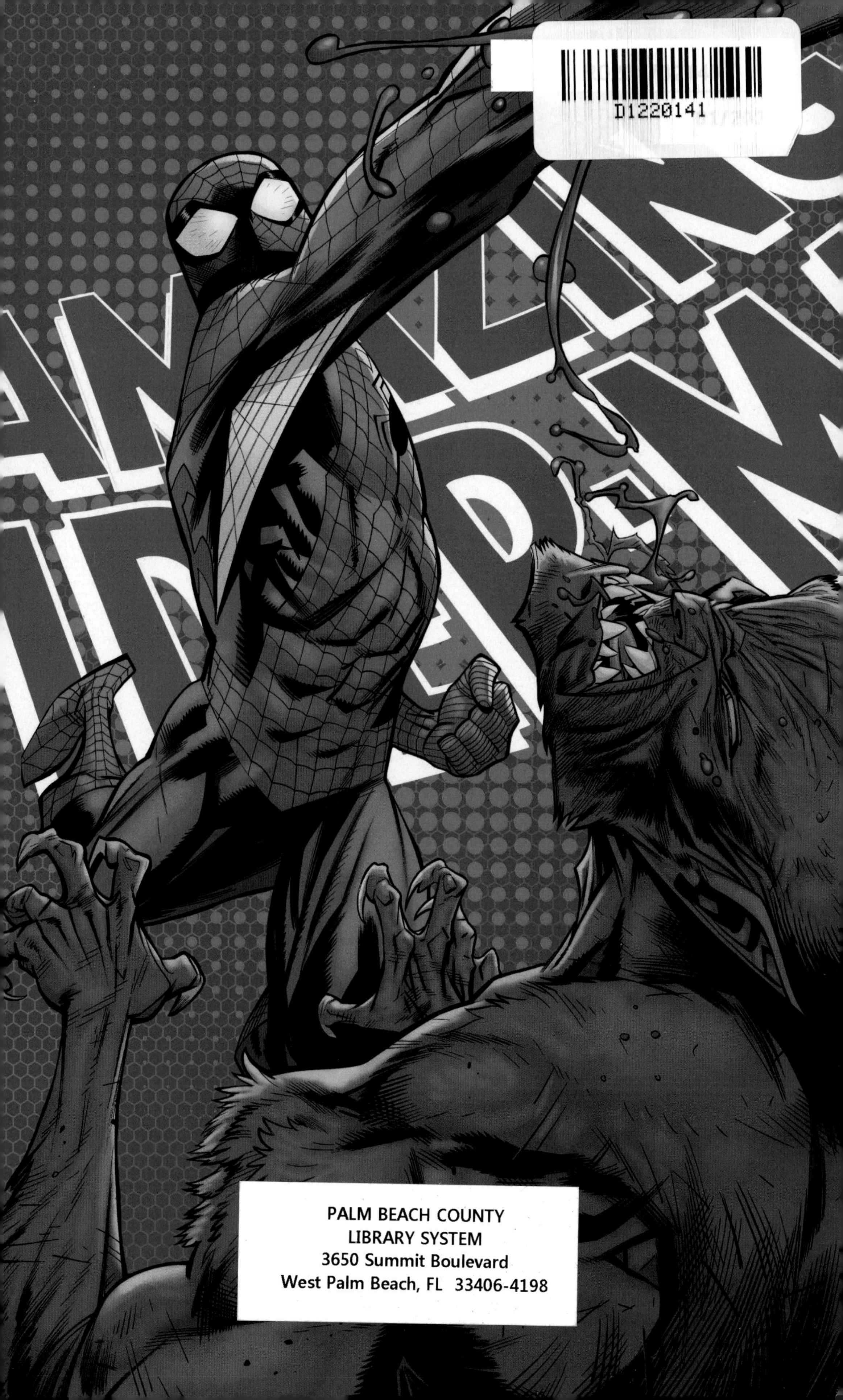

New York City is safe again, thanks to Spider-Man and a little help from the Spider-Man of the year 2099 and an incredible device created by one of Peter Parker's classmates at Empire State University: the Clairvoyant. It surveys the Multiverse, collating decisions our counterparts have already made to predict likely outcomes of our actions. When Miguel O'Hara (Spidey 2099) left the present, it caused an energy surge that powered the Clairvoyant, which Spidey used to get the city and himself out of certain doom (by getting a certain Doom out of the city). So the city is safe again! Let's just keep saying it!

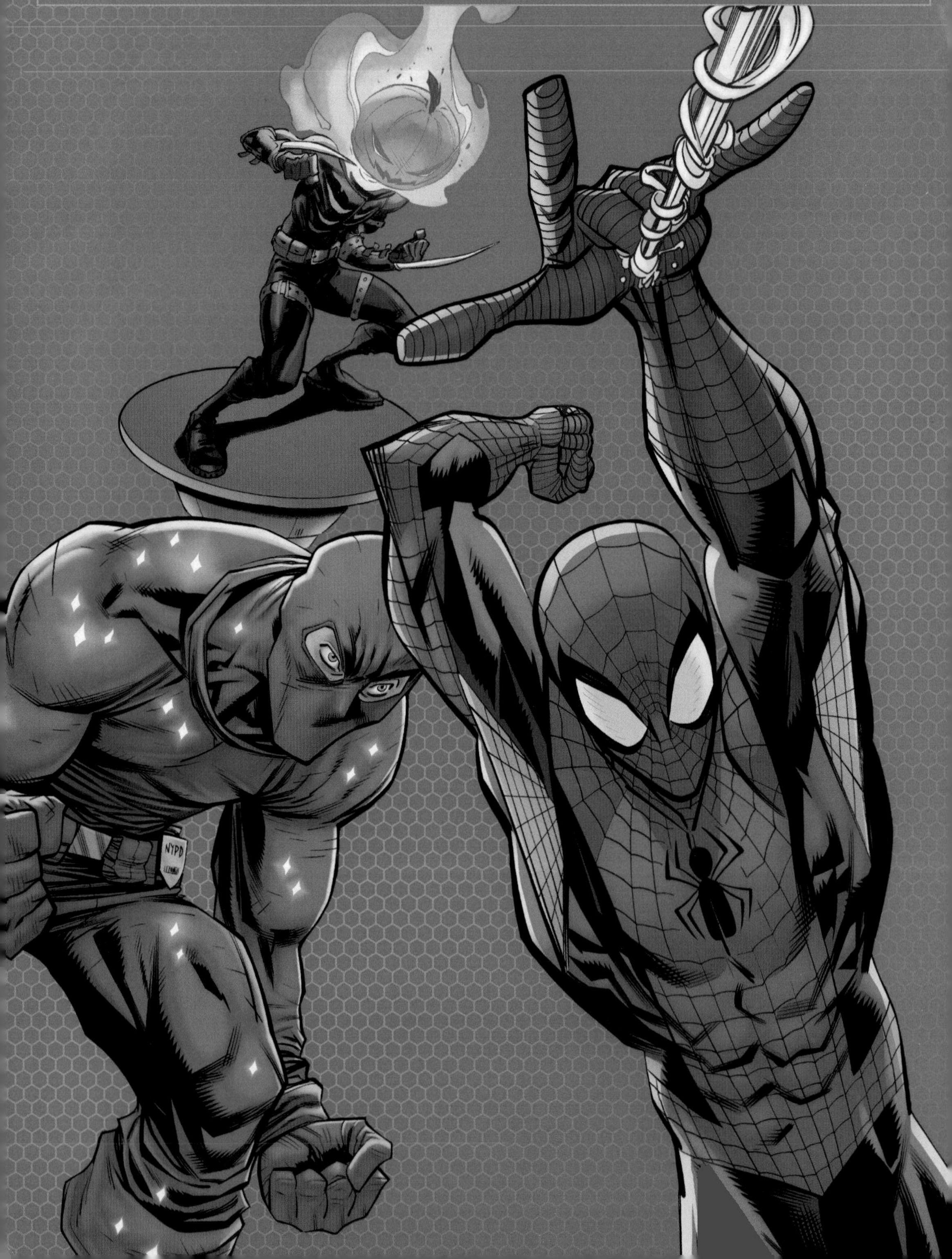
NYPD

THREATS & MENACES

WRITER **NICK SPENCER**

AMAZING SPIDER-MAN #37 & #41-43

PENCILER	**RYAN OTTLEY**
INKERS	**CLIFF RATHBURN** WITH **RYAN OTTLEY** (#43)
COLORISTS	**NATHAN FAIRBAIRN** WITH **DEE CUNNIFFE** (#43)
COVER ART	**RYAN OTTLEY & NATHAN FAIRBAIRN**

AMAZING SPIDER-MAN #38-40

ARTISTS	**IBAN COELLO** WITH **ZÉ CARLOS** (#40)
COLORISTS	**BRIAN REBER** WITH **PETE PANTAZIS** (#40)
COVER ART	**PATRICK GLEASON & MORRY HOLLOWELL** (#38); **PATRICK GLEASON & MARTE GRACIA** (#39) AND **RYAN OTTLEY & NATHAN FAIRBAIRN** (#40)

"THE SINS OF OVERDRIVE," "THE SINS OF THE LETHAL LEGION" & "THE SINS OF..."

NICK SPENCER	**FRANCESCO MOBILI**	**ERICK ARCINIEGA**
WRITER	ARTIST	COLOR ARTIST

VC'S JOE CARAMAGNA	**KATHLEEN WISNESKI**	**NICK LOWE**
LETTERER	ASSOCIATE EDITOR	EDITOR

SPIDER-MAN CREATED BY STAN LEE & STEVE DITKO

COLLECTION EDITOR **JENNIFER GRÜNWALD**
ASSISTANT MANAGING EDITOR **MAIA LOY** ❖ ASSISTANT MANAGING EDITOR **LISA MONTALBANO**
EDITOR, SPECIAL PROJECTS **MARK D. BEAZLEY** ❖ VP PRODUCTION & SPECIAL PROJECTS **JEFF YOUNGQUIST**
BOOK DESIGNERS **STACIE ZUCKER** WITH **JAY BOWEN**
SVP PRINT, SALES & MARKETING **DAVID GABRIEL** ❖ EDITOR IN CHIEF **C.B. CEBULSKI**

AMAZING SPIDER-MAN BY NICK SPENCER VOL. 8: THREATS & MENACES. Contains material originally published in magazine form as AMAZING SPIDER-MAN (2018) #37-43. First printing 2020. ISBN 978-1-302-92023-4. Published by MARVEL WORLDWIDE, INC., a subsidiary of MARVEL ENTERTAINMENT, LLC. OFFICE OF PUBLICATION: 1290 Avenue of the Americas, New York, NY 10104. © 2020 MARVEL No similarity between any of the names, characters, persons, and/or institutions in this magazine with those of any living or dead person or institution is intended, and any such similarity which may exist is purely coincidental. **Printed in the U.S.A.** KEVIN FEIGE, Chief Creative Officer; DAN BUCKLEY, President, Marvel Entertainment; JOHN NEE, Publisher; JOE QUESADA, EVP & Creative Director; TOM BREVOORT, SVP of Publishing; DAVID BOGART, Associate Publisher & SVP of Talent Affairs; Publishing & Partnership; DAVID GABRIEL, VP of Print & Digital Publishing; JEFF YOUNGQUIST, VP of Production & Special Projects; DAN CARR, Executive Director of Publishing Technology; ALEX MORALES, Director of Publishing Operations; DAN EDINGTON, Managing Editor; SUSAN CRESPI, Production Manager; STAN LEE, Chairman Emeritus. For information regarding advertising in Marvel Comics or on Marvel.com, please contact Vit DeBellis, Custom Solutions & Integrated Advertising Manager, at vdebellis@marvel.com. For Marvel subscription inquiries, please call 888-511-5480. **Manufactured between 7/10/2020 and 8/11/2020 by LSC COMMUNICATIONS INC., KENDALLVILLE, IN, USA.**
10 9 8 7 6 5 4 3 2 1

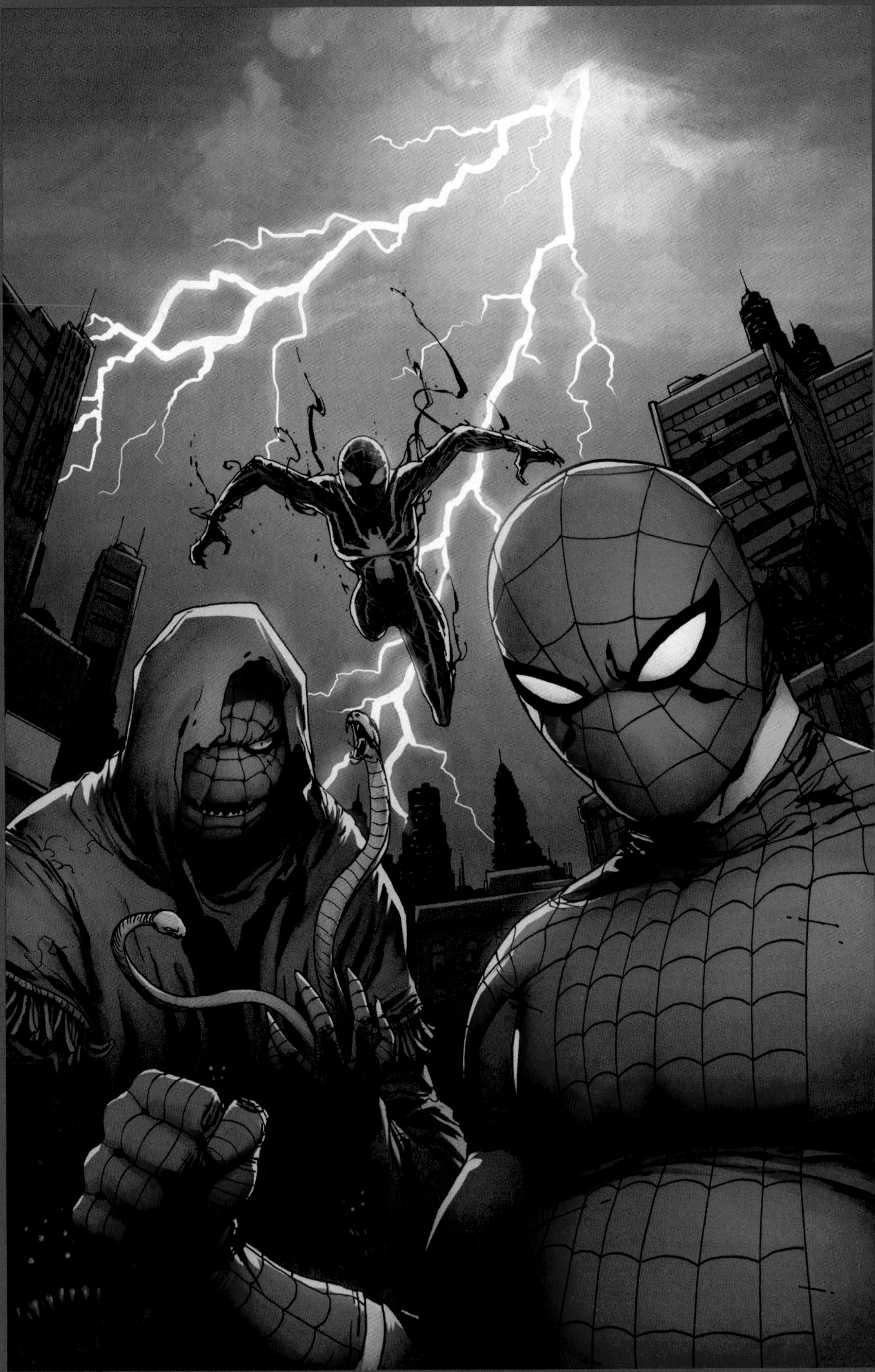

#37 MARVELS X VARIANT BY GIUSEPPE CAMUNCOLI & JEAN-FRANÇOIS BEAULIEU

37

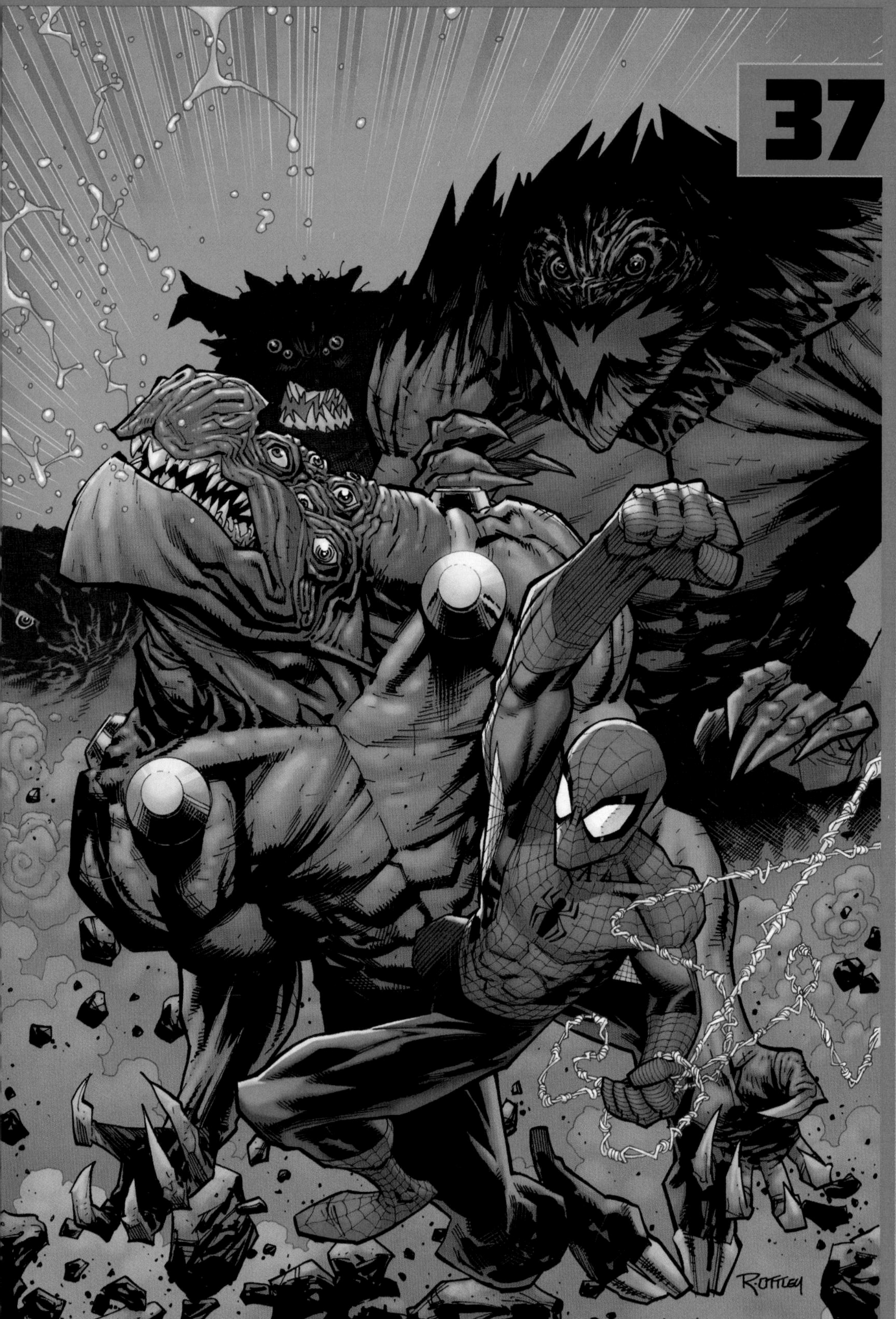
R.OTTLEY

TIME, FOR A CHANGE

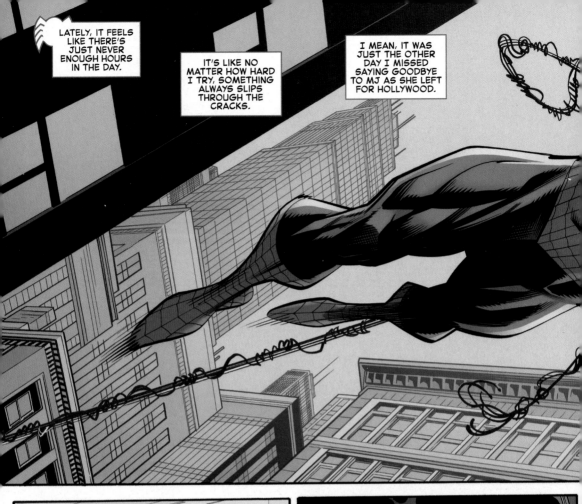

LATELY, IT FEELS LIKE THERE'S JUST NEVER ENOUGH HOURS IN THE DAY.

IT'S LIKE NO MATTER HOW HARD I TRY, SOMETHING ALWAYS SLIPS THROUGH THE CRACKS.

I MEAN, IT WAS JUST THE OTHER DAY I MISSED SAYING GOODBYE TO MJ AS SHE LEFT FOR HOLLYWOOD.

NOW, SURE, I HAVE A LOT GOING ON RIGHT NOW. I'M BACK AT *EMPIRE STATE*, STUDYING HARD--

--THEN I'M HELPING AUNT MAY GET THE *F.E.A.S.T. CENTER* BACK OPEN--

--AND ALONG THE WAY, DODGING CALLS FROM OLD FRIENDS. THEN, OF COURSE--

PETE, IT'S BETTY AGAIN, FOR THE SEVENTEENTH TIME! GOT SOMETHING YOU MIGHT BE INTERESTED IN...

YOU HAVE SEVENTEEN NEW MESSAGES.

--THERE'S THE *USUAL*.

PEOPLE TRAPPED IN FIRES...

HEEELPPP!

THAT WAS *TOUGH.*

...BANK ROBBERS WEARING ROLLER SKATES...

IT'S ROBBIN' TIME!

RAAARGH!

...AND, *UH,* PEOPLE TURNED INTO DINOSAURS BY A STEGRON VIRUS.

OKAY, MAYBE *THAT* ONE'S NOT SO USUAL.

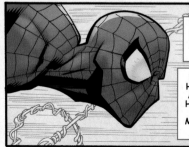

SO YEAH, IT'S NOT LIKE I DON'T HAVE A LOT TO DEAL WITH.

BUT STILL, I CAN'T HELP BUT HEAR THIS ANGRY VOICE IN MY HEAD YELLING AT ME FOR LETTING SO MANY PEOPLE DOWN. TELLING ME TO--

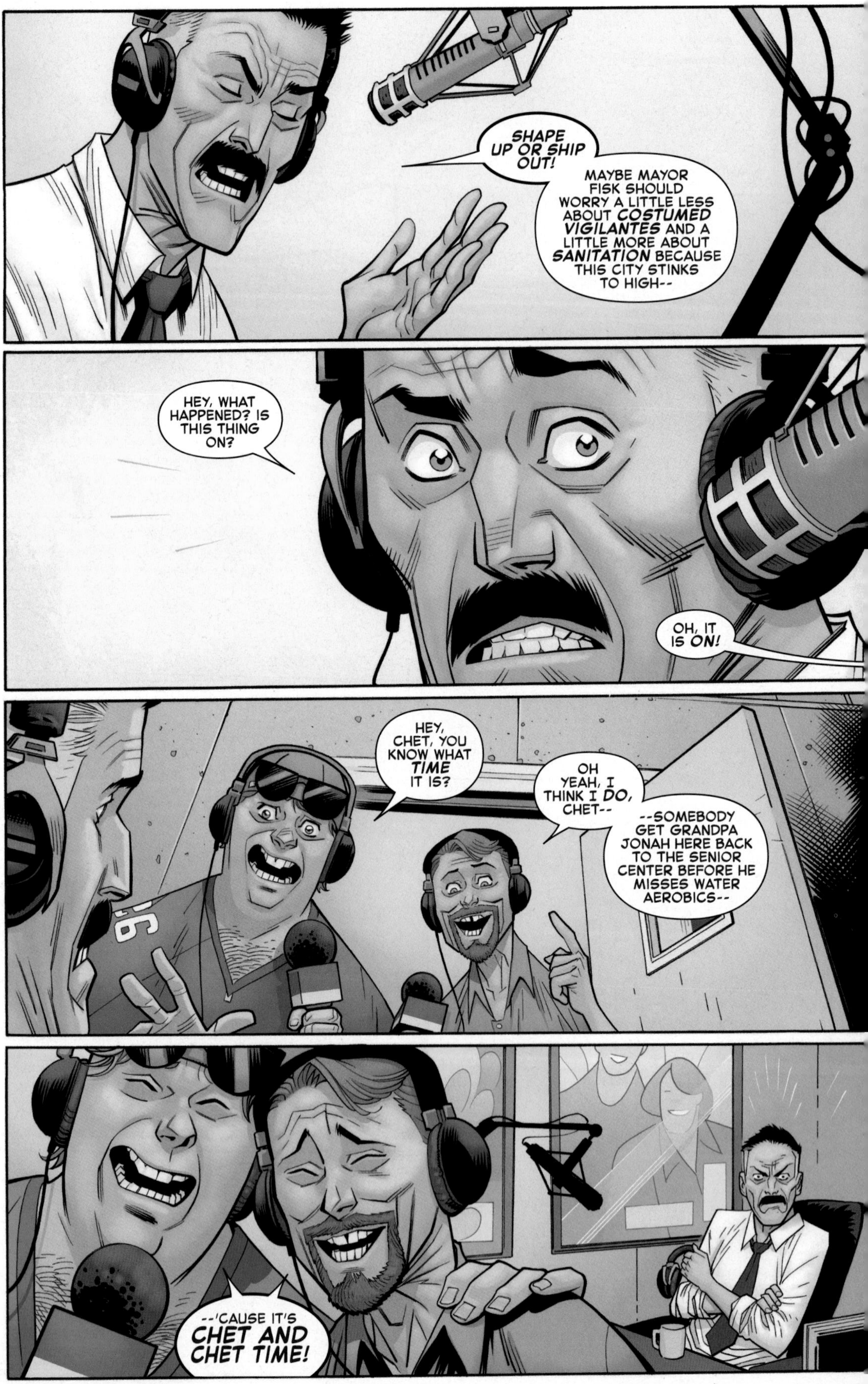
SHAPE UP OR SHIP OUT!
MAYBE MAYOR FISK SHOULD WORRY A LITTLE LESS ABOUT COSTUMED VIGILANTES AND A LITTLE MORE ABOUT SANITATION BECAUSE THIS CITY STINKS TO HIGH--
HEY, WHAT HAPPENED? IS THIS THING ON?
OH, IT IS ON!
HEY, CHET, YOU KNOW WHAT TIME IT IS?
OH YEAH, I THINK I DO, CHET--
--SOMEBODY GET GRANDPA JONAH HERE BACK TO THE SENIOR CENTER BEFORE HE MISSES WATER AEROBICS--
--'CAUSE IT'S CHET AND CHET TIME!

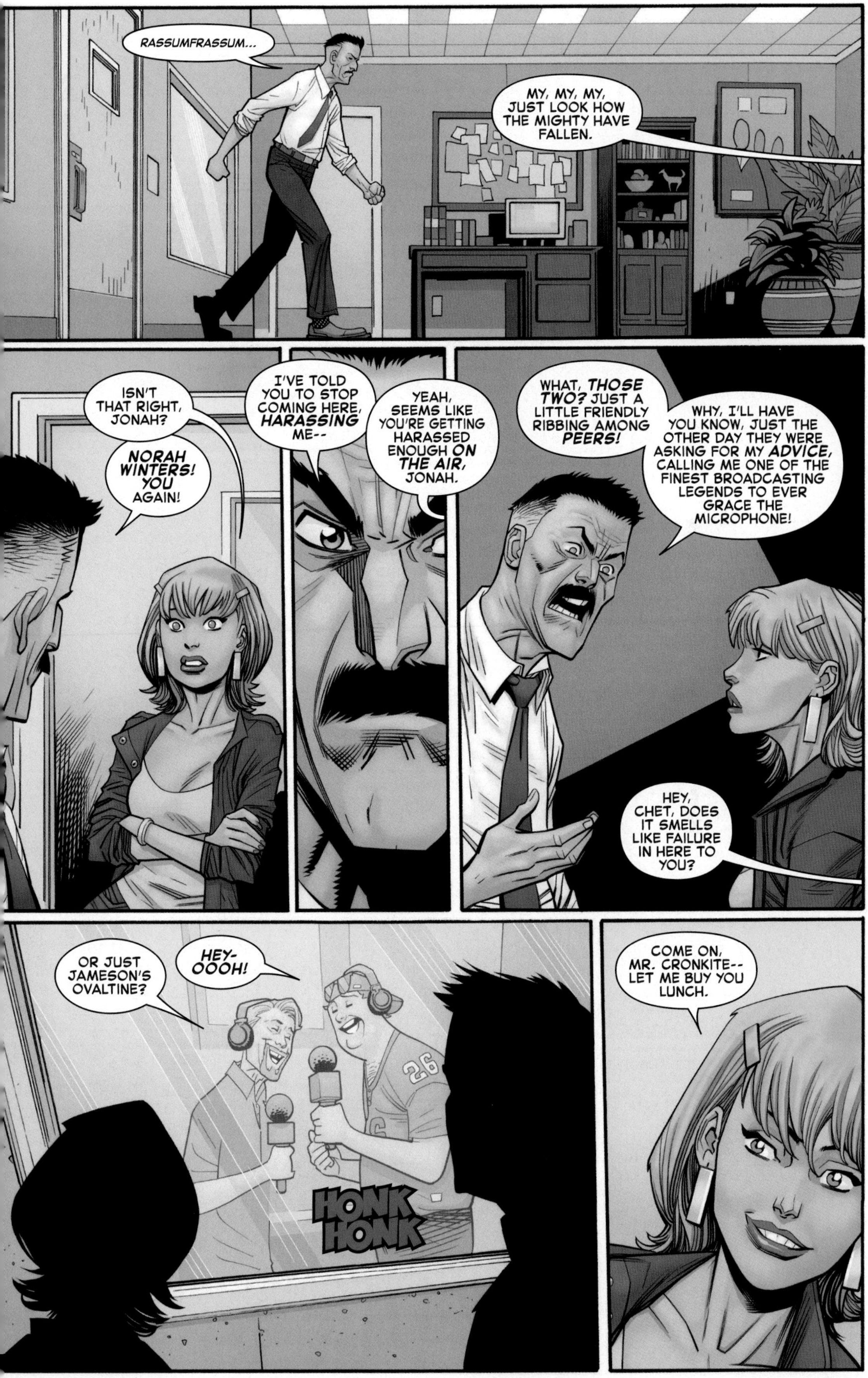
RASSUMFRASSUM...
MY, MY, MY, JUST LOOK HOW THE MIGHTY HAVE FALLEN.
ISN'T THAT RIGHT, JONAH?
NORAH WINTERS! YOU AGAIN!
I'VE TOLD YOU TO STOP COMING HERE, HARASSING ME--
YEAH, SEEMS LIKE YOU'RE GETTING HARASSED ENOUGH ON THE AIR, JONAH.
WHAT, THOSE TWO? JUST A LITTLE FRIENDLY RIBBING AMONG PEERS!
WHY, I'LL HAVE YOU KNOW, JUST THE OTHER DAY THEY WERE ASKING FOR MY ADVICE, CALLING ME ONE OF THE FINEST BROADCASTING LEGENDS TO EVER GRACE THE MICROPHONE!
HEY, CHET, DOES IT SMELLS LIKE FAILURE IN HERE TO YOU?
OR JUST JAMESON'S OVALTINE?
HEY-OOOH!
HONK HONK
COME ON, MR. CRONKITE-- LET ME BUY YOU LUNCH.

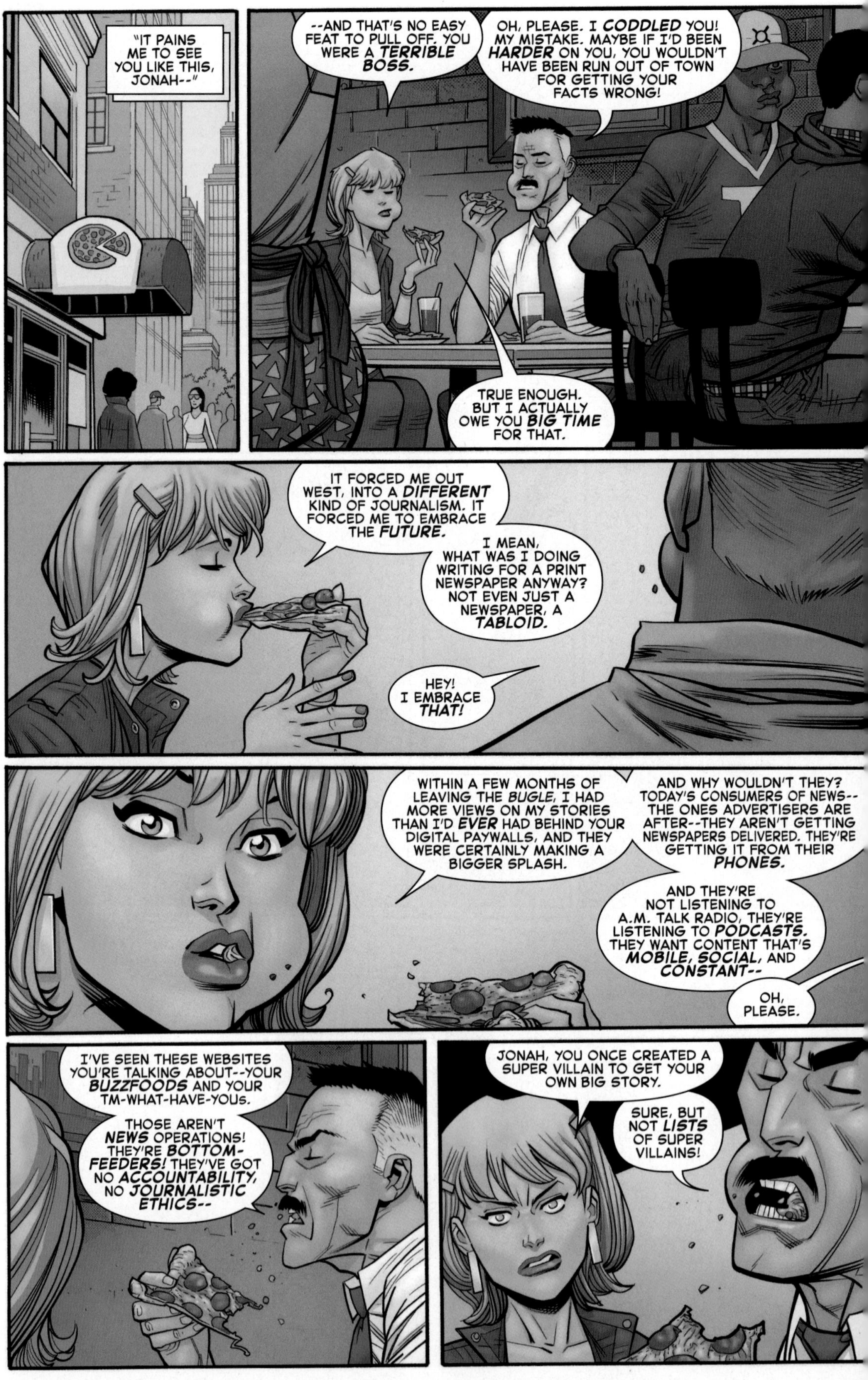
"IT PAINS ME TO SEE YOU LIKE THIS, JONAH--"
--AND THAT'S NO EASY FEAT TO PULL OFF. YOU WERE A TERRIBLE BOSS.
OH, PLEASE. I CODDLED YOU! MY MISTAKE. MAYBE IF I'D BEEN HARDER ON YOU, YOU WOULDN'T HAVE BEEN RUN OUT OF TOWN FOR GETTING YOUR FACTS WRONG!
TRUE ENOUGH. BUT I ACTUALLY OWE YOU BIG TIME FOR THAT.
IT FORCED ME OUT WEST, INTO A DIFFERENT KIND OF JOURNALISM. IT FORCED ME TO EMBRACE THE FUTURE.
I MEAN, WHAT WAS I DOING WRITING FOR A PRINT NEWSPAPER ANYWAY? NOT EVEN JUST A NEWSPAPER, A TABLOID.
HEY! I EMBRACE THAT!
WITHIN A FEW MONTHS OF LEAVING THE BUGLE, I HAD MORE VIEWS ON MY STORIES THAN I'D EVER HAD BEHIND YOUR DIGITAL PAYWALLS, AND THEY WERE CERTAINLY MAKING A BIGGER SPLASH.
AND WHY WOULDN'T THEY? TODAY'S CONSUMERS OF NEWS-- THE ONES ADVERTISERS ARE AFTER--THEY AREN'T GETTING NEWSPAPERS DELIVERED. THEY'RE GETTING IT FROM THEIR PHONES.
AND THEY'RE NOT LISTENING TO A.M. TALK RADIO, THEY'RE LISTENING TO PODCASTS. THEY WANT CONTENT THAT'S MOBILE, SOCIAL, AND CONSTANT--
OH, PLEASE.
I'VE SEEN THESE WEBSITES YOU'RE TALKING ABOUT--YOUR BUZZFOODS AND YOUR TM-WHAT-HAVE-YOUS.
THOSE AREN'T NEWS OPERATIONS! THEY'RE BOTTOM-FEEDERS! THEY'VE GOT NO ACCOUNTABILITY, NO JOURNALISTIC ETHICS--
JONAH, YOU ONCE CREATED A SUPER VILLAIN TO GET YOUR OWN BIG STORY.
SURE, BUT NOT LISTS OF SUPER VILLAINS!

I'M HONESTLY SURPRISED YOU FEEL THAT WAY, JJJ. I MEAN, YOU PRACTICALLY *INVENTED* THIS STUFF.

YOU WERE DOING CLICKBAIT BEFORE THERE WERE CLICKS! I MEAN, SPIDER-MAN: THREAT OR MENACE!

I DON'T DO THAT ANYMORE!

SPIDER-MAN IS A *HERO.*

HE'S IN A PERMANENT STATE OF *CANCELED* IS WHAT HE IS, THANKS TO *YOU.* AND YOU DIDN'T EVEN NEED SOCIAL MEDIA TO DO IT! WHICH IS WHY I'M MAKING YOU THIS OFFER--

I DON'T NEED TO HEAR IT! *PASS!* LISTEN, NORAH, YOU GO BACK TO THOSE SNOT-NOSED SILICON VALLEY PUNKS AND YOU TELL THEM-- J. JONAH JAMESON IS A *NEWSPAPERMAN,* EVEN WHEN HE'S ON THE RADIO!

SO WHATEVER YOUR "OFFER" IS, YOU CAN SHOVE IT.

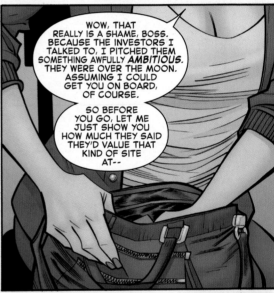

WOW, THAT REALLY IS A SHAME, BOSS. BECAUSE THE INVESTORS I TALKED TO, I PITCHED THEM SOMETHING AWFULLY *AMBITIOUS.* THEY WERE OVER THE MOON. ASSUMING I COULD GET YOU ON BOARD, OF COURSE.

SO BEFORE YOU GO, LET ME JUST SHOW YOU HOW MUCH THEY SAID THEY'D VALUE THAT KIND OF SITE AT--

I'M IN!

AND WHO CAN BLAME HIM?

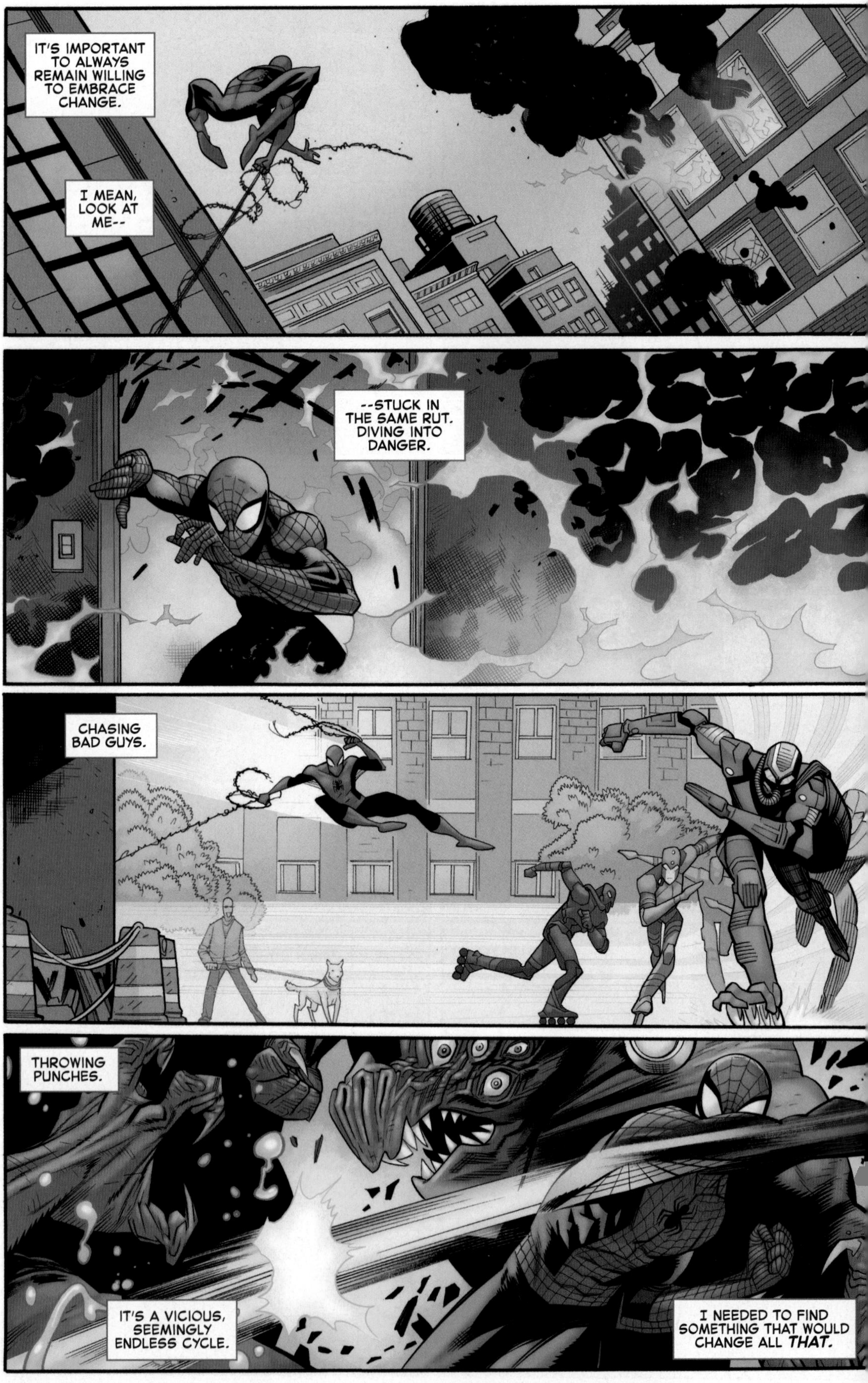
IT'S IMPORTANT TO ALWAYS REMAIN WILLING TO EMBRACE CHANGE.
I MEAN, LOOK AT ME--
--STUCK IN THE SAME RUT. DIVING INTO DANGER.
CHASING BAD GUYS.
THROWING PUNCHES.
IT'S A VICIOUS, SEEMINGLY ENDLESS CYCLE.
I NEEDED TO FIND SOMETHING THAT WOULD CHANGE ALL THAT.

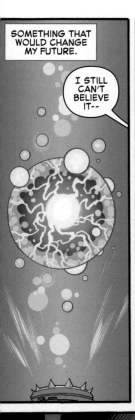

SOMETHING THAT WOULD CHANGE MY FUTURE.

I STILL CAN'T BELIEVE IT--

--YOU REALLY FIXED THE CLAIRVOYANT'S *POWER SOURCE* PROBLEM!

WELL, *FOR NOW.*

THE SOLUTION I FOUND IS JUST TEMPORARY, THERE WON'T BE MORE WHERE *THAT* CAME FROM.

BUT IT LOOKS LIKE IT'S ENOUGH TO RUN SOME DECENT LARGE-SCALE BETA TESTS, GET SOME BENCHMARKS ON THIS THING--

AMAZING WORK. I KNEW I WAS RIGHT BRINGING YOU ON BOARD, PETE!

IT'LL DO IN SHORT DOSES. I DID HAVE A *QUESTION* FOR YOU, THOUGH, JAMIE. WHEN I WAS TESTING IT IN THE FIELD--

AND BY "TESTING" I MEAN "HELPING SAVE THE CITY FROM AN ARMY OF DOOMBOTS."

PROBABLY BEST TO LEAVE THAT PART OUT FOR NOW.

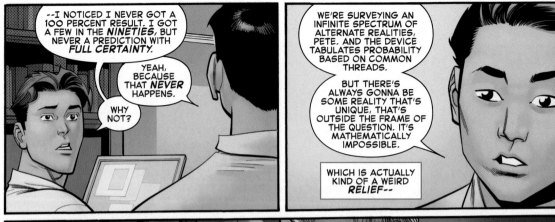

--I NOTICED I NEVER GOT A 100 PERCENT RESULT. I GOT A FEW IN THE *NINETIES*, BUT NEVER A PREDICTION WITH *FULL CERTAINTY*.

YEAH, BECAUSE THAT *NEVER* HAPPENS.

WHY NOT?

WE'RE SURVEYING AN INFINITE SPECTRUM OF ALTERNATE REALITIES, PETE. AND THE DEVICE TABULATES PROBABILITY BASED ON COMMON THREADS.

BUT THERE'S ALWAYS GONNA BE SOME REALITY THAT'S UNIQUE, THAT'S OUTSIDE THE FRAME OF THE QUESTION. IT'S MATHEMATICALLY IMPOSSIBLE.

WHICH IS ACTUALLY KIND OF A WEIRD *RELIEF*--

--BECAUSE THE LAST TIME WE FOUND SOMETHING THAT COULD TELL THE FUTURE--

--THINGS GOT A LITTLE *HEATED.*

I DON'T WANNA GO INTO THIS BLIND. USING IT WHEN DOOM INVADED WAS ONE THING--THAT WAS AN *EMERGENCY.*

WITH A LITTLE TIME TO BREATHE, I USED IT TO ASK THE PEOPLE I TRUST WHAT *THEY* THOUGHT I SHOULD DO...

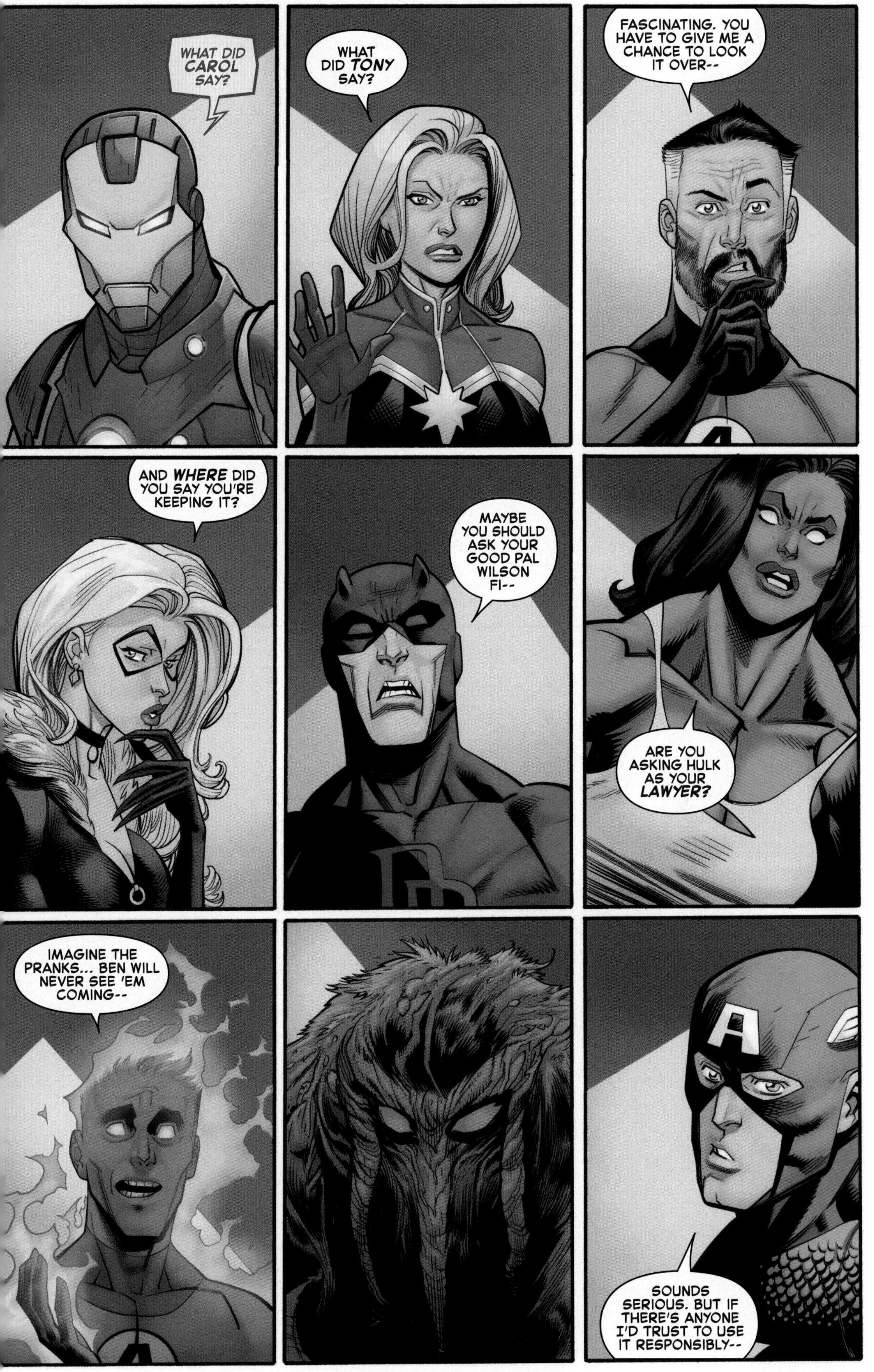
WHAT DID CAROL SAY?
WHAT DID TONY SAY?
FASCINATING. YOU HAVE TO GIVE ME A CHANCE TO LOOK IT OVER--
AND WHERE DID YOU SAY YOU'RE KEEPING IT?
MAYBE YOU SHOULD ASK YOUR GOOD PAL WILSON FI--
ARE YOU ASKING HULK AS YOUR LAWYER?
IMAGINE THE PRANKS... BEN WILL NEVER SEE 'EM COMING--
SOUNDS SERIOUS. BUT IF THERE'S ANYONE I'D TRUST TO USE IT RESPONSIBLY--

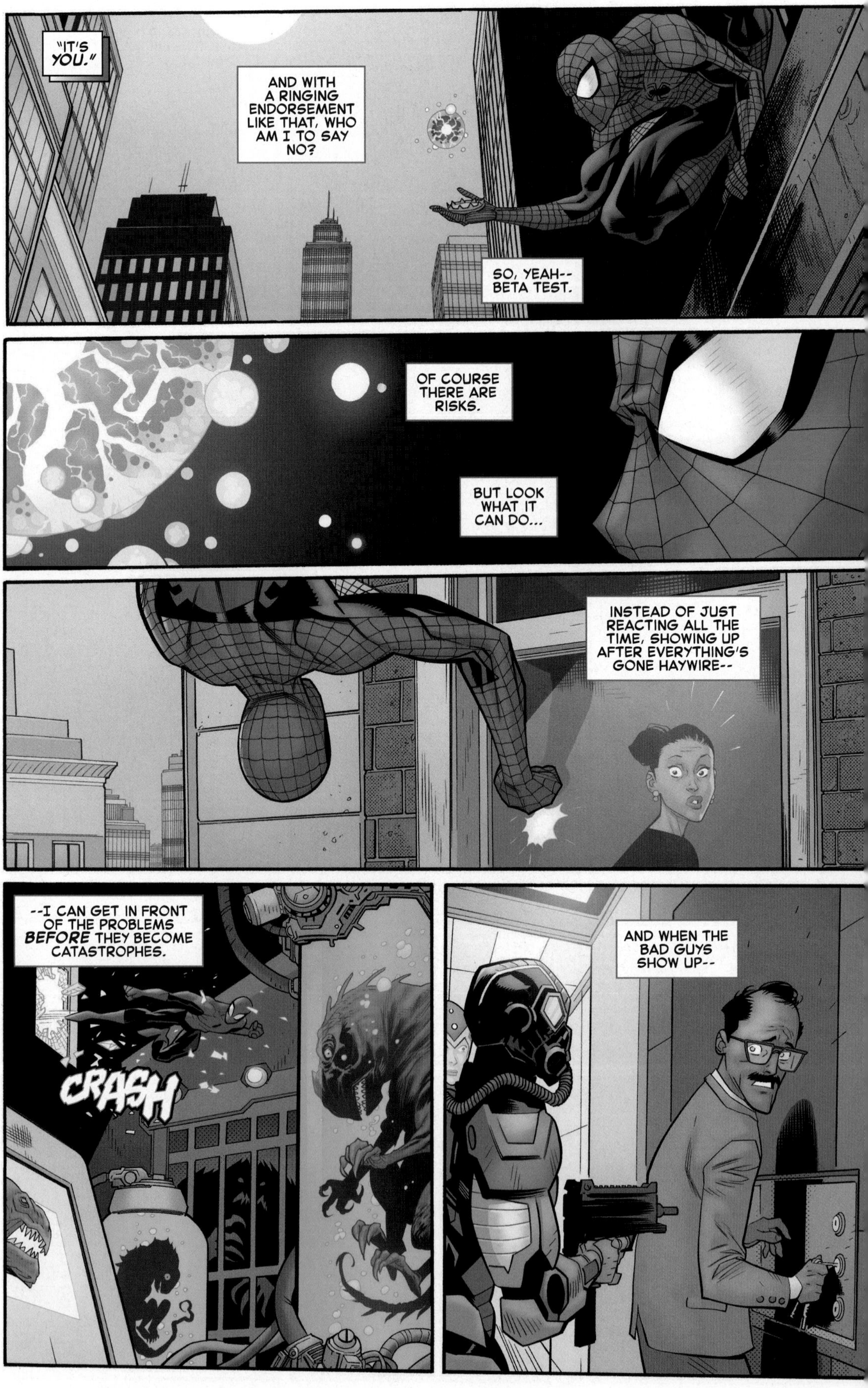
"IT'S YOU."
AND WITH A RINGING ENDORSEMENT LIKE THAT, WHO AM I TO SAY NO?
SO, YEAH-- BETA TEST.
OF COURSE THERE ARE RISKS.
BUT LOOK WHAT IT CAN DO...
INSTEAD OF JUST REACTING ALL THE TIME, SHOWING UP AFTER EVERYTHING'S GONE HAYWIRE--
--I CAN GET IN FRONT OF THE PROBLEMS BEFORE THEY BECOME CATASTROPHES.
CRASH
AND WHEN THE BAD GUYS SHOW UP--

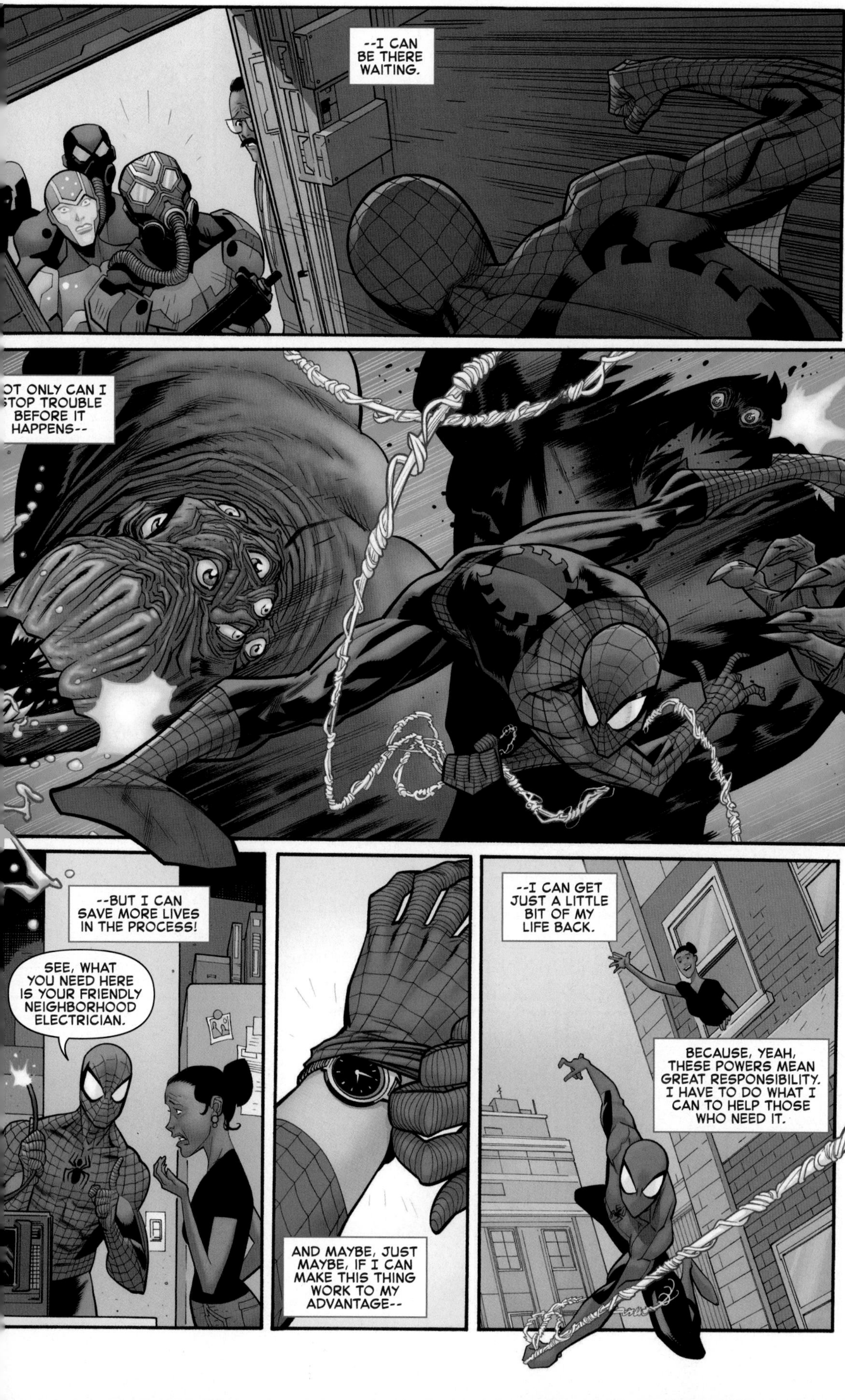
--I CAN BE THERE WAITING.
OT ONLY CAN I STOP TROUBLE BEFORE IT HAPPENS--
--BUT I CAN SAVE MORE LIVES IN THE PROCESS!
SEE, WHAT YOU NEED HERE IS YOUR FRIENDLY NEIGHBORHOOD ELECTRICIAN.
AND MAYBE, JUST MAYBE, IF I CAN MAKE THIS THING WORK TO MY ADVANTAGE--
--I CAN GET JUST A LITTLE BIT OF MY LIFE BACK.
BECAUSE, YEAH, THESE POWERS MEAN GREAT RESPONSIBILITY. I HAVE TO DO WHAT I CAN TO HELP THOSE WHO NEED IT.

BUT WHAT ABOUT THE PEOPLE *IN* MY LIFE? THE PEOPLE WHO CARE ABOUT ME? WHAT ABOUT MY RESPONSIBILITY TO THEM?

THE ONES I'M ALWAYS LETTING DOWN.

WELL, NOT TODAY!

TODAY, PETER PARKER AND SPIDER-MAN *BOTH* WIN!

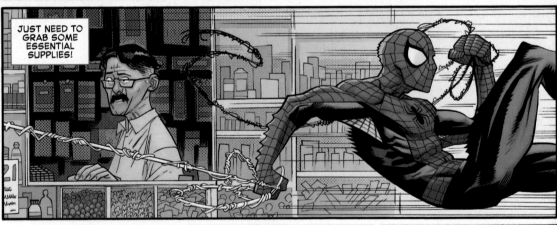

JUST NEED TO GRAB SOME ESSENTIAL SUPPLIES!

SALTe CHIPS

SUGAR

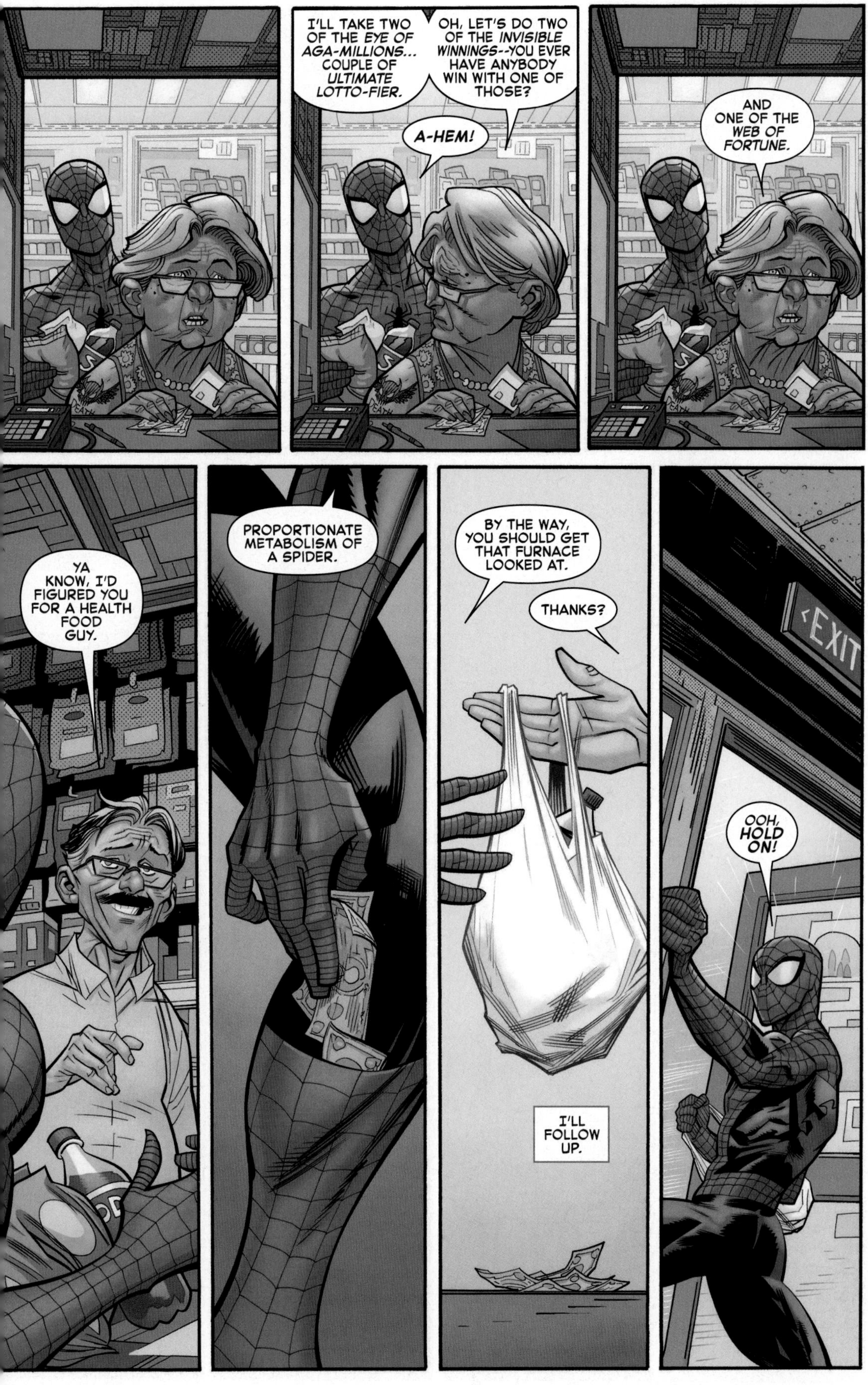
I'LL TAKE TWO OF THE EYE OF AGA-MILLIONS... COUPLE OF ULTIMATE LOTTO-FIER.
OH, LET'S DO TWO OF THE INVISIBLE WINNINGS--YOU EVER HAVE ANYBODY WIN WITH ONE OF THOSE?
A-HEM!
AND ONE OF THE WEB OF FORTUNE.
YA KNOW, I'D FIGURED YOU FOR A HEALTH FOOD GUY.
PROPORTIONATE METABOLISM OF A SPIDER.
BY THE WAY, YOU SHOULD GET THAT FURNACE LOOKED AT.
THANKS?
I'LL FOLLOW UP.
EXIT
OOH, HOLD ON!

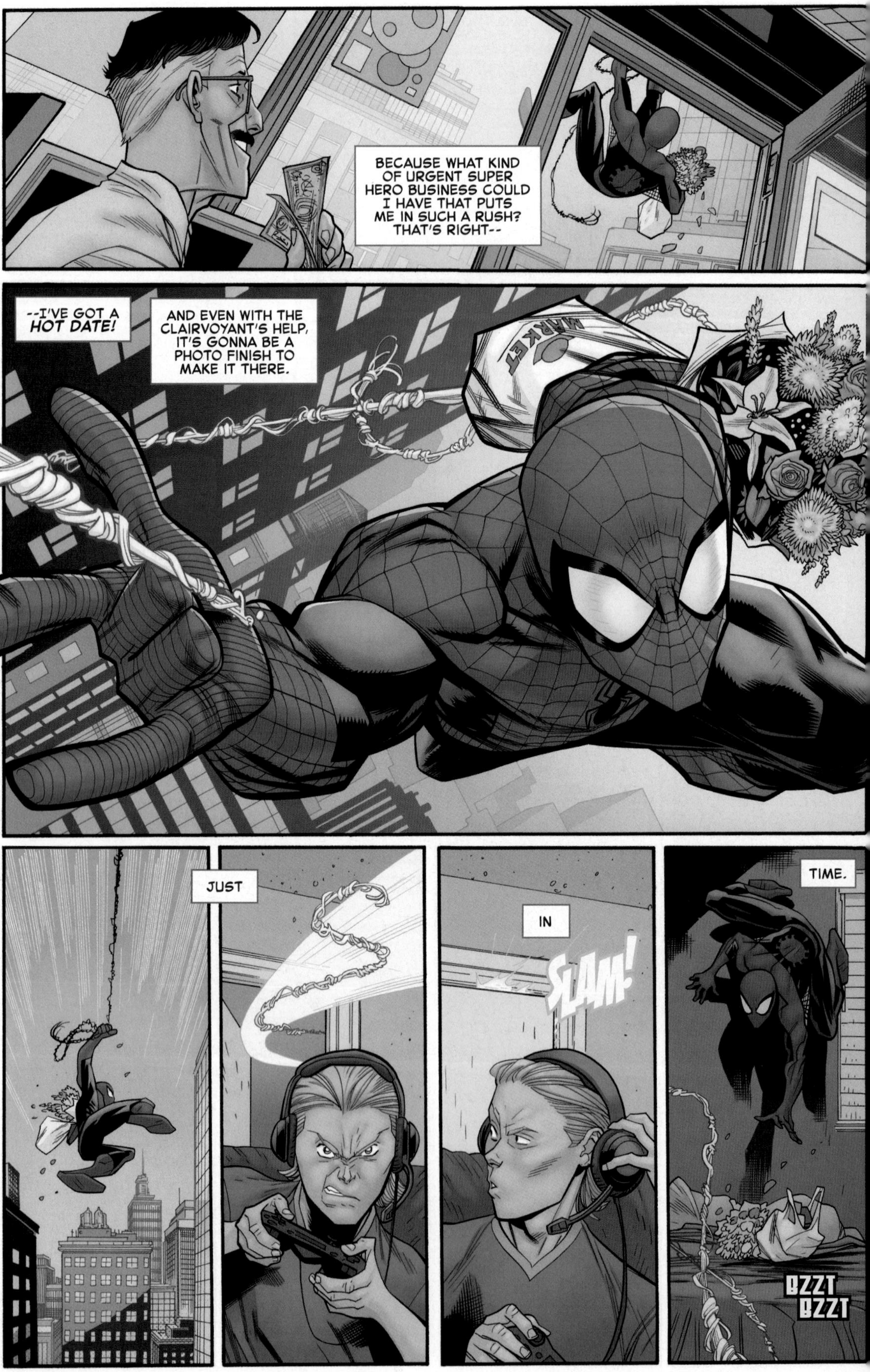

BECAUSE WHAT KIND OF URGENT SUPER HERO BUSINESS COULD I HAVE THAT PUTS ME IN SUCH A RUSH? THAT'S RIGHT--
--I'VE GOT A HOT DATE!
AND EVEN WITH THE CLAIRVOYANT'S HELP, IT'S GONNA BE A PHOTO FINISH TO MAKE IT THERE.
MARKET
JUST
IN
SLAM!
TIME.
BZZT BZZT

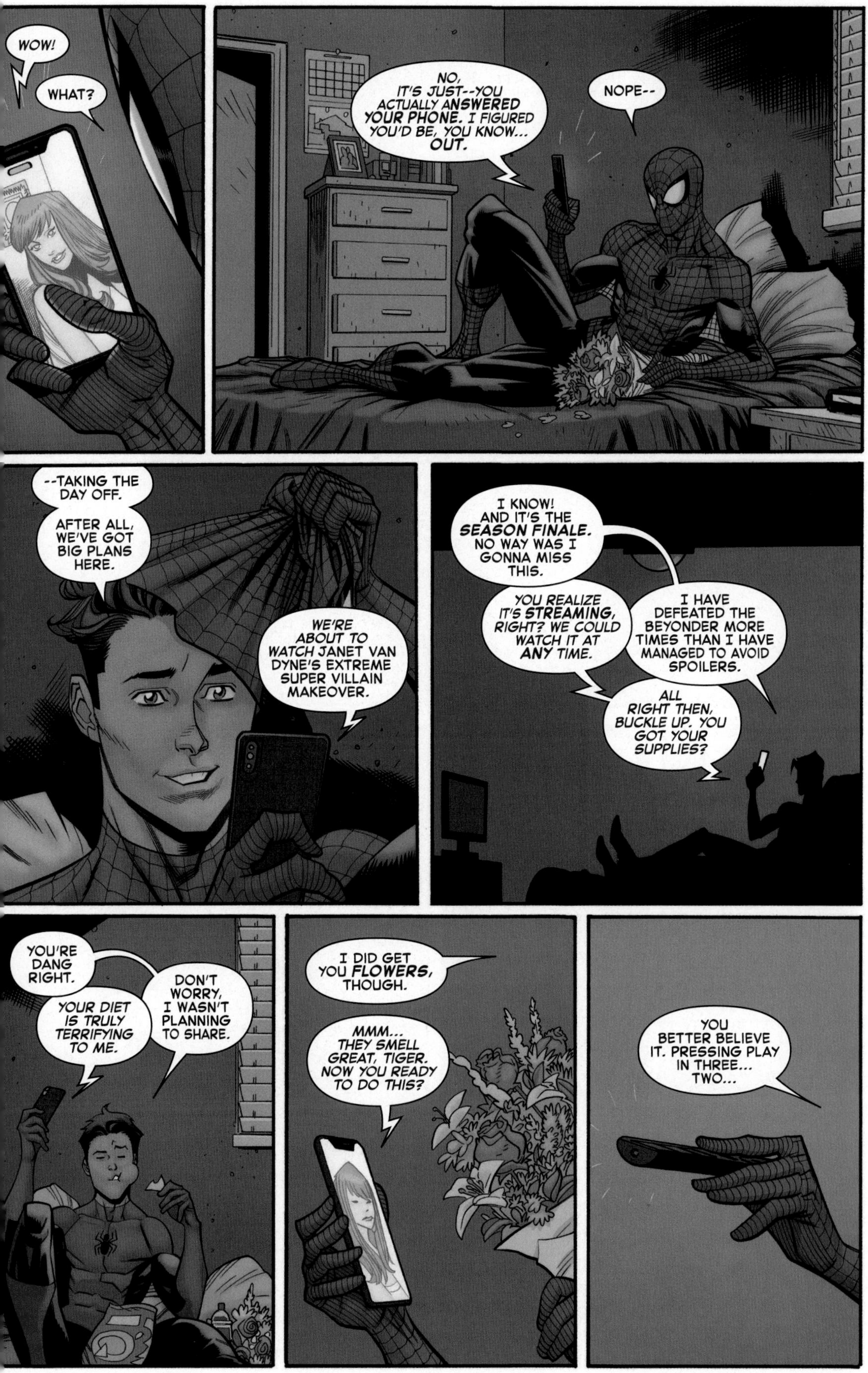
WOW!
WHAT?
NO, IT'S JUST--YOU ACTUALLY ANSWERED YOUR PHONE. I FIGURED YOU'D BE, YOU KNOW... OUT.
NOPE--
--TAKING THE DAY OFF.
AFTER ALL, WE'VE GOT BIG PLANS HERE.
WE'RE ABOUT TO WATCH JANET VAN DYNE'S EXTREME SUPER VILLAIN MAKEOVER.
I KNOW! AND IT'S THE SEASON FINALE. NO WAY WAS I GONNA MISS THIS.
YOU REALIZE IT'S STREAMING, RIGHT? WE COULD WATCH IT AT ANY TIME.
I HAVE DEFEATED THE BEYONDER MORE TIMES THAN I HAVE MANAGED TO AVOID SPOILERS.
ALL RIGHT THEN, BUCKLE UP. YOU GOT YOUR SUPPLIES?
YOU'RE DANG RIGHT.
YOUR DIET IS TRULY TERRIFYING TO ME.
DON'T WORRY, I WASN'T PLANNING TO SHARE.
I DID GET YOU FLOWERS, THOUGH.
MMM... THEY SMELL GREAT, TIGER. NOW YOU READY TO DO THIS?
YOU BETTER BELIEVE IT. PRESSING PLAY IN THREE... TWO...

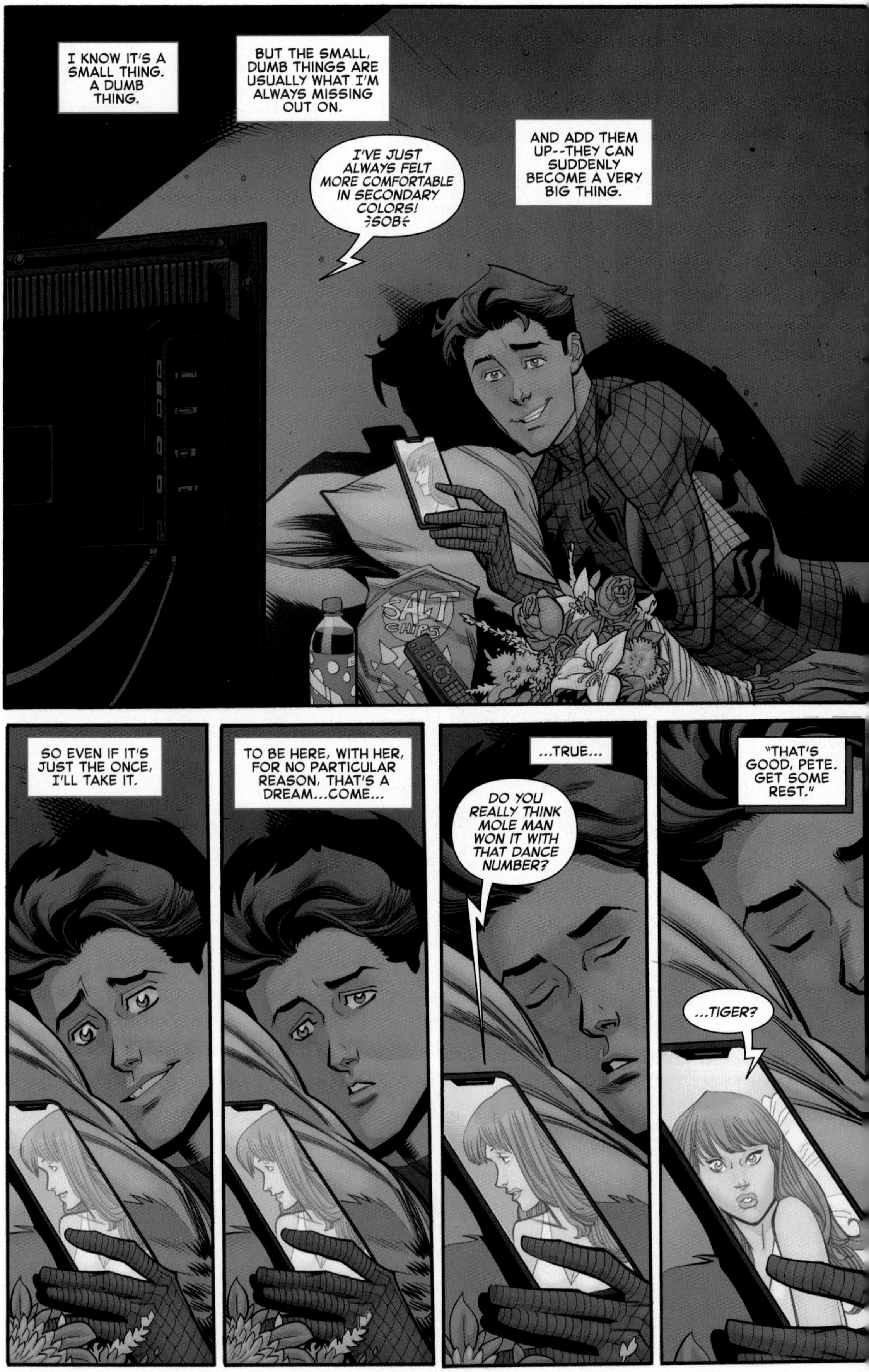
I KNOW IT'S A SMALL THING. A DUMB THING.
BUT THE SMALL, DUMB THINGS ARE USUALLY WHAT I'M ALWAYS MISSING OUT ON.
I'VE JUST ALWAYS FELT MORE COMFORTABLE IN SECONDARY COLORS! ⁑SOB⁑
AND ADD THEM UP--THEY CAN SUDDENLY BECOME A VERY BIG THING.
SALT CHIPS
SO EVEN IF IT'S JUST THE ONCE, I'LL TAKE IT.
TO BE HERE, WITH HER, FOR NO PARTICULAR REASON, THAT'S A DREAM...COME...
...TRUE...
DO YOU REALLY THINK MOLE MAN WON IT WITH THAT DANCE NUMBER?
"THAT'S GOOD, PETE. GET SOME REST."
...TIGER?

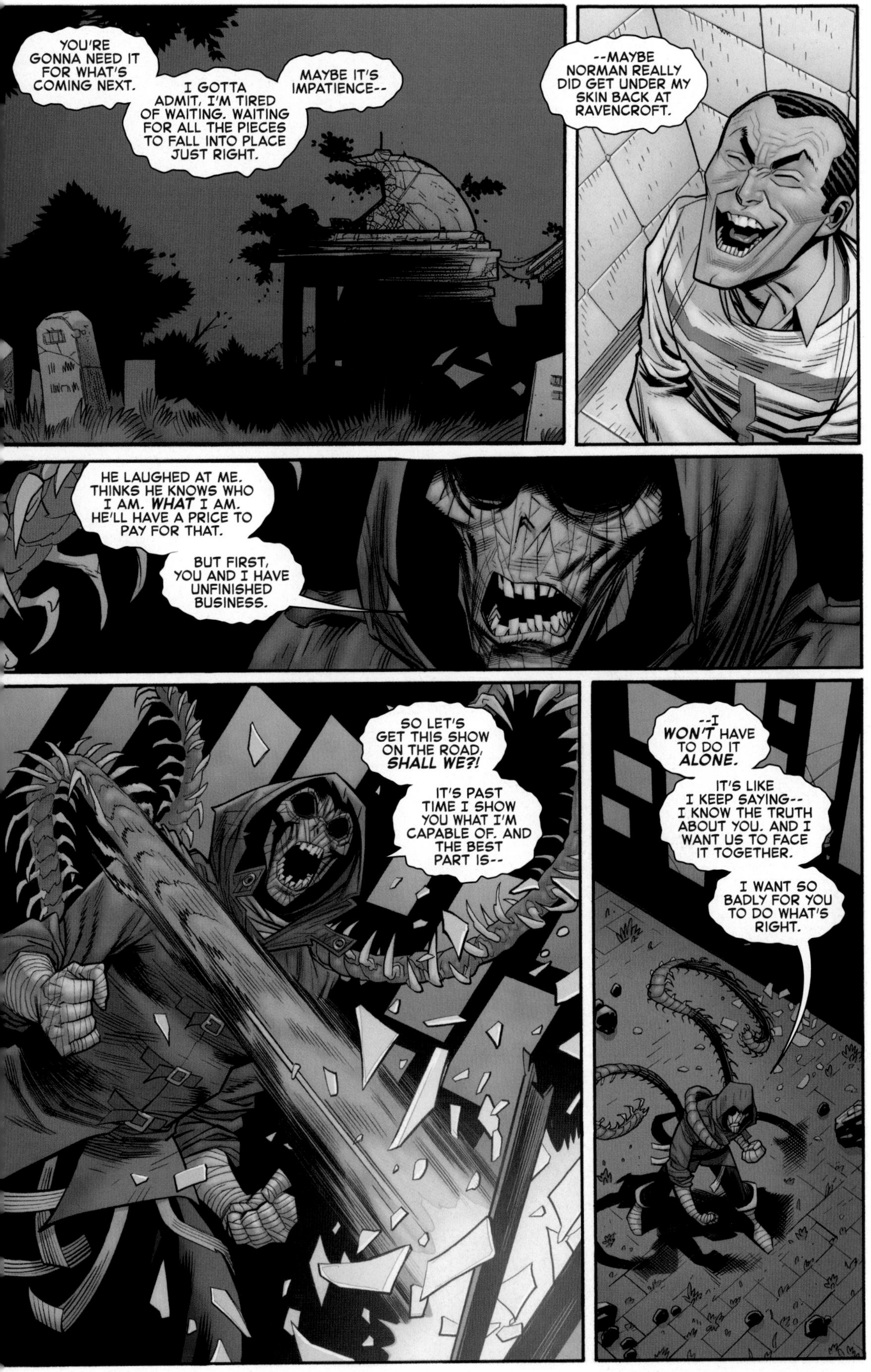

YOU'RE GONNA NEED IT FOR WHAT'S COMING NEXT.
I GOTTA ADMIT, I'M TIRED OF WAITING. WAITING FOR ALL THE PIECES TO FALL INTO PLACE JUST RIGHT.
MAYBE IT'S IMPATIENCE--
--MAYBE NORMAN REALLY DID GET UNDER MY SKIN BACK AT RAVENCROFT.
HE LAUGHED AT ME. THINKS HE KNOWS WHO I AM. WHAT I AM. HE'LL HAVE A PRICE TO PAY FOR THAT.
BUT FIRST, YOU AND I HAVE UNFINISHED BUSINESS.
SO LET'S GET THIS SHOW ON THE ROAD, SHALL WE?!
IT'S PAST TIME I SHOW YOU WHAT I'M CAPABLE OF. AND THE BEST PART IS--
--I WON'T HAVE TO DO IT ALONE.
IT'S LIKE I KEEP SAYING-- I KNOW THE TRUTH ABOUT YOU. AND I WANT US TO FACE IT TOGETHER.
I WANT SO BADLY FOR YOU TO DO WHAT'S RIGHT.

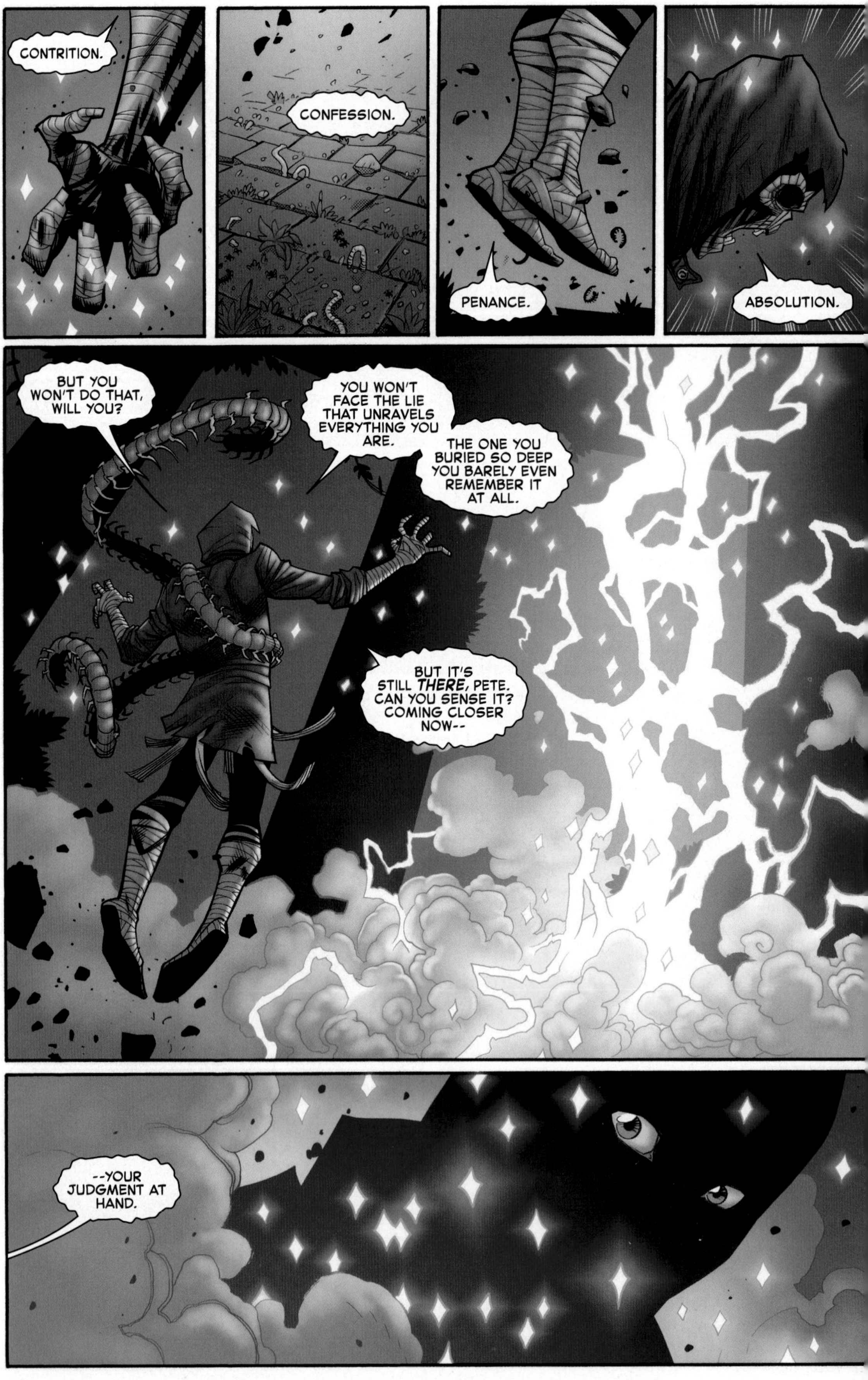

CONTRITION.
CONFESSION.
PENANCE.
ABSOLUTION.
BUT YOU WON'T DO THAT, WILL YOU?
YOU WON'T FACE THE LIE THAT UNRAVELS EVERYTHING YOU ARE.
THE ONE YOU BURIED SO DEEP YOU BARELY EVEN REMEMBER IT AT ALL.
BUT IT'S STILL THERE, PETE. CAN YOU SENSE IT? COMING CLOSER NOW--
--YOUR JUDGMENT AT HAND.

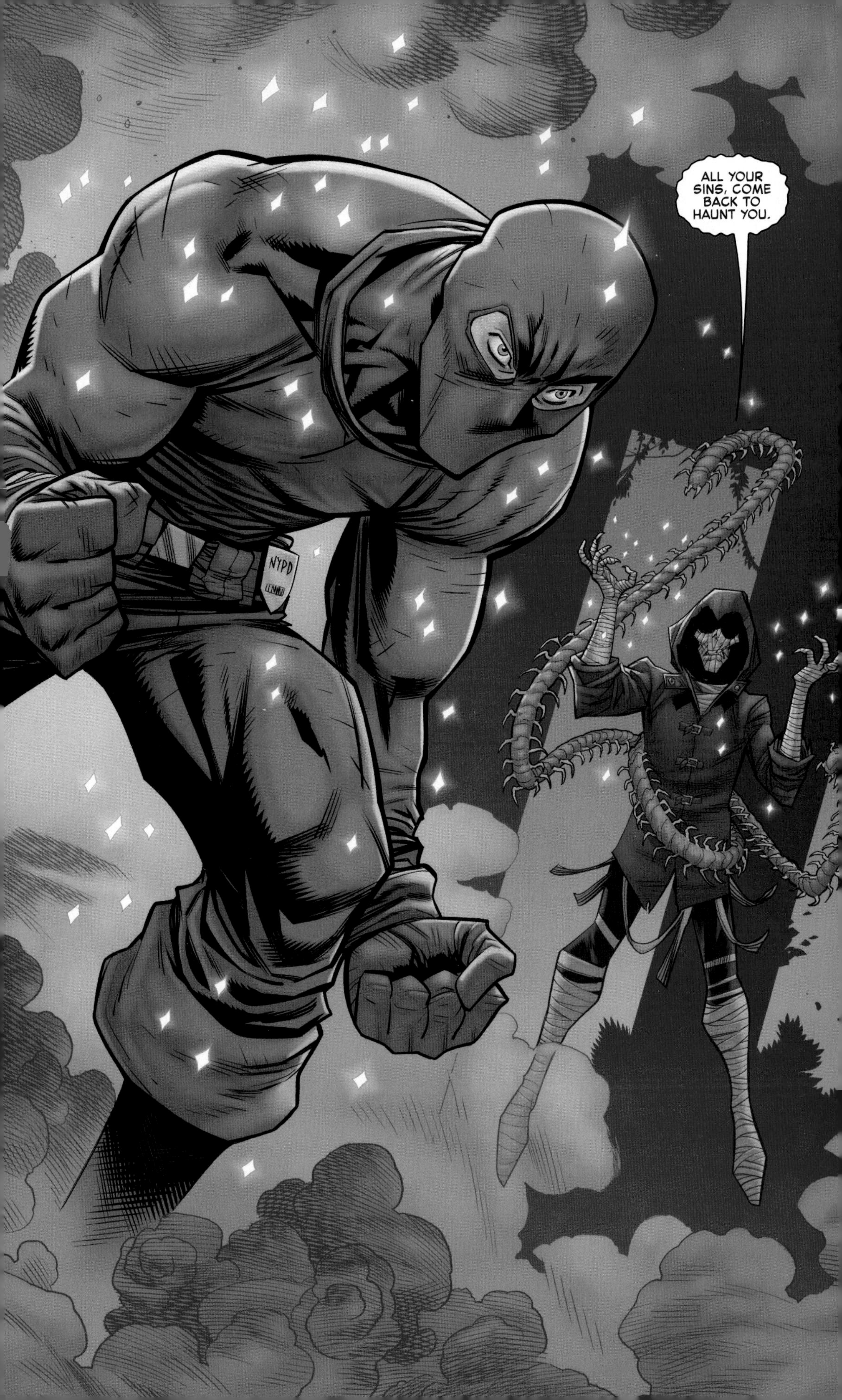
ALL YOUR SINS, COME BACK TO HAUNT YOU.
NYPD

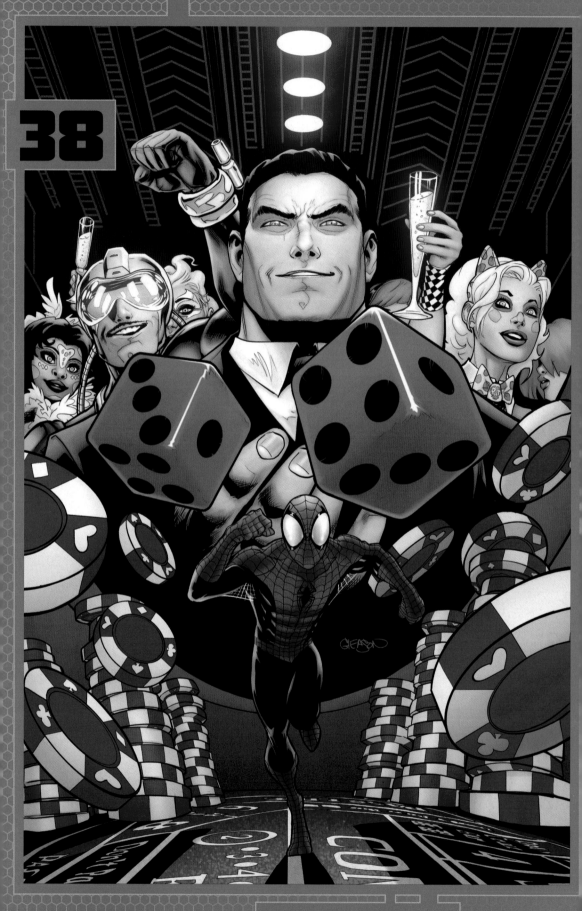

38

BREAKING NEWS PART 1

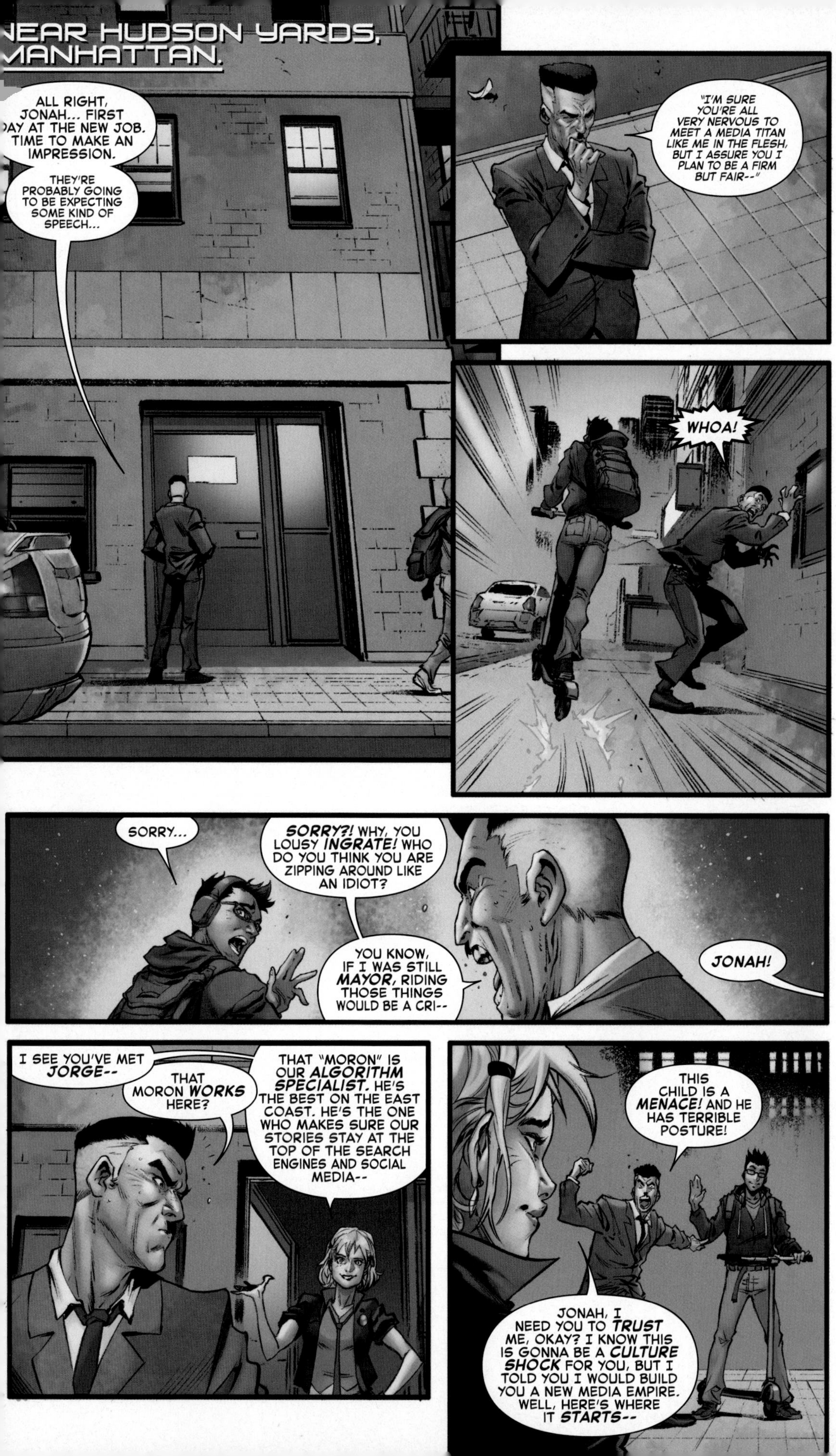
NEAR HUDSON YARDS, MANHATTAN.
ALL RIGHT, JONAH... FIRST DAY AT THE NEW JOB. TIME TO MAKE AN IMPRESSION.
THEY'RE PROBABLY GOING TO BE EXPECTING SOME KIND OF SPEECH...
"I'M SURE YOU'RE ALL VERY NERVOUS TO MEET A MEDIA TITAN LIKE ME IN THE FLESH, BUT I ASSURE YOU I PLAN TO BE A FIRM BUT FAIR--"
WHOA!
SORRY...
SORRY?! WHY, YOU LOUSY INGRATE! WHO DO YOU THINK YOU ARE ZIPPING AROUND LIKE AN IDIOT?
YOU KNOW, IF I WAS STILL MAYOR, RIDING THOSE THINGS WOULD BE A CRI--
JONAH!
I SEE YOU'VE MET JORGE--
THAT MORON WORKS HERE?
THAT "MORON" IS OUR ALGORITHM SPECIALIST. HE'S THE BEST ON THE EAST COAST. HE'S THE ONE WHO MAKES SURE OUR STORIES STAY AT THE TOP OF THE SEARCH ENGINES AND SOCIAL MEDIA--
THIS CHILD IS A MENACE! AND HE HAS TERRIBLE POSTURE!
JONAH, I NEED YOU TO TRUST ME, OKAY? I KNOW THIS IS GONNA BE A CULTURE SHOCK FOR YOU, BUT I TOLD YOU I WOULD BUILD YOU A NEW MEDIA EMPIRE. WELL, HERE'S WHERE IT STARTS--

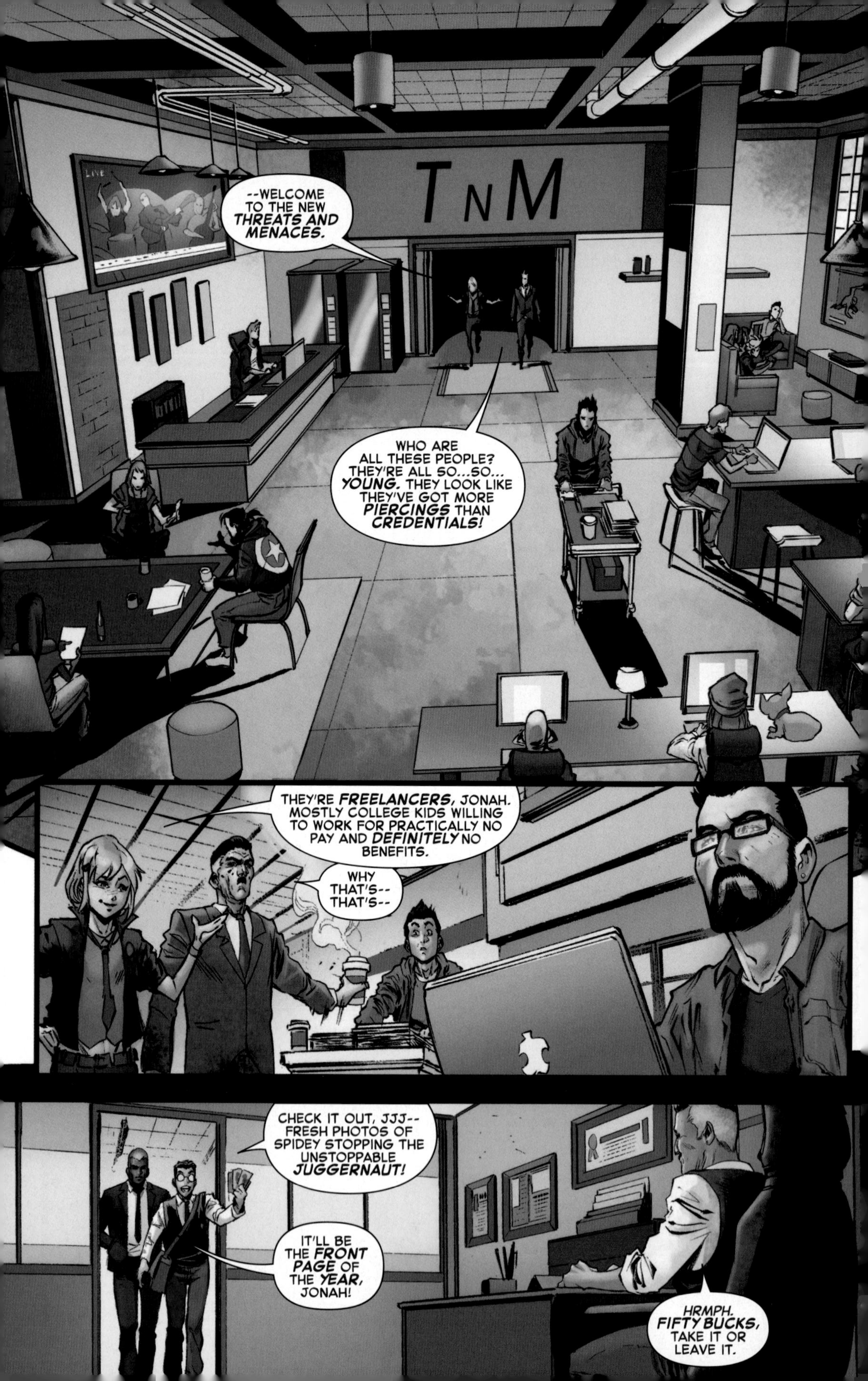
--WELCOME TO THE NEW THREATS AND MENACES.
TnM
WHO ARE ALL THESE PEOPLE? THEY'RE ALL SO...SO... YOUNG. THEY LOOK LIKE THEY'VE GOT MORE PIERCINGS THAN CREDENTIALS!
THEY'RE FREELANCERS, JONAH. MOSTLY COLLEGE KIDS WILLING TO WORK FOR PRACTICALLY NO PAY AND DEFINITELY NO BENEFITS.
WHY THAT'S-- THAT'S--
CHECK IT OUT, JJJ-- FRESH PHOTOS OF SPIDEY STOPPING THE UNSTOPPABLE JUGGERNAUT!
IT'LL BE THE FRONT PAGE OF THE YEAR, JONAH!
HRMPH. FIFTY BUCKS, TAKE IT OR LEAVE IT.

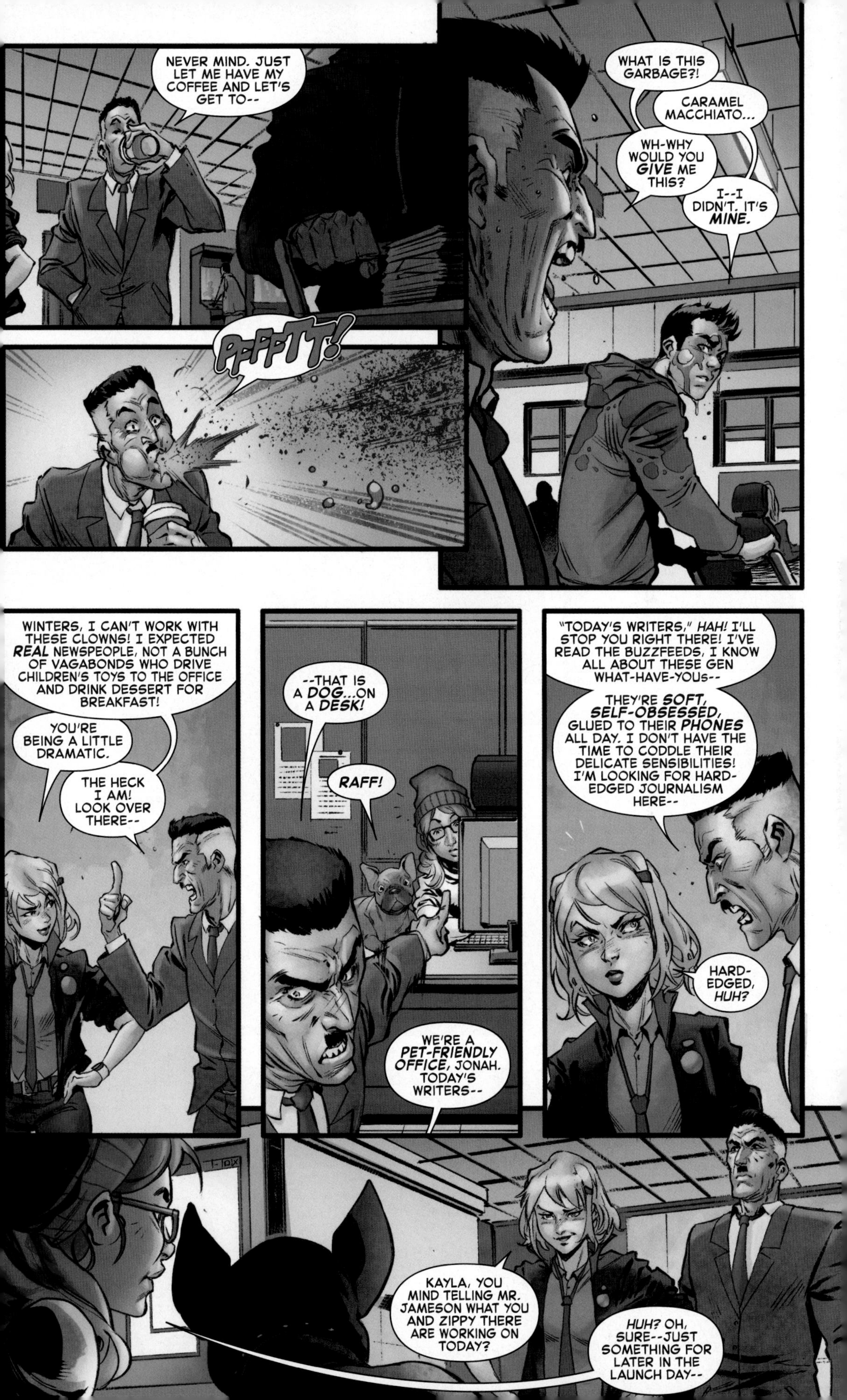

NEVER MIND. JUST LET ME HAVE MY COFFEE AND LET'S GET TO--
PFFFTT!
WHAT IS THIS GARBAGE?!
CARAMEL MACCHIATO...
WH-WHY WOULD YOU GIVE ME THIS?
I--I DIDN'T. IT'S MINE.
WINTERS, I CAN'T WORK WITH THESE CLOWNS! I EXPECTED REAL NEWSPEOPLE, NOT A BUNCH OF VAGABONDS WHO DRIVE CHILDREN'S TOYS TO THE OFFICE AND DRINK DESSERT FOR BREAKFAST!
YOU'RE BEING A LITTLE DRAMATIC.
THE HECK I AM! LOOK OVER THERE--
--THAT IS A DOG...ON A DESK!
RAFF!
WE'RE A PET-FRIENDLY OFFICE, JONAH. TODAY'S WRITERS--
"TODAY'S WRITERS," HAH! I'LL STOP YOU RIGHT THERE! I'VE READ THE BUZZFEEDS, I KNOW ALL ABOUT THESE GEN WHAT-HAVE-YOUs--
THEY'RE SOFT, SELF-OBSESSED, GLUED TO THEIR PHONES ALL DAY. I DON'T HAVE THE TIME TO CODDLE THEIR DELICATE SENSIBILITIES! I'M LOOKING FOR HARD-EDGED JOURNALISM HERE--
HARD-EDGED, HUH?
KAYLA, YOU MIND TELLING MR. JAMESON WHAT YOU AND ZIPPY THERE ARE WORKING ON TODAY?
HUH? OH, SURE--JUST SOMETHING FOR LATER IN THE LAUNCH DAY--

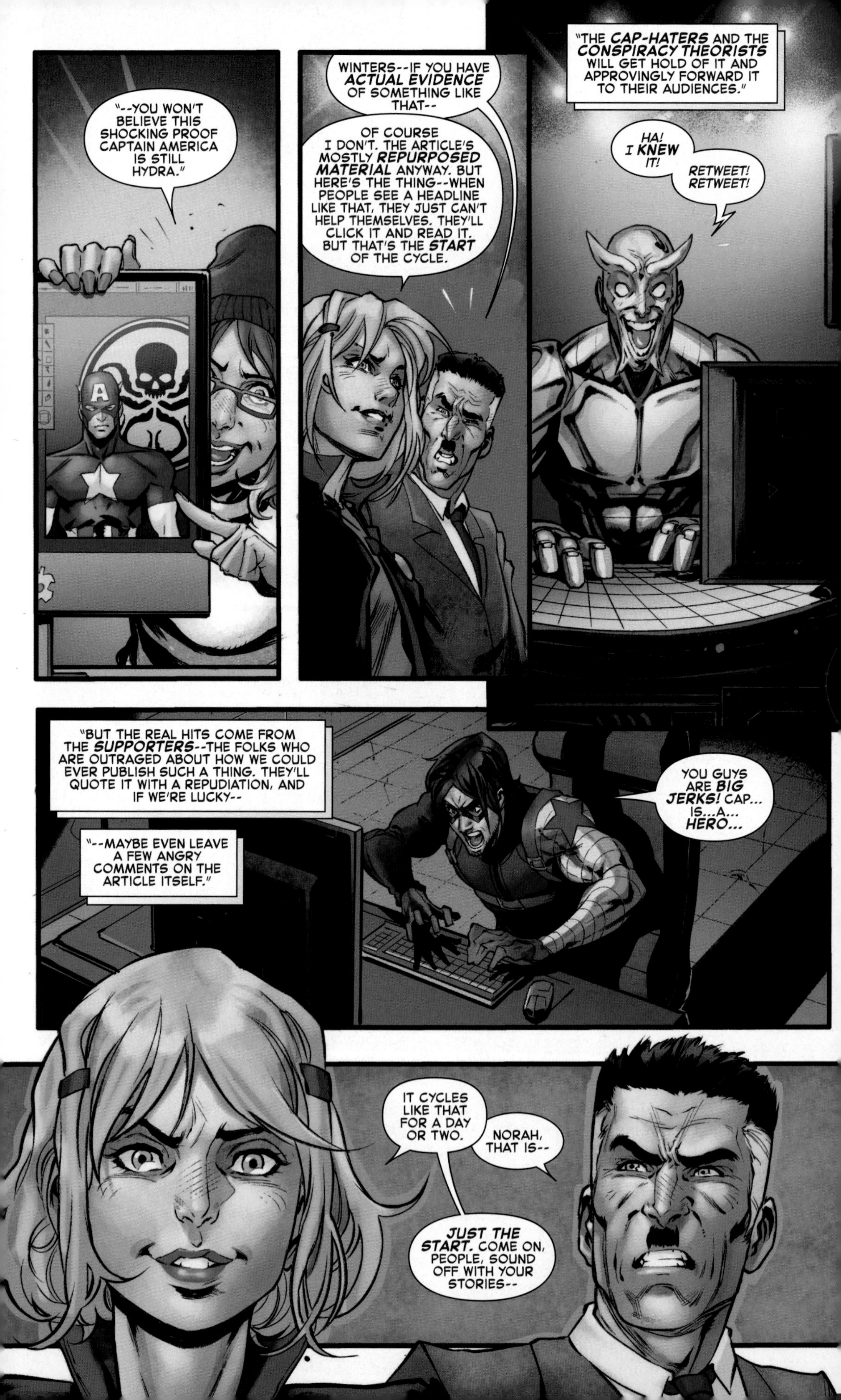

"--YOU WON'T BELIEVE THIS SHOCKING PROOF CAPTAIN AMERICA IS STILL HYDRA."
WINTERS--IF YOU HAVE ACTUAL EVIDENCE OF SOMETHING LIKE THAT--
OF COURSE I DON'T. THE ARTICLE'S MOSTLY REPURPOSED MATERIAL ANYWAY. BUT HERE'S THE THING--WHEN PEOPLE SEE A HEADLINE LIKE THAT, THEY JUST CAN'T HELP THEMSELVES. THEY'LL CLICK IT AND READ IT. BUT THAT'S THE START OF THE CYCLE.
"THE CAP-HATERS AND THE CONSPIRACY THEORISTS WILL GET HOLD OF IT AND APPROVINGLY FORWARD IT TO THEIR AUDIENCES."
HA! I KNEW IT!
RETWEET! RETWEET!
"BUT THE REAL HITS COME FROM THE SUPPORTERS--THE FOLKS WHO ARE OUTRAGED ABOUT HOW WE COULD EVER PUBLISH SUCH A THING. THEY'LL QUOTE IT WITH A REPUDIATION, AND IF WE'RE LUCKY--
"--MAYBE EVEN LEAVE A FEW ANGRY COMMENTS ON THE ARTICLE ITSELF."
YOU GUYS ARE BIG JERKS! CAP... IS...A... HERO...
IT CYCLES LIKE THAT FOR A DAY OR TWO.
NORAH, THAT IS--
JUST THE START. COME ON, PEOPLE, SOUND OFF WITH YOUR STORIES--

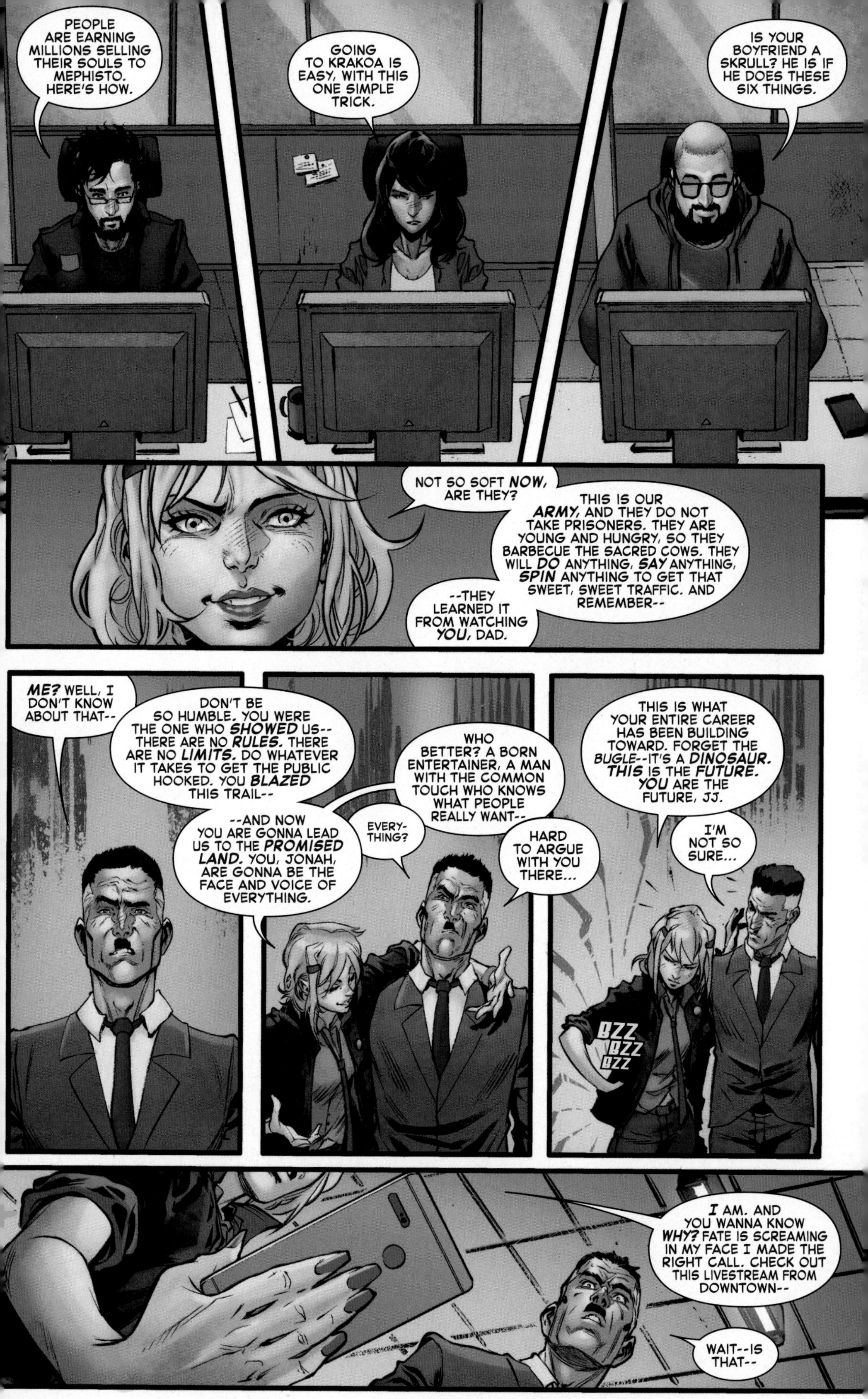
PEOPLE ARE EARNING MILLIONS SELLING THEIR SOULS TO MEPHISTO. HERE'S HOW.
GOING TO KRAKOA IS EASY, WITH THIS ONE SIMPLE TRICK.
IS YOUR BOYFRIEND A SKRULL? HE IS IF HE DOES THESE SIX THINGS.
NOT SO SOFT NOW, ARE THEY?
THIS IS OUR ARMY, AND THEY DO NOT TAKE PRISONERS. THEY ARE YOUNG AND HUNGRY, SO THEY BARBECUE THE SACRED COWS. THEY WILL DO ANYTHING, SAY ANYTHING, SPIN ANYTHING TO GET THAT SWEET, SWEET TRAFFIC. AND REMEMBER--
--THEY LEARNED IT FROM WATCHING YOU, DAD.
ME? WELL, I DON'T KNOW ABOUT THAT--
DON'T BE SO HUMBLE. YOU WERE THE ONE WHO SHOWED US-- THERE ARE NO RULES. THERE ARE NO LIMITS. DO WHATEVER IT TAKES TO GET THE PUBLIC HOOKED. YOU BLAZED THIS TRAIL--
--AND NOW YOU ARE GONNA LEAD US TO THE PROMISED LAND. YOU, JONAH, ARE GONNA BE THE FACE AND VOICE OF EVERYTHING.
EVERY-THING?
WHO BETTER? A BORN ENTERTAINER, A MAN WITH THE COMMON TOUCH WHO KNOWS WHAT PEOPLE REALLY WANT--
HARD TO ARGUE WITH YOU THERE...
THIS IS WHAT YOUR ENTIRE CAREER HAS BEEN BUILDING TOWARD. FORGET THE BUGLE--IT'S A DINOSAUR. THIS IS THE FUTURE. YOU ARE THE FUTURE, JJ.
I'M NOT SO SURE...
BZZ BZZ BZZ
I AM. AND YOU WANNA KNOW WHY? FATE IS SCREAMING IN MY FACE I MADE THE RIGHT CALL. CHECK OUT THIS LIVESTREAM FROM DOWNTOWN--
WAIT--IS THAT--

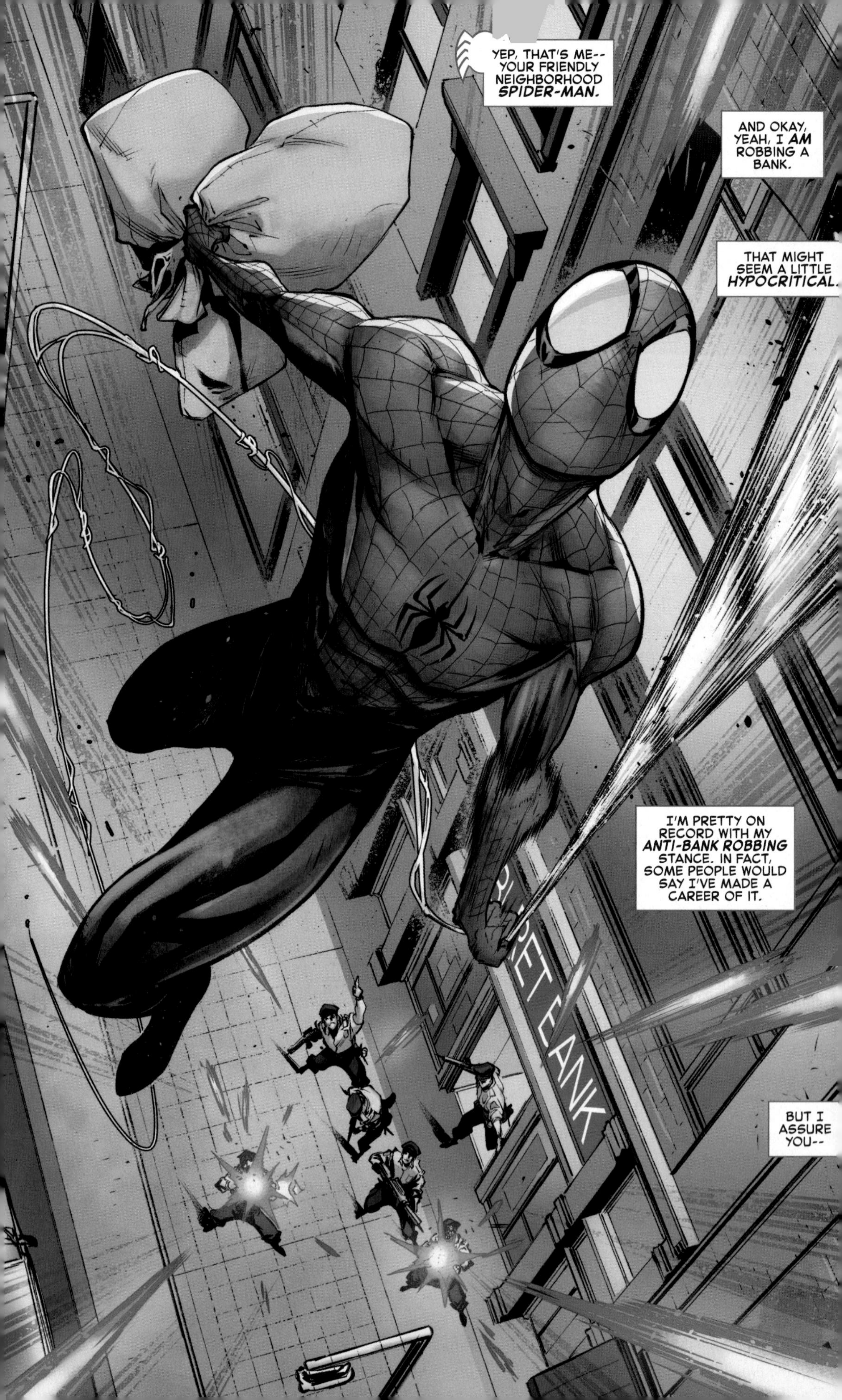

YEP, THAT'S ME--
YOUR FRIENDLY
NEIGHBORHOOD
SPIDER-MAN.
AND OKAY, YEAH, I AM ROBBING A BANK.
THAT MIGHT SEEM A LITTLE HYPOCRITICAL.
I'M PRETTY ON RECORD WITH MY ANTI-BANK ROBBING STANCE. IN FACT, SOME PEOPLE WOULD SAY I'VE MADE A CAREER OF IT.
BUT I ASSURE YOU--

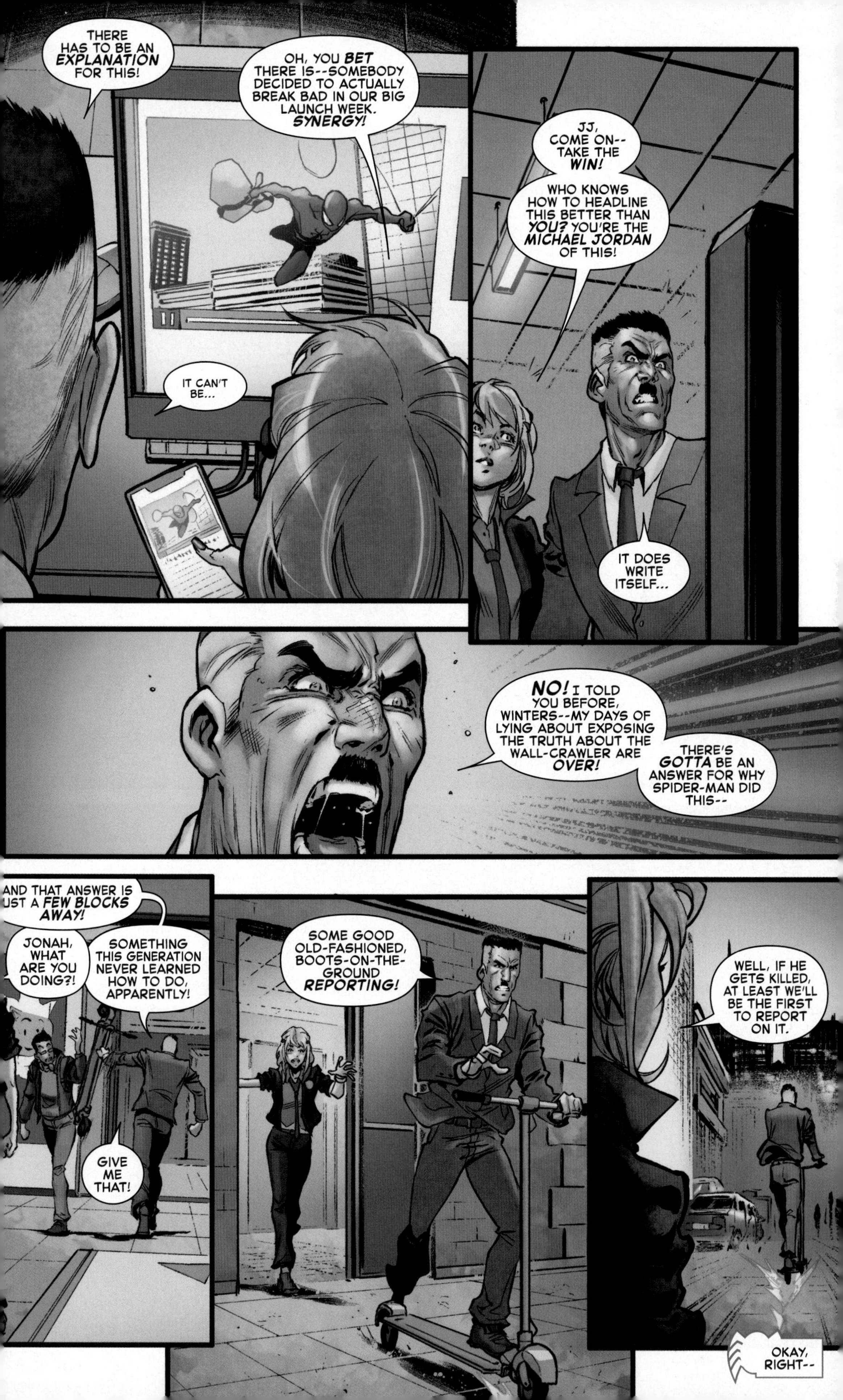
THERE HAS TO BE AN *EXPLANATION* FOR THIS!
OH, YOU *BET* THERE IS--SOMEBODY DECIDED TO ACTUALLY BREAK BAD IN OUR BIG LAUNCH WEEK. *SYNERGY!*
IT CAN'T BE...
JJ, COME ON--TAKE THE *WIN!*
WHO KNOWS HOW TO HEADLINE THIS BETTER THAN *YOU?* YOU'RE THE *MICHAEL JORDAN* OF THIS!
IT DOES WRITE ITSELF...
NO! I TOLD YOU BEFORE, WINTERS--MY DAYS OF LYING ABOUT EXPOSING THE TRUTH ABOUT THE WALL-CRAWLER ARE *OVER!*
THERE'S *GOTTA* BE AN ANSWER FOR WHY SPIDER-MAN DID THIS--
AND THAT ANSWER IS JUST A *FEW BLOCKS AWAY!*
JONAH, WHAT ARE YOU DOING?!
SOMETHING THIS GENERATION NEVER LEARNED HOW TO DO, APPARENTLY!
GIVE ME THAT!
SOME GOOD OLD-FASHIONED, BOOTS-ON-THE-GROUND *REPORTING!*
WELL, IF HE GETS KILLED, AT LEAST WE'LL BE THE FIRST TO REPORT ON IT.
OKAY, RIGHT--

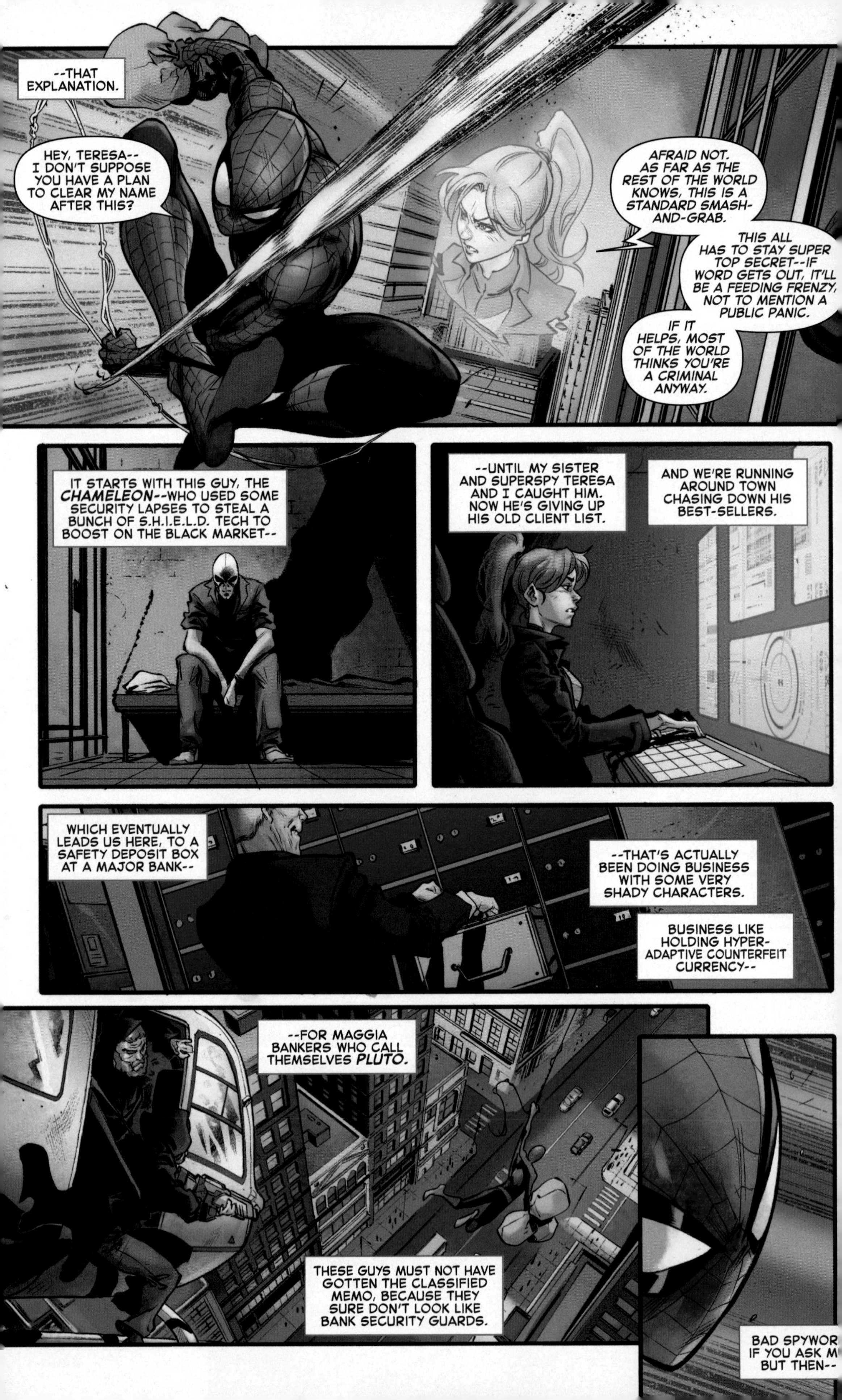

--THAT EXPLANATION.
HEY, TERESA-- I DON'T SUPPOSE YOU HAVE A PLAN TO CLEAR MY NAME AFTER THIS?
AFRAID NOT. AS FAR AS THE REST OF THE WORLD KNOWS, THIS IS A STANDARD SMASH-AND-GRAB.
THIS ALL HAS TO STAY SUPER TOP SECRET--IF WORD GETS OUT, IT'LL BE A FEEDING FRENZY, NOT TO MENTION A PUBLIC PANIC.
IF IT HELPS, MOST OF THE WORLD THINKS YOU'RE A CRIMINAL ANYWAY.
IT STARTS WITH THIS GUY, THE *CHAMELEON*--WHO USED SOME SECURITY LAPSES TO STEAL A BUNCH OF S.H.I.E.L.D. TECH TO BOOST ON THE BLACK MARKET--
--UNTIL MY SISTER AND SUPERSPY TERESA AND I CAUGHT HIM. NOW HE'S GIVING UP HIS OLD CLIENT LIST.
AND WE'RE RUNNING AROUND TOWN CHASING DOWN HIS BEST-SELLERS.
WHICH EVENTUALLY LEADS US HERE, TO A SAFETY DEPOSIT BOX AT A MAJOR BANK--
--THAT'S ACTUALLY BEEN DOING BUSINESS WITH SOME VERY SHADY CHARACTERS.
BUSINESS LIKE HOLDING HYPER-ADAPTIVE COUNTERFEIT CURRENCY--
--FOR MAGGIA BANKERS WHO CALL THEMSELVES *PLUTO*.
THESE GUYS MUST NOT HAVE GOTTEN THE CLASSIFIED MEMO, BECAUSE THEY SURE DON'T LOOK LIKE BANK SECURITY GUARDS.
BAD SPYWOR IF YOU ASK M BUT THEN--

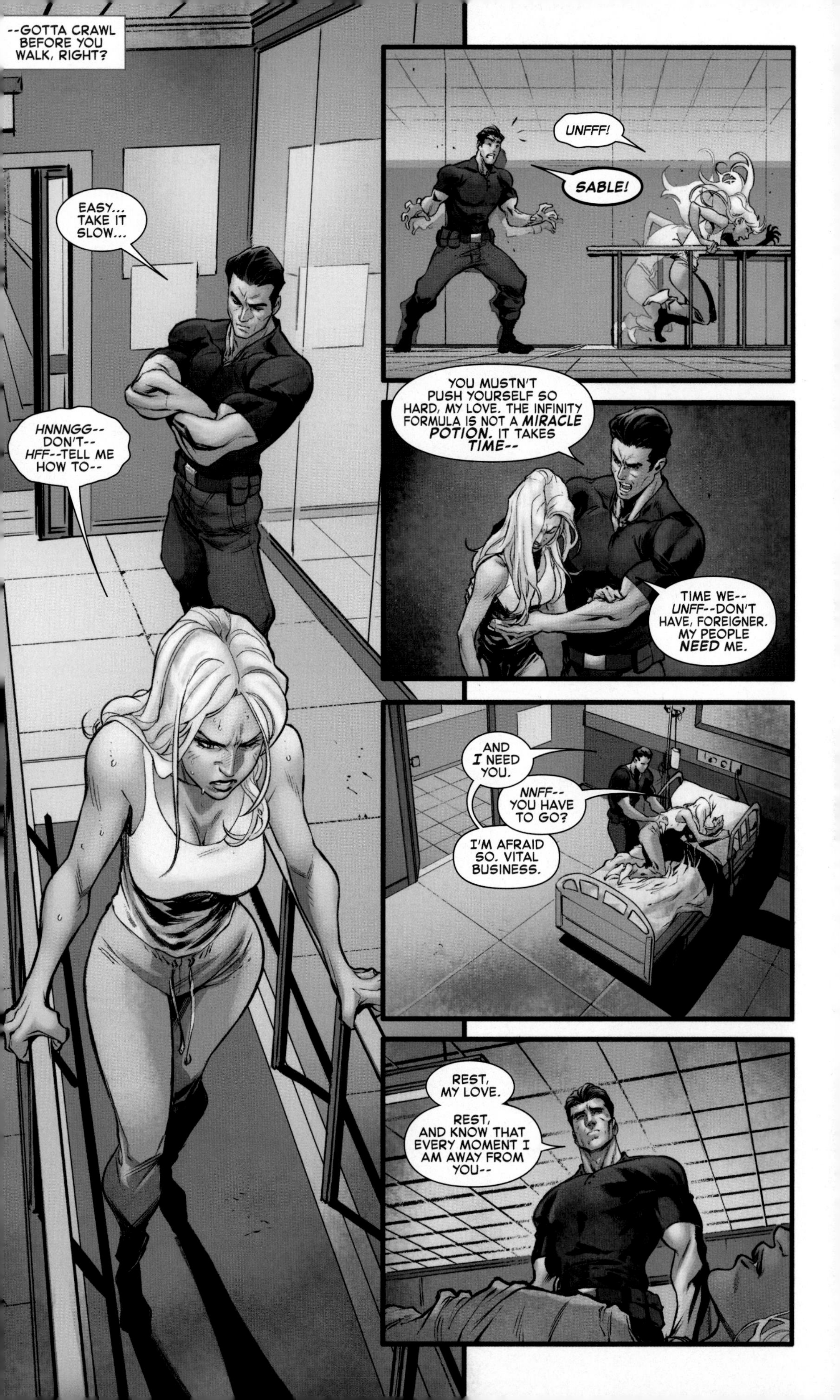

--GOTTA CRAWL BEFORE YOU WALK, RIGHT?
EASY... TAKE IT SLOW...
HNNNGG--DON'T--HFF--TELL ME HOW TO--
UNFFF!
SABLE!
YOU MUSTN'T PUSH YOURSELF SO HARD, MY LOVE. THE INFINITY FORMULA IS NOT A MIRACLE POTION. IT TAKES TIME--
TIME WE--UNFF--DON'T HAVE, FOREIGNER. MY PEOPLE NEED ME.
AND I NEED YOU.
NNFF--YOU HAVE TO GO?
I'M AFRAID SO. VITAL BUSINESS.
REST, MY LOVE.
REST, AND KNOW THAT EVERY MOMENT I AM AWAY FROM YOU--

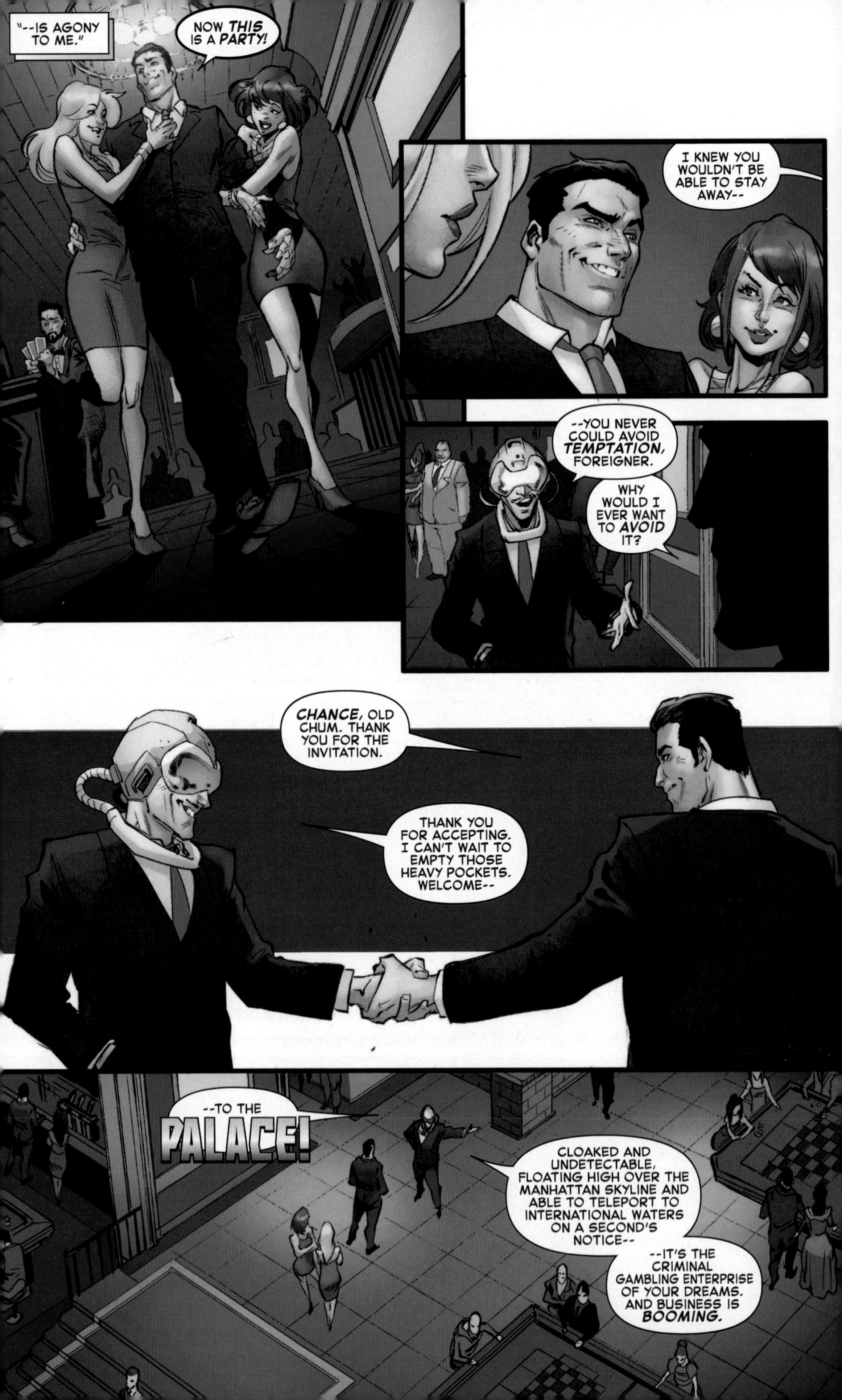
"--IS AGONY TO ME."
NOW THIS IS A PARTY!
I KNEW YOU WOULDN'T BE ABLE TO STAY AWAY--
--YOU NEVER COULD AVOID TEMPTATION, FOREIGNER.
WHY WOULD I EVER WANT TO AVOID IT?
CHANCE, OLD CHUM. THANK YOU FOR THE INVITATION.
THANK YOU FOR ACCEPTING. I CAN'T WAIT TO EMPTY THOSE HEAVY POCKETS. WELCOME--
--TO THE PALACE!
CLOAKED AND UNDETECTABLE, FLOATING HIGH OVER THE MANHATTAN SKYLINE AND ABLE TO TELEPORT TO INTERNATIONAL WATERS ON A SECOND'S NOTICE--
--IT'S THE CRIMINAL GAMBLING ENTERPRISE OF YOUR DREAMS. AND BUSINESS IS BOOMING.

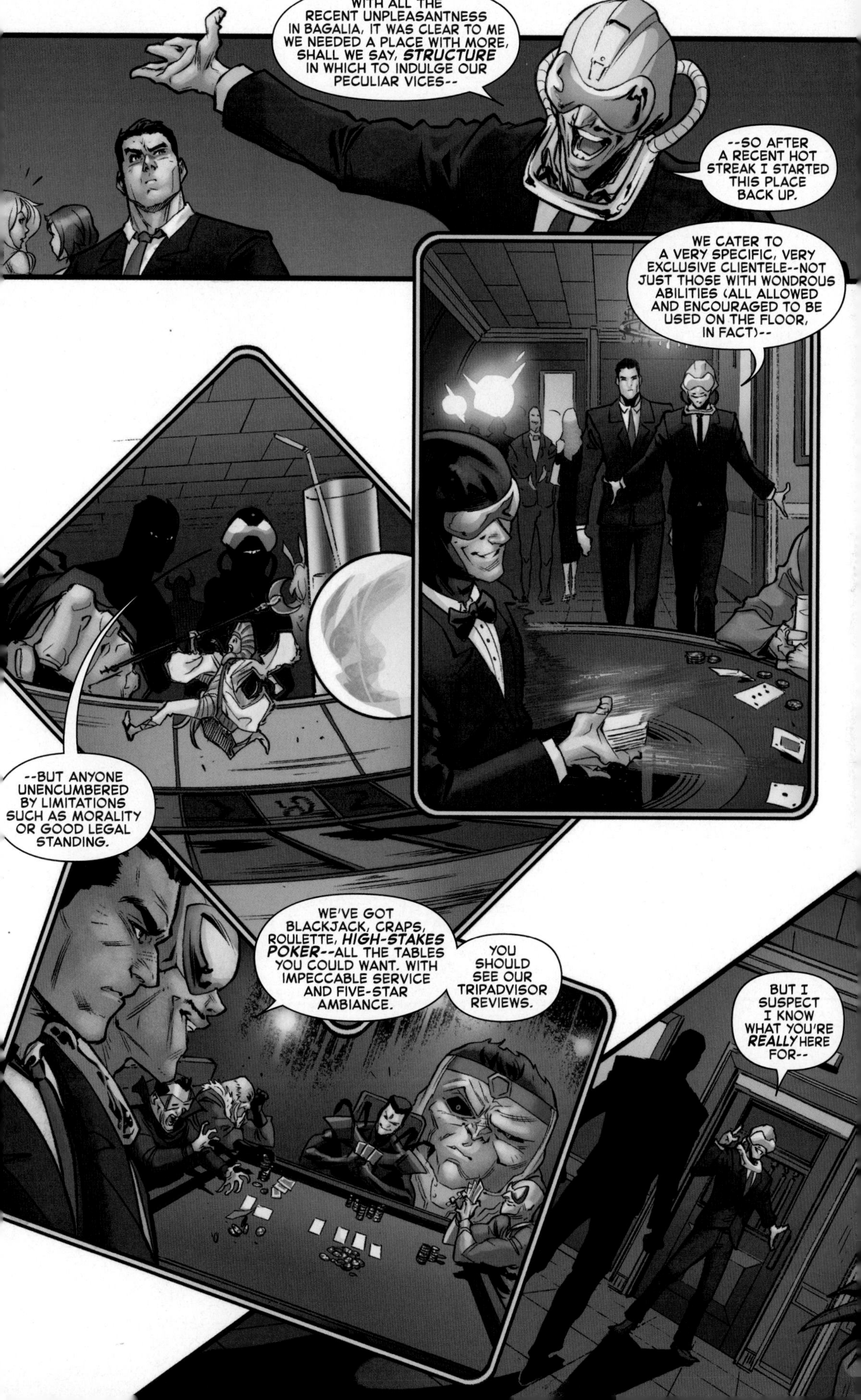
WITH ALL THE RECENT UNPLEASANTNESS IN BAGALIA, IT WAS CLEAR TO ME WE NEEDED A PLACE WITH MORE, SHALL WE SAY, *STRUCTURE* IN WHICH TO INDULGE OUR PECULIAR VICES--
--SO AFTER A RECENT HOT STREAK I STARTED THIS PLACE BACK UP.
WE CATER TO A VERY SPECIFIC, VERY EXCLUSIVE CLIENTELE--NOT JUST THOSE WITH WONDROUS ABILITIES (ALL ALLOWED AND ENCOURAGED TO BE USED ON THE FLOOR, IN FACT)--
--BUT ANYONE UNENCUMBERED BY LIMITATIONS SUCH AS MORALITY OR GOOD LEGAL STANDING.
WE'VE GOT BLACKJACK, CRAPS, ROULETTE, *HIGH-STAKES POKER*--ALL THE TABLES YOU COULD WANT. WITH IMPECCABLE SERVICE AND FIVE-STAR AMBIANCE.
YOU SHOULD SEE OUR TRIPADVISOR REVIEWS.
BUT I SUSPECT I KNOW WHAT YOU'RE *REALLY* HERE FOR--

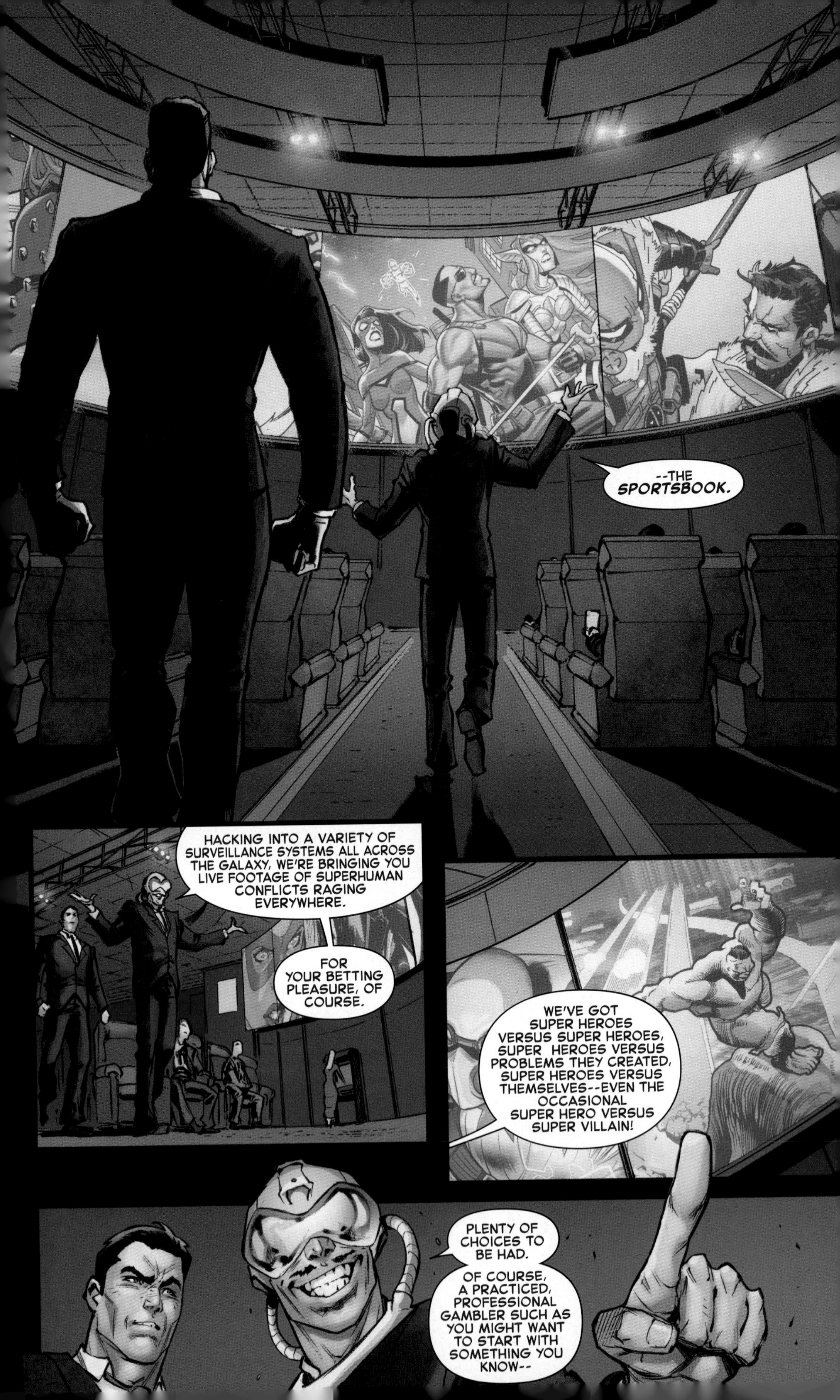
--THE SPORTSBOOK.
HACKING INTO A VARIETY OF SURVEILLANCE SYSTEMS ALL ACROSS THE GALAXY, WE'RE BRINGING YOU LIVE FOOTAGE OF SUPERHUMAN CONFLICTS RAGING EVERYWHERE.
FOR YOUR BETTING PLEASURE, OF COURSE.
WE'VE GOT SUPER HEROES VERSUS SUPER HEROES, SUPER HEROES VERSUS PROBLEMS THEY CREATED, SUPER HEROES VERSUS THEMSELVES--EVEN THE OCCASIONAL SUPER HERO VERSUS SUPER VILLAIN!
PLENTY OF CHOICES TO BE HAD.
OF COURSE, A PRACTICED, PROFESSIONAL GAMBLER SUCH AS YOU MIGHT WANT TO START WITH SOMETHING YOU KNOW--

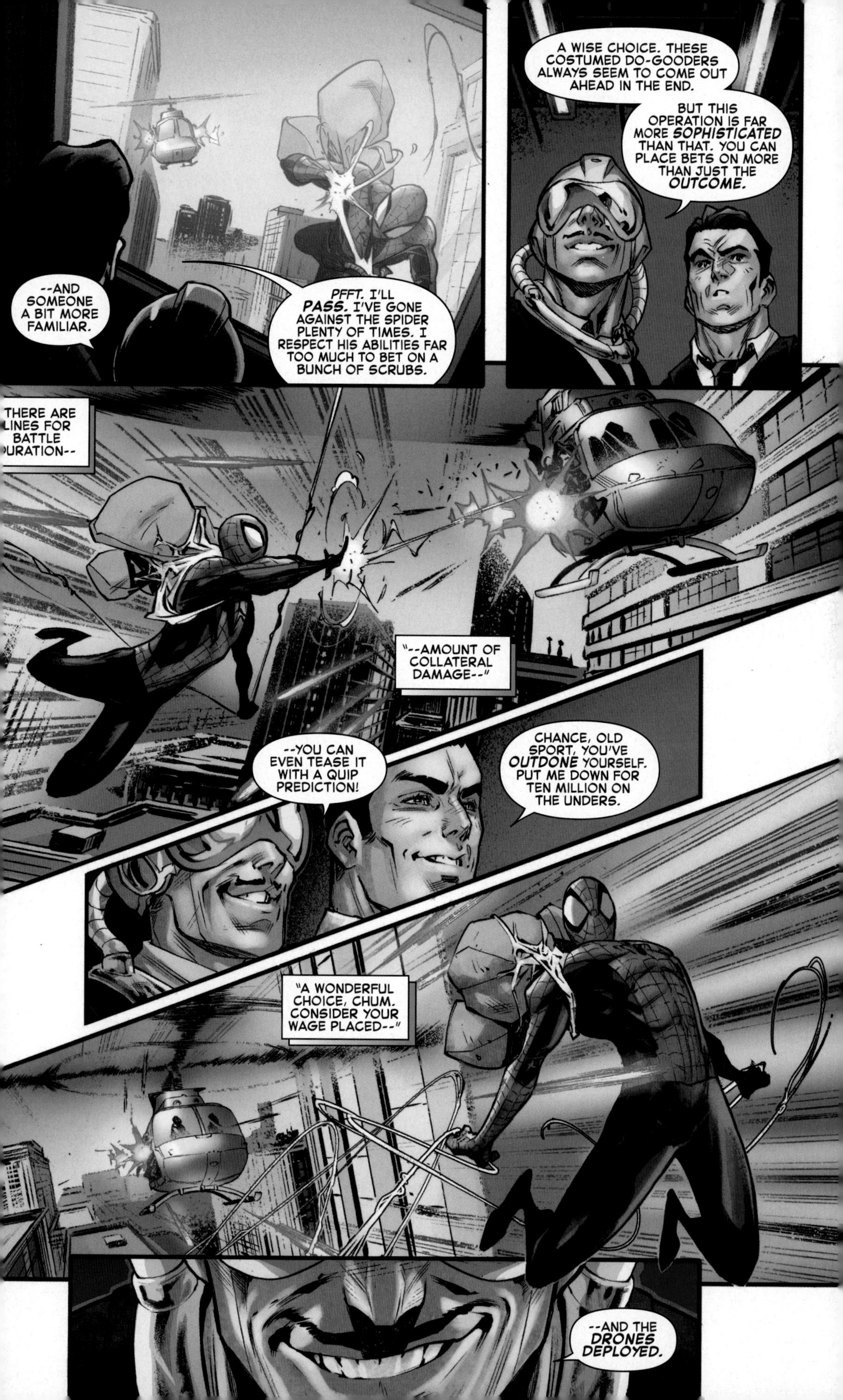
--AND SOMEONE A BIT MORE FAMILIAR.
PFFT. I'LL PASS. I'VE GONE AGAINST THE SPIDER PLENTY OF TIMES. I RESPECT HIS ABILITIES FAR TOO MUCH TO BET ON A BUNCH OF SCRUBS.
A WISE CHOICE. THESE COSTUMED DO-GOODERS ALWAYS SEEM TO COME OUT AHEAD IN THE END.
BUT THIS OPERATION IS FAR MORE SOPHISTICATED THAN THAT. YOU CAN PLACE BETS ON MORE THAN JUST THE OUTCOME.
THERE ARE LINES FOR BATTLE DURATION--
"--AMOUNT OF COLLATERAL DAMAGE--"
--YOU CAN EVEN TEASE IT WITH A QUIP PREDICTION!
CHANCE, OLD SPORT, YOU'VE OUTDONE YOURSELF. PUT ME DOWN FOR TEN MILLION ON THE UNDERS.
"A WONDERFUL CHOICE, CHUM. CONSIDER YOUR WAGE PLACED--"
--AND THE DRONES DEPLOYED.

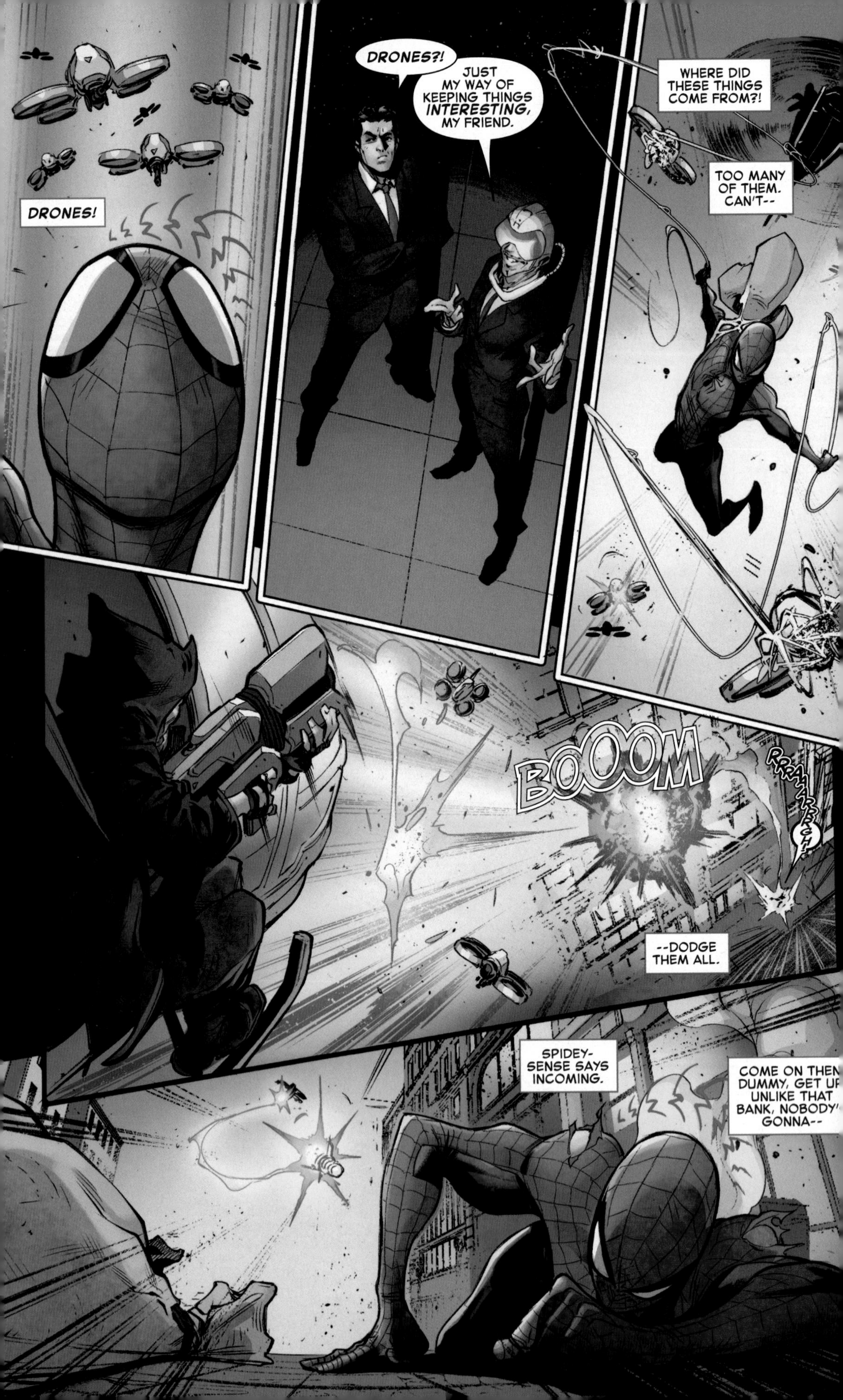
DRONES!
DRONES?!
JUST MY WAY OF KEEPING THINGS INTERESTING, MY FRIEND.
WHERE DID THESE THINGS COME FROM?!
TOO MANY OF THEM. CAN'T--
BOOOOM
RRRAAARRGH!
--DODGE THEM ALL.
SPIDEY-SENSE SAYS INCOMING.
COME ON THEN DUMMY, GET UP UNLIKE THAT BANK, NOBODY'S GONNA--

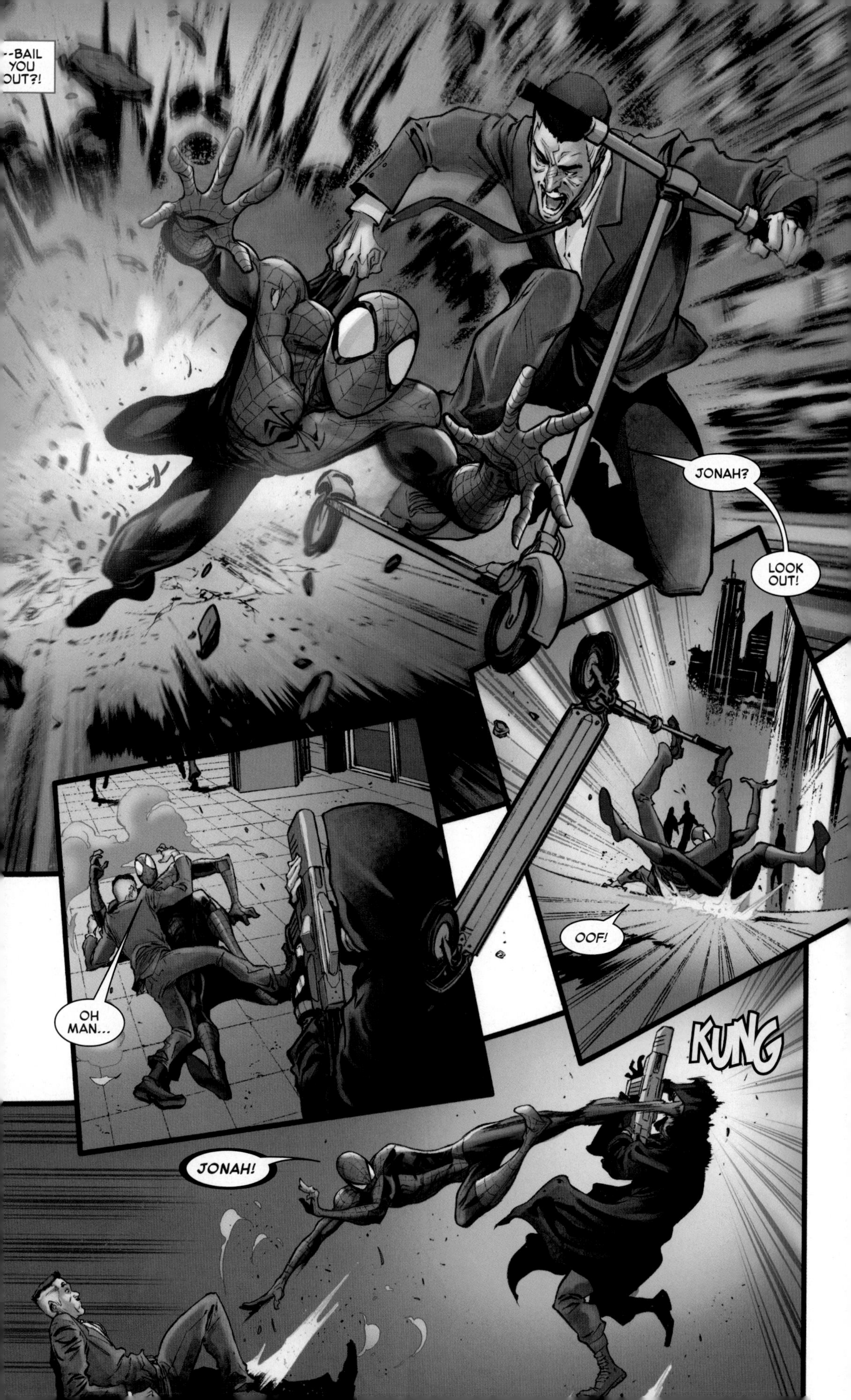
--BAIL YOU OUT?!
JONAH?
LOOK OUT!
OOF!
OH MAN...
KUNG
JONAH!

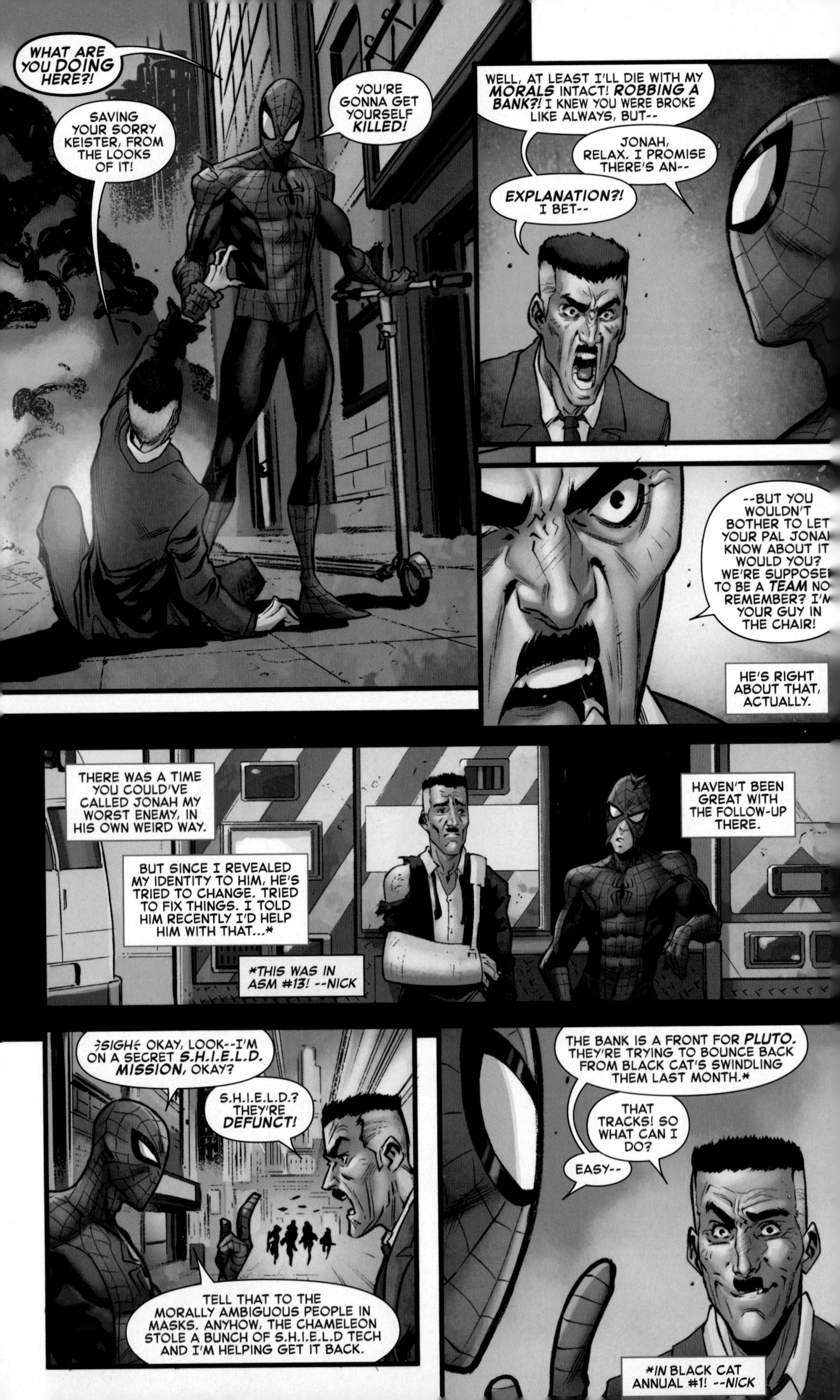
WHAT ARE YOU DOING HERE?!
YOU'RE GONNA GET YOURSELF KILLED!
SAVING YOUR SORRY KEISTER, FROM THE LOOKS OF IT!
WELL, AT LEAST I'LL DIE WITH MY MORALS INTACT! ROBBING A BANK?! I KNEW YOU WERE BROKE LIKE ALWAYS, BUT--
JONAH, RELAX. I PROMISE THERE'S AN--
EXPLANATION?! I BET--
--BUT YOU WOULDN'T BOTHER TO LET YOUR PAL JONAH KNOW ABOUT IT WOULD YOU? WE'RE SUPPOSED TO BE A TEAM NOW REMEMBER? I'M YOUR GUY IN THE CHAIR!
HE'S RIGHT ABOUT THAT, ACTUALLY.
THERE WAS A TIME YOU COULD'VE CALLED JONAH MY WORST ENEMY, IN HIS OWN WEIRD WAY.
BUT SINCE I REVEALED MY IDENTITY TO HIM, HE'S TRIED TO CHANGE. TRIED TO FIX THINGS. I TOLD HIM RECENTLY I'D HELP HIM WITH THAT...*
*THIS WAS IN ASM #13! --NICK
HAVEN'T BEEN GREAT WITH THE FOLLOW-UP THERE.
⥽SIGH⥼ OKAY, LOOK--I'M ON A SECRET S.H.I.E.L.D. MISSION, OKAY?
S.H.I.E.L.D.? THEY'RE DEFUNCT!
TELL THAT TO THE MORALLY AMBIGUOUS PEOPLE IN MASKS. ANYHOW, THE CHAMELEON STOLE A BUNCH OF S.H.I.E.L.D TECH AND I'M HELPING GET IT BACK.
THE BANK IS A FRONT FOR PLUTO. THEY'RE TRYING TO BOUNCE BACK FROM BLACK CAT'S SWINDLING THEM LAST MONTH.*
THAT TRACKS! SO WHAT CAN I DO?
EASY--
*IN BLACK CAT ANNUAL #1! --NICK

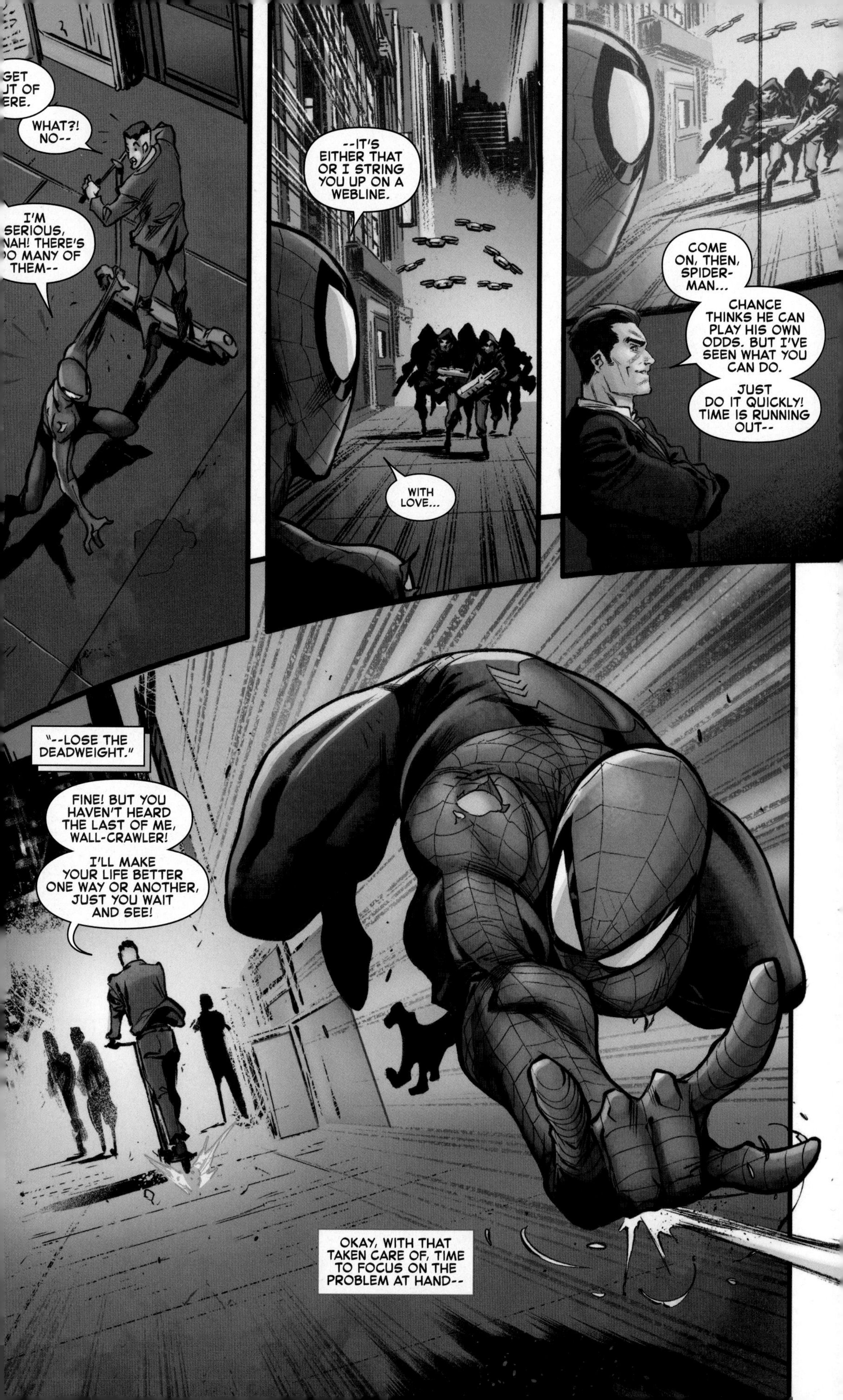

GET
UT OF
ERE.
WHAT?! NO--
I'M SERIOUS, NAH! THERE'S O MANY OF THEM--
--IT'S EITHER THAT OR I STRING YOU UP ON A WEBLINE.
WITH LOVE...
COME ON, THEN, SPIDER-MAN...
CHANCE THINKS HE CAN PLAY HIS OWN ODDS. BUT I'VE SEEN WHAT YOU CAN DO.
JUST DO IT QUICKLY! TIME IS RUNNING OUT--
"--LOSE THE DEADWEIGHT."
FINE! BUT YOU HAVEN'T HEARD THE LAST OF ME, WALL-CRAWLER!
I'LL MAKE YOUR LIFE BETTER ONE WAY OR ANOTHER, JUST YOU WAIT AND SEE!
OKAY, WITH THAT TAKEN CARE OF, TIME TO FOCUS ON THE PROBLEM AT HAND--

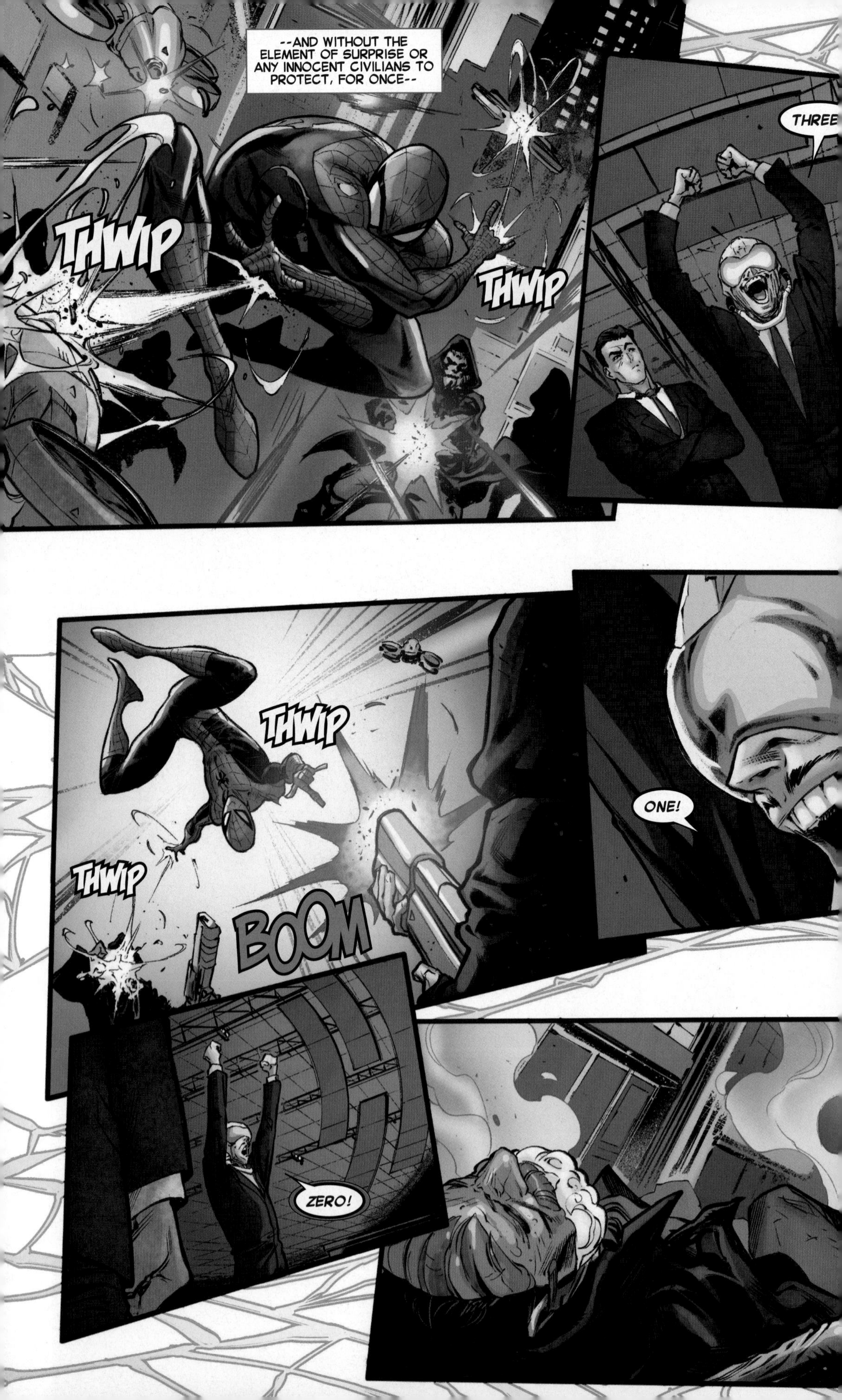
--AND WITHOUT THE ELEMENT OF SURPRISE OR ANY INNOCENT CIVILIANS TO PROTECT, FOR ONCE--
THWIP
THWIP
THREE
THWIP
THWIP
BOOM
ONE!
ZERO!

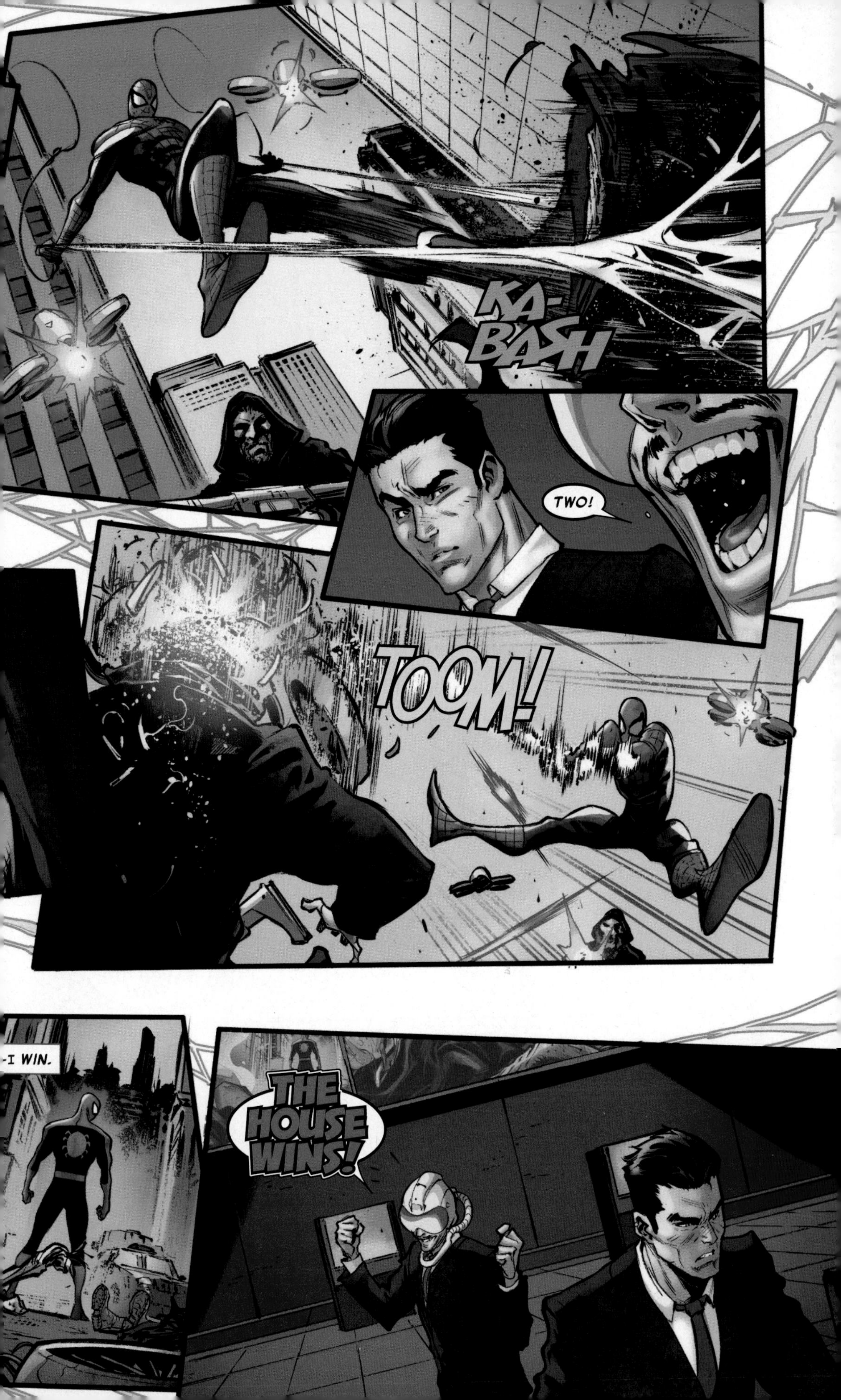
KA-BASH
TWO!
TOOM!
-I WIN.
THE HOUSE WINS!

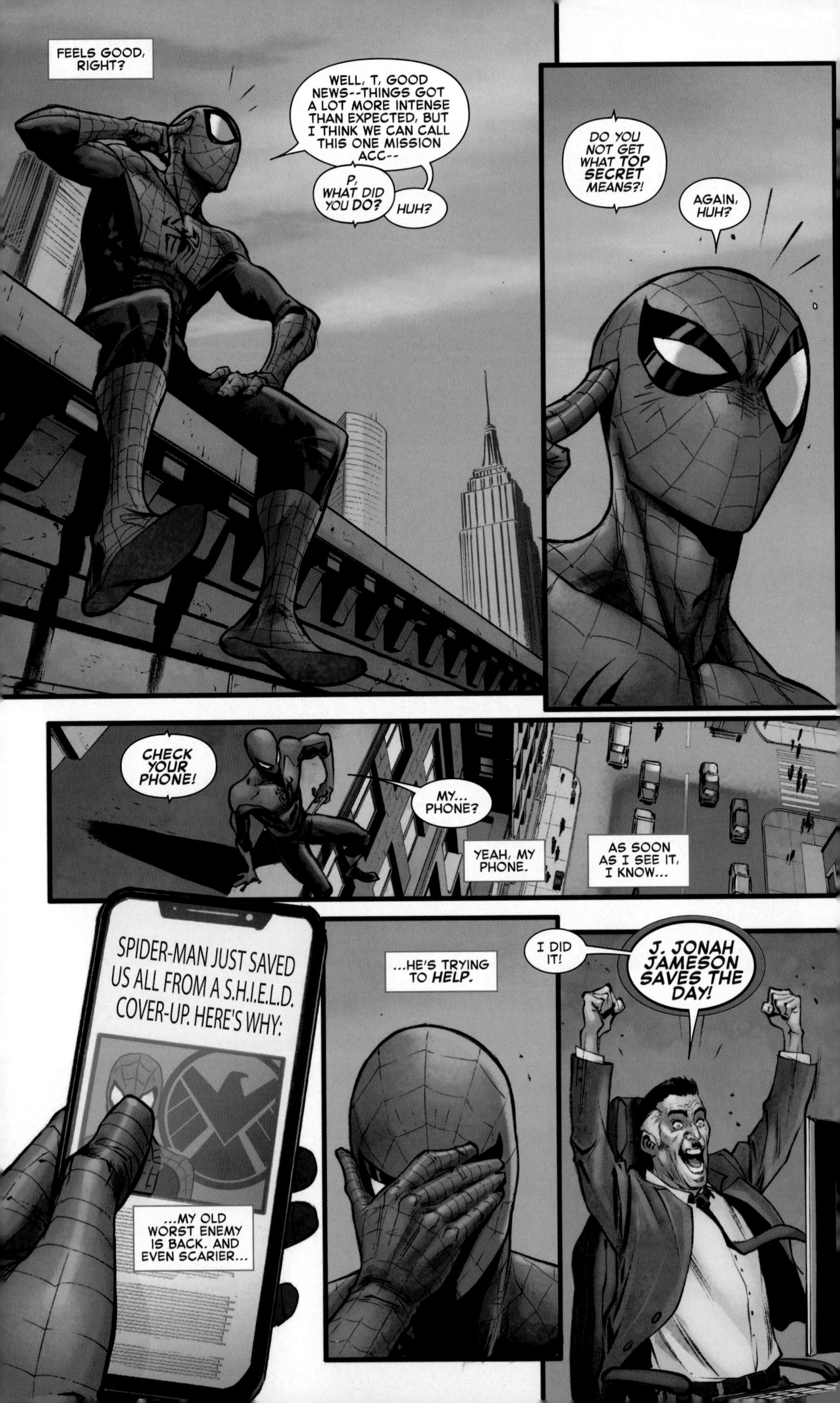

FEELS GOOD, RIGHT?
WELL, T, GOOD NEWS--THINGS GOT A LOT MORE INTENSE THAN EXPECTED, BUT I THINK WE CAN CALL THIS ONE MISSION ACC--
P, WHAT DID YOU DO?
HUH?
DO YOU NOT GET WHAT TOP SECRET MEANS?!
AGAIN, HUH?
CHECK YOUR PHONE!
MY... PHONE?
YEAH, MY PHONE.
AS SOON AS I SEE IT, I KNOW...
SPIDER-MAN JUST SAVED US ALL FROM A S.H.I.E.L.D. COVER-UP. HERE'S WHY:
...MY OLD WORST ENEMY IS BACK. AND EVEN SCARIER...
...HE'S TRYING TO HELP.
I DID IT!
J. JONAH JAMESON SAVES THE DAY!

39

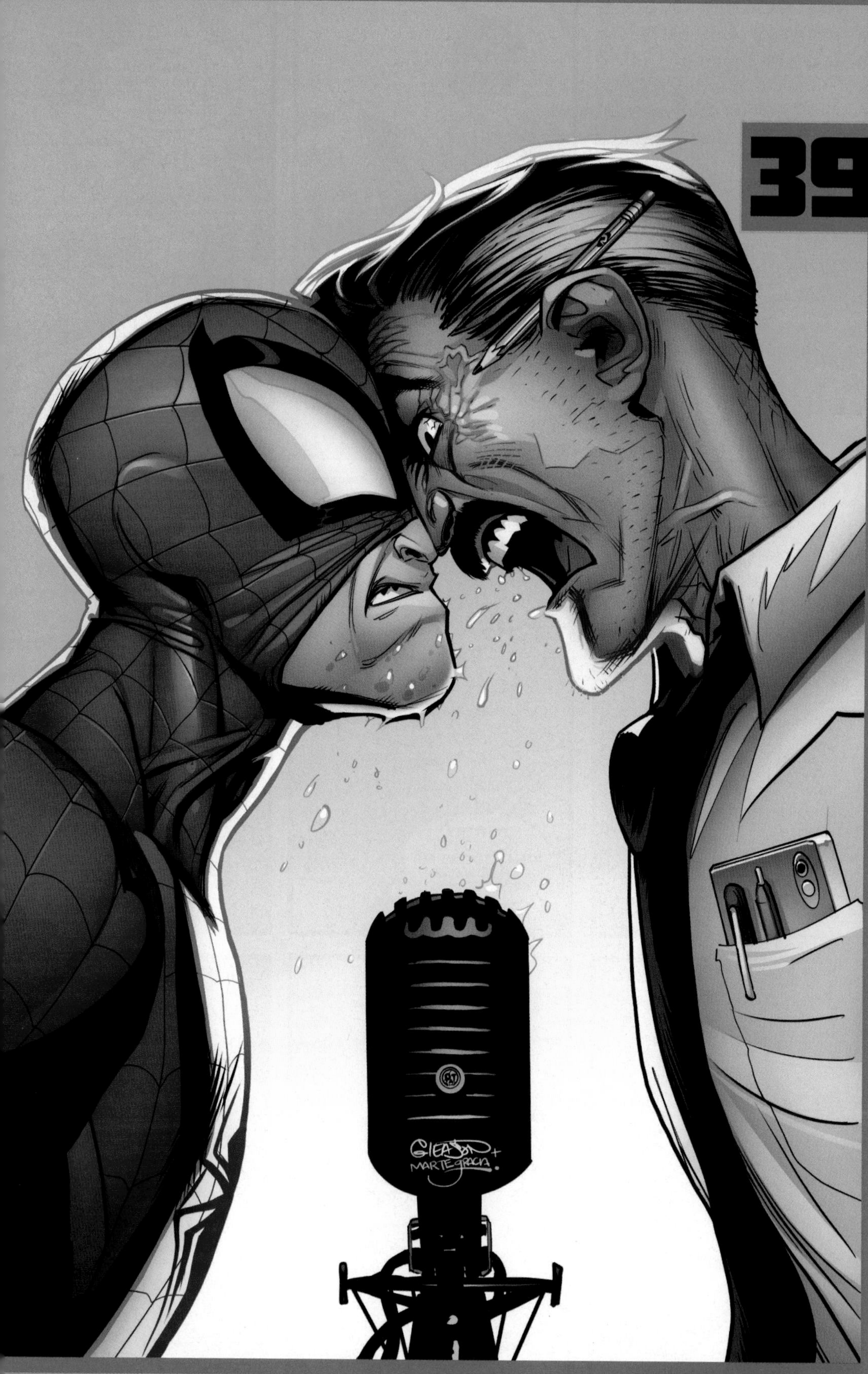
GLEASON +
MARTEGRACIA

BREAKING NEWS PART 2

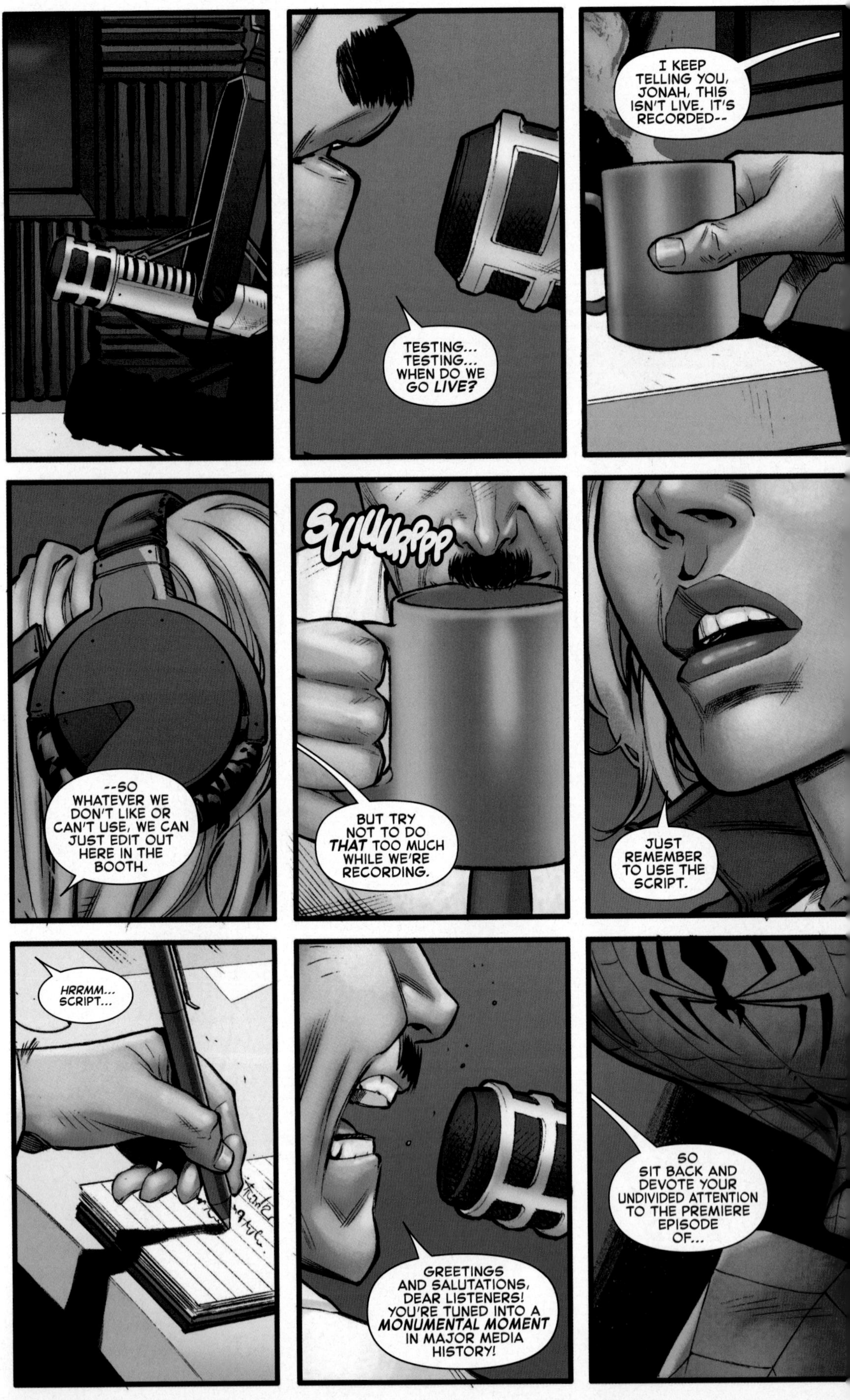
TESTING... TESTING... WHEN DO WE GO *LIVE?*
I KEEP TELLING YOU, JONAH, THIS ISN'T LIVE. IT'S RECORDED--
--SO WHATEVER WE DON'T LIKE OR CAN'T USE, WE CAN JUST EDIT OUT HERE IN THE BOOTH.
SLUUURPPP
BUT TRY NOT TO DO *THAT* TOO MUCH WHILE WE'RE RECORDING.
JUST REMEMBER TO USE THE SCRIPT.
HRRMM... SCRIPT...
GREETINGS AND SALUTATIONS, DEAR LISTENERS! YOU'RE TUNED INTO A ***MONUMENTAL MOMENT*** IN MAJOR MEDIA HISTORY!
SO SIT BACK AND DEVOTE YOUR UNDIVIDED ATTENTION TO THE PREMIERE EPISODE OF...

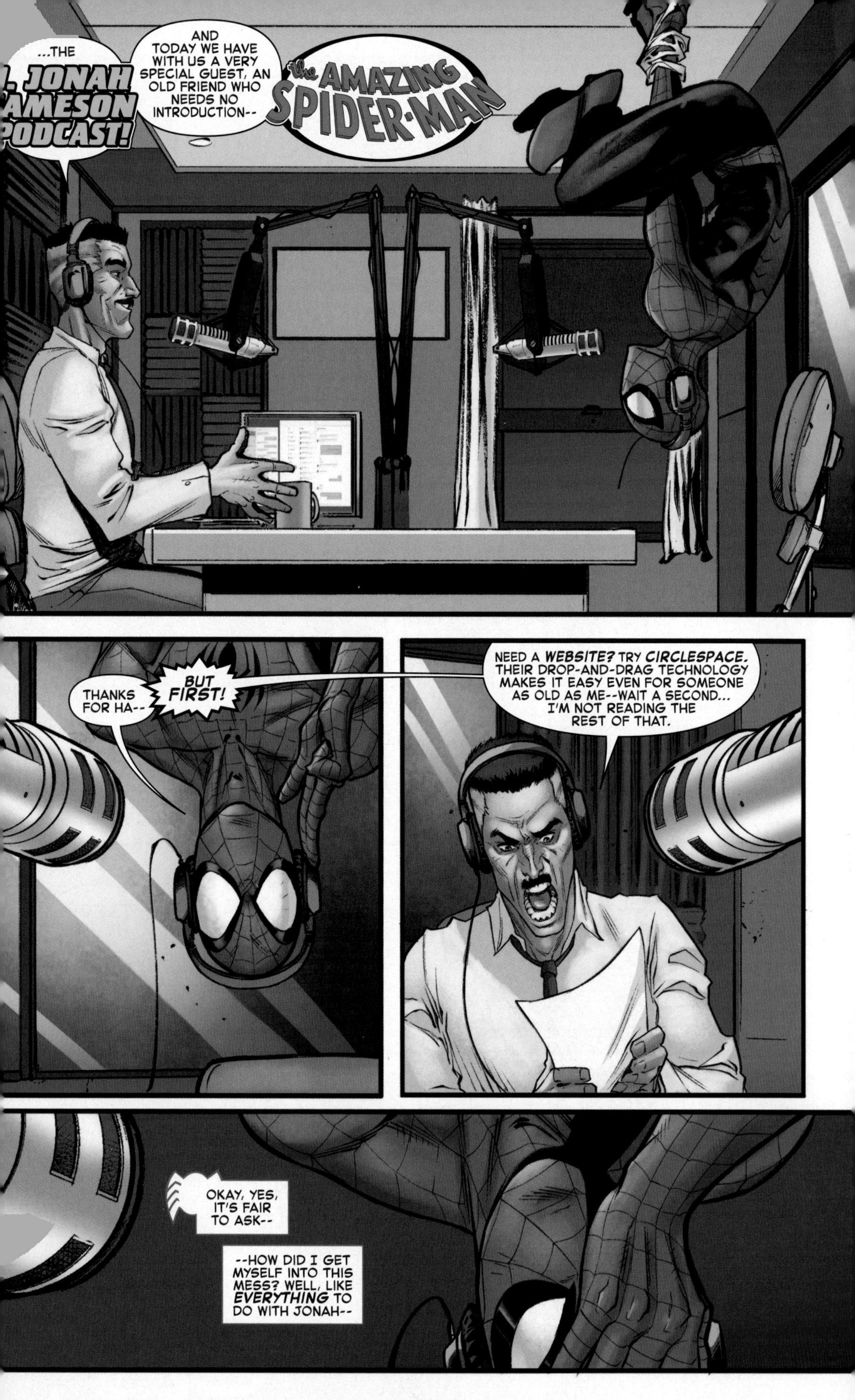
...THE J. JONAH JAMESON PODCAST!
AND TODAY WE HAVE WITH US A VERY SPECIAL GUEST, AN OLD FRIEND WHO NEEDS NO INTRODUCTION--
THE AMAZING SPIDER-MAN
THANKS FOR HA--
BUT FIRST!
NEED A WEBSITE? TRY CIRCLESPACE. THEIR DROP-AND-DRAG TECHNOLOGY MAKES IT EASY EVEN FOR SOMEONE AS OLD AS ME--WAIT A SECOND... I'M NOT READING THE REST OF THAT.
OKAY, YES, IT'S FAIR TO ASK--
--HOW DID I GET MYSELF INTO THIS MESS? WELL, LIKE EVERYTHING TO DO WITH JONAH--

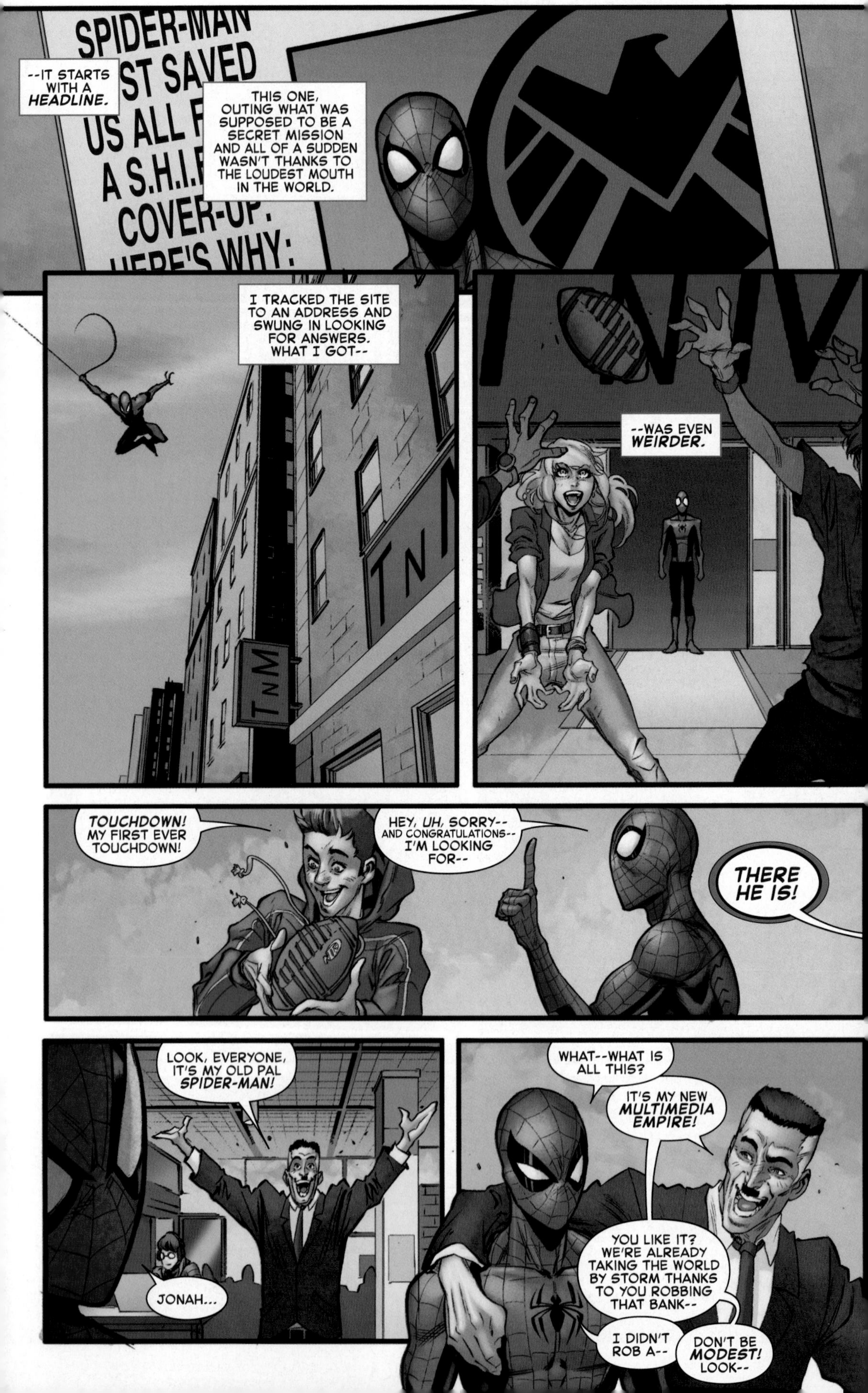
SPIDER-MAN
ST SAVED
US ALL F
A S.H.I.F
COVER-UP.
--IT STARTS WITH A HEADLINE.
THIS ONE, OUTING WHAT WAS SUPPOSED TO BE A SECRET MISSION AND ALL OF A SUDDEN WASN'T THANKS TO THE LOUDEST MOUTH IN THE WORLD.
I TRACKED THE SITE TO AN ADDRESS AND SWUNG IN LOOKING FOR ANSWERS. WHAT I GOT--
TNM
--WAS EVEN WEIRDER.
TOUCHDOWN! MY FIRST EVER TOUCHDOWN!
HEY, UH, SORRY-- AND CONGRATULATIONS-- I'M LOOKING FOR--
THERE HE IS!
LOOK, EVERYONE, IT'S MY OLD PAL SPIDER-MAN!
JONAH...
WHAT--WHAT IS ALL THIS?
IT'S MY NEW MULTIMEDIA EMPIRE!
YOU LIKE IT? WE'RE ALREADY TAKING THE WORLD BY STORM THANKS TO YOU ROBBING THAT BANK--
I DIDN'T ROB A--
DON'T BE MODEST! LOOK--

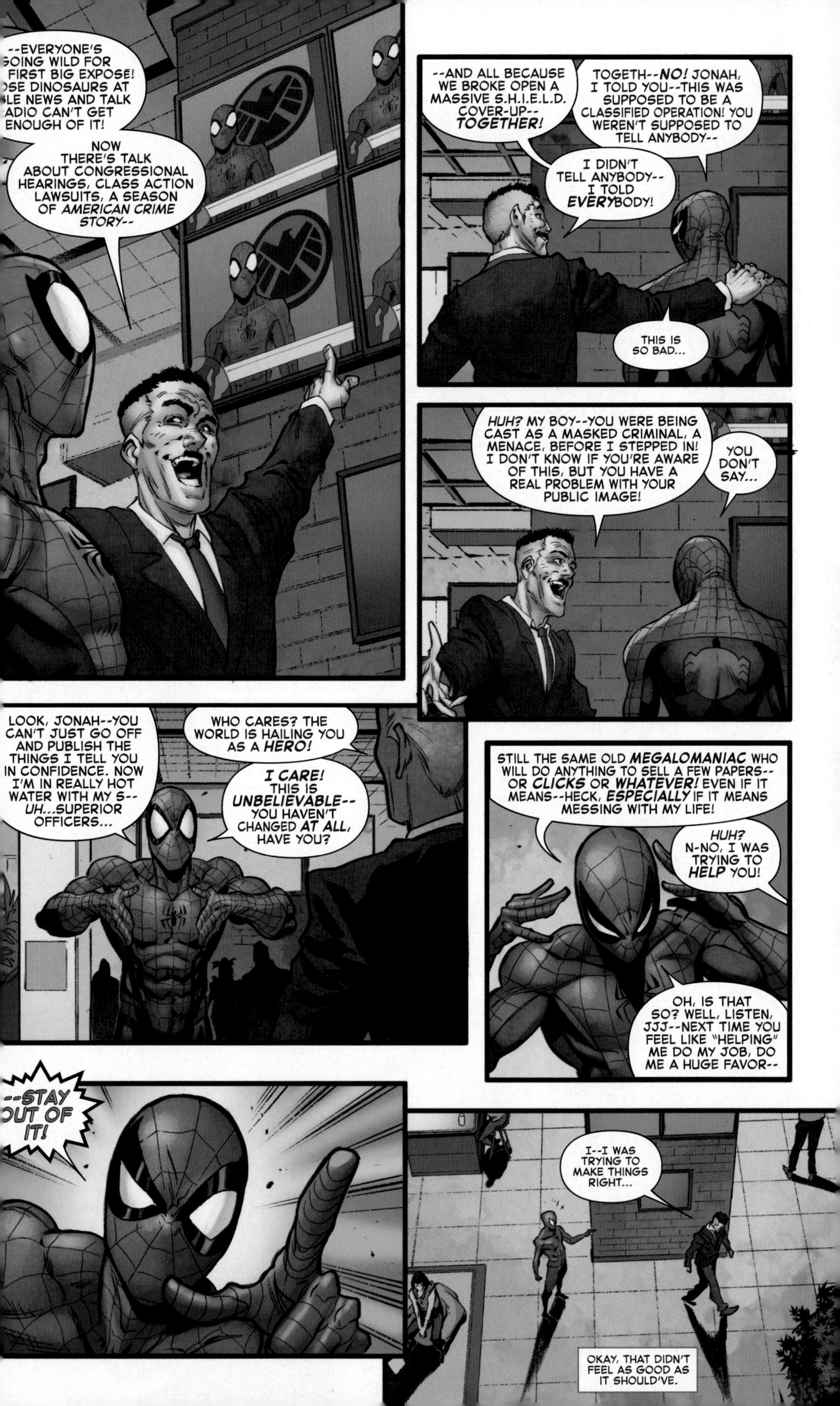

--EVERYONE'S GOING WILD FOR FIRST BIG EXPOSE! OSE DINOSAURS AT BLE NEWS AND TALK ADIO CAN'T GET ENOUGH OF IT!
NOW THERE'S TALK ABOUT CONGRESSIONAL HEARINGS, CLASS ACTION LAWSUITS, A SEASON OF AMERICAN CRIME STORY--
--AND ALL BECAUSE WE BROKE OPEN A MASSIVE S.H.I.E.L.D. COVER-UP-- TOGETHER!
TOGETH--NO! JONAH, I TOLD YOU--THIS WAS SUPPOSED TO BE A CLASSIFIED OPERATION! YOU WEREN'T SUPPOSED TO TELL ANYBODY--
I DIDN'T TELL ANYBODY-- I TOLD EVERYBODY!
THIS IS SO BAD...
HUH? MY BOY--YOU WERE BEING CAST AS A MASKED CRIMINAL, A MENACE, BEFORE I STEPPED IN! I DON'T KNOW IF YOU'RE AWARE OF THIS, BUT YOU HAVE A REAL PROBLEM WITH YOUR PUBLIC IMAGE!
YOU DON'T SAY...
LOOK, JONAH--YOU CAN'T JUST GO OFF AND PUBLISH THE THINGS I TELL YOU IN CONFIDENCE. NOW I'M IN REALLY HOT WATER WITH MY S-- UH...SUPERIOR OFFICERS...
WHO CARES? THE WORLD IS HAILING YOU AS A HERO!
I CARE! THIS IS UNBELIEVABLE-- YOU HAVEN'T CHANGED AT ALL, HAVE YOU?
STILL THE SAME OLD MEGALOMANIAC WHO WILL DO ANYTHING TO SELL A FEW PAPERS-- OR CLICKS OR WHATEVER! EVEN IF IT MEANS--HECK, ESPECIALLY IF IT MEANS MESSING WITH MY LIFE!
HUH? N-NO, I WAS TRYING TO HELP YOU!
OH, IS THAT SO? WELL, LISTEN, JJJ--NEXT TIME YOU FEEL LIKE "HELPING" ME DO MY JOB, DO ME A HUGE FAVOR--
--STAY OUT OF IT!
I--I WAS TRYING TO MAKE THINGS RIGHT...
OKAY, THAT DIDN'T FEEL AS GOOD AS IT SHOULD'VE.

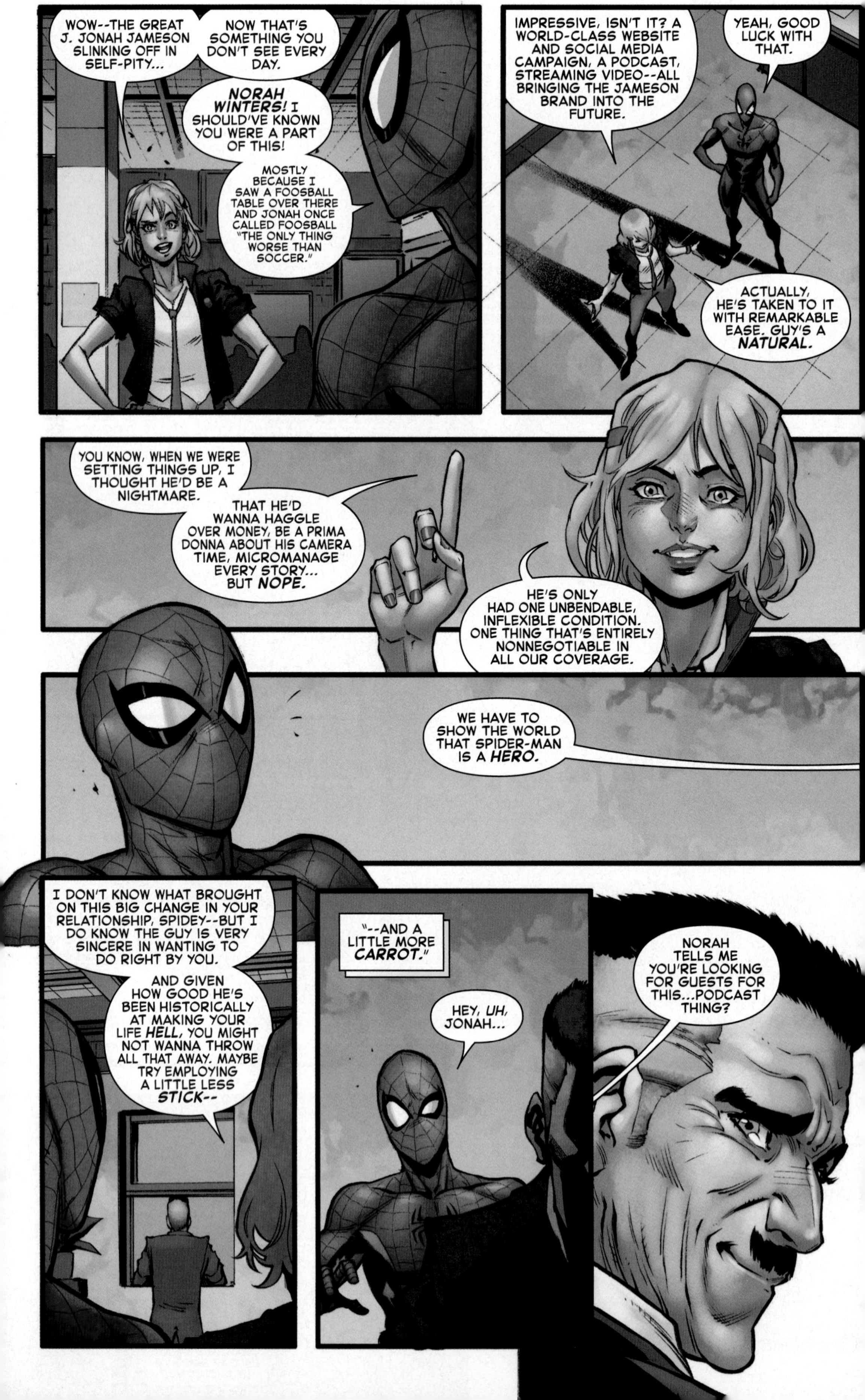
WOW--THE GREAT J. JONAH JAMESON SLINKING OFF IN SELF-PITY...
NOW THAT'S SOMETHING YOU DON'T SEE EVERY DAY.
NORAH WINTERS! I SHOULD'VE KNOWN YOU WERE A PART OF THIS!
MOSTLY BECAUSE I SAW A FOOSBALL TABLE OVER THERE AND JONAH ONCE CALLED FOOSBALL "THE ONLY THING WORSE THAN SOCCER."
IMPRESSIVE, ISN'T IT? A WORLD-CLASS WEBSITE AND SOCIAL MEDIA CAMPAIGN, A PODCAST, STREAMING VIDEO--ALL BRINGING THE JAMESON BRAND INTO THE FUTURE.
YEAH, GOOD LUCK WITH THAT.
ACTUALLY, HE'S TAKEN TO IT WITH REMARKABLE EASE. GUY'S A NATURAL.
YOU KNOW, WHEN WE WERE SETTING THINGS UP, I THOUGHT HE'D BE A NIGHTMARE.
THAT HE'D WANNA HAGGLE OVER MONEY, BE A PRIMA DONNA ABOUT HIS CAMERA TIME, MICROMANAGE EVERY STORY... BUT NOPE.
HE'S ONLY HAD ONE UNBENDABLE, INFLEXIBLE CONDITION. ONE THING THAT'S ENTIRELY NONNEGOTIABLE IN ALL OUR COVERAGE.
WE HAVE TO SHOW THE WORLD THAT SPIDER-MAN IS A HERO.
I DON'T KNOW WHAT BROUGHT ON THIS BIG CHANGE IN YOUR RELATIONSHIP, SPIDEY--BUT I DO KNOW THE GUY IS VERY SINCERE IN WANTING TO DO RIGHT BY YOU.
AND GIVEN HOW GOOD HE'S BEEN HISTORICALLY AT MAKING YOUR LIFE HELL, YOU MIGHT NOT WANNA THROW ALL THAT AWAY. MAYBE TRY EMPLOYING A LITTLE LESS STICK--
"--AND A LITTLE MORE CARROT."
HEY, UH, JONAH...
NORAH TELLS ME YOU'RE LOOKING FOR GUESTS FOR THIS...PODCAST THING?

I MEAN, I DID OWE HIM AN INTERVIEW AFTER ALL.

WE SAT DOWN TO TALK A WHILE BACK, BUT THINGS GOT SIDETRACKED*--

*SEE PPSSM VOL. 6 #3!

--WHEN I DECIDED TO REVEAL MY SECRET IDENTITY TO HIM.

IT'S BEEN A BUMPY ROAD SINCE THEN.

BUT RECENTLY WE CAME TO AN UNDERSTANDING.*

HE REALLY DOES WANT TO SET THINGS RIGHT, SO HEY--

*IN ASM VOL. 5, #13, AVAILABLE IN THE COLLECTION LIFETIME ACHIEVEMENT! --IN-THE-KNOW NICK LOWE

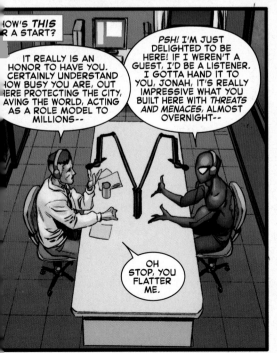

HOW'S THIS FOR A START?

IT REALLY IS AN HONOR TO HAVE YOU. I CERTAINLY UNDERSTAND HOW BUSY YOU ARE, OUT THERE PROTECTING THE CITY, SAVING THE WORLD, ACTING AS A ROLE MODEL TO MILLIONS--

PSH! I'M JUST DELIGHTED TO BE HERE! IF I WEREN'T A GUEST, I'D BE A LISTENER. I GOTTA HAND IT TO YOU, JONAH, IT'S REALLY IMPRESSIVE WHAT YOU BUILT HERE WITH THREATS AND MENACES, ALMOST OVERNIGHT--

OH STOP, YOU FLATTER ME.

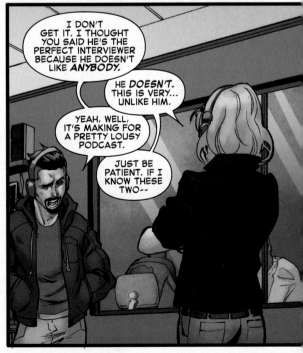

I DON'T GET IT. I THOUGHT YOU SAID HE'S THE PERFECT INTERVIEWER BECAUSE HE DOESN'T LIKE ANYBODY.

HE DOESN'T. THIS IS VERY... UNLIKE HIM.

YEAH, WELL, IT'S MAKING FOR A PRETTY LOUSY PODCAST.

JUST BE PATIENT. IF I KNOW THESE TWO--

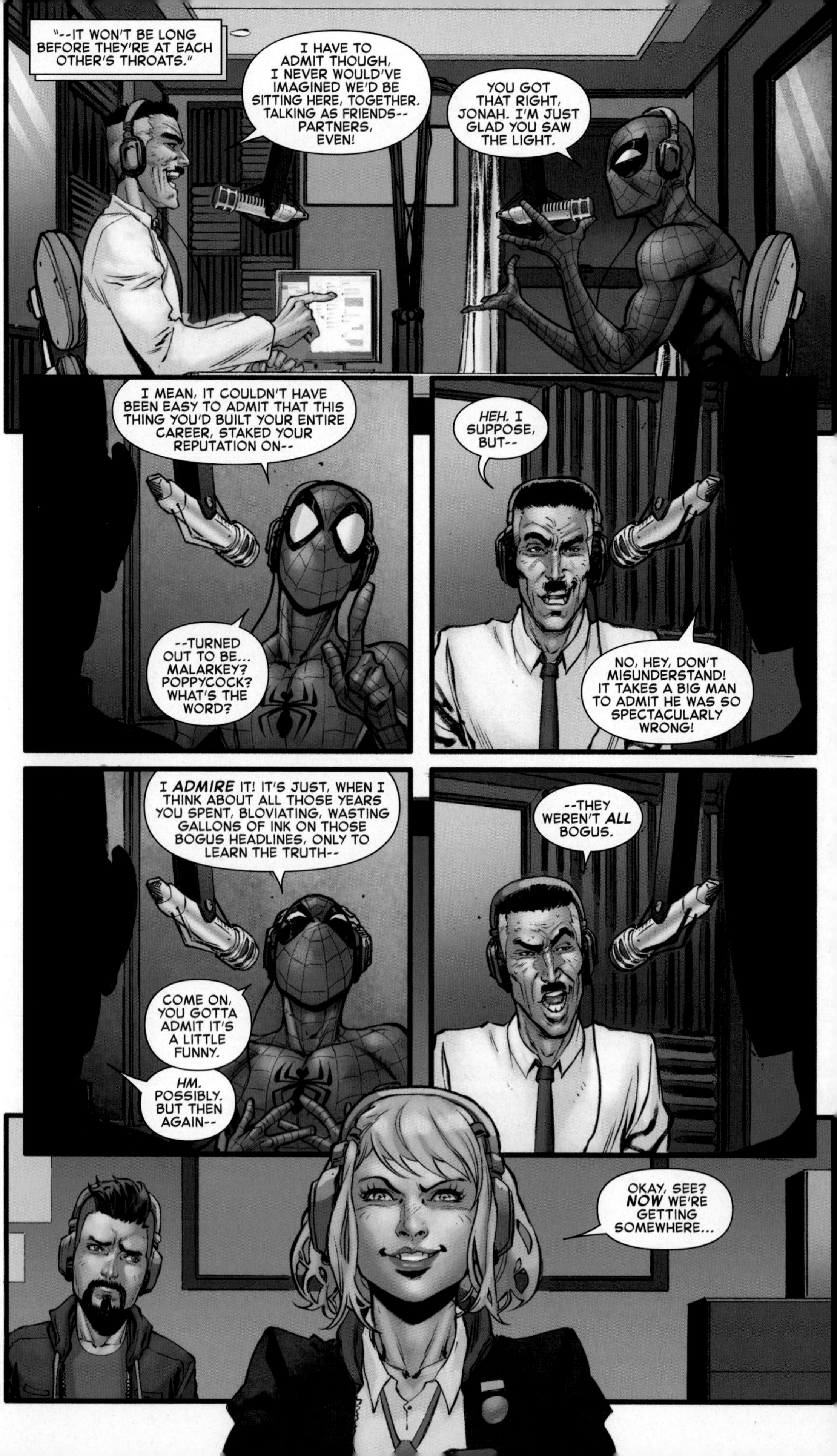
"--IT WON'T BE LONG BEFORE THEY'RE AT EACH OTHER'S THROATS."
I HAVE TO ADMIT THOUGH, I NEVER WOULD'VE IMAGINED WE'D BE SITTING HERE, TOGETHER. TALKING AS FRIENDS-- PARTNERS, EVEN!
YOU GOT THAT RIGHT, JONAH. I'M JUST GLAD YOU SAW THE LIGHT.
I MEAN, IT COULDN'T HAVE BEEN EASY TO ADMIT THAT THIS THING YOU'D BUILT YOUR ENTIRE CAREER, STAKED YOUR REPUTATION ON--
--TURNED OUT TO BE... MALARKEY? POPPYCOCK? WHAT'S THE WORD?
HEH. I SUPPOSE, BUT--
NO, HEY, DON'T MISUNDERSTAND! IT TAKES A BIG MAN TO ADMIT HE WAS SO SPECTACULARLY WRONG!
I *ADMIRE* IT! IT'S JUST, WHEN I THINK ABOUT ALL THOSE YEARS YOU SPENT, BLOVIATING, WASTING GALLONS OF INK ON THOSE BOGUS HEADLINES, ONLY TO LEARN THE TRUTH--
--THEY WEREN'T *ALL* BOGUS.
COME ON, YOU GOTTA ADMIT IT'S A LITTLE FUNNY.
HM. POSSIBLY. BUT THEN AGAIN--
OKAY, SEE? *NOW* WE'RE GETTING SOMEWHERE...

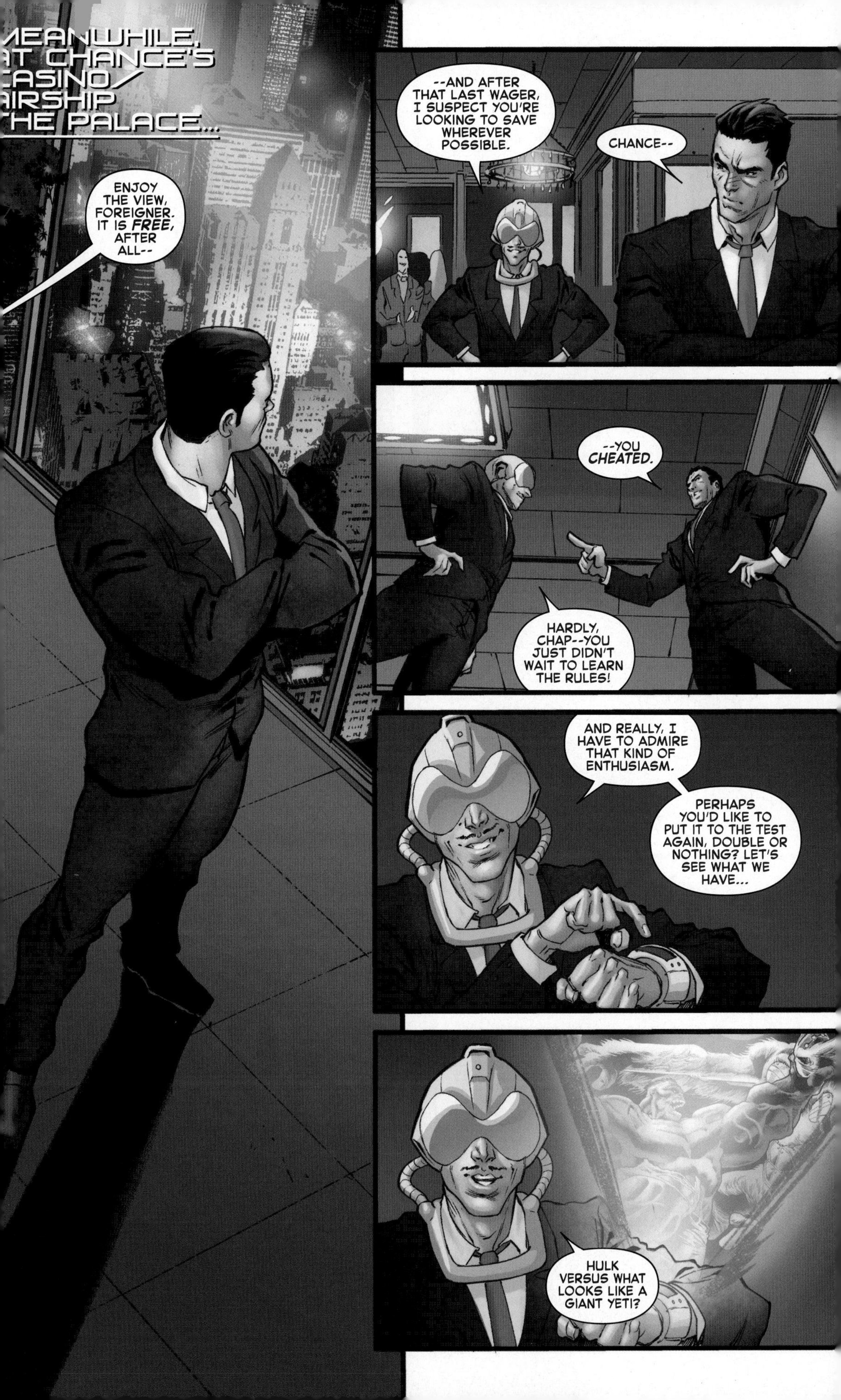

MEANWHILE, AT CHANCE'S CASINO/ AIRSHIP THE PALACE...
ENJOY THE VIEW, FOREIGNER. IT IS FREE, AFTER ALL--
--AND AFTER THAT LAST WAGER, I SUSPECT YOU'RE LOOKING TO SAVE WHEREVER POSSIBLE.
CHANCE--
--YOU CHEATED.
HARDLY, CHAP--YOU JUST DIDN'T WAIT TO LEARN THE RULES!
AND REALLY, I HAVE TO ADMIRE THAT KIND OF ENTHUSIASM.
PERHAPS YOU'D LIKE TO PUT IT TO THE TEST AGAIN, DOUBLE OR NOTHING? LET'S SEE WHAT WE HAVE...
HULK VERSUS WHAT LOOKS LIKE A GIANT YETI?

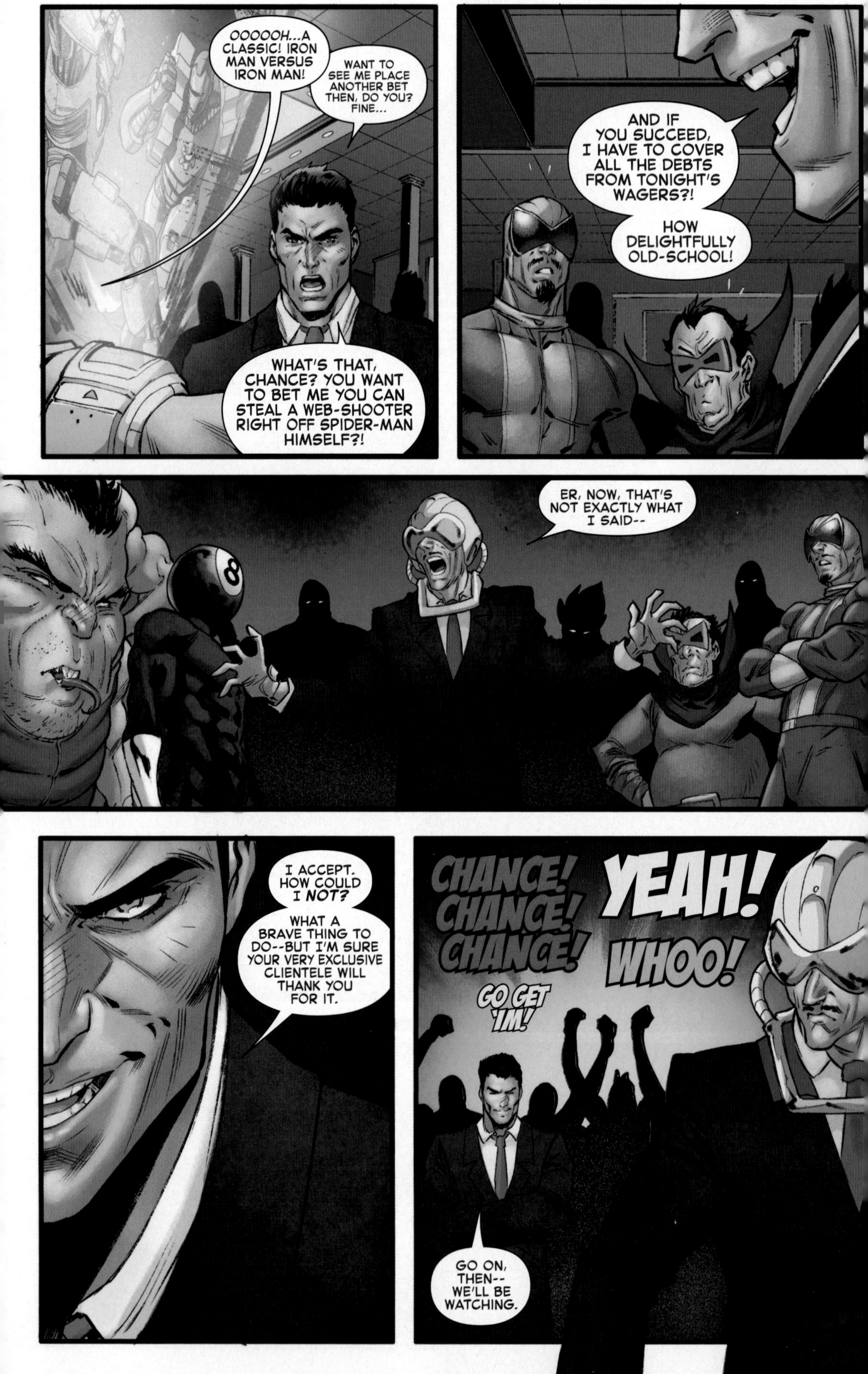
OOOOOH...A CLASSIC! IRON MAN VERSUS IRON MAN!
WANT TO SEE ME PLACE ANOTHER BET THEN, DO YOU? FINE...
WHAT'S THAT, CHANCE? YOU WANT TO BET ME YOU CAN STEAL A WEB-SHOOTER RIGHT OFF SPIDER-MAN HIMSELF?!
AND IF YOU SUCCEED, I HAVE TO COVER ALL THE DEBTS FROM TONIGHT'S WAGERS?!
HOW DELIGHTFULLY OLD-SCHOOL!
ER, NOW, THAT'S NOT EXACTLY WHAT I SAID--
I ACCEPT. HOW COULD I *NOT?*
WHAT A BRAVE THING TO DO--BUT I'M SURE YOUR VERY EXCLUSIVE CLIENTELE WILL THANK YOU FOR IT.
CHANCE! CHANCE! CHANCE!
YEAH!
WHOO!
GO GET 'IM!
GO ON, THEN-- WE'LL BE WATCHING.

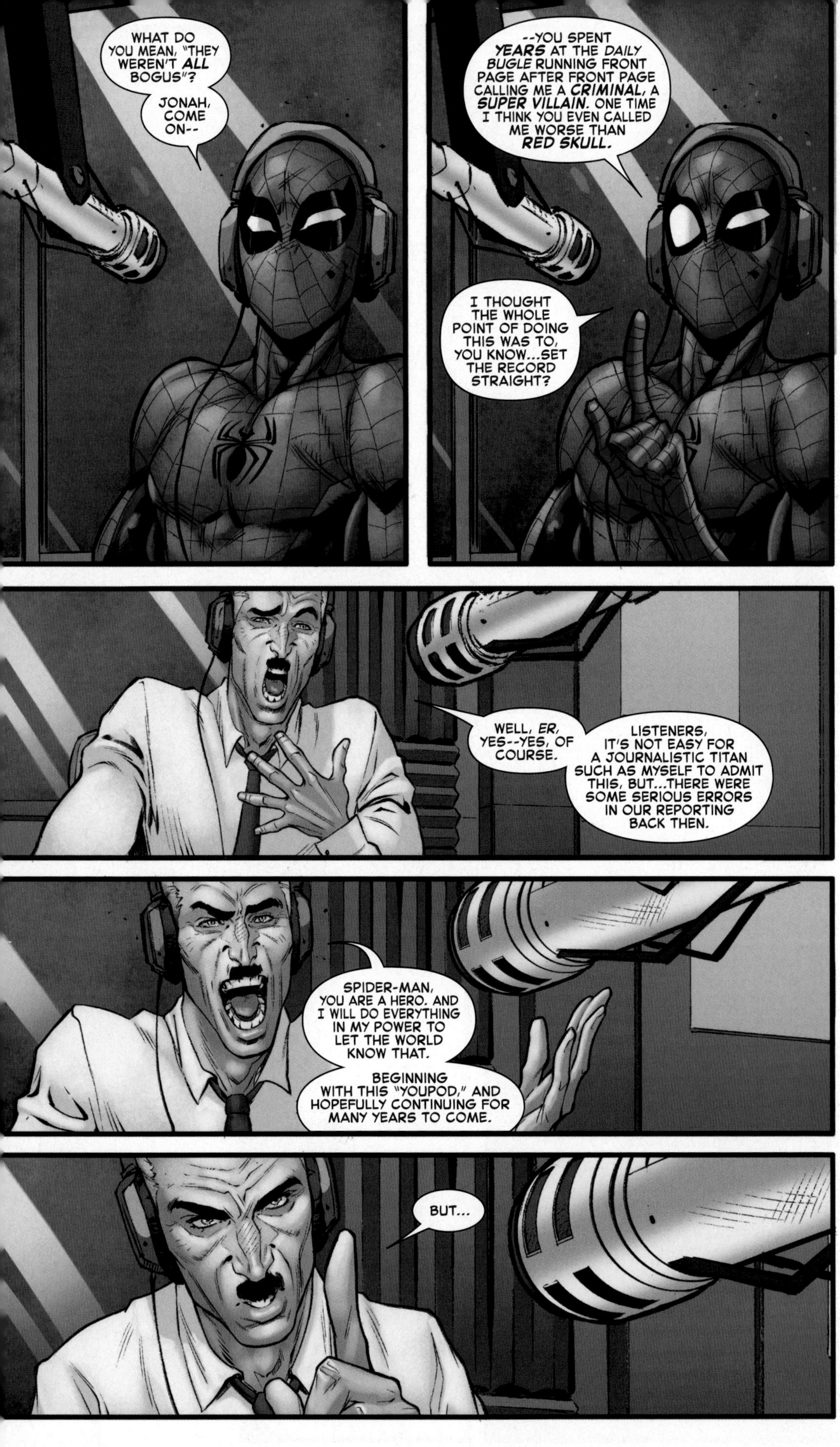

WHAT DO YOU MEAN, "THEY WEREN'T ALL BOGUS"?
JONAH, COME ON--
--YOU SPENT YEARS AT THE DAILY BUGLE RUNNING FRONT PAGE AFTER FRONT PAGE CALLING ME A CRIMINAL, A SUPER VILLAIN. ONE TIME I THINK YOU EVEN CALLED ME WORSE THAN RED SKULL.
I THOUGHT THE WHOLE POINT OF DOING THIS WAS TO, YOU KNOW...SET THE RECORD STRAIGHT?
WELL, ER, YES--YES, OF COURSE.
LISTENERS, IT'S NOT EASY FOR A JOURNALISTIC TITAN SUCH AS MYSELF TO ADMIT THIS, BUT...THERE WERE SOME SERIOUS ERRORS IN OUR REPORTING BACK THEN.
SPIDER-MAN, YOU ARE A HERO. AND I WILL DO EVERYTHING IN MY POWER TO LET THE WORLD KNOW THAT.
BEGINNING WITH THIS "YOUPOD," AND HOPEFULLY CONTINUING FOR MANY YEARS TO COME.
BUT...

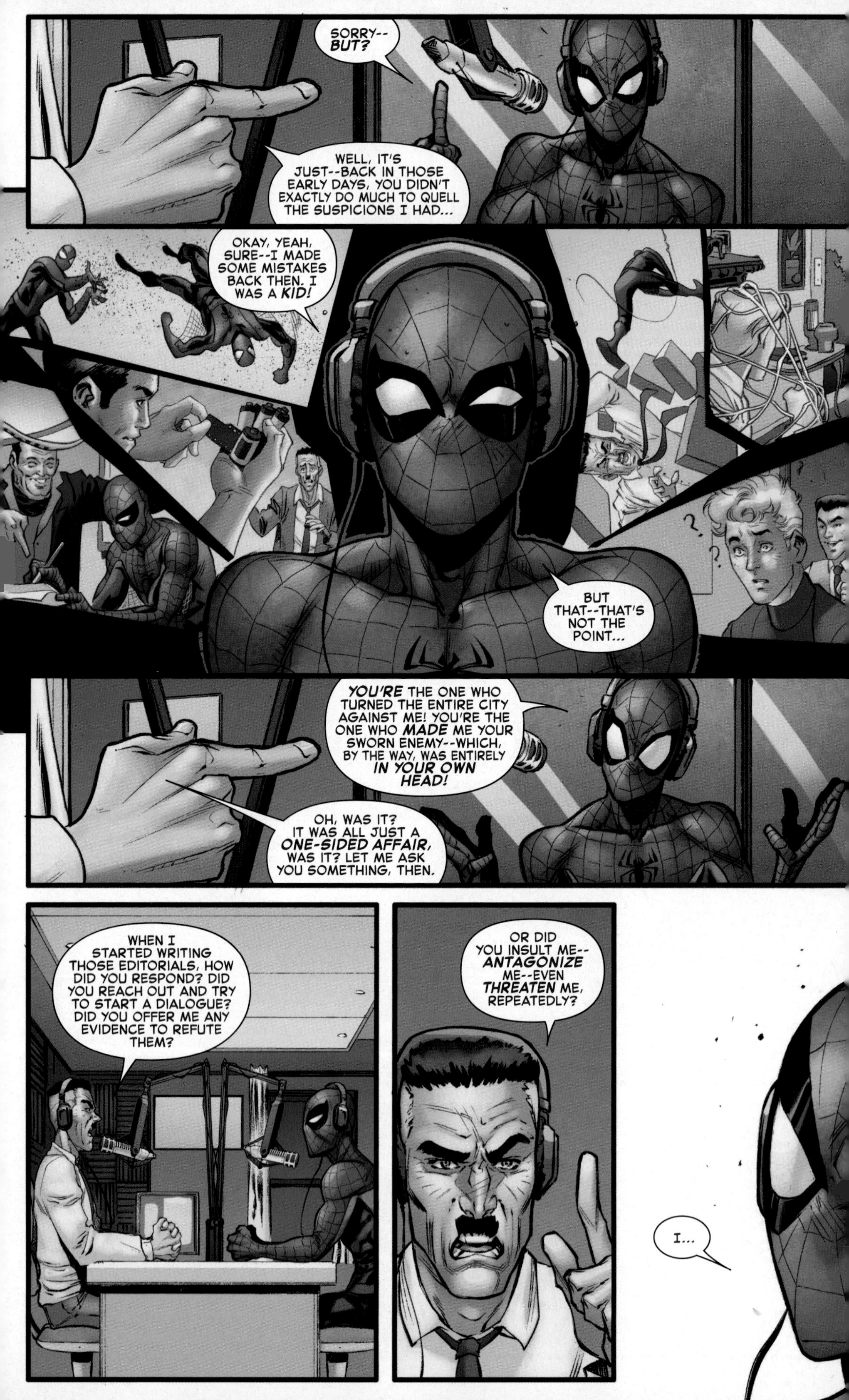

SORRY-- BUT?
WELL, IT'S JUST--BACK IN THOSE EARLY DAYS, YOU DIDN'T EXACTLY DO MUCH TO QUELL THE SUSPICIONS I HAD...
OKAY, YEAH, SURE--I MADE SOME MISTAKES BACK THEN. I WAS A KID!
BUT THAT--THAT'S NOT THE POINT...
YOU'RE THE ONE WHO TURNED THE ENTIRE CITY AGAINST ME! YOU'RE THE ONE WHO MADE ME YOUR SWORN ENEMY--WHICH, BY THE WAY, WAS ENTIRELY IN YOUR OWN HEAD!
OH, WAS IT? IT WAS ALL JUST A ONE-SIDED AFFAIR, WAS IT? LET ME ASK YOU SOMETHING, THEN.
WHEN I STARTED WRITING THOSE EDITORIALS, HOW DID YOU RESPOND? DID YOU REACH OUT AND TRY TO START A DIALOGUE? DID YOU OFFER ME ANY EVIDENCE TO REFUTE THEM?
OR DID YOU INSULT ME--ANTAGONIZE ME--EVEN THREATEN ME, REPEATEDLY?
I...

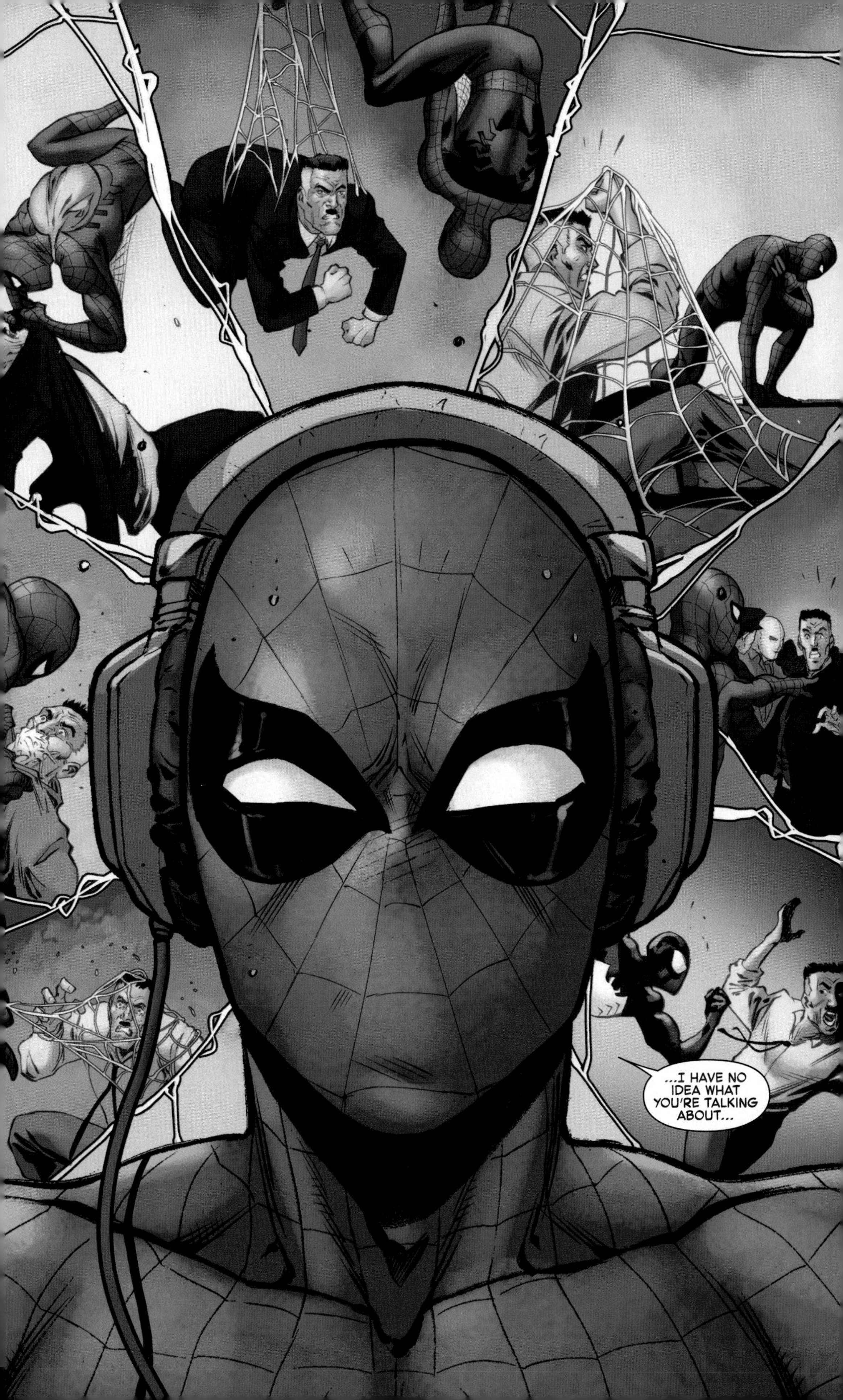
...I HAVE NO IDEA WHAT YOU'RE TALKING ABOUT...

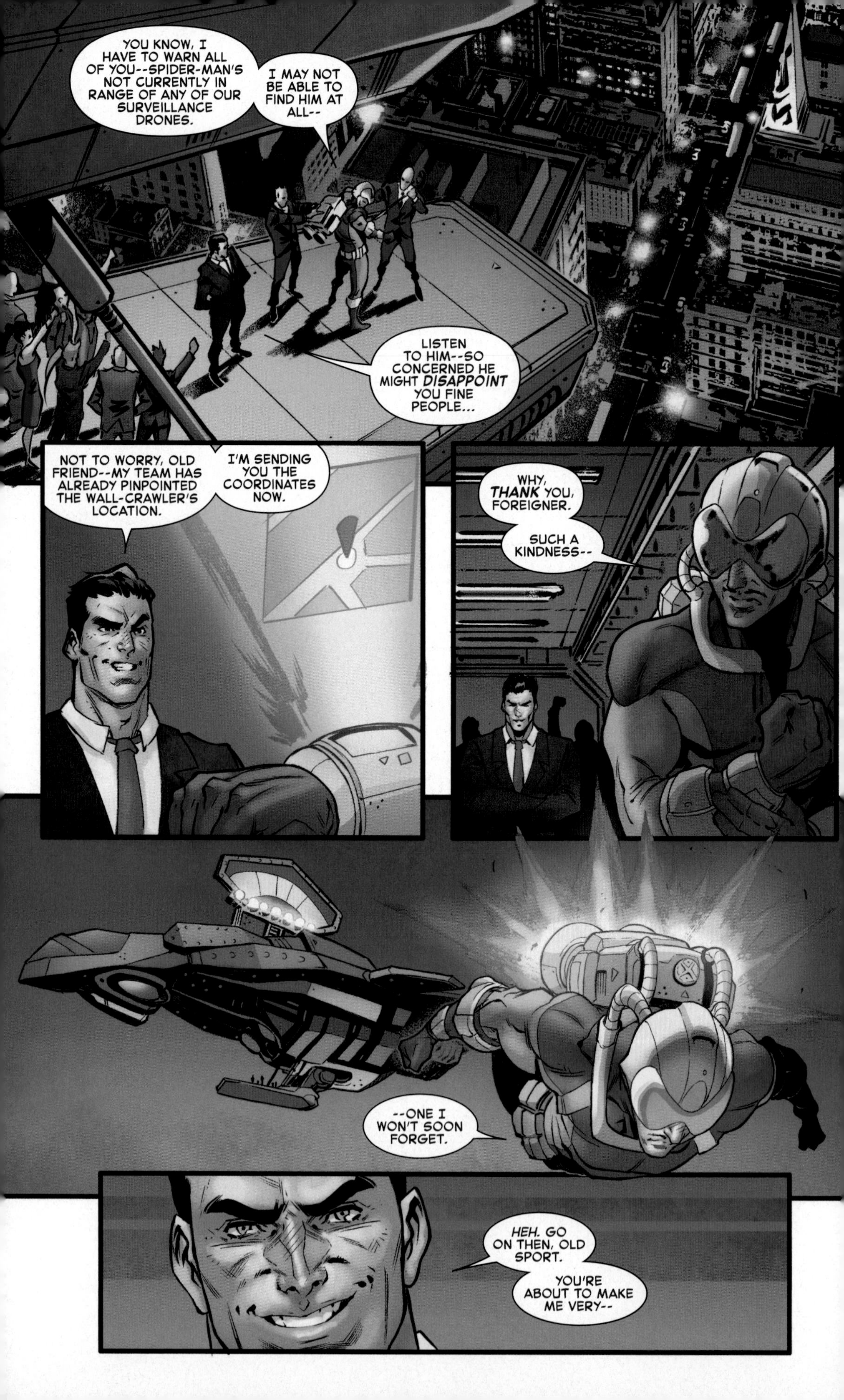
YOU KNOW, I HAVE TO WARN ALL OF YOU--SPIDER-MAN'S NOT CURRENTLY IN RANGE OF ANY OF OUR SURVEILLANCE DRONES.
I MAY NOT BE ABLE TO FIND HIM AT ALL--
LISTEN TO HIM--SO CONCERNED HE MIGHT *DISAPPOINT* YOU FINE PEOPLE...
NOT TO WORRY, OLD FRIEND--MY TEAM HAS ALREADY PINPOINTED THE WALL-CRAWLER'S LOCATION.
I'M SENDING YOU THE COORDINATES NOW.
WHY, **THANK** YOU, FOREIGNER.
SUCH A KINDNESS--
--ONE I WON'T SOON FORGET.
HEH. GO ON THEN, OLD SPORT.
YOU'RE ABOUT TO MAKE ME VERY--

RICH! WE'RE GONNA BE **RICH!**

EVERY MINUTE THOSE TWO SPEND ARGUING IS PODCAST GOLD. THIS IS BETTER THAN STERN.

AND I HAVE A FEELING IT'S ONLY GONNA GET WORSE.

I MEAN BETTER.

DO YOU HAVE ANY IDEA HOW HARD IT IS TO GET **WEBBING** OUT OF A **MUSTACHE?!**

I CAN'T BELIEVE YOU'RE TRYING TO TURN THIS AROUND ON **ME!**

AND I CAN'T BELIEVE YOU WON'T TAKE **RESPONSIBILITY** FOR YOUR OWN PART IN ALL THIS!

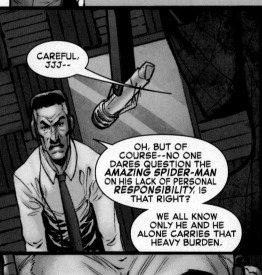

CAREFUL, JJJ--

OH, BUT OF COURSE--NO ONE DARES QUESTION THE **AMAZING SPIDER-MAN** ON HIS LACK OF PERSONAL **RESPONSIBILITY,** IS THAT RIGHT?

WE ALL KNOW ONLY HE AND HE ALONE CARRIES THAT HEAVY BURDEN.

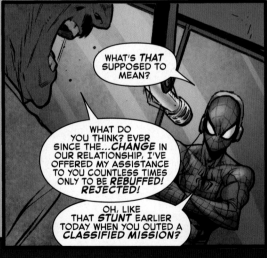

WHAT'S **THAT** SUPPOSED TO MEAN?

WHAT DO YOU THINK? EVER SINCE THE...**CHANGE** IN OUR RELATIONSHIP, I'VE OFFERED MY ASSISTANCE TO YOU COUNTLESS TIMES ONLY TO BE **REBUFFED! REJECTED!**

OH, LIKE THAT **STUNT** EARLIER TODAY WHEN YOU OUTED A **CLASSIFIED MISSION?**

TO **CLEAR YOUR NAME!** YOU KNOW, A LOT OF OTHER SUPER HEROES OUT THERE WOULD LOVE TO HAVE A PUBLIC RELATIONS GENIUS LIKE MYSELF HELPING THEM--

NO, YOU WON'T.

YEAH, I'LL ASK AROUND.

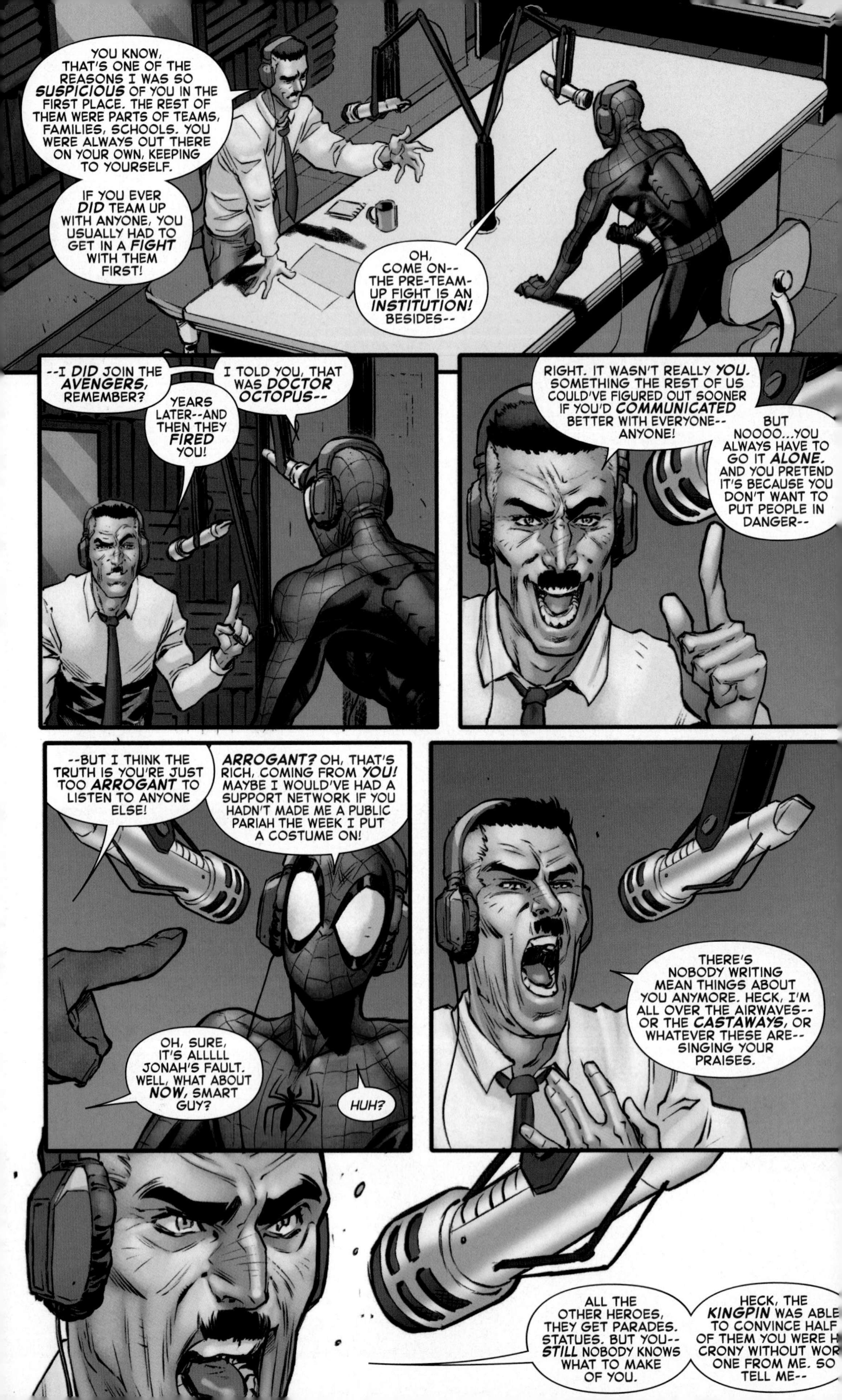
YOU KNOW, THAT'S ONE OF THE REASONS I WAS SO SUSPICIOUS OF YOU IN THE FIRST PLACE. THE REST OF THEM WERE PARTS OF TEAMS, FAMILIES, SCHOOLS. YOU WERE ALWAYS OUT THERE ON YOUR OWN, KEEPING TO YOURSELF.
IF YOU EVER DID TEAM UP WITH ANYONE, YOU USUALLY HAD TO GET IN A FIGHT WITH THEM FIRST!
OH, COME ON-- THE PRE-TEAM-UP FIGHT IS AN INSTITUTION! BESIDES--
--I DID JOIN THE AVENGERS, REMEMBER?
YEARS LATER--AND THEN THEY FIRED YOU!
I TOLD YOU, THAT WAS DOCTOR OCTOPUS--
RIGHT. IT WASN'T REALLY YOU. SOMETHING THE REST OF US COULD'VE FIGURED OUT SOONER IF YOU'D COMMUNICATED BETTER WITH EVERYONE-- ANYONE!
BUT NOOOO...YOU ALWAYS HAVE TO GO IT ALONE. AND YOU PRETEND IT'S BECAUSE YOU DON'T WANT TO PUT PEOPLE IN DANGER--
--BUT I THINK THE TRUTH IS YOU'RE JUST TOO ARROGANT TO LISTEN TO ANYONE ELSE!
ARROGANT? OH, THAT'S RICH, COMING FROM YOU! MAYBE I WOULD'VE HAD A SUPPORT NETWORK IF YOU HADN'T MADE ME A PUBLIC PARIAH THE WEEK I PUT A COSTUME ON!
OH, SURE, IT'S ALLLLL JONAH'S FAULT. WELL, WHAT ABOUT NOW, SMART GUY?
HUH?
THERE'S NOBODY WRITING MEAN THINGS ABOUT YOU ANYMORE. HECK, I'M ALL OVER THE AIRWAVES-- OR THE CASTAWAYS, OR WHATEVER THESE ARE-- SINGING YOUR PRAISES.
ALL THE OTHER HEROES, THEY GET PARADES. STATUES. BUT YOU-- STILL NOBODY KNOWS WHAT TO MAKE OF YOU.
HECK, THE KINGPIN WAS ABLE TO CONVINCE HALF OF THEM YOU WERE H CRONY WITHOUT WOR ONE FROM ME. SO TELL ME--

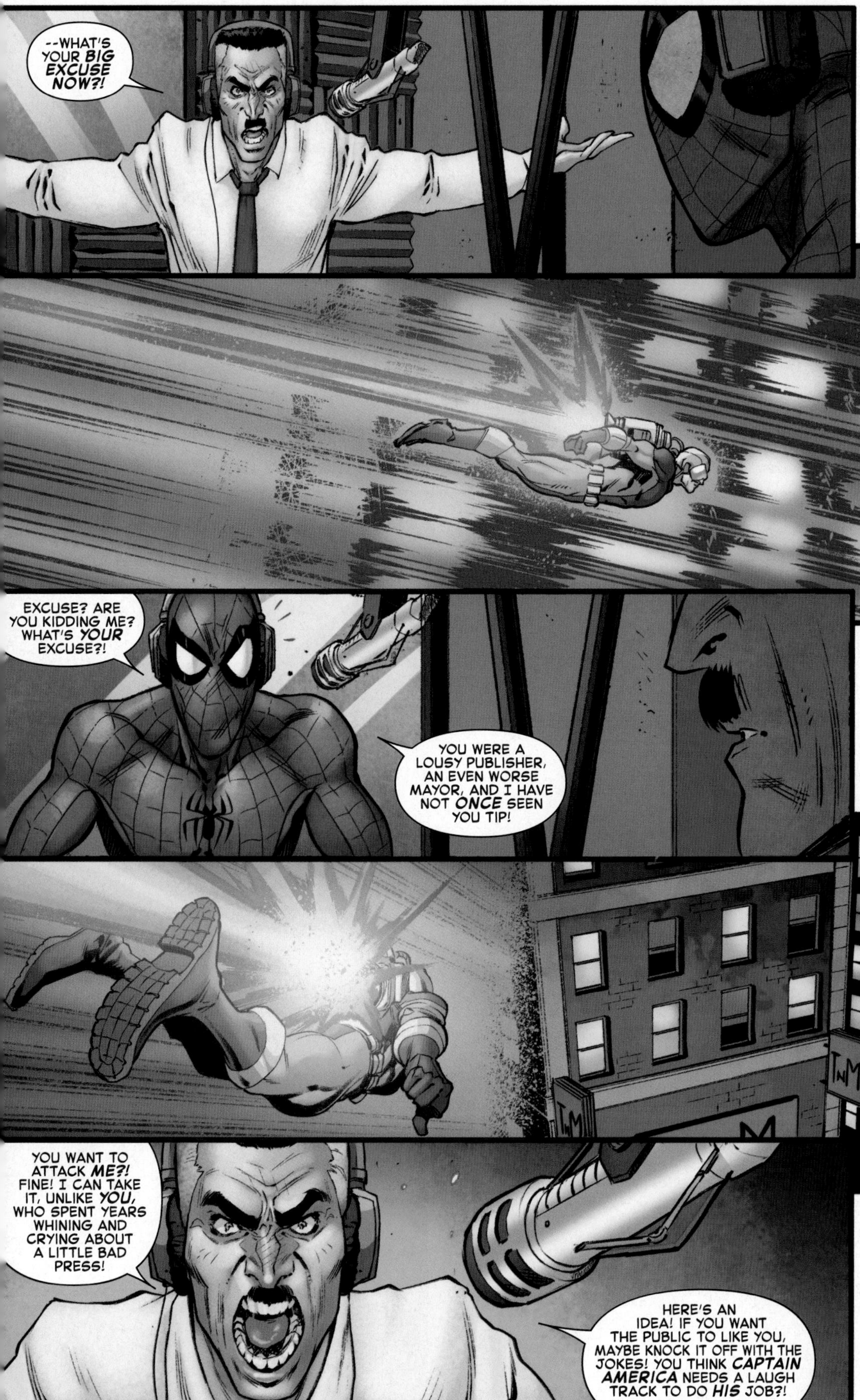
--WHAT'S YOUR BIG EXCUSE NOW?!
EXCUSE? ARE YOU KIDDING ME? WHAT'S YOUR EXCUSE?!
YOU WERE A LOUSY PUBLISHER, AN EVEN WORSE MAYOR, AND I HAVE NOT ONCE SEEN YOU TIP!
TNM
TNM
YOU WANT TO ATTACK ME?! FINE! I CAN TAKE IT, UNLIKE YOU, WHO SPENT YEARS WHINING AND CRYING ABOUT A LITTLE BAD PRESS!
HERE'S AN IDEA! IF YOU WANT THE PUBLIC TO LIKE YOU, MAYBE KNOCK IT OFF WITH THE JOKES! YOU THINK CAPTAIN AMERICA NEEDS A LAUGH TRACK TO DO HIS JOB?!

AND ANOTHER THING--THE **WEBS?!** THEY'RE EVERYWHERE, DIRTYING UP HALF THE BLOCKS IN MANHATTAN! YOU SAY THEY DISSOLVE IN AN HOUR? YOU SHOULD ASK THE JANITORS IN THIS CITY!

STOP--

OH, ARE YOU THREATENING ME NOW?

I'M NOT AFRAID OF YOU, YOU WEBBED MENA--

WHOA-- IS HE ABOUT TO--

OH GOD, PLEASE-- PLEASE--

FIIIIGHT

BUT NO, EVEN IF I MIGHT **WANT** TO.

NOTHING COULD EVER BE THAT SIMPLE WITH ME AND JONAH.

BUT THEN, IF TI IS THE END O OUR BURGEON PARTNERSHIP-

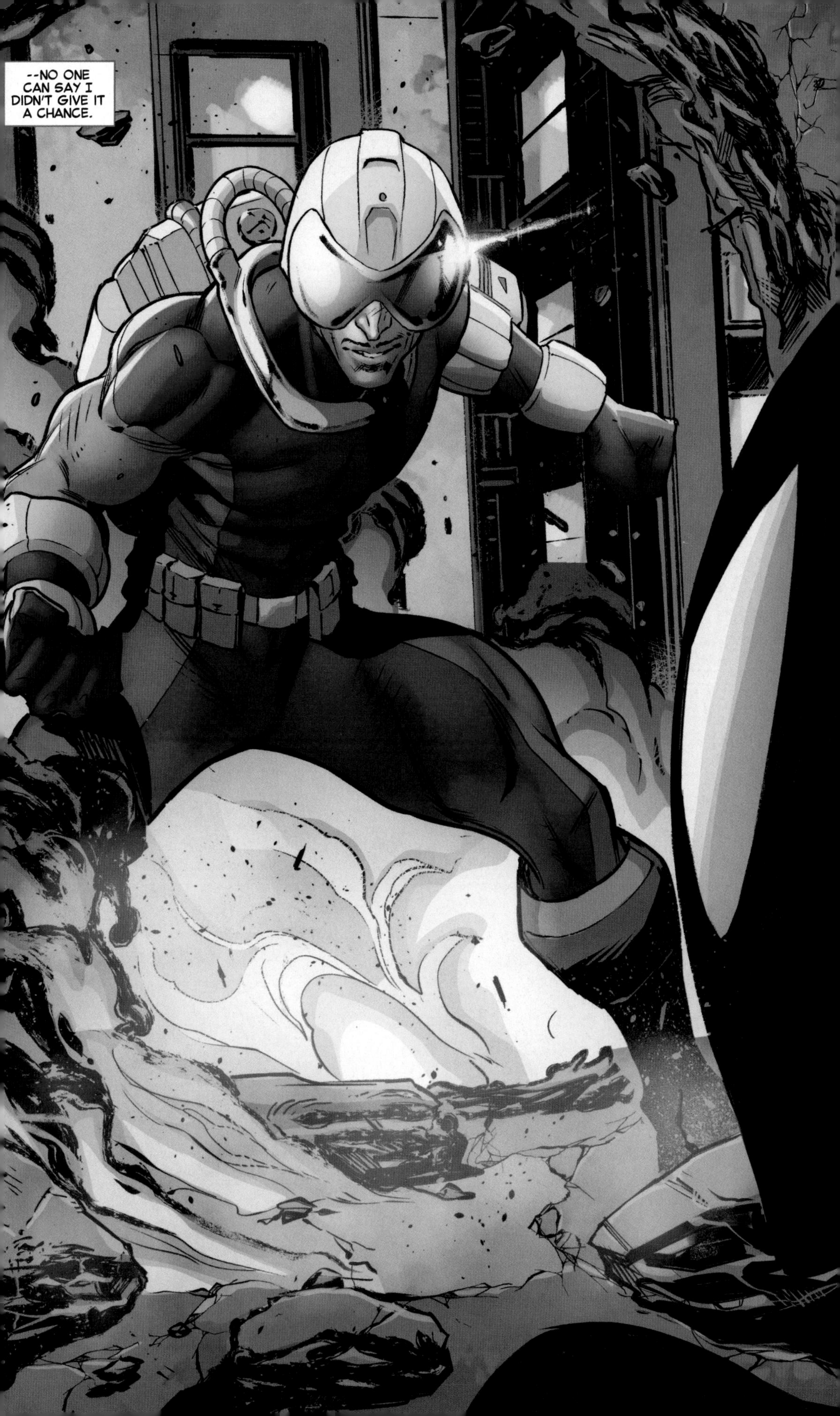
--NO ONE CAN SAY I DIDN'T GIVE IT A CHANCE.

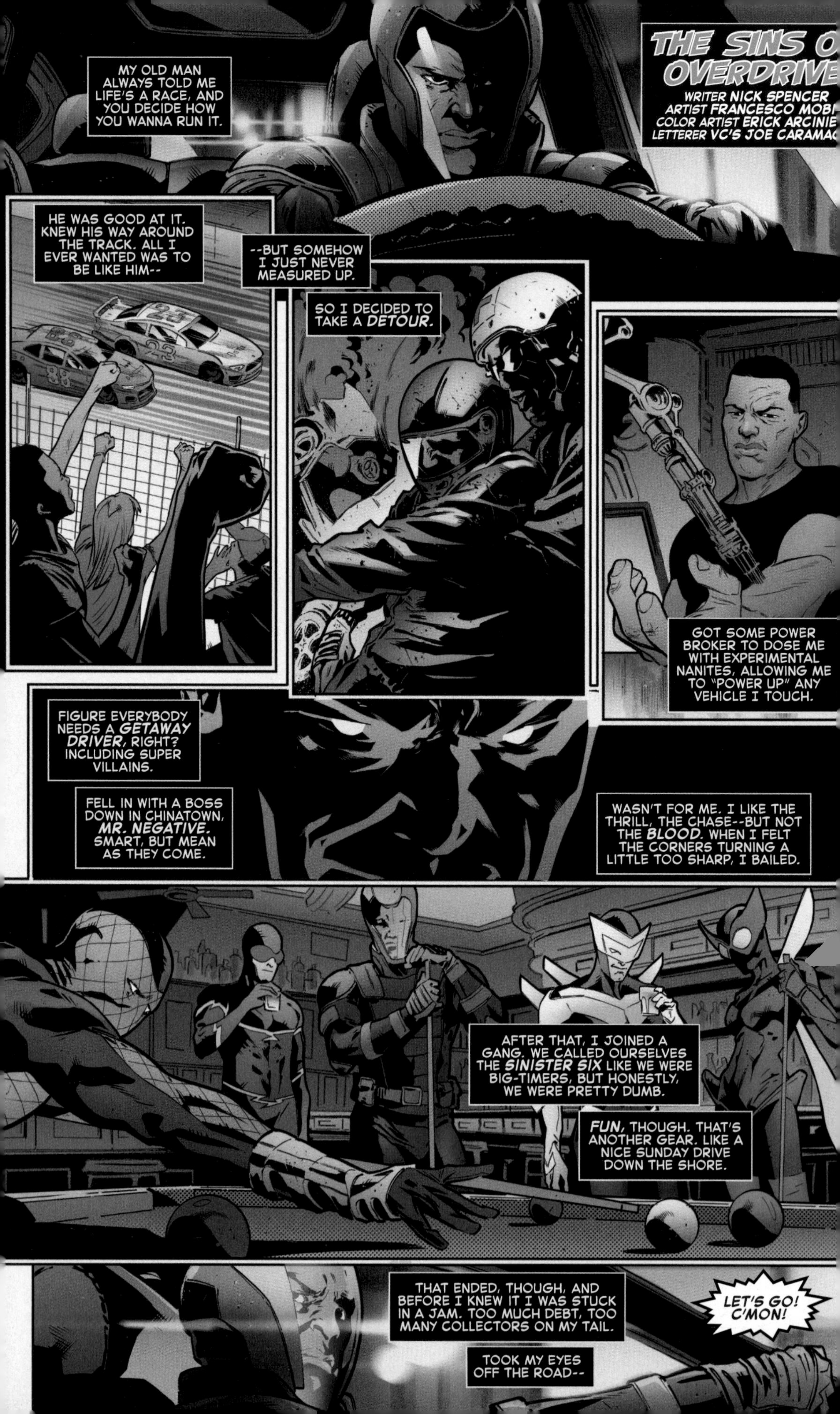

THE SINS OF OVERDRIVE
WRITER NICK SPENCER
ARTIST FRANCESCO MOBI
COLOR ARTIST ERICK ARCINIE
LETTERER VC'S JOE CARAMAG
MY OLD MAN ALWAYS TOLD ME LIFE'S A RACE, AND YOU DECIDE HOW YOU WANNA RUN IT.
HE WAS GOOD AT IT. KNEW HIS WAY AROUND THE TRACK. ALL I EVER WANTED WAS TO BE LIKE HIM--
--BUT SOMEHOW I JUST NEVER MEASURED UP.
SO I DECIDED TO TAKE A DETOUR.
GOT SOME POWER BROKER TO DOSE ME WITH EXPERIMENTAL NANITES, ALLOWING ME TO "POWER UP" ANY VEHICLE I TOUCH.
FIGURE EVERYBODY NEEDS A GETAWAY DRIVER, RIGHT? INCLUDING SUPER VILLAINS.
FELL IN WITH A BOSS DOWN IN CHINATOWN, MR. NEGATIVE. SMART, BUT MEAN AS THEY COME.
WASN'T FOR ME. I LIKE THE THRILL, THE CHASE--BUT NOT THE BLOOD. WHEN I FELT THE CORNERS TURNING A LITTLE TOO SHARP, I BAILED.
AFTER THAT, I JOINED A GANG. WE CALLED OURSELVES THE SINISTER SIX LIKE WE WERE BIG-TIMERS, BUT HONESTLY, WE WERE PRETTY DUMB.
FUN, THOUGH. THAT'S ANOTHER GEAR. LIKE A NICE SUNDAY DRIVE DOWN THE SHORE.
THAT ENDED, THOUGH, AND BEFORE I KNEW IT I WAS STUCK IN A JAM. TOO MUCH DEBT, TOO MANY COLLECTORS ON MY TAIL.
LET'S GO! C'MON!
TOOK MY EYES OFF THE ROAD--

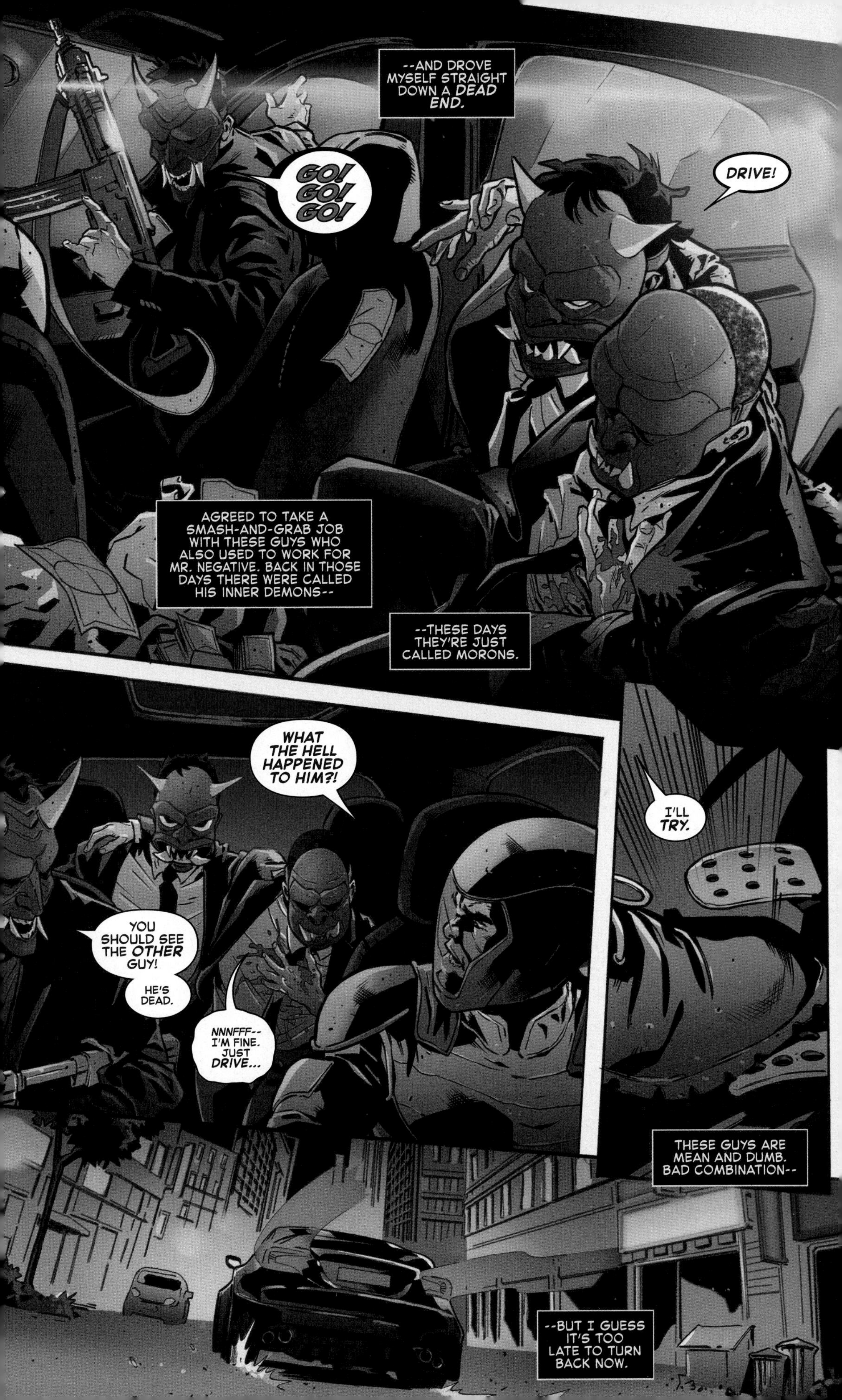

--AND DROVE MYSELF STRAIGHT DOWN A DEAD END.
GO! GO! GO!
DRIVE!
AGREED TO TAKE A SMASH-AND-GRAB JOB WITH THESE GUYS WHO ALSO USED TO WORK FOR MR. NEGATIVE. BACK IN THOSE DAYS THERE WERE CALLED HIS INNER DEMONS--
--THESE DAYS THEY'RE JUST CALLED MORONS.
WHAT THE HELL HAPPENED TO HIM?!
YOU SHOULD SEE THE OTHER GUY!
HE'S DEAD.
NNNFFF-- I'M FINE. JUST DRIVE...
I'LL TRY.
THESE GUYS ARE MEAN AND DUMB. BAD COMBINATION--
--BUT I GUESS IT'S TOO LATE TO TURN BACK NOW.

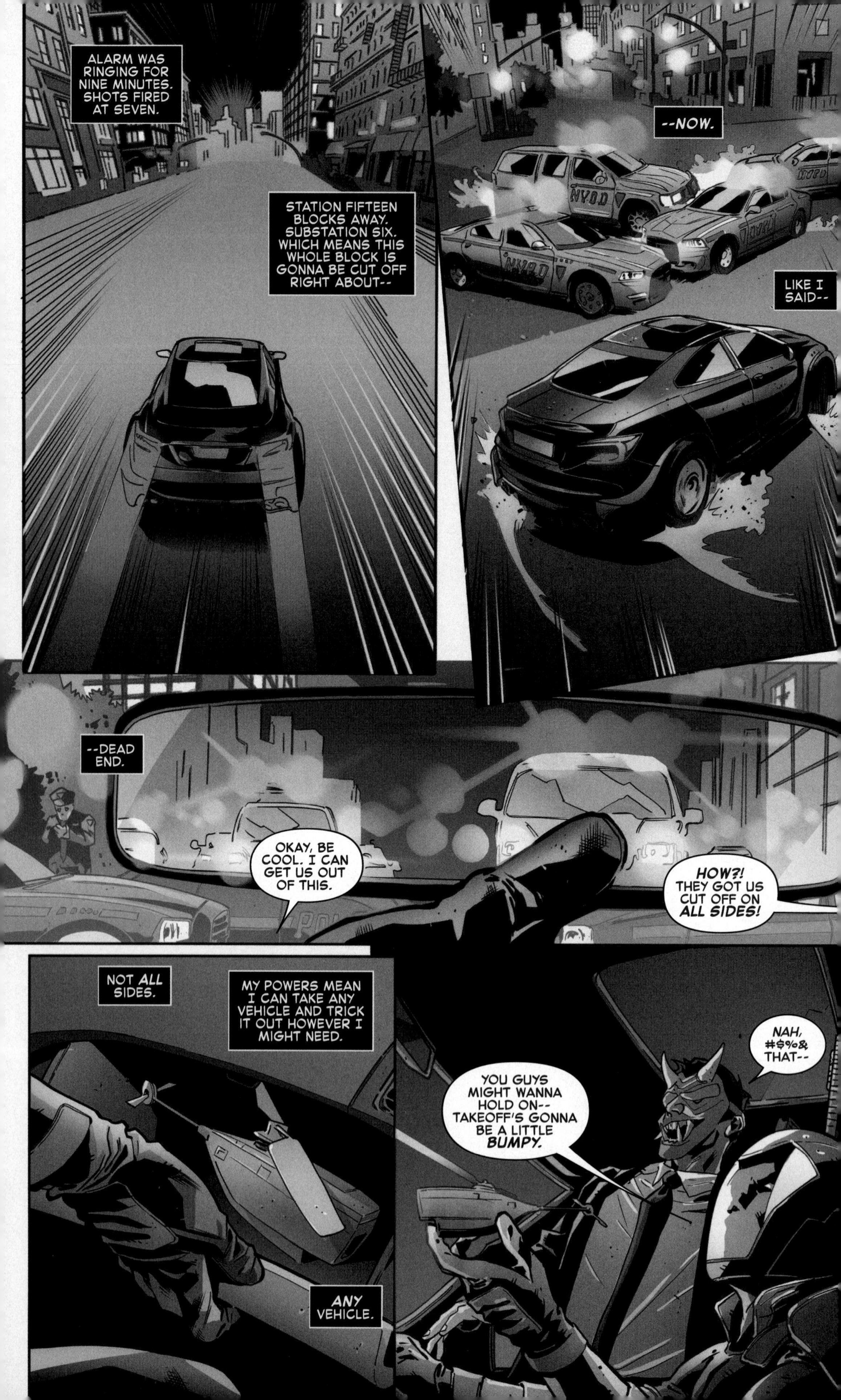
ALARM WAS RINGING FOR NINE MINUTES. SHOTS FIRED AT SEVEN.
STATION FIFTEEN BLOCKS AWAY. SUBSTATION SIX. WHICH MEANS THIS WHOLE BLOCK IS GONNA BE CUT OFF RIGHT ABOUT--
--NOW.
NYPD
LIKE I SAID--
--DEAD END.
OKAY, BE COOL. I CAN GET US OUT OF THIS.
HOW?! THEY GOT US CUT OFF ON ALL SIDES!
NOT ALL SIDES.
MY POWERS MEAN I CAN TAKE ANY VEHICLE AND TRICK IT OUT HOWEVER I MIGHT NEED.
ANY VEHICLE.
YOU GUYS MIGHT WANNA HOLD ON-- TAKEOFF'S GONNA BE A LITTLE BUMPY.
NAH, #$%& THAT--

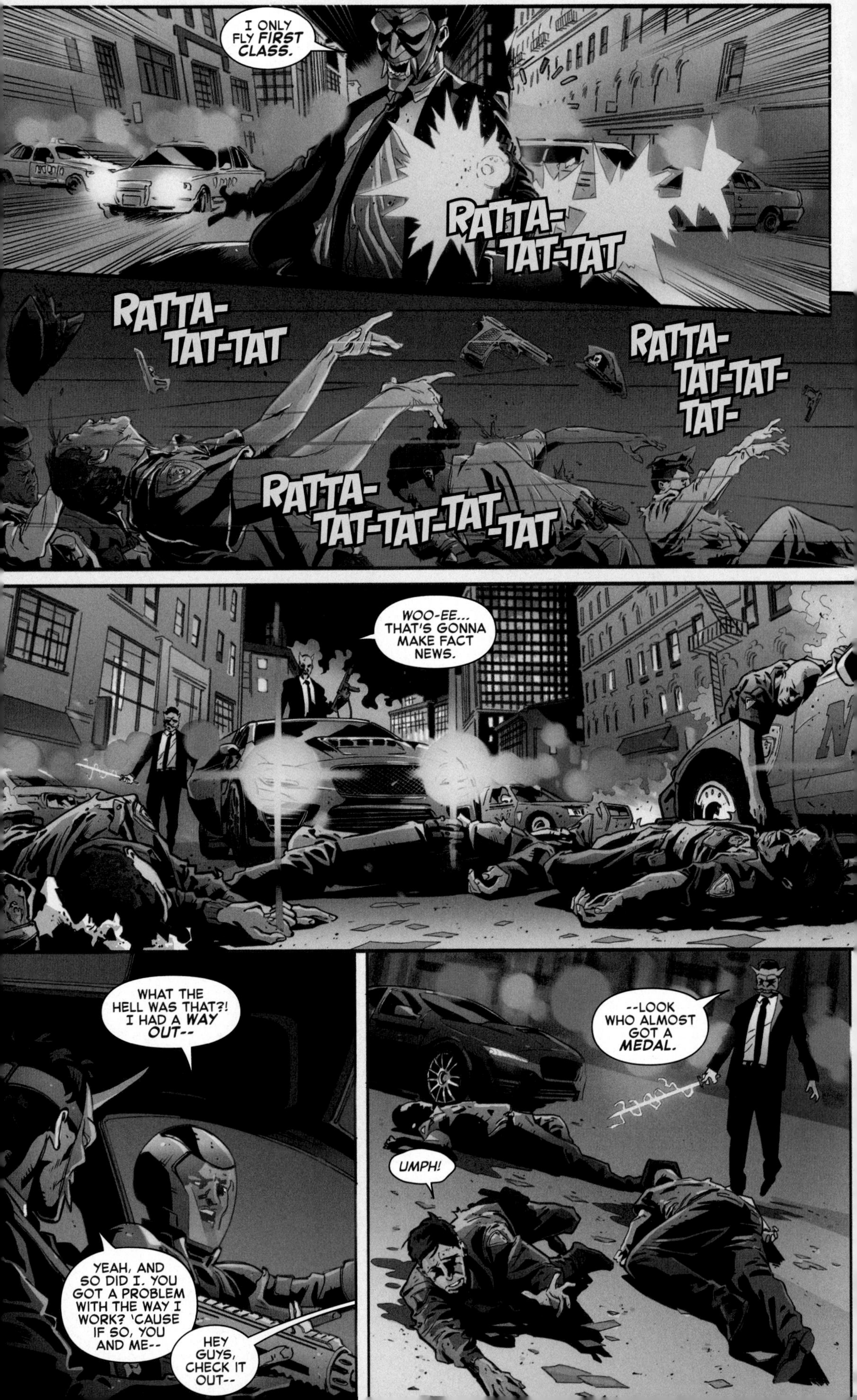
I ONLY FLY FIRST CLASS.
RATTA-TAT-TAT
RATTA-TAT-TAT
RATTA-TAT-TAT-TAT-
RATTA-TAT-TAT-TAT-TAT
WOO-EE... THAT'S GONNA MAKE FACT NEWS.
WHAT THE HELL WAS THAT?! I HAD A WAY OUT--
YEAH, AND SO DID I. YOU GOT A PROBLEM WITH THE WAY I WORK? 'CAUSE IF SO, YOU AND ME--
HEY GUYS, CHECK IT OUT--
--LOOK WHO ALMOST GOT A MEDAL.
UMPH!

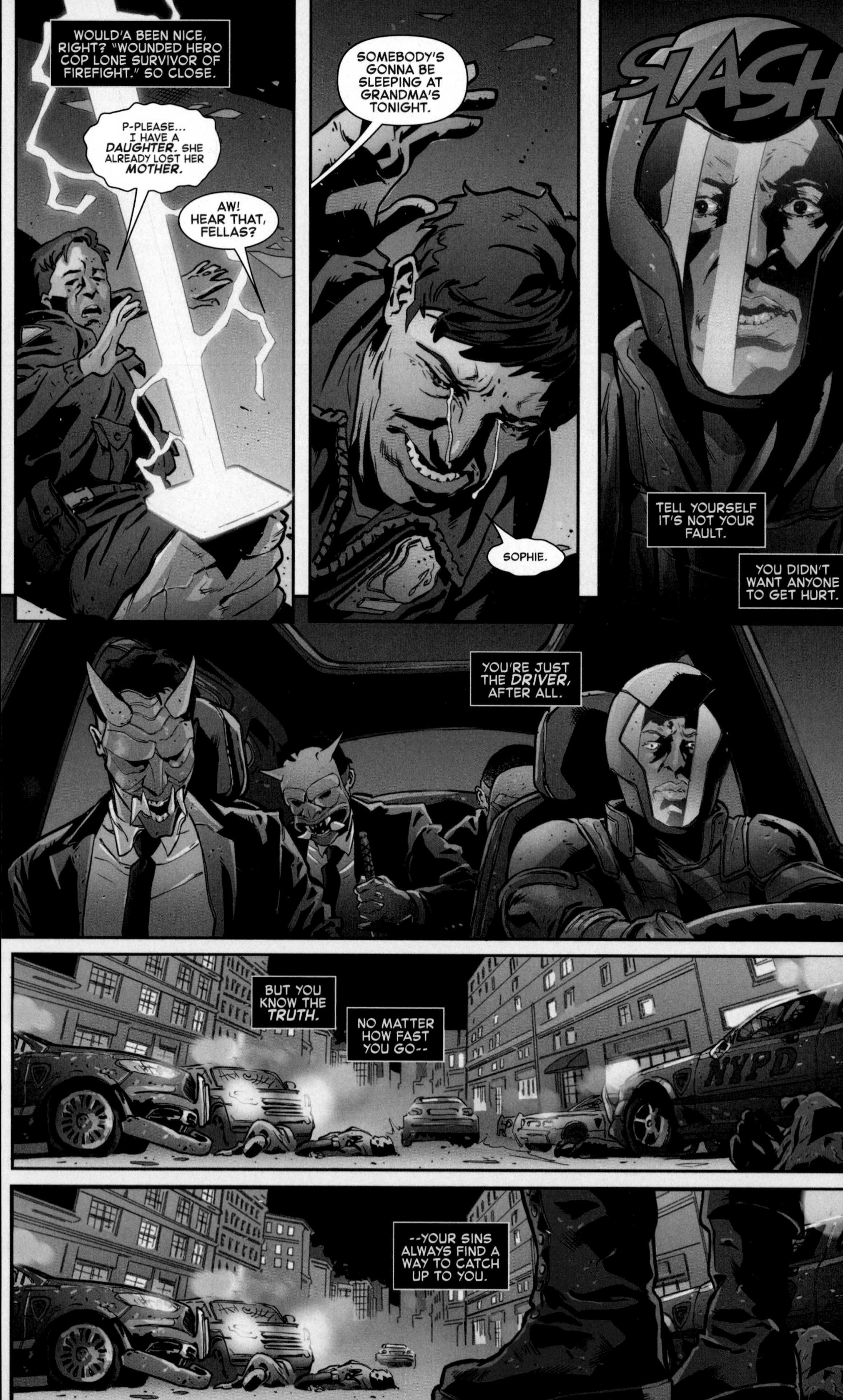
WOULD'A BEEN NICE, RIGHT? "WOUNDED HERO COP LONE SURVIVOR OF FIREFIGHT." SO CLOSE.
P-PLEASE... I HAVE A *DAUGHTER.* SHE ALREADY LOST HER *MOTHER.*
AW! HEAR THAT, FELLAS?
SOMEBODY'S GONNA BE SLEEPING AT GRANDMA'S TONIGHT.
SOPHIE.
SLASH
TELL YOURSELF IT'S NOT YOUR FAULT.
YOU DIDN'T WANT ANYONE TO GET HURT.
YOU'RE JUST THE *DRIVER,* AFTER ALL.
BUT YOU KNOW THE *TRUTH.*
NO MATTER HOW FAST YOU GO--
NYPD
--YOUR SINS ALWAYS FIND A WAY TO CATCH UP TO YOU.

40

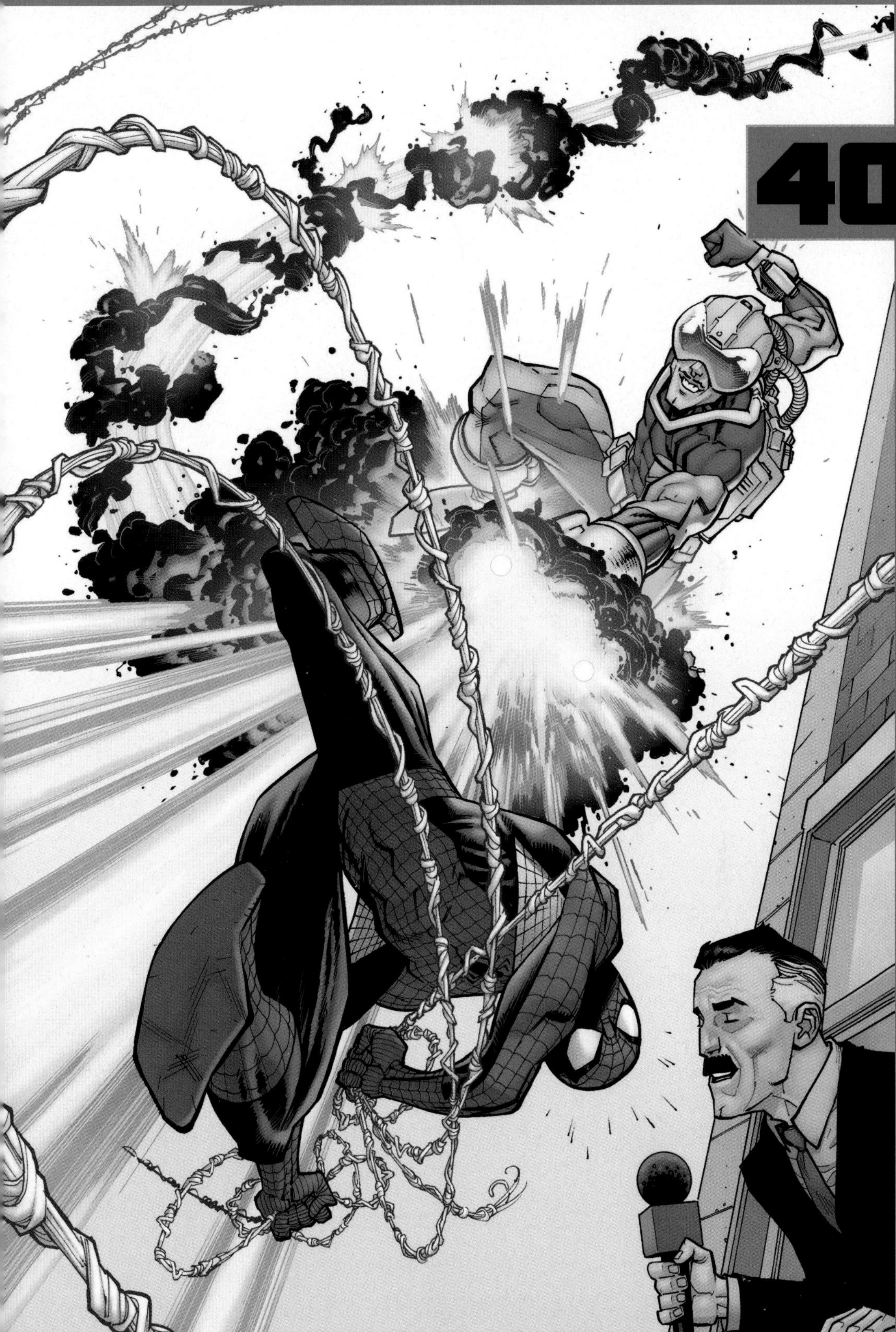

BREAKING NEWS PART 3

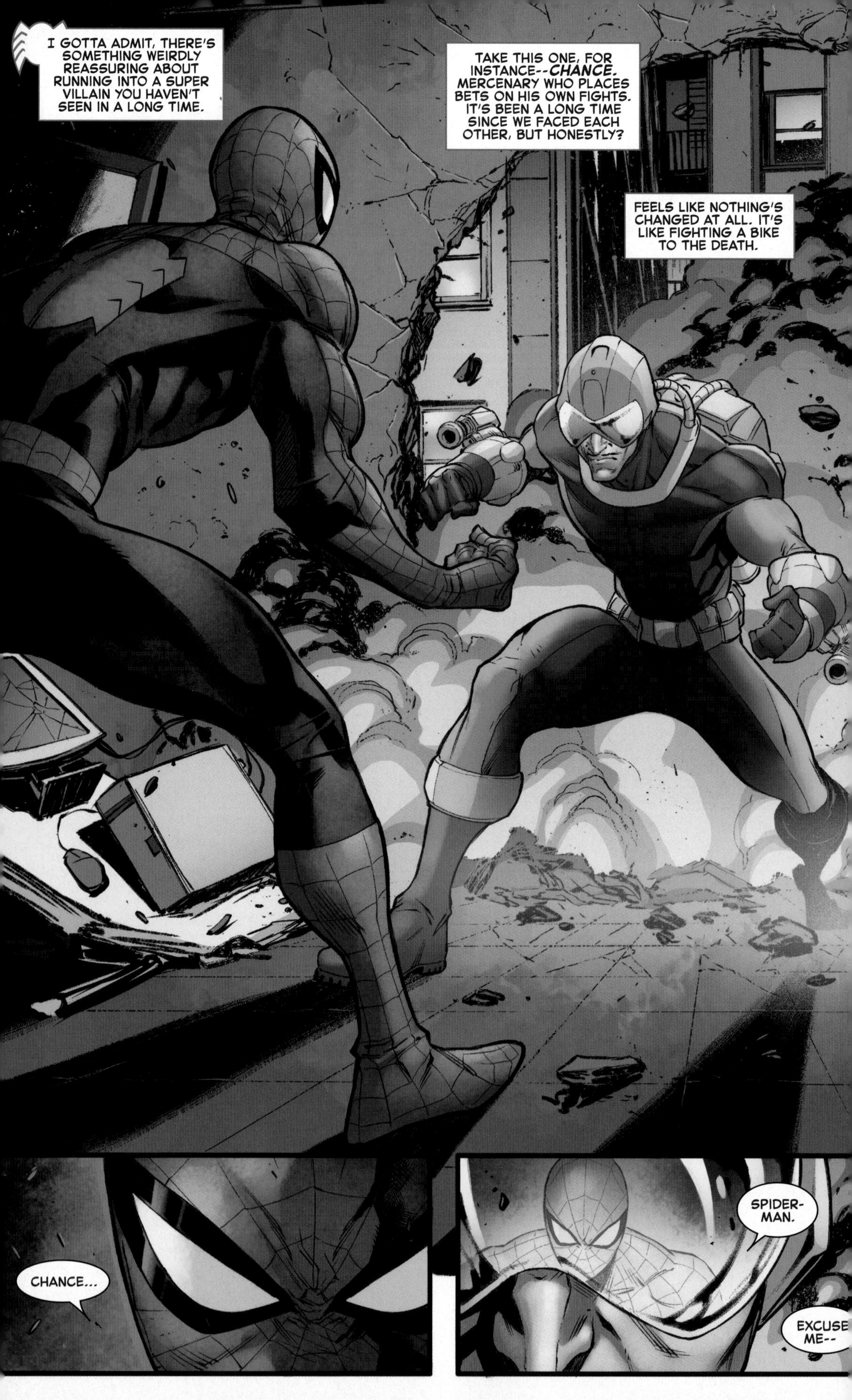

I GOTTA ADMIT, THERE'S SOMETHING WEIRDLY REASSURING ABOUT RUNNING INTO A SUPER VILLAIN YOU HAVEN'T SEEN IN A LONG TIME.
TAKE THIS ONE, FOR INSTANCE--CHANCE. MERCENARY WHO PLACES BETS ON HIS OWN FIGHTS. IT'S BEEN A LONG TIME SINCE WE FACED EACH OTHER, BUT HONESTLY?
FEELS LIKE NOTHING'S CHANGED AT ALL. IT'S LIKE FIGHTING A BIKE TO THE DEATH.
CHANCE...
SPIDER-MAN.
EXCUSE ME--

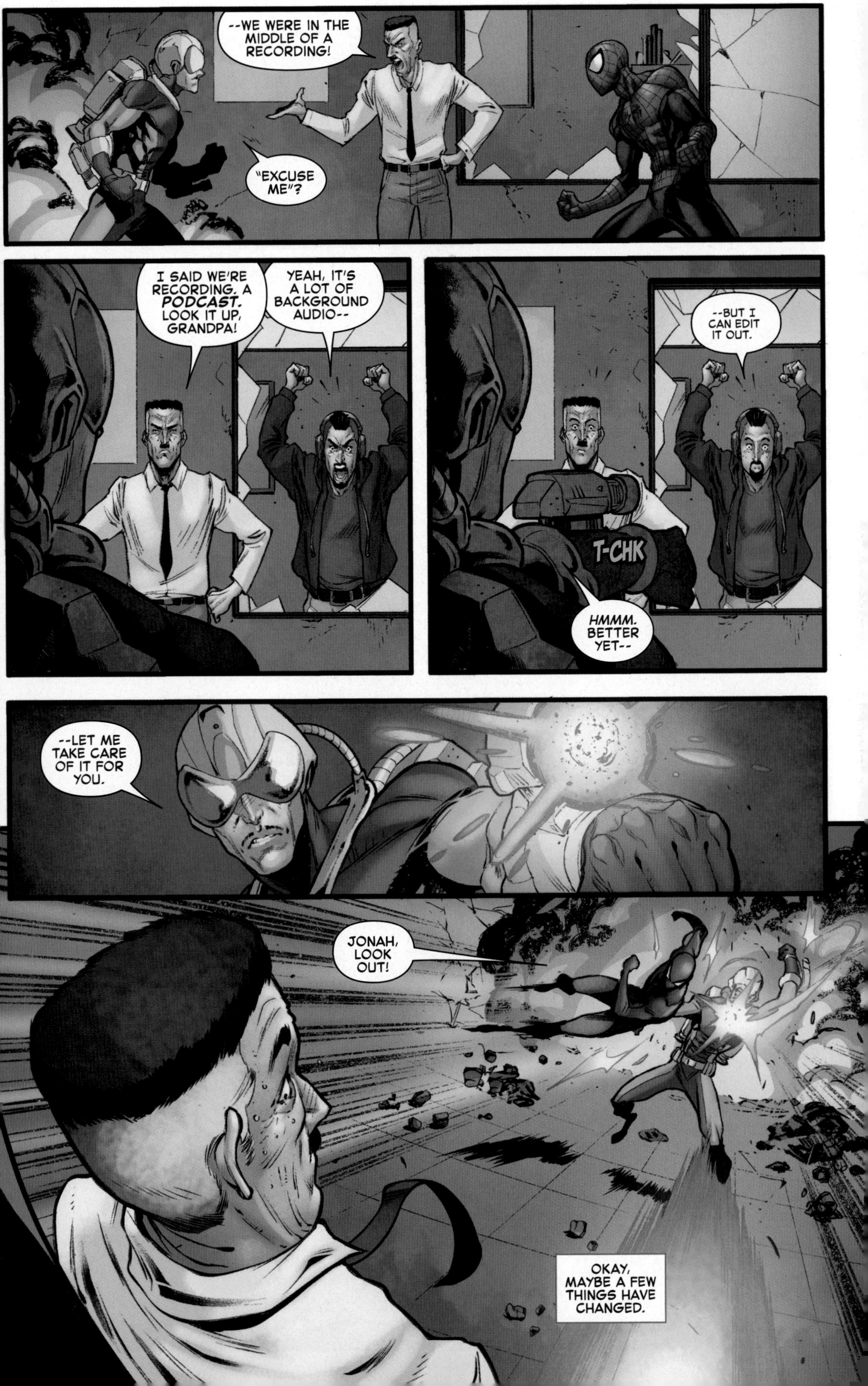
--WE WERE IN THE MIDDLE OF A RECORDING!
"EXCUSE ME"?
I SAID WE'RE RECORDING. A *PODCAST.* LOOK IT UP, GRANDPA!
YEAH, IT'S A LOT OF BACKGROUND AUDIO--
--BUT I CAN EDIT IT OUT.
T-CHK
HMMM. BETTER YET--
--LET ME TAKE CARE OF IT FOR YOU.
JONAH, LOOK OUT!
OKAY, MAYBE A FEW THINGS HAVE CHANGED.

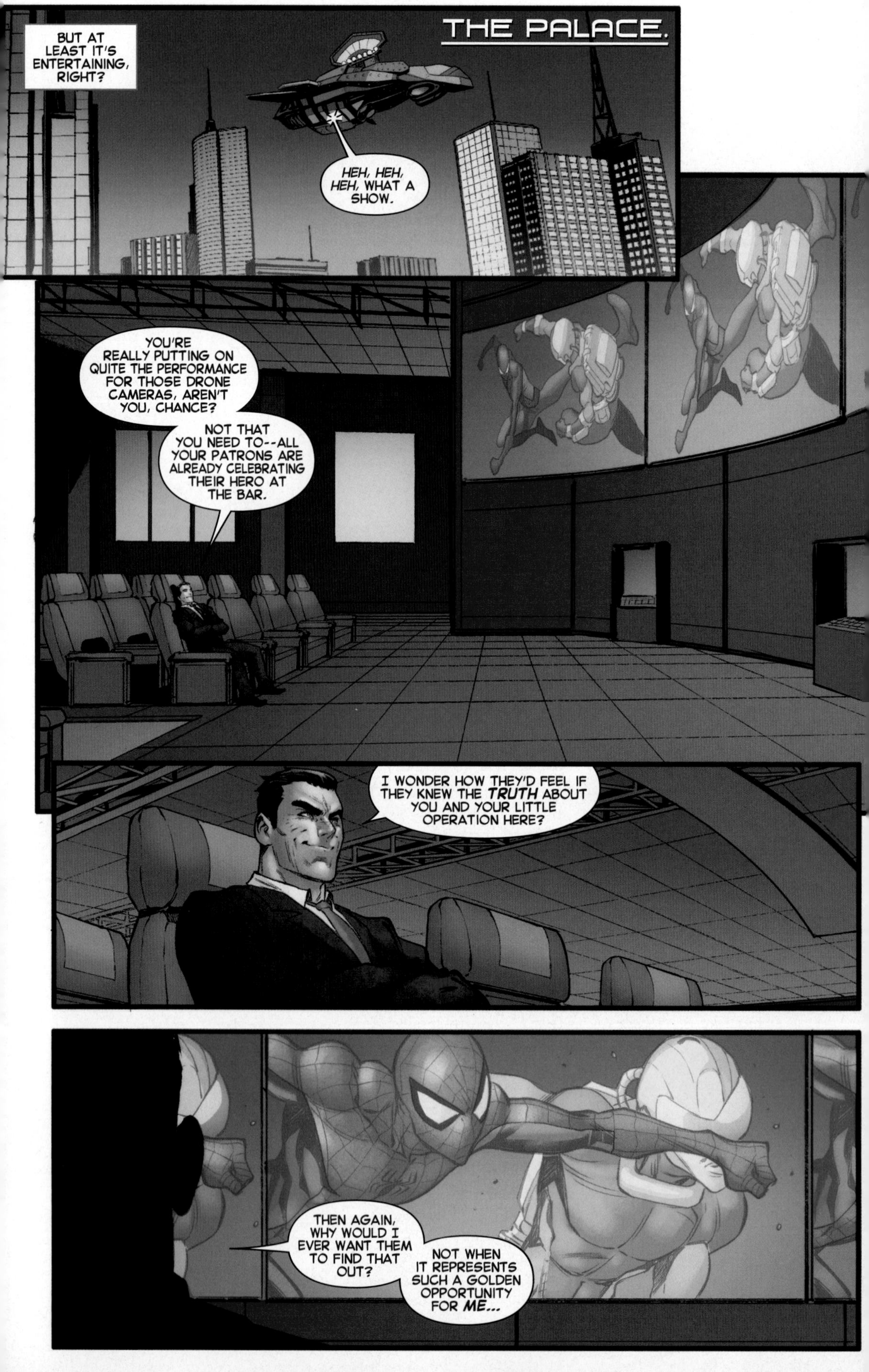
THE PALACE.
BUT AT LEAST IT'S ENTERTAINING, RIGHT?
HEH, HEH, HEH, WHAT A SHOW.
YOU'RE REALLY PUTTING ON QUITE THE PERFORMANCE FOR THOSE DRONE CAMERAS, AREN'T YOU, CHANCE?
NOT THAT YOU NEED TO--ALL YOUR PATRONS ARE ALREADY CELEBRATING THEIR HERO AT THE BAR.
I WONDER HOW THEY'D FEEL IF THEY KNEW THE TRUTH ABOUT YOU AND YOUR LITTLE OPERATION HERE?
THEN AGAIN, WHY WOULD I EVER WANT THEM TO FIND THAT OUT?
NOT WHEN IT REPRESENTS SUCH A GOLDEN OPPORTUNITY FOR ME...

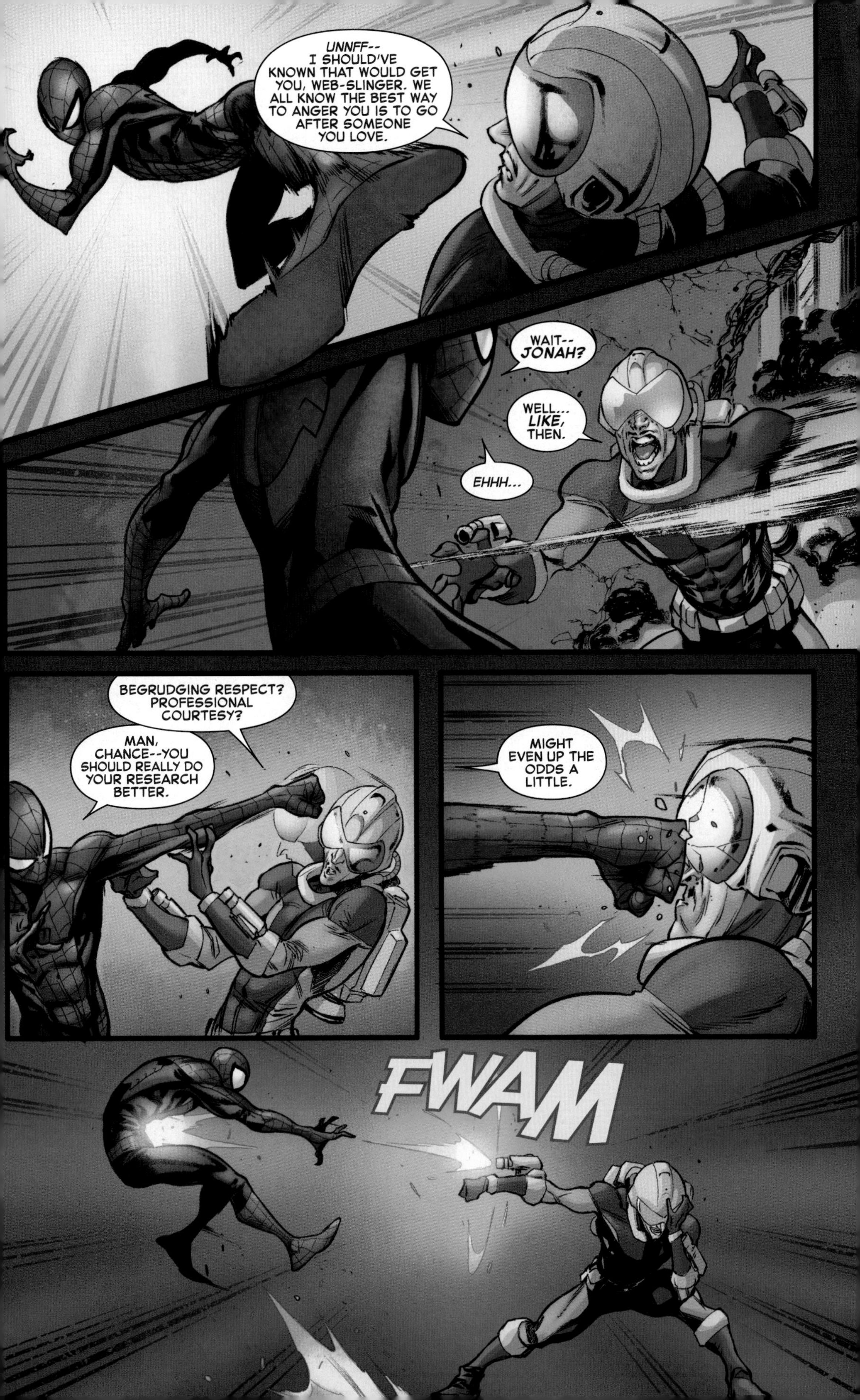
UNNFF-- I SHOULD'VE KNOWN THAT WOULD GET YOU, WEB-SLINGER. WE ALL KNOW THE BEST WAY TO ANGER YOU IS TO GO AFTER SOMEONE YOU LOVE.
WAIT-- JONAH?
WELL... LIKE, THEN.
EHHH...
BEGRUDGING RESPECT? PROFESSIONAL COURTESY?
MAN, CHANCE--YOU SHOULD REALLY DO YOUR RESEARCH BETTER.
MIGHT EVEN UP THE ODDS A LITTLE.
FWAM

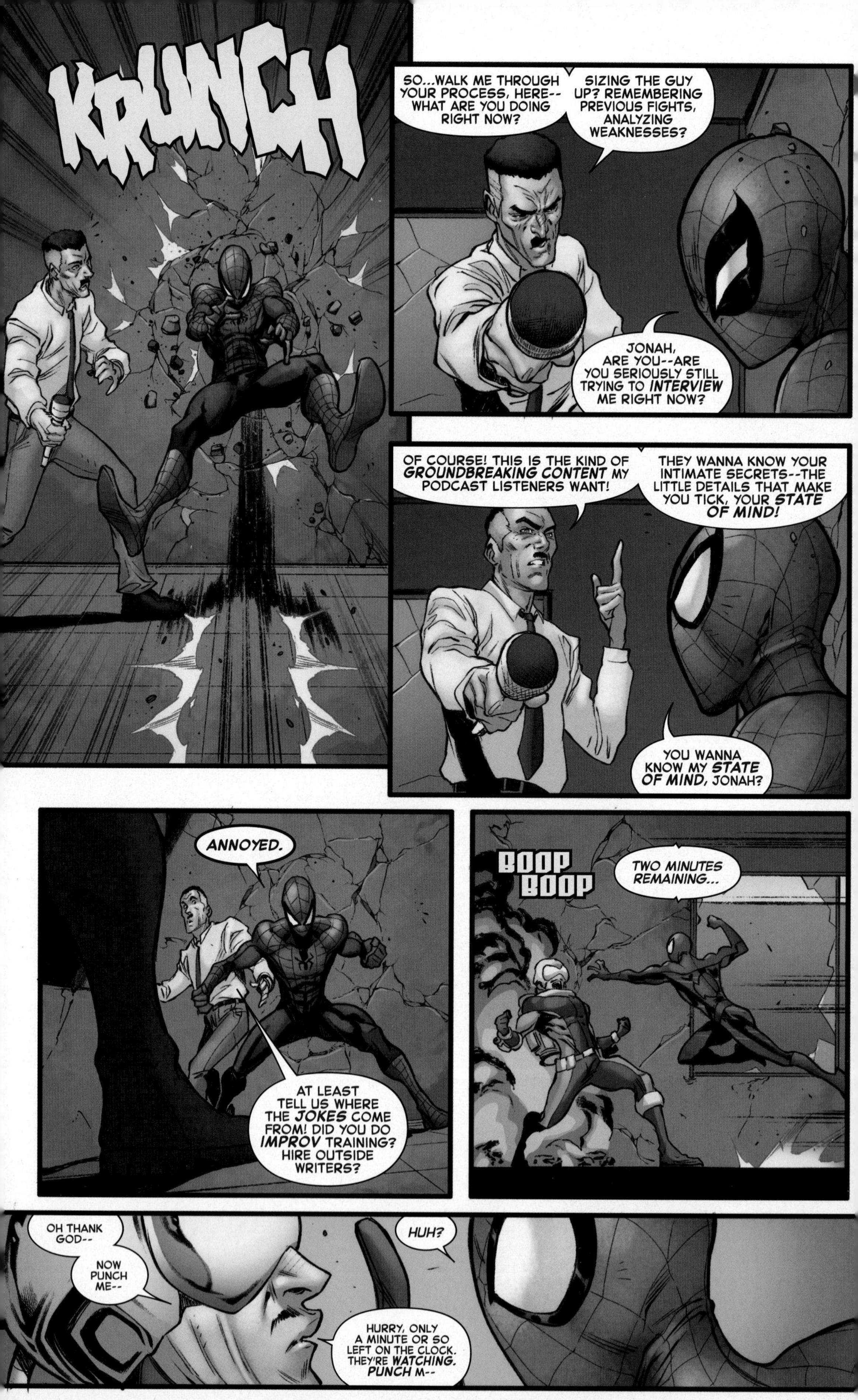
KRUNCH
SO...WALK ME THROUGH YOUR PROCESS, HERE-- WHAT ARE YOU DOING RIGHT NOW?
SIZING THE GUY UP? REMEMBERING PREVIOUS FIGHTS, ANALYZING WEAKNESSES?
JONAH, ARE YOU--ARE YOU SERIOUSLY STILL TRYING TO INTERVIEW ME RIGHT NOW?
OF COURSE! THIS IS THE KIND OF GROUNDBREAKING CONTENT MY PODCAST LISTENERS WANT!
THEY WANNA KNOW YOUR INTIMATE SECRETS--THE LITTLE DETAILS THAT MAKE YOU TICK, YOUR STATE OF MIND!
YOU WANNA KNOW MY STATE OF MIND, JONAH?
ANNOYED.
AT LEAST TELL US WHERE THE JOKES COME FROM! DID YOU DO IMPROV TRAINING? HIRE OUTSIDE WRITERS?
BOOP BOOP
TWO MINUTES REMAINING...
OH THANK GOD--
NOW PUNCH ME--
HUH?
HURRY, ONLY A MINUTE OR SO LEFT ON THE CLOCK. THEY'RE WATCHING. PUNCH M--

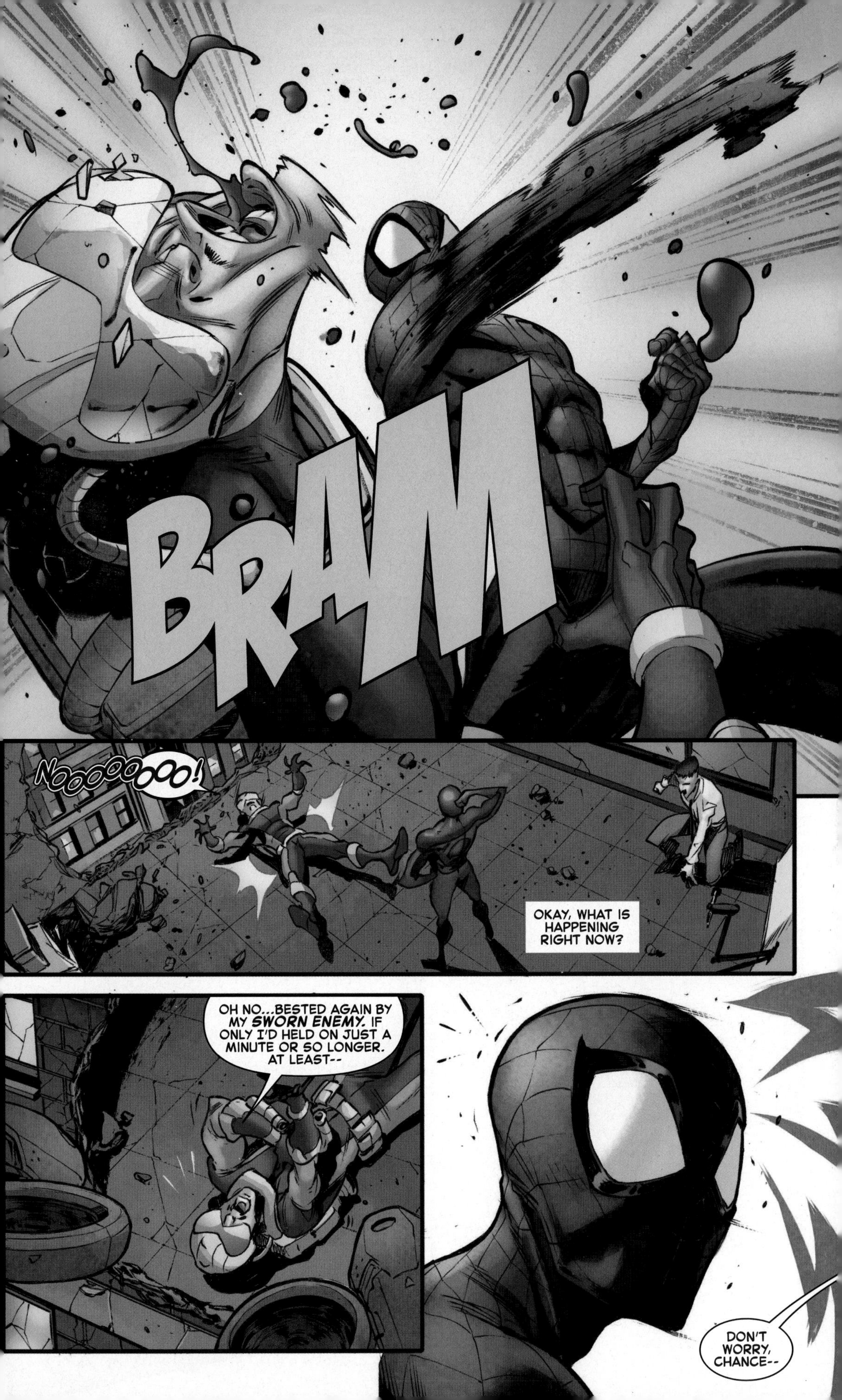
BRAM
NOOOOOOOO!
OKAY, WHAT IS HAPPENING RIGHT NOW?
OH NO...BESTED AGAIN BY MY SWORN ENEMY. IF ONLY I'D HELD ON JUST A MINUTE OR SO LONGER. AT LEAST--
DON'T WORRY, CHANCE--

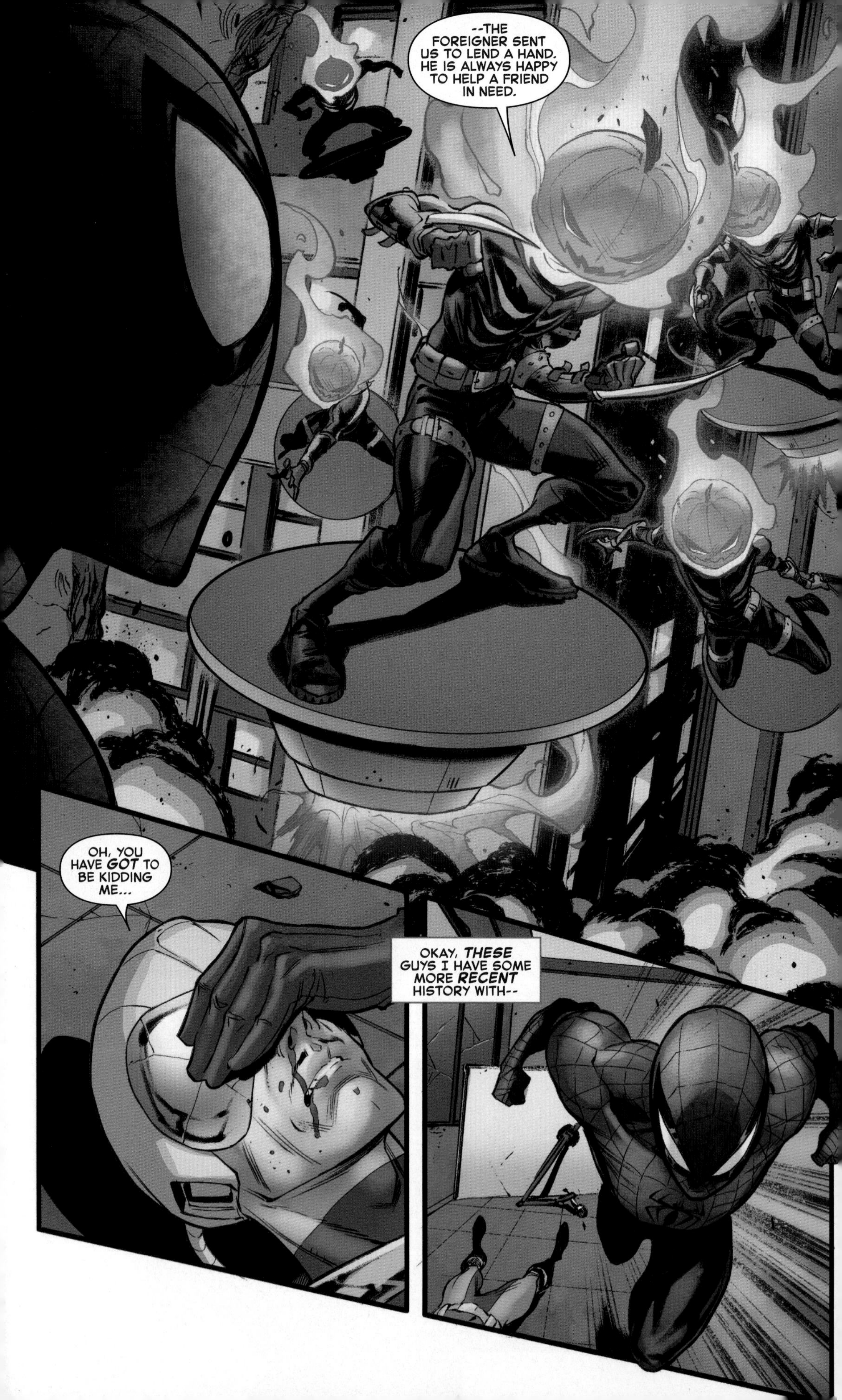
--THE FOREIGNER SENT US TO LEND A HAND. HE IS ALWAYS HAPPY TO HELP A FRIEND IN NEED.
OH, YOU HAVE GOT TO BE KIDDING ME...
OKAY, THESE GUYS I HAVE SOME MORE RECENT HISTORY WITH--

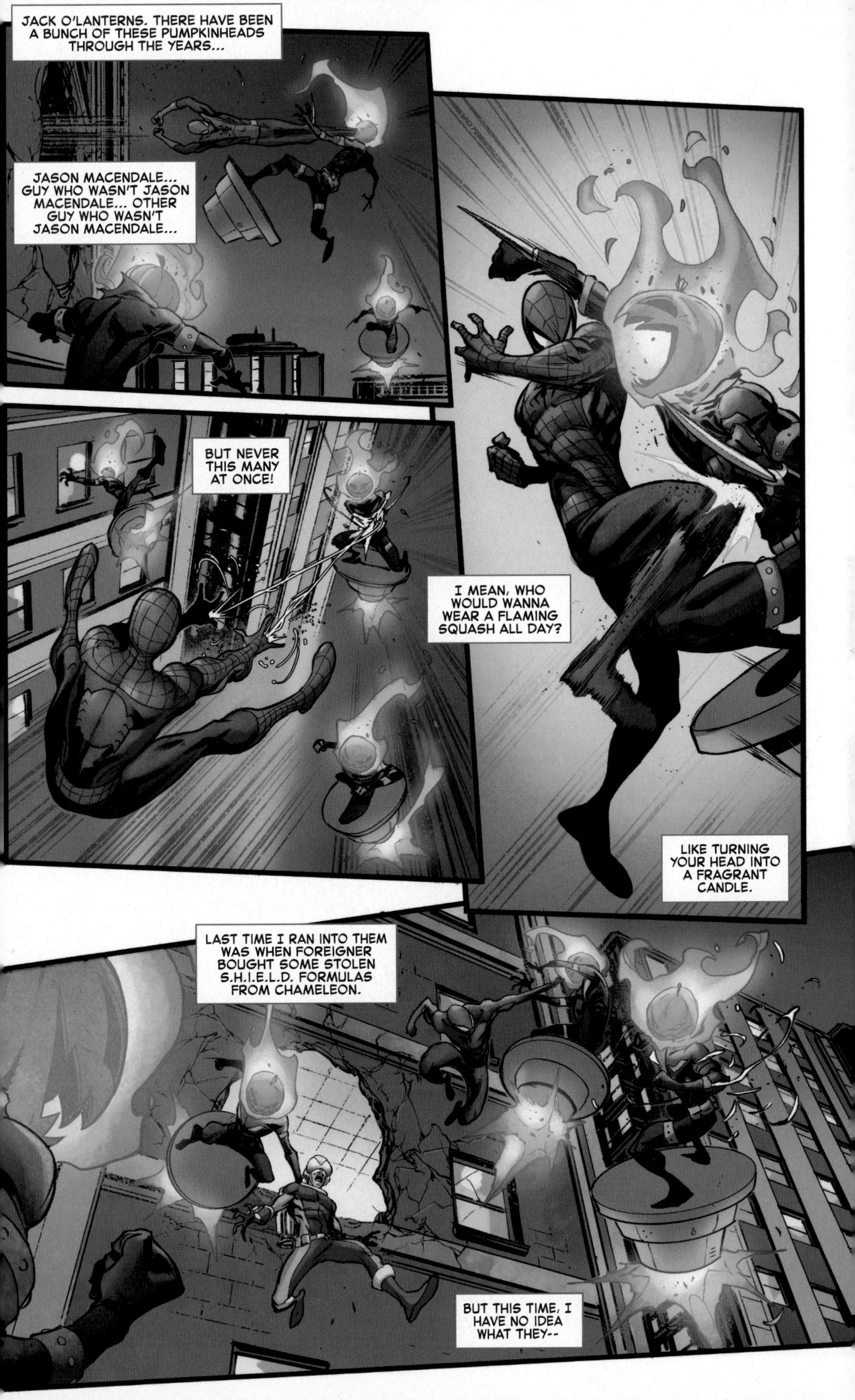
JACK O'LANTERNS. THERE HAVE BEEN A BUNCH OF THESE PUMPKINHEADS THROUGH THE YEARS...
JASON MACENDALE... GUY WHO WASN'T JASON MACENDALE... OTHER GUY WHO WASN'T JASON MACENDALE...
BUT NEVER THIS MANY AT ONCE!
I MEAN, WHO WOULD WANNA WEAR A FLAMING SQUASH ALL DAY?
LIKE TURNING YOUR HEAD INTO A FRAGRANT CANDLE.
LAST TIME I RAN INTO THEM WAS WHEN FOREIGNER BOUGHT SOME STOLEN S.H.I.E.L.D. FORMULAS FROM CHAMELEON.
BUT THIS TIME, I HAVE NO IDEA WHAT THEY--

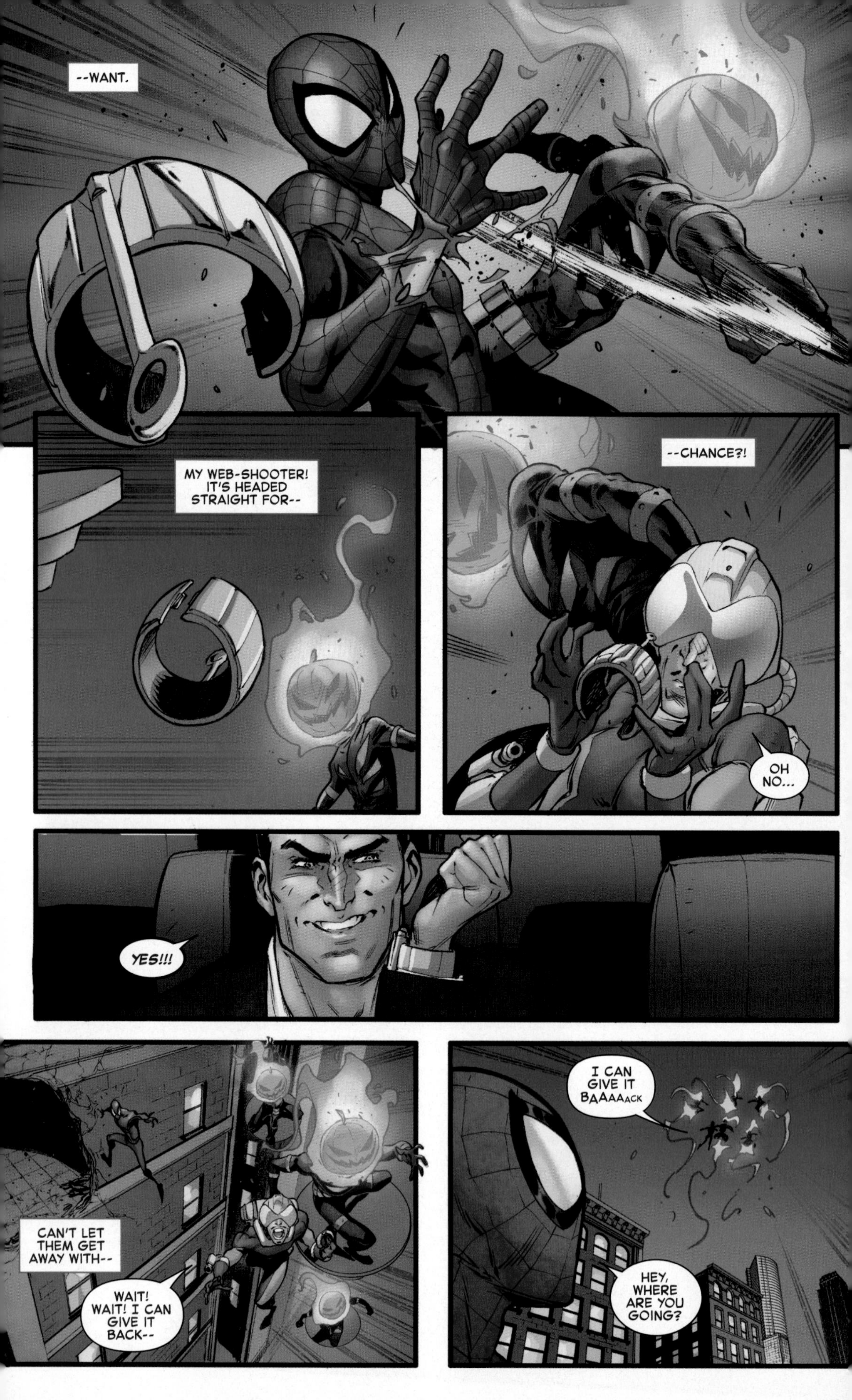
--WANT.
MY WEB-SHOOTER! IT'S HEADED STRAIGHT FOR--
--CHANCE?!
OH NO...
YES!!!
CAN'T LET THEM GET AWAY WITH--
WAIT! WAIT! I CAN GIVE IT BACK--
I CAN GIVE IT BAAAAACK
HEY, WHERE ARE YOU GOING?

GOTTA FOLLOW THEM--FIND OUT WHAT THEY'RE UP TO BEFORE--

AH, *THERE* IT IS. THE EXCUSE. I KNOW WHAT THIS IS.

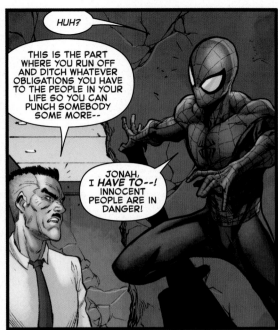

HUH?

THIS IS THE PART WHERE YOU RUN OFF AND DITCH WHATEVER OBLIGATIONS YOU HAVE TO THE PEOPLE IN YOUR LIFE SO YOU CAN PUNCH SOMEBODY SOME MORE--

JONAH, I *HAVE TO*--! INNOCENT PEOPLE ARE IN DANGER!

WAIT A SECOND-- RE THEY? I MEAN, OSE GUYS MOSTLY EEMED TO HAVE A PROBLEM WITH *EACH OTHER.*

WORST IT SEEMED KE A SUPER VILLAIN SCAVENGER HUNT. WHICH SOUNDS TERRIFYING. BUT THEN, MAYBE--

⸗SIGH⸗ OKAY, JONAH.

--SO IS THIS.

LET'S TALK.

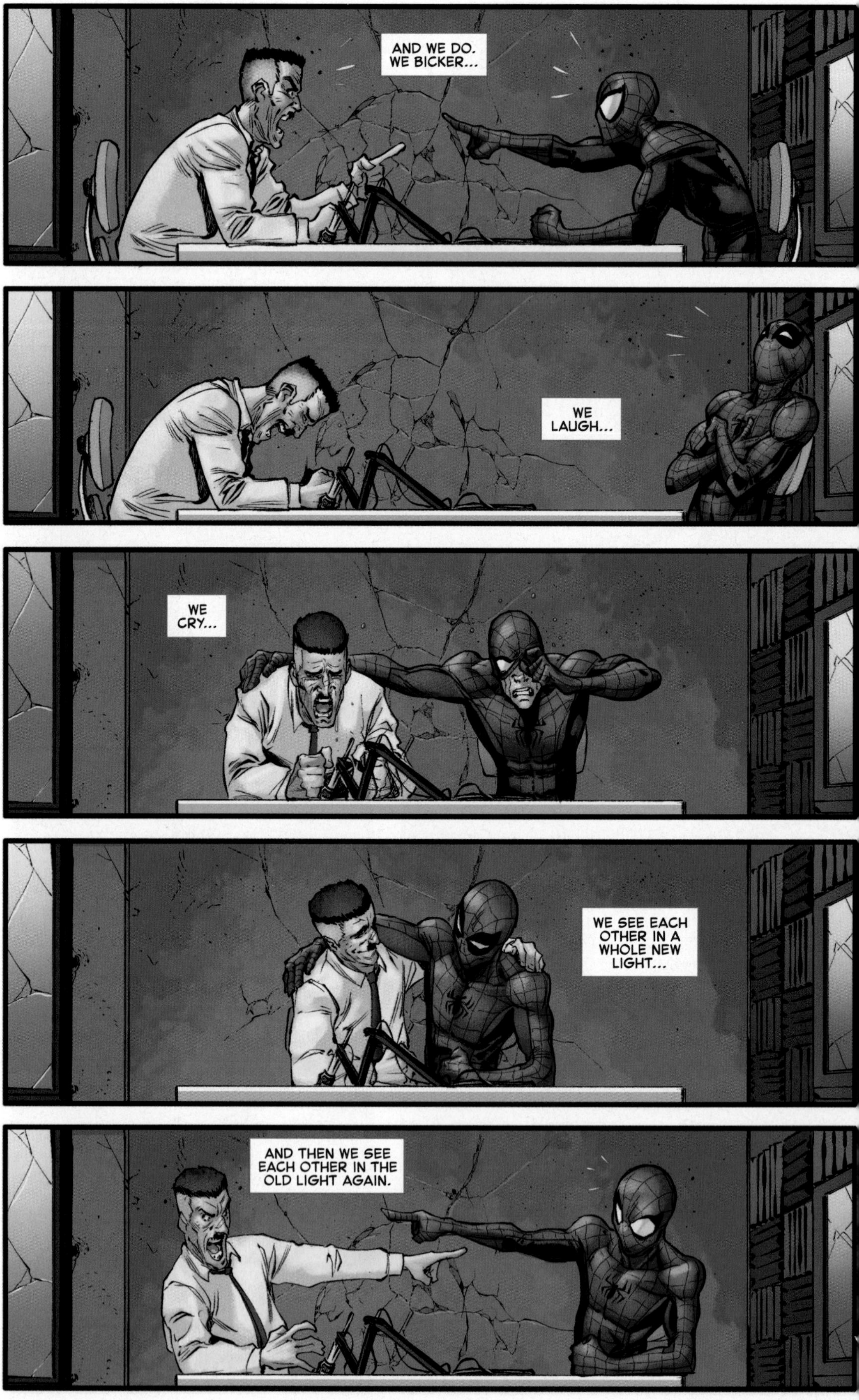
AND WE DO. WE BICKER...
WE LAUGH...
WE CRY...
WE SEE EACH OTHER IN A WHOLE NEW LIGHT...
AND THEN WE SEE EACH OTHER IN THE OLD LIGHT AGAIN.

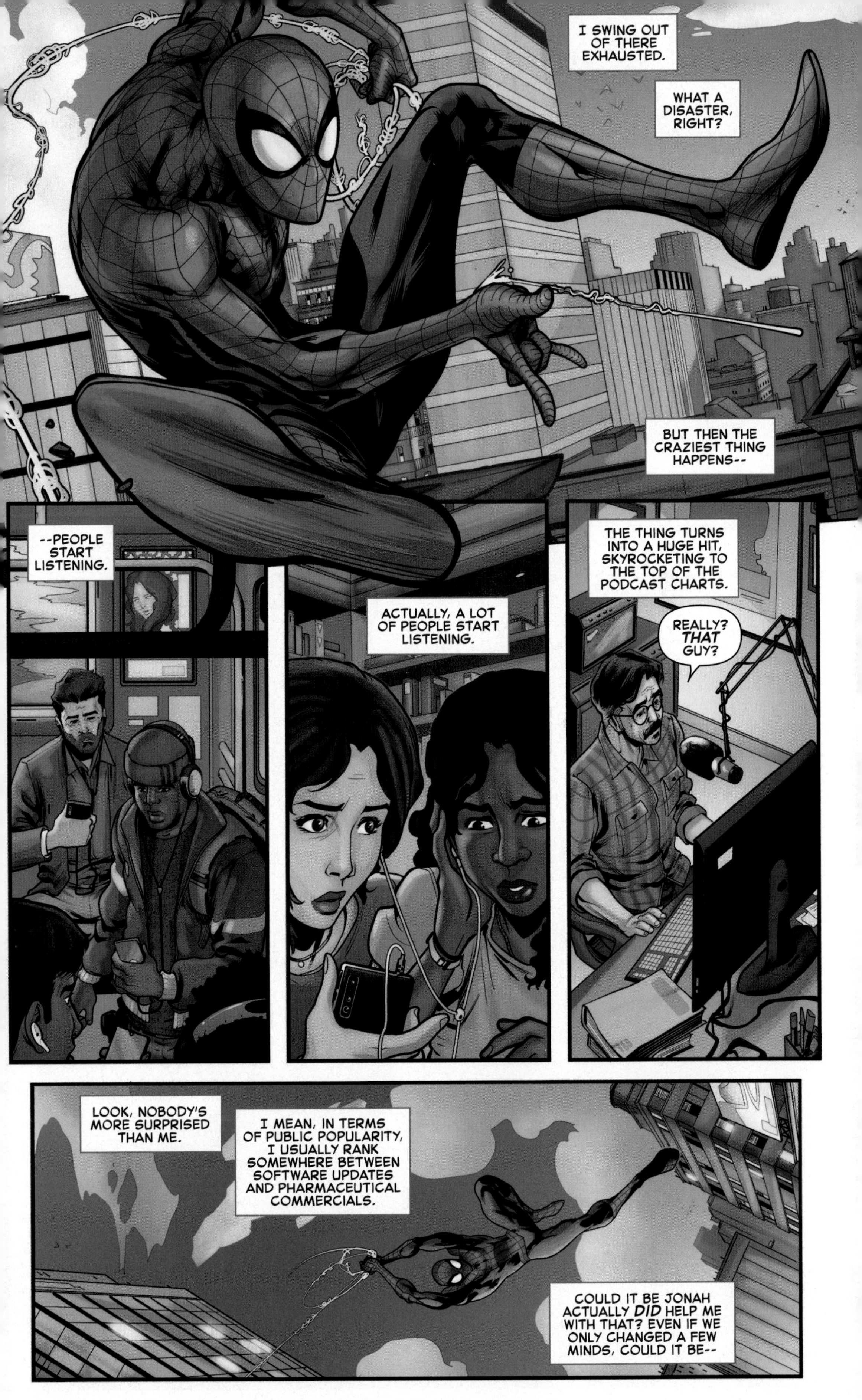
I SWING OUT OF THERE EXHAUSTED.
WHAT A DISASTER, RIGHT?
BUT THEN THE CRAZIEST THING HAPPENS--
--PEOPLE START LISTENING.
ACTUALLY, A LOT OF PEOPLE START LISTENING.
THE THING TURNS INTO A HUGE HIT, SKYROCKETING TO THE TOP OF THE PODCAST CHARTS.
REALLY? *THAT* GUY?
LOOK, NOBODY'S MORE SURPRISED THAN ME.
I MEAN, IN TERMS OF PUBLIC POPULARITY, I USUALLY RANK SOMEWHERE BETWEEN SOFTWARE UPDATES AND PHARMACEUTICAL COMMERCIALS.
COULD IT BE JONAH ACTUALLY *DID* HELP ME WITH THAT? EVEN IF WE ONLY CHANGED A FEW MINDS, COULD IT BE--

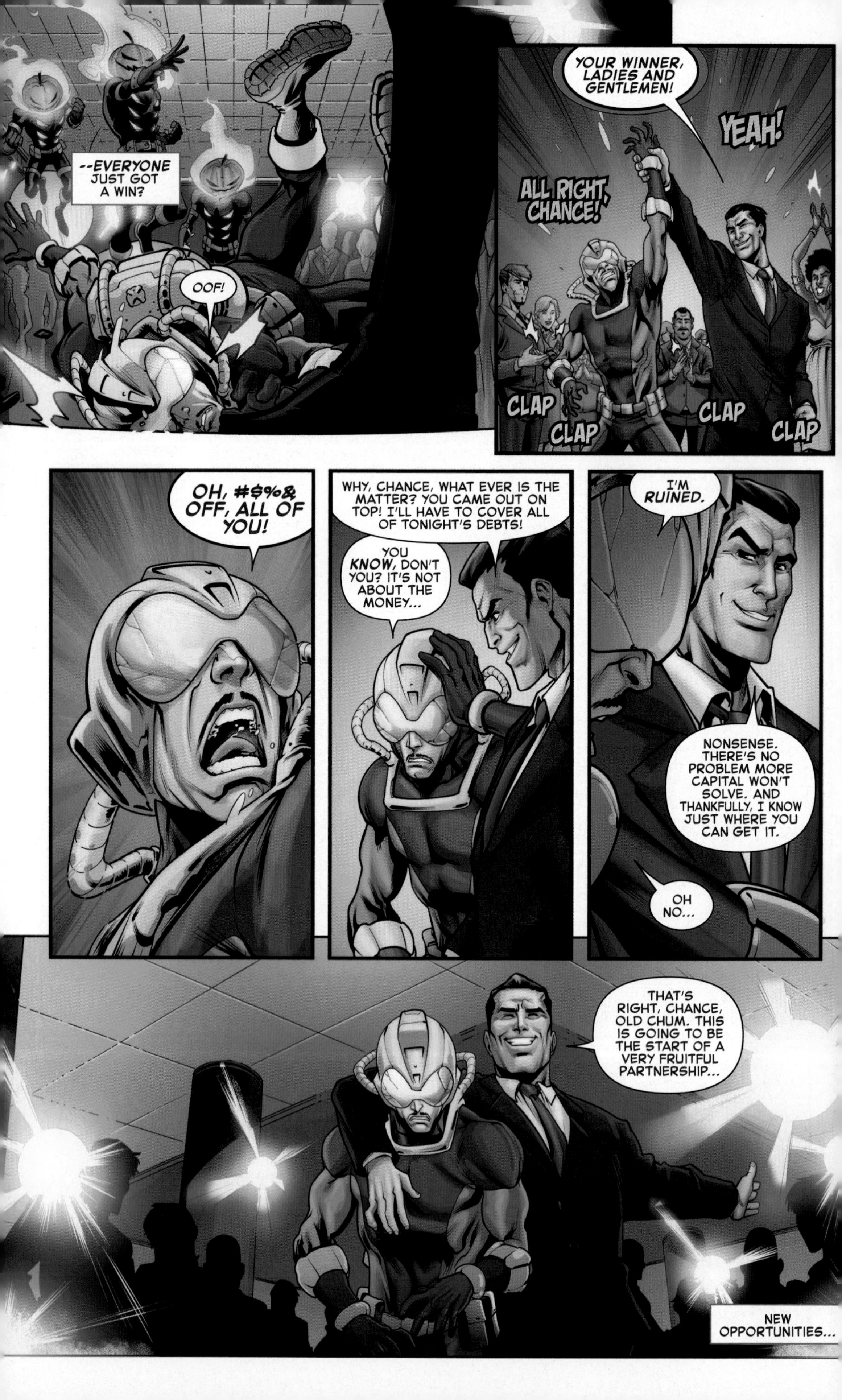
--EVERYONE JUST GOT A WIN?
OOF!
YOUR WINNER, LADIES AND GENTLEMEN!
YEAH!
ALL RIGHT, CHANCE!
CLAP
CLAP
CLAP
CLAP
OH, #$%& OFF, ALL OF YOU!
WHY, CHANCE, WHAT EVER IS THE MATTER? YOU CAME OUT ON TOP! I'LL HAVE TO COVER ALL OF TONIGHT'S DEBTS!
YOU KNOW, DON'T YOU? IT'S NOT ABOUT THE MONEY...
I'M RUINED.
NONSENSE. THERE'S NO PROBLEM MORE CAPITAL WON'T SOLVE. AND THANKFULLY, I KNOW JUST WHERE YOU CAN GET IT.
OH NO...
THAT'S RIGHT, CHANCE, OLD CHUM. THIS IS GOING TO BE THE START OF A VERY FRUITFUL PARTNERSHIP...
NEW OPPORTUNITIES...

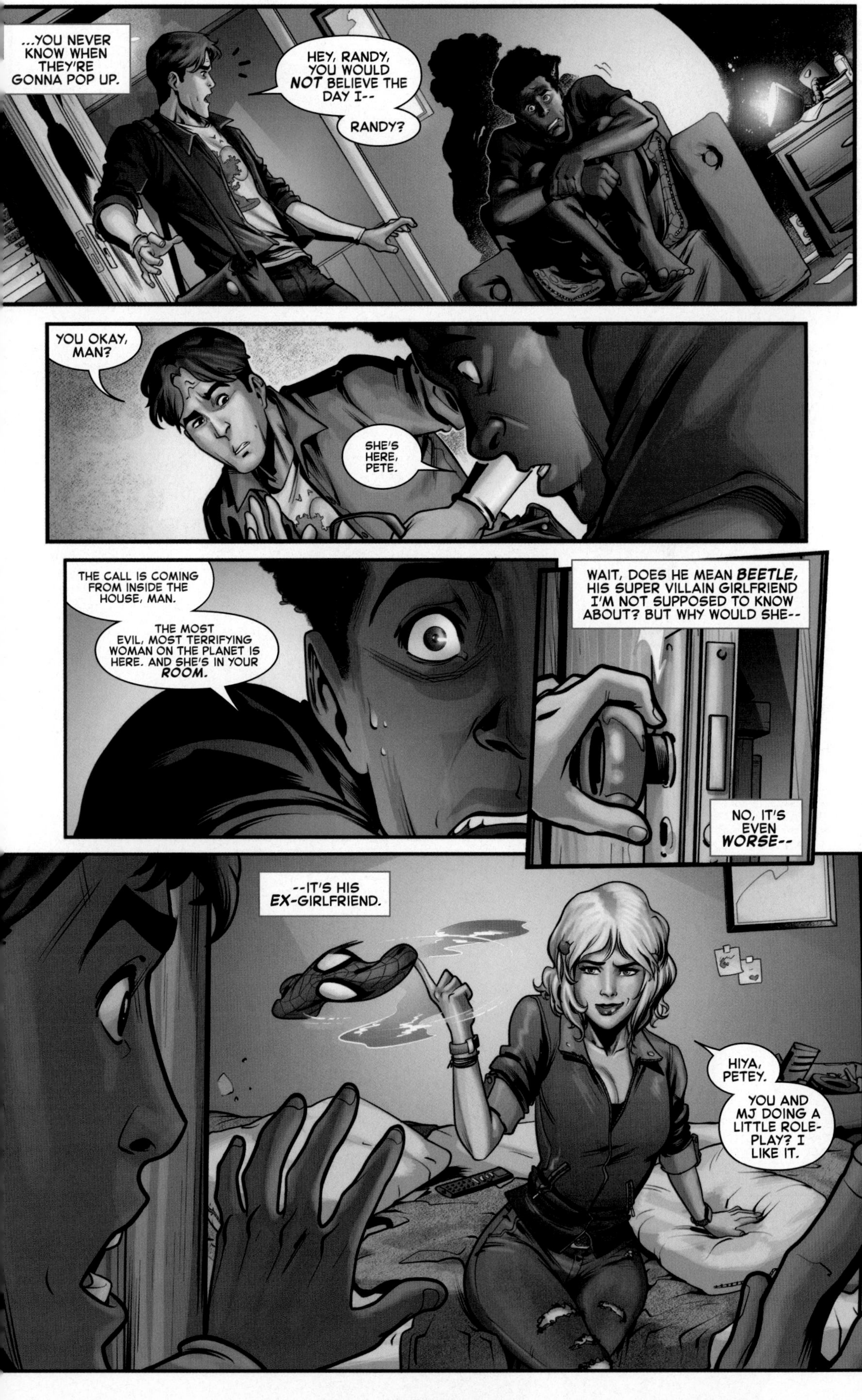
...YOU NEVER KNOW WHEN THEY'RE GONNA POP UP.
HEY, RANDY, YOU WOULD NOT BELIEVE THE DAY I--
RANDY?
YOU OKAY, MAN?
SHE'S HERE, PETE.
THE CALL IS COMING FROM INSIDE THE HOUSE, MAN.
THE MOST EVIL, MOST TERRIFYING WOMAN ON THE PLANET IS HERE. AND SHE'S IN YOUR ROOM.
WAIT, DOES HE MEAN BEETLE, HIS SUPER VILLAIN GIRLFRIEND I'M NOT SUPPOSED TO KNOW ABOUT? BUT WHY WOULD SHE--
NO, IT'S EVEN WORSE--
--IT'S HIS EX-GIRLFRIEND.
HIYA, PETEY.
YOU AND MJ DOING A LITTLE ROLE-PLAY? I LIKE IT.

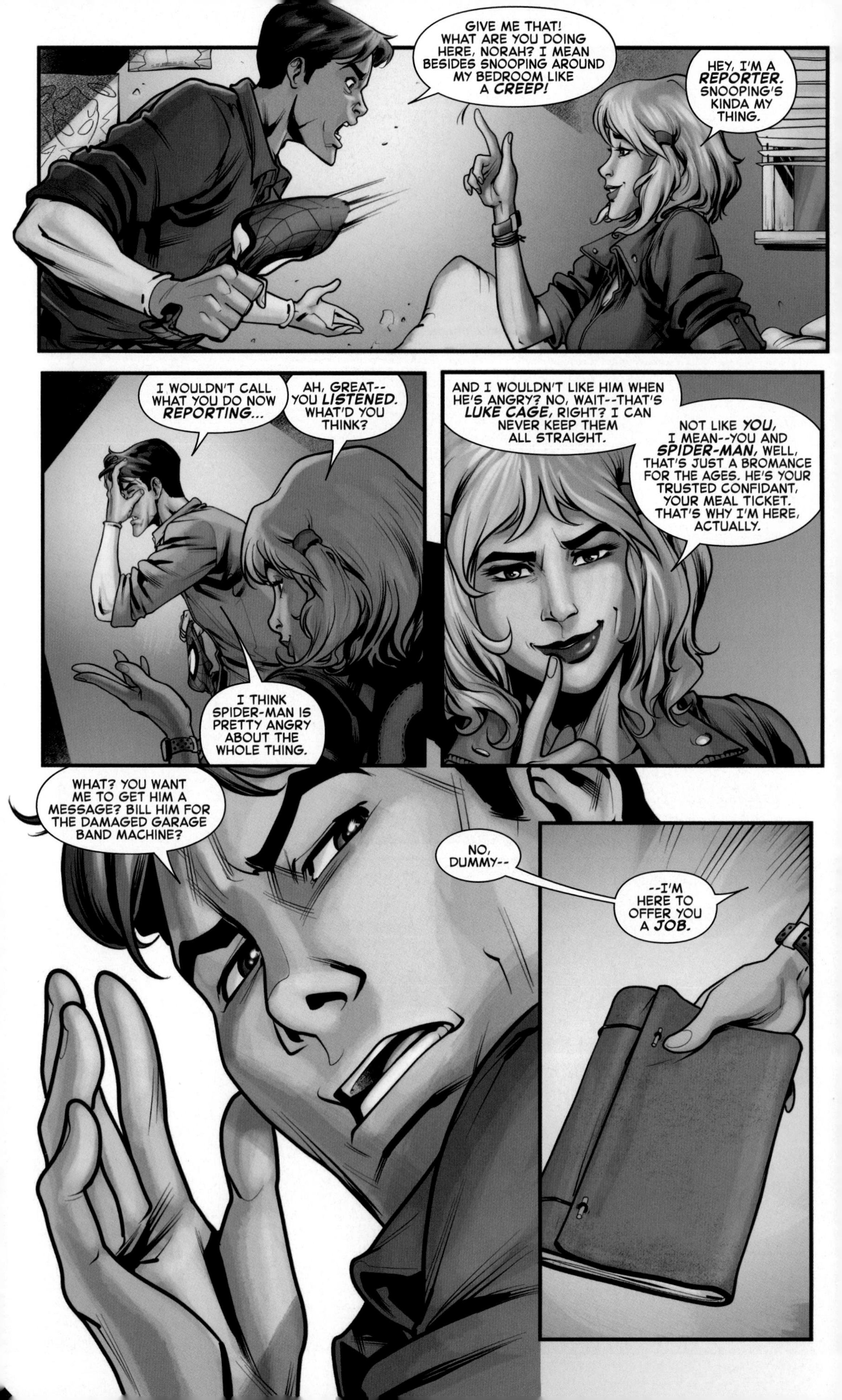

GIVE ME THAT! WHAT ARE YOU DOING HERE, NORAH? I MEAN BESIDES SNOOPING AROUND MY BEDROOM LIKE A CREEP!
HEY, I'M A REPORTER. SNOOPING'S KINDA MY THING.
I WOULDN'T CALL WHAT YOU DO NOW REPORTING...
AH, GREAT--YOU LISTENED. WHAT'D YOU THINK?
I THINK SPIDER-MAN IS PRETTY ANGRY ABOUT THE WHOLE THING.
AND I WOULDN'T LIKE HIM WHEN HE'S ANGRY? NO, WAIT--THAT'S LUKE CAGE, RIGHT? I CAN NEVER KEEP THEM ALL STRAIGHT.
NOT LIKE YOU, I MEAN--YOU AND SPIDER-MAN, WELL, THAT'S JUST A BROMANCE FOR THE AGES. HE'S YOUR TRUSTED CONFIDANT, YOUR MEAL TICKET. THAT'S WHY I'M HERE, ACTUALLY.
WHAT? YOU WANT ME TO GET HIM A MESSAGE? BILL HIM FOR THE DAMAGED GARAGE BAND MACHINE?
NO, DUMMY--
--I'M HERE TO OFFER YOU A JOB.

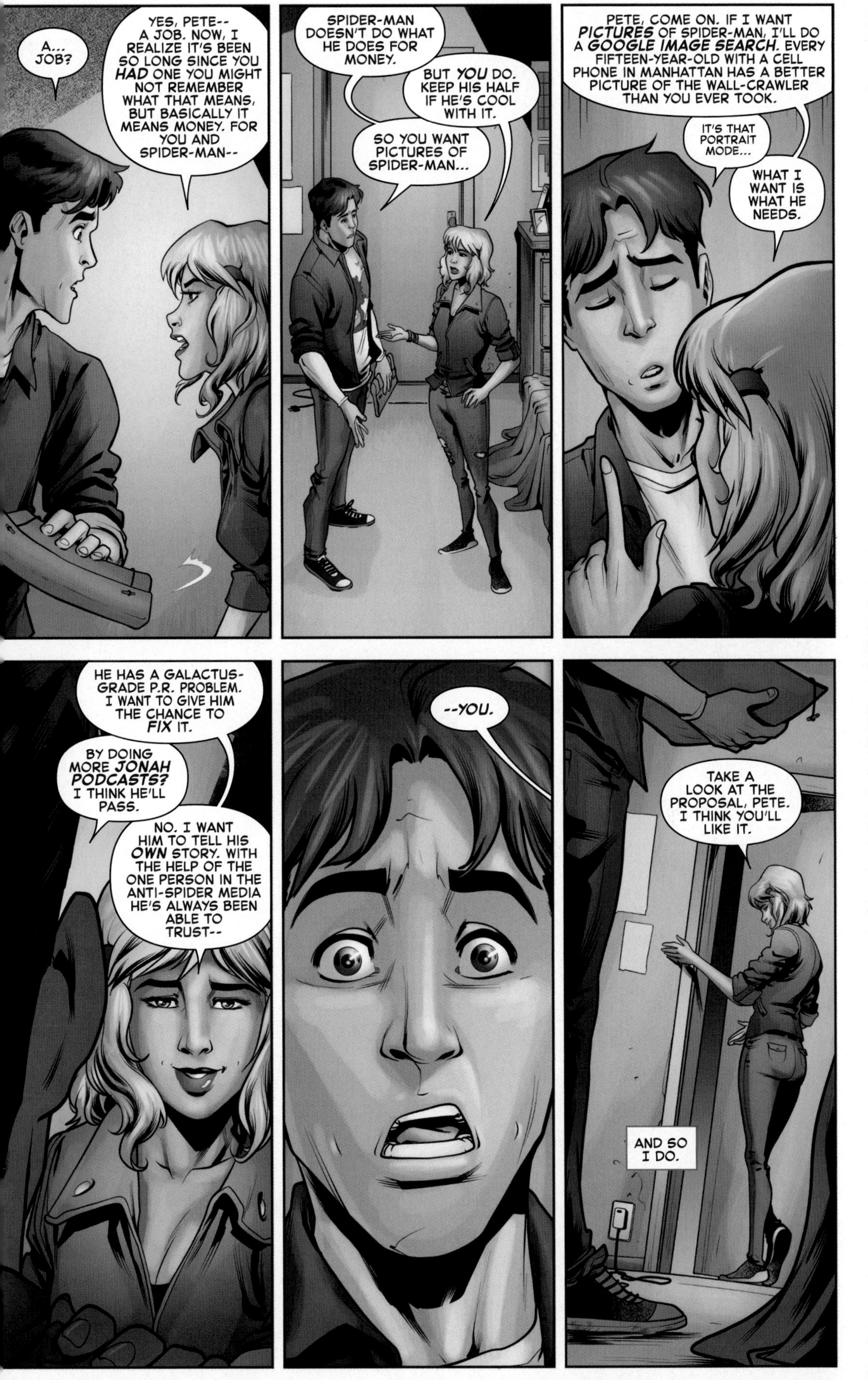
A... JOB?
YES, PETE-- A JOB. NOW, I REALIZE IT'S BEEN SO LONG SINCE YOU HAD ONE YOU MIGHT NOT REMEMBER WHAT THAT MEANS, BUT BASICALLY IT MEANS MONEY. FOR YOU AND SPIDER-MAN--
SPIDER-MAN DOESN'T DO WHAT HE DOES FOR MONEY.
BUT YOU DO. KEEP HIS HALF IF HE'S COOL WITH IT.
SO YOU WANT PICTURES OF SPIDER-MAN...
PETE, COME ON. IF I WANT PICTURES OF SPIDER-MAN, I'LL DO A GOOGLE IMAGE SEARCH. EVERY FIFTEEN-YEAR-OLD WITH A CELL PHONE IN MANHATTAN HAS A BETTER PICTURE OF THE WALL-CRAWLER THAN YOU EVER TOOK.
IT'S THAT PORTRAIT MODE...
WHAT I WANT IS WHAT HE NEEDS.
HE HAS A GALACTUS-GRADE P.R. PROBLEM. I WANT TO GIVE HIM THE CHANCE TO FIX IT.
BY DOING MORE JONAH PODCASTS? I THINK HE'LL PASS.
NO. I WANT HIM TO TELL HIS OWN STORY. WITH THE HELP OF THE ONE PERSON IN THE ANTI-SPIDER MEDIA HE'S ALWAYS BEEN ABLE TO TRUST--
--YOU.
TAKE A LOOK AT THE PROPOSAL, PETE. I THINK YOU'LL LIKE IT.
AND SO I DO.

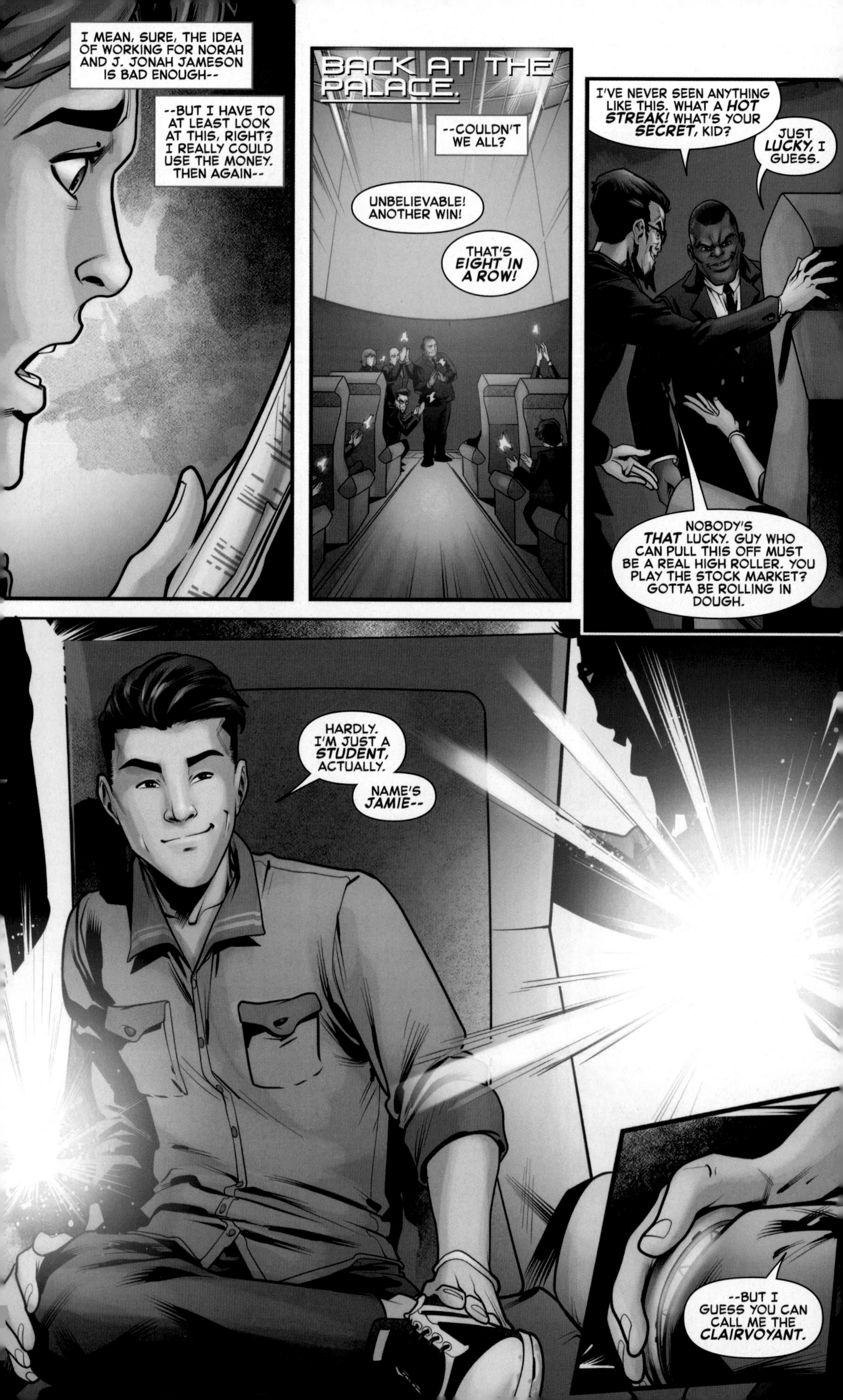

I MEAN, SURE, THE IDEA OF WORKING FOR NORAH AND J. JONAH JAMESON IS BAD ENOUGH--
--BUT I HAVE TO AT LEAST LOOK AT THIS, RIGHT? I REALLY COULD USE THE MONEY. THEN AGAIN--
BACK AT THE PALACE.
--COULDN'T WE ALL?
UNBELIEVABLE! ANOTHER WIN!
THAT'S EIGHT IN A ROW!
I'VE NEVER SEEN ANYTHING LIKE THIS. WHAT A HOT STREAK! WHAT'S YOUR SECRET, KID?
JUST LUCKY, I GUESS.
NOBODY'S THAT LUCKY. GUY WHO CAN PULL THIS OFF MUST BE A REAL HIGH ROLLER. YOU PLAY THE STOCK MARKET? GOTTA BE ROLLING IN DOUGH.
HARDLY. I'M JUST A STUDENT, ACTUALLY.
NAME'S JAMIE--
--BUT I GUESS YOU CAN CALL ME THE CLAIRVOYANT.

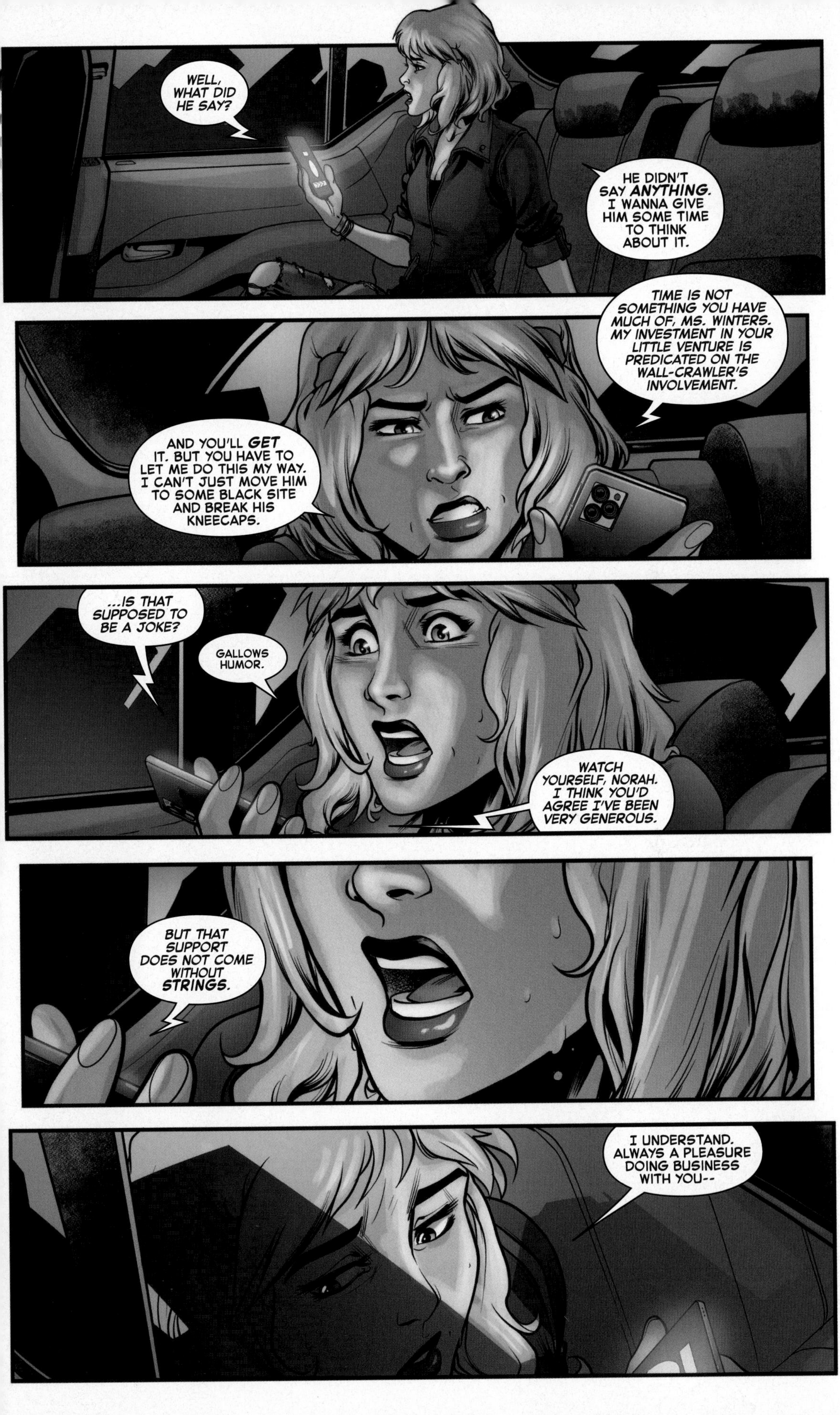
WELL, WHAT DID HE SAY?
HE DIDN'T SAY ANYTHING. I WANNA GIVE HIM SOME TIME TO THINK ABOUT IT.
TIME IS NOT SOMETHING YOU HAVE MUCH OF, MS. WINTERS. MY INVESTMENT IN YOUR LITTLE VENTURE IS PREDICATED ON THE WALL-CRAWLER'S INVOLVEMENT.
AND YOU'LL GET IT. BUT YOU HAVE TO LET ME DO THIS MY WAY. I CAN'T JUST MOVE HIM TO SOME BLACK SITE AND BREAK HIS KNEECAPS.
...IS THAT SUPPOSED TO BE A JOKE?
GALLOWS HUMOR.
WATCH YOURSELF, NORAH. I THINK YOU'D AGREE I'VE BEEN VERY GENEROUS.
BUT THAT SUPPORT DOES NOT COME WITHOUT STRINGS.
I UNDERSTAND. ALWAYS A PLEASURE DOING BUSINESS WITH YOU--

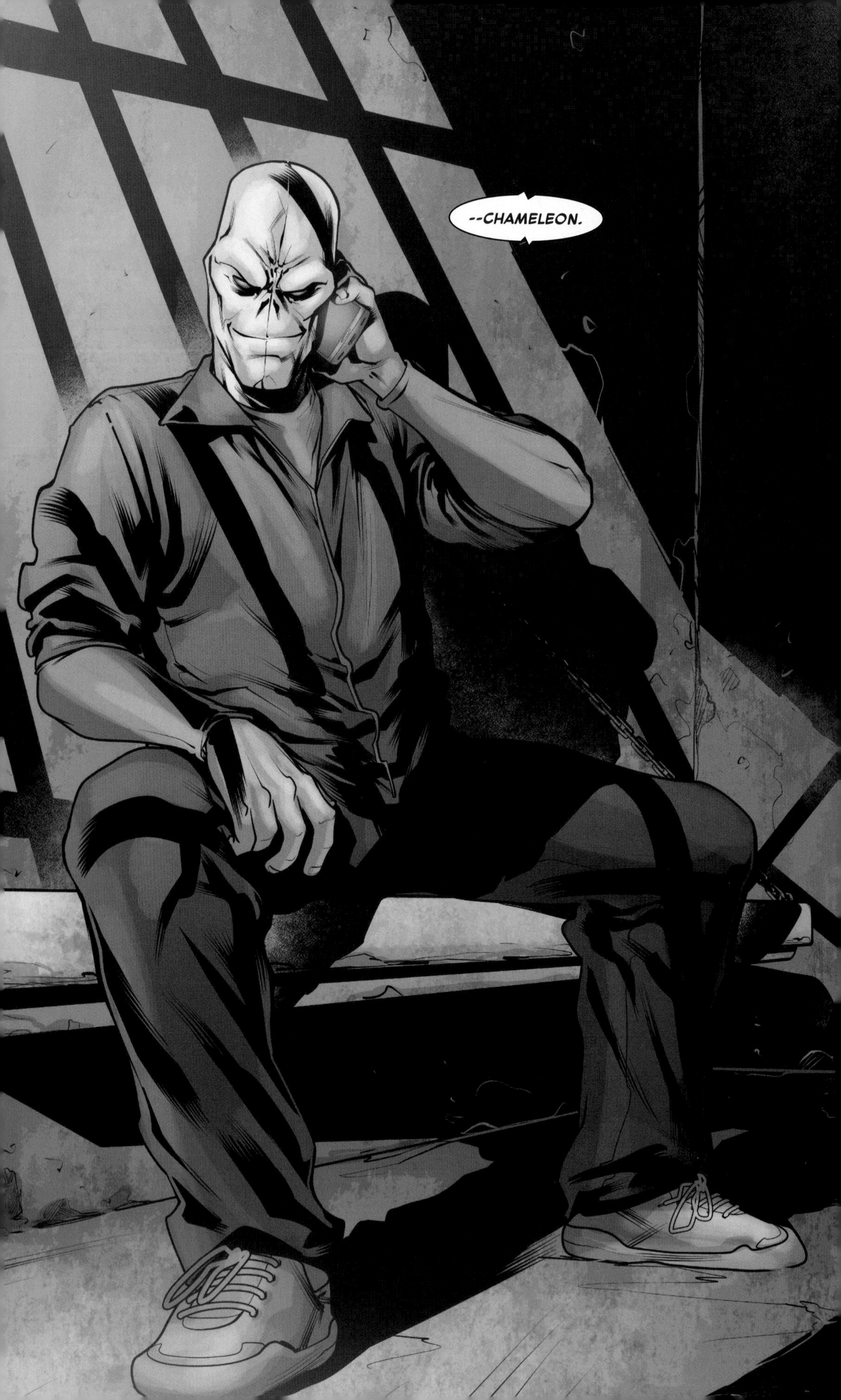
--CHAMELEON.

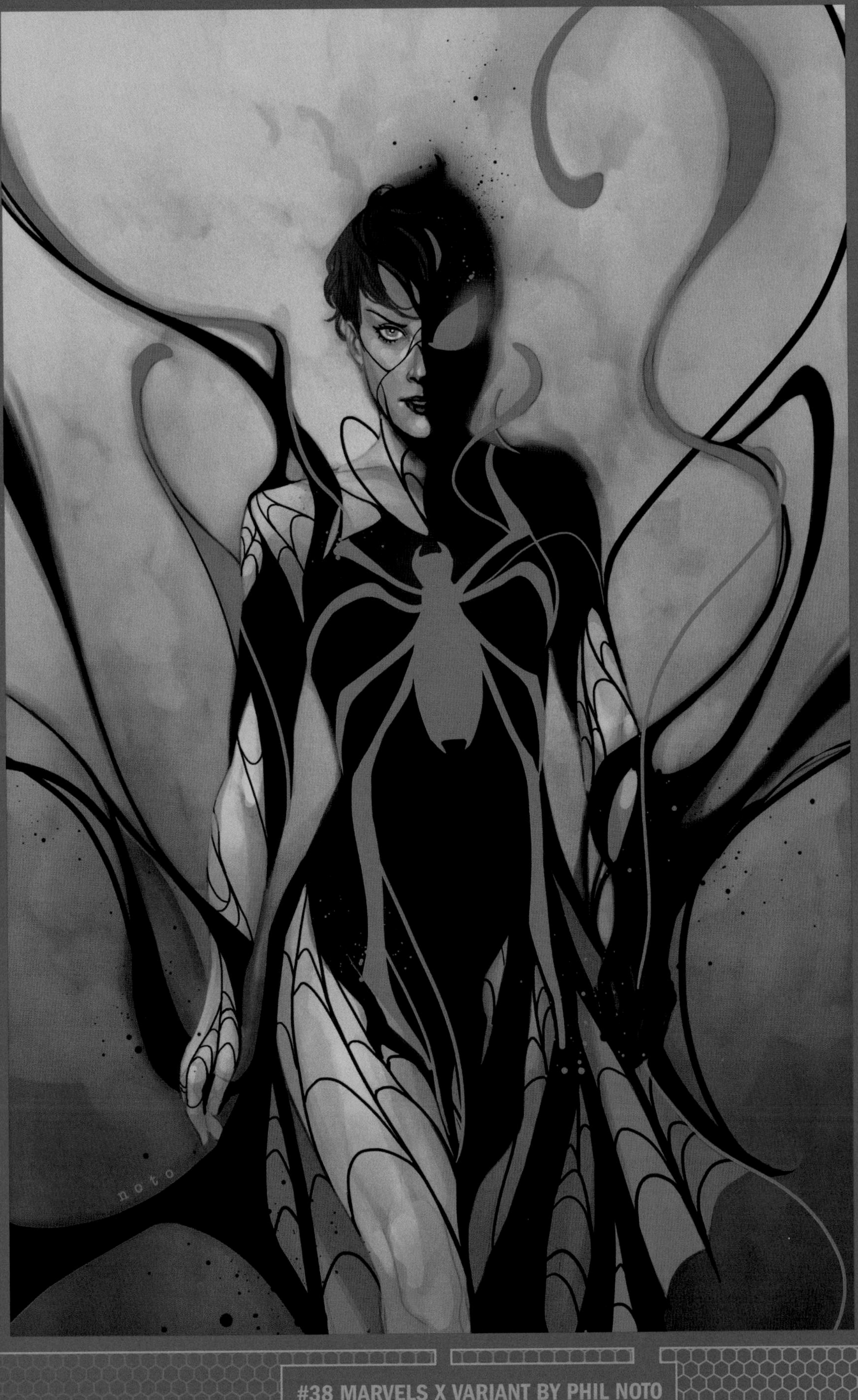
noto

#38 MARVELS X VARIANT BY PHIL NOTO

41

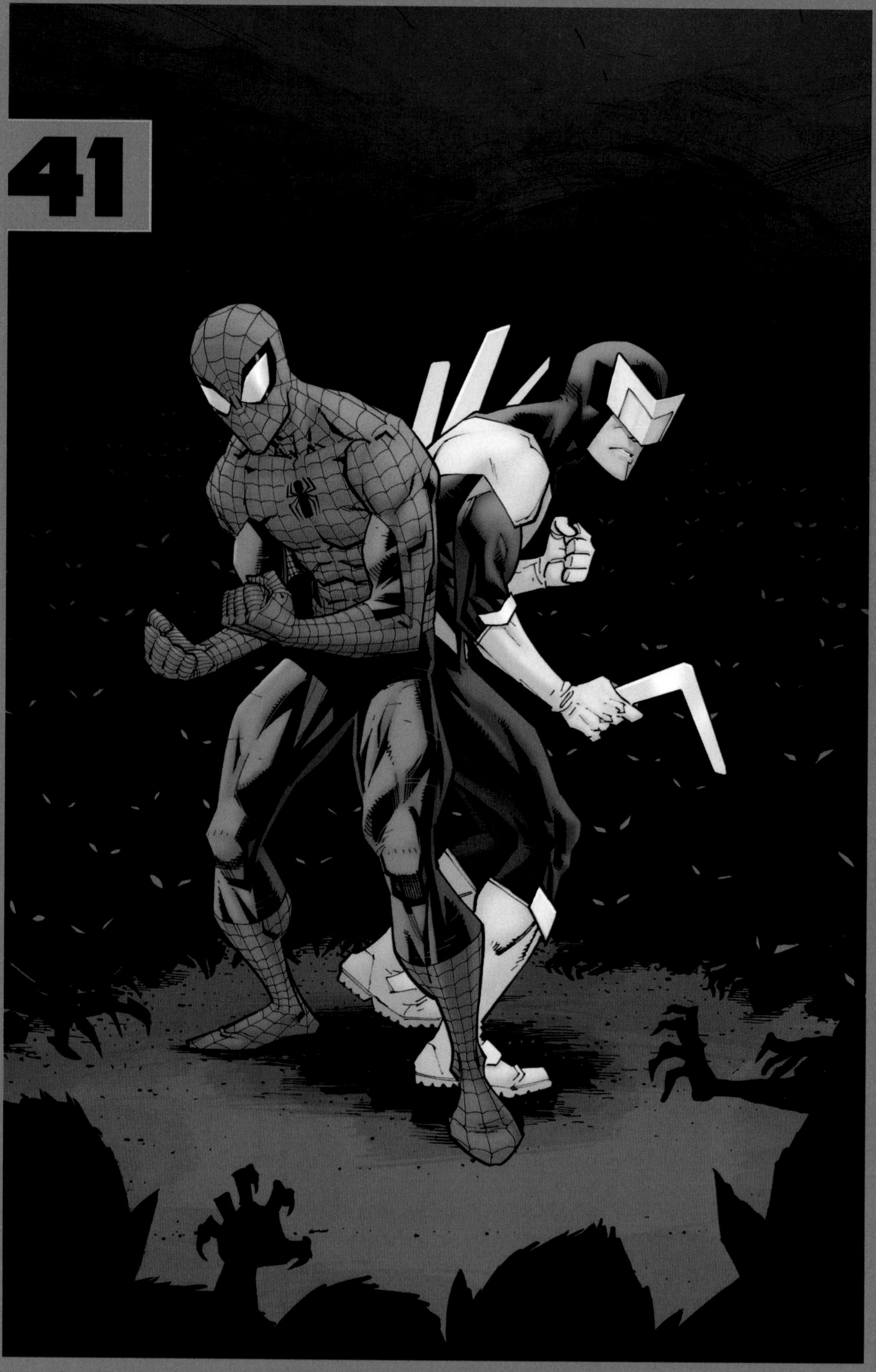

TRUE COMPANIONS PART 1

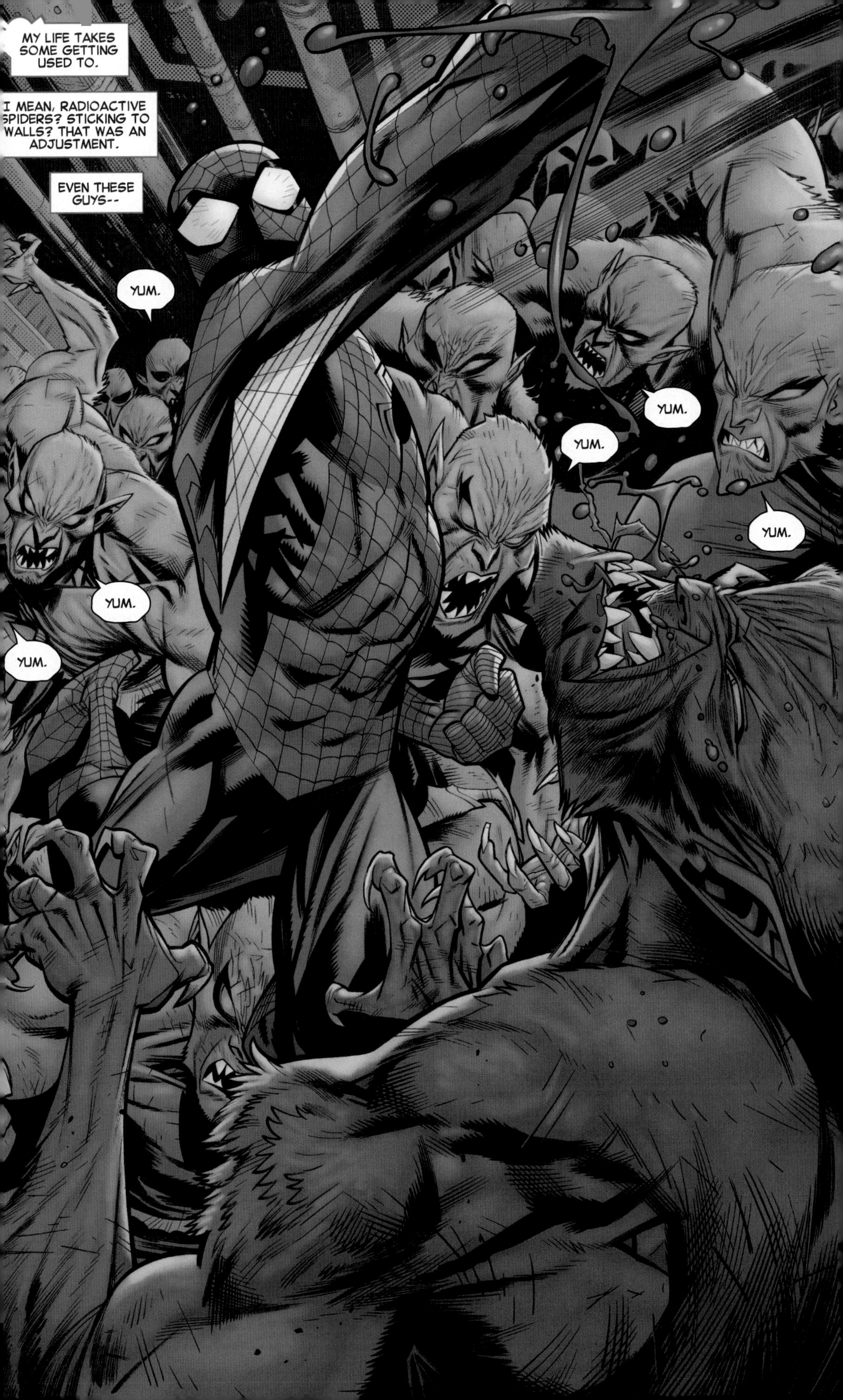
MY LIFE TAKES SOME GETTING USED TO.
I MEAN, RADIOACTIVE SPIDERS? STICKING TO WALLS? THAT WAS AN ADJUSTMENT.
EVEN THESE GUYS--
YUM.
YUM.
YUM.
YUM.
YUM.
YUM.

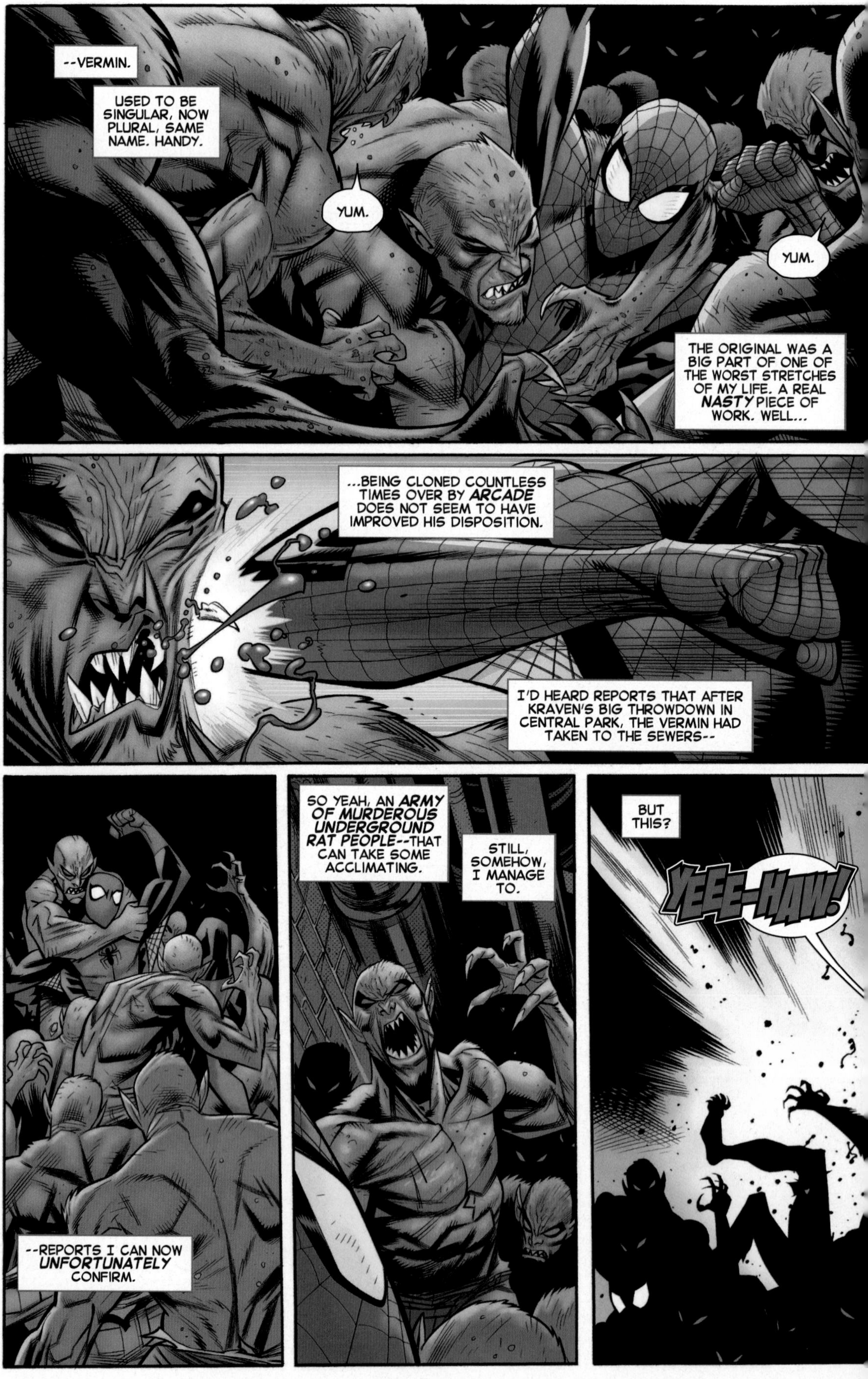
--VERMIN.
USED TO BE SINGULAR, NOW PLURAL, SAME NAME. HANDY.
YUM.
YUM.
THE ORIGINAL WAS A BIG PART OF ONE OF THE WORST STRETCHES OF MY LIFE. A REAL NASTY PIECE OF WORK. WELL...
...BEING CLONED COUNTLESS TIMES OVER BY ARCADE DOES NOT SEEM TO HAVE IMPROVED HIS DISPOSITION.
I'D HEARD REPORTS THAT AFTER KRAVEN'S BIG THROWDOWN IN CENTRAL PARK, THE VERMIN HAD TAKEN TO THE SEWERS--
--REPORTS I CAN NOW UNFORTUNATELY CONFIRM.
SO YEAH, AN ARMY OF MURDEROUS UNDERGROUND RAT PEOPLE--THAT CAN TAKE SOME ACCLIMATING.
STILL, SOMEHOW, I MANAGE TO.
BUT THIS?
YEEE-HAW!

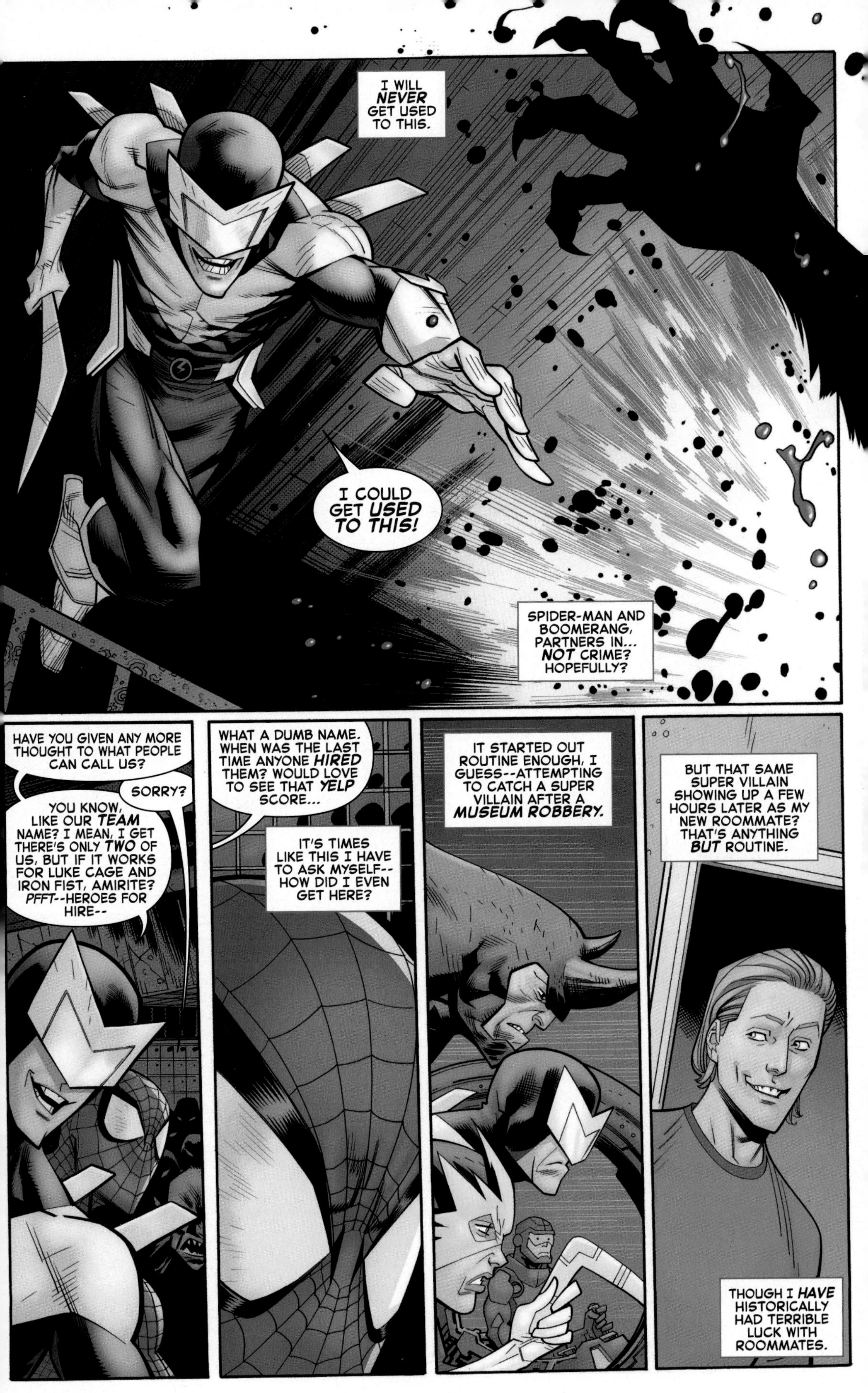

I WILL NEVER GET USED TO THIS.
I COULD GET USED TO THIS!
SPIDER-MAN AND BOOMERANG, PARTNERS IN... NOT CRIME? HOPEFULLY?
HAVE YOU GIVEN ANY MORE THOUGHT TO WHAT PEOPLE CAN CALL US?
SORRY?
YOU KNOW, LIKE OUR TEAM NAME? I MEAN, I GET THERE'S ONLY TWO OF US, BUT IF IT WORKS FOR LUKE CAGE AND IRON FIST, AMIRITE? PFFT--HEROES FOR HIRE--
WHAT A DUMB NAME. WHEN WAS THE LAST TIME ANYONE HIRED THEM? WOULD LOVE TO SEE THAT YELP SCORE...
IT'S TIMES LIKE THIS I HAVE TO ASK MYSELF-- HOW DID I EVEN GET HERE?
IT STARTED OUT ROUTINE ENOUGH, I GUESS--ATTEMPTING TO CATCH A SUPER VILLAIN AFTER A MUSEUM ROBBERY.
BUT THAT SAME SUPER VILLAIN SHOWING UP A FEW HOURS LATER AS MY NEW ROOMMATE? THAT'S ANYTHING BUT ROUTINE.
THOUGH I HAVE HISTORICALLY HAD TERRIBLE LUCK WITH ROOMMATES.

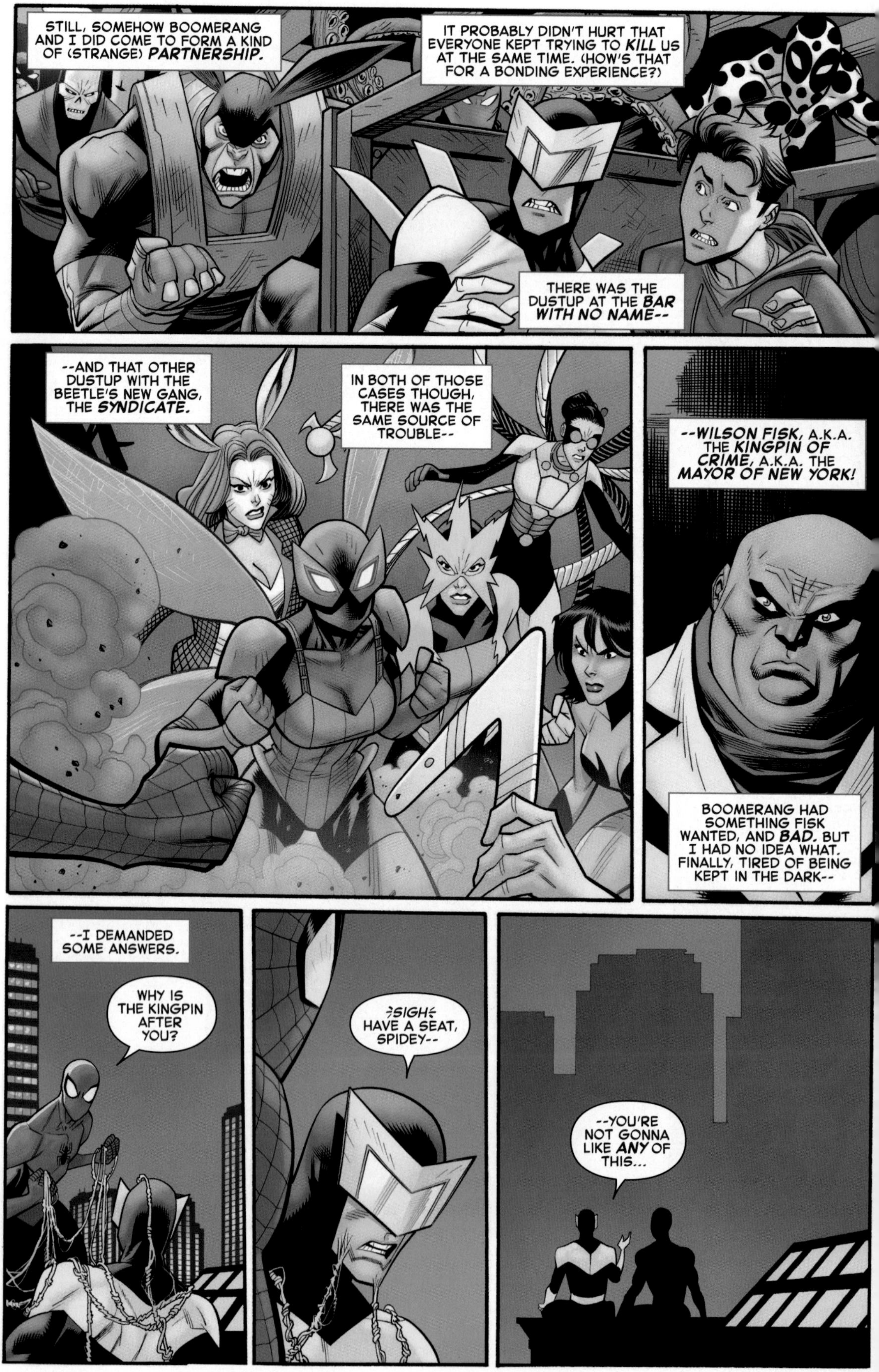
STILL, SOMEHOW BOOMERANG AND I DID COME TO FORM A KIND OF (STRANGE) PARTNERSHIP.
IT PROBABLY DIDN'T HURT THAT EVERYONE KEPT TRYING TO KILL US AT THE SAME TIME. (HOW'S THAT FOR A BONDING EXPERIENCE?)
THERE WAS THE DUSTUP AT THE BAR WITH NO NAME--
--AND THAT OTHER DUSTUP WITH THE BEETLE'S NEW GANG, THE SYNDICATE.
IN BOTH OF THOSE CASES THOUGH, THERE WAS THE SAME SOURCE OF TROUBLE--
--WILSON FISK, A.K.A. THE KINGPIN OF CRIME, A.K.A. THE MAYOR OF NEW YORK!
BOOMERANG HAD SOMETHING FISK WANTED, AND BAD. BUT I HAD NO IDEA WHAT. FINALLY, TIRED OF BEING KEPT IN THE DARK--
--I DEMANDED SOME ANSWERS.
WHY IS THE KINGPIN AFTER YOU?
SIGH HAVE A SEAT, SPIDEY--
--YOU'RE NOT GONNA LIKE ANY OF THIS...

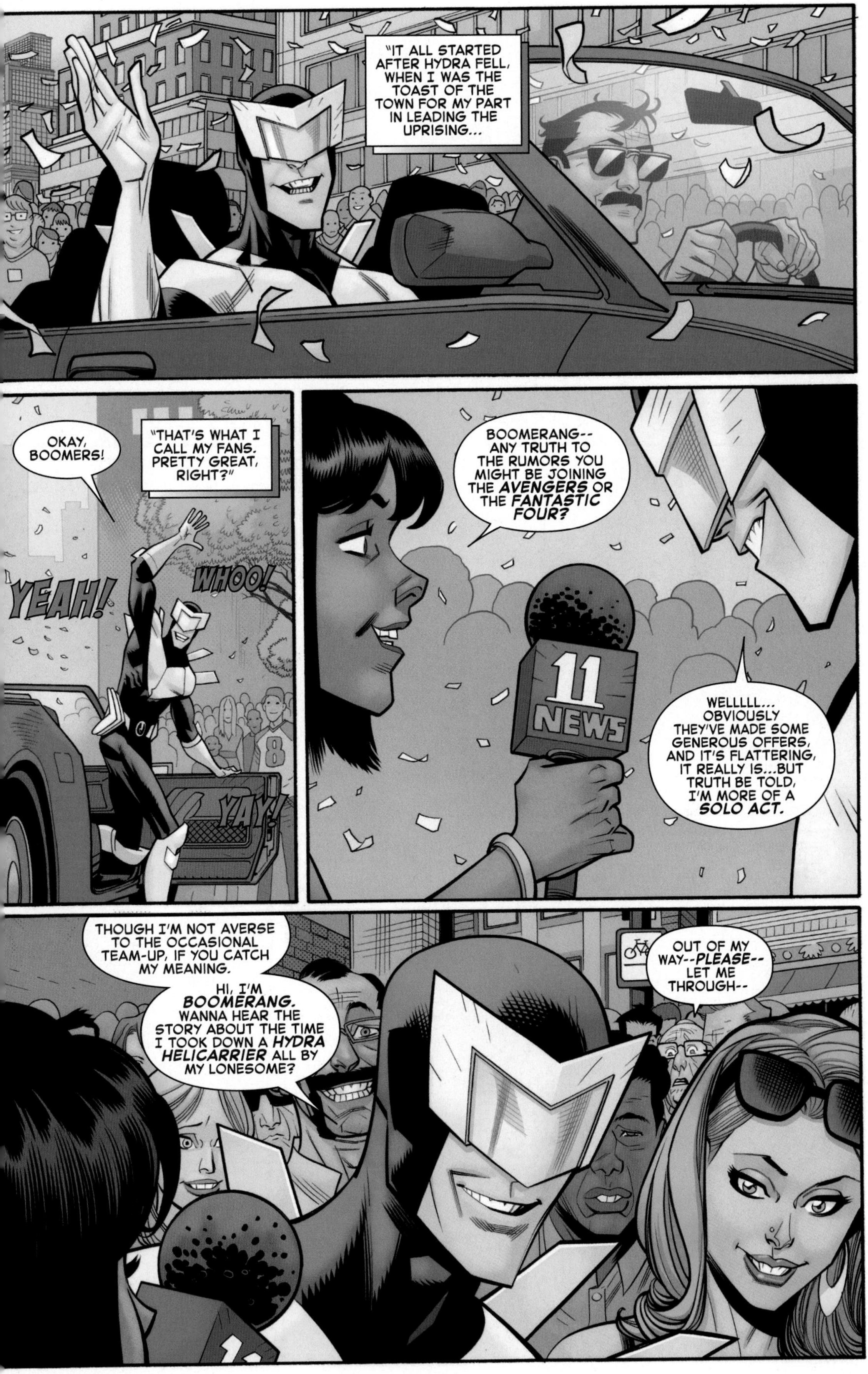
"IT ALL STARTED AFTER HYDRA FELL, WHEN I WAS THE TOAST OF THE TOWN FOR MY PART IN LEADING THE UPRISING...
OKAY, BOOMERS!
"THAT'S WHAT I CALL MY FANS. PRETTY GREAT, RIGHT?"
YEAH!
WHOO!
YAY!
BOOMERANG-- ANY TRUTH TO THE RUMORS YOU MIGHT BE JOINING THE AVENGERS OR THE FANTASTIC FOUR?
11 NEWS
WELLLLL... OBVIOUSLY THEY'VE MADE SOME GENEROUS OFFERS, AND IT'S FLATTERING, IT REALLY IS...BUT TRUTH BE TOLD, I'M MORE OF A SOLO ACT.
THOUGH I'M NOT AVERSE TO THE OCCASIONAL TEAM-UP, IF YOU CATCH MY MEANING.
HI, I'M BOOMERANG. WANNA HEAR THE STORY ABOUT THE TIME I TOOK DOWN A HYDRA HELICARRIER ALL BY MY LONESOME?
OUT OF MY WAY--PLEASE-- LET ME THROUGH--

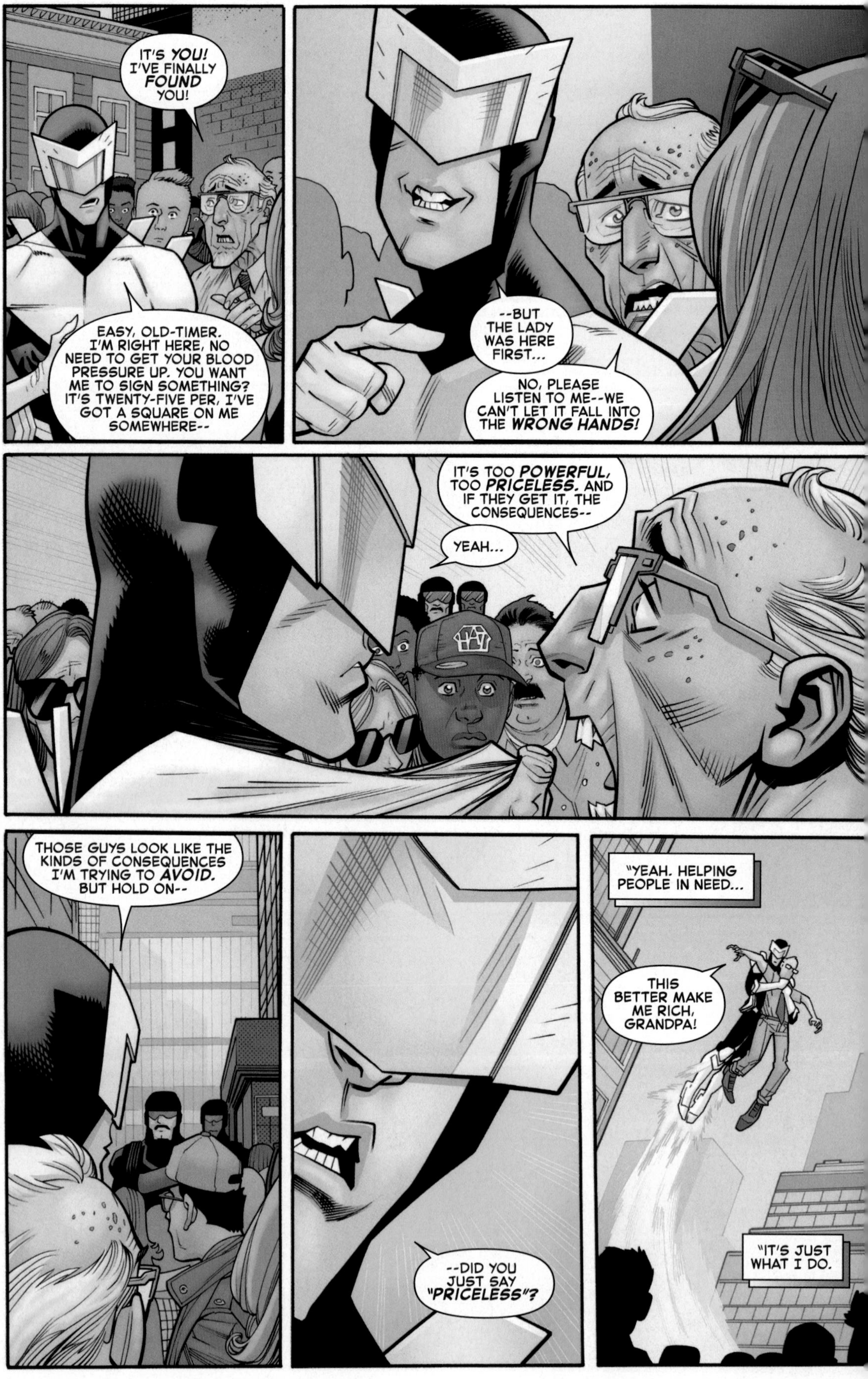
IT'S YOU! I'VE FINALLY FOUND YOU!
EASY, OLD-TIMER. I'M RIGHT HERE, NO NEED TO GET YOUR BLOOD PRESSURE UP. YOU WANT ME TO SIGN SOMETHING? IT'S TWENTY-FIVE PER, I'VE GOT A SQUARE ON ME SOMEWHERE--
--BUT THE LADY WAS HERE FIRST...
NO, PLEASE LISTEN TO ME--WE CAN'T LET IT FALL INTO THE WRONG HANDS!
IT'S TOO POWERFUL, TOO PRICELESS. AND IF THEY GET IT, THE CONSEQUENCES--
YEAH...
THOSE GUYS LOOK LIKE THE KINDS OF CONSEQUENCES I'M TRYING TO AVOID. BUT HOLD ON--
--DID YOU JUST SAY "PRICELESS"?
"YEAH. HELPING PEOPLE IN NEED...
THIS BETTER MAKE ME RICH, GRANDPA!
"IT'S JUST WHAT I DO.

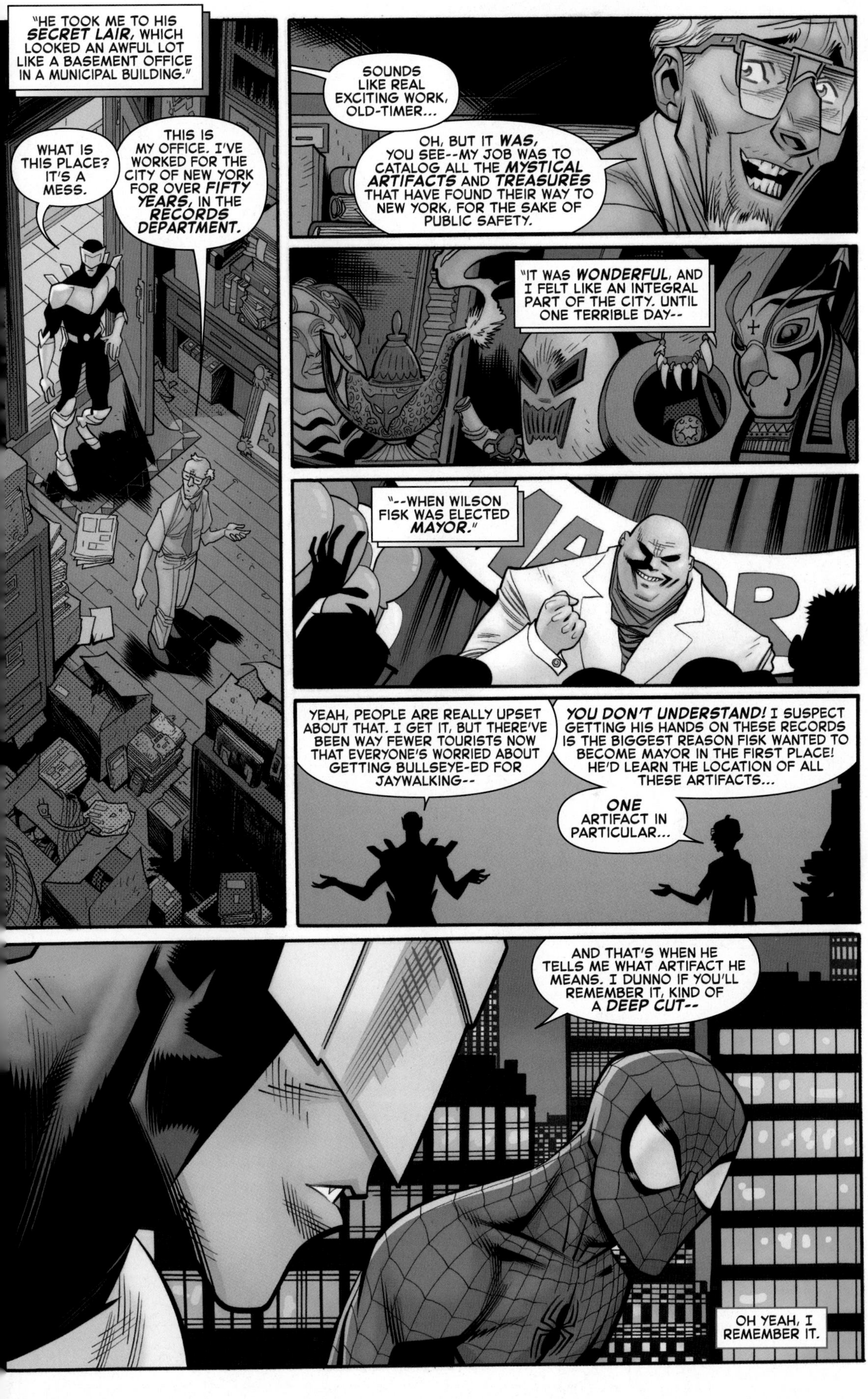
"HE TOOK ME TO HIS SECRET LAIR, WHICH LOOKED AN AWFUL LOT LIKE A BASEMENT OFFICE IN A MUNICIPAL BUILDING."
WHAT IS THIS PLACE? IT'S A MESS.
THIS IS MY OFFICE. I'VE WORKED FOR THE CITY OF NEW YORK FOR OVER FIFTY YEARS, IN THE RECORDS DEPARTMENT.
SOUNDS LIKE REAL EXCITING WORK, OLD-TIMER...
OH, BUT IT WAS, YOU SEE--MY JOB WAS TO CATALOG ALL THE MYSTICAL ARTIFACTS AND TREASURES THAT HAVE FOUND THEIR WAY TO NEW YORK, FOR THE SAKE OF PUBLIC SAFETY.
"IT WAS WONDERFUL, AND I FELT LIKE AN INTEGRAL PART OF THE CITY. UNTIL ONE TERRIBLE DAY--
"--WHEN WILSON FISK WAS ELECTED MAYOR."
YEAH, PEOPLE ARE REALLY UPSET ABOUT THAT. I GET IT, BUT THERE'VE BEEN WAY FEWER TOURISTS NOW THAT EVERYONE'S WORRIED ABOUT GETTING BULLSEYE-ED FOR JAYWALKING--
YOU DON'T UNDERSTAND! I SUSPECT GETTING HIS HANDS ON THESE RECORDS IS THE BIGGEST REASON FISK WANTED TO BECOME MAYOR IN THE FIRST PLACE! HE'D LEARN THE LOCATION OF ALL THESE ARTIFACTS...
ONE ARTIFACT IN PARTICULAR...
AND THAT'S WHEN HE TELLS ME WHAT ARTIFACT HE MEANS. I DUNNO IF YOU'LL REMEMBER IT, KIND OF A DEEP CUT--
OH YEAH, I REMEMBER IT.

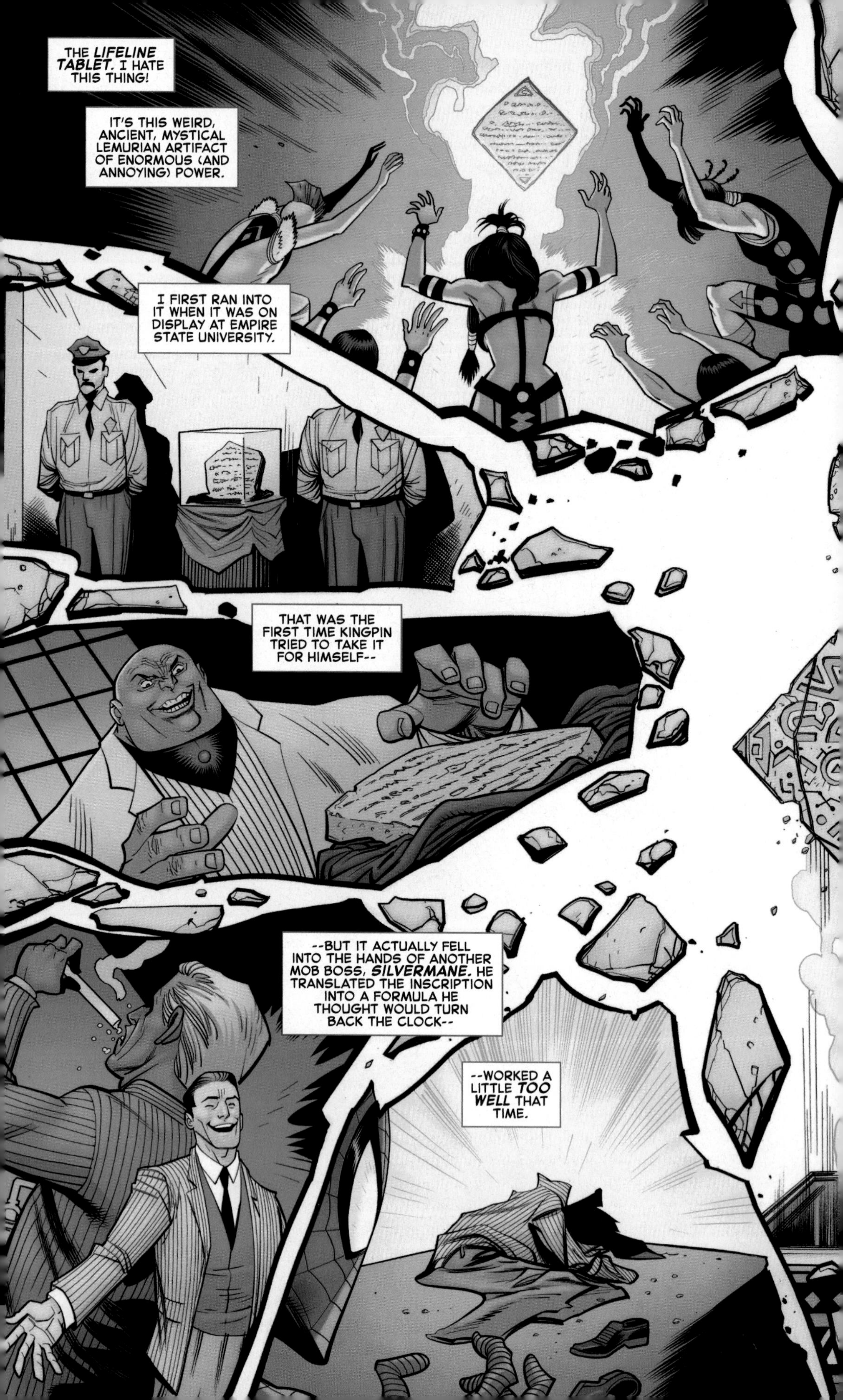
THE *LIFELINE TABLET.* I HATE THIS THING!
IT'S THIS WEIRD, ANCIENT, MYSTICAL LEMURIAN ARTIFACT OF ENORMOUS (AND ANNOYING) POWER.
I FIRST RAN INTO IT WHEN IT WAS ON DISPLAY AT EMPIRE STATE UNIVERSITY.
THAT WAS THE FIRST TIME KINGPIN TRIED TO TAKE IT FOR HIMSELF--
--BUT IT ACTUALLY FELL INTO THE HANDS OF ANOTHER MOB BOSS, *SILVERMANE.* HE TRANSLATED THE INSCRIPTION INTO A FORMULA HE THOUGHT WOULD TURN BACK THE CLOCK--
--WORKED A LITTLE *TOO WELL* THAT TIME.

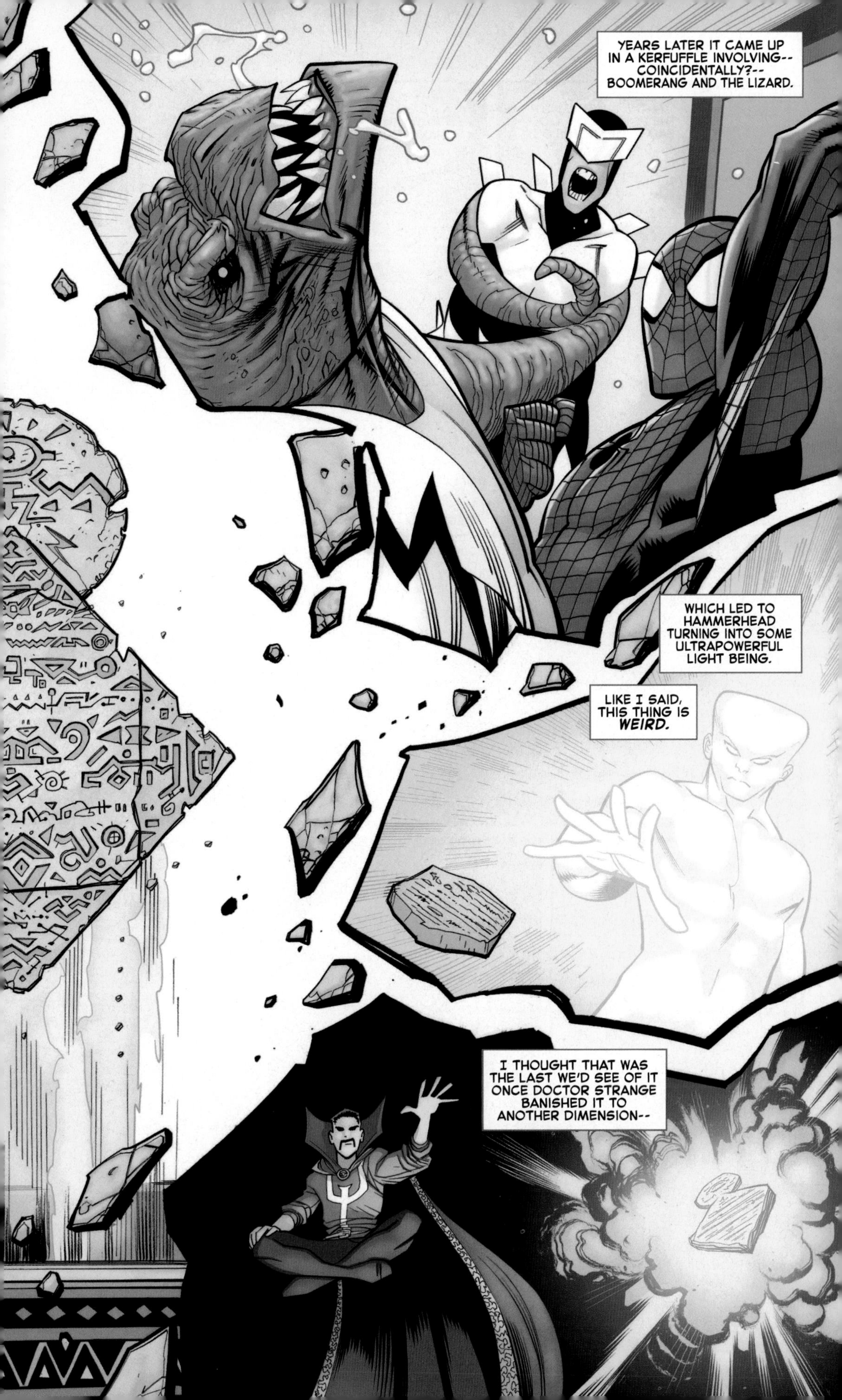
YEARS LATER IT CAME UP IN A KERFUFFLE INVOLVING-- COINCIDENTALLY?-- BOOMERANG AND THE LIZARD.
WHICH LED TO HAMMERHEAD TURNING INTO SOME ULTRAPOWERFUL LIGHT BEING.
LIKE I SAID, THIS THING IS *WEIRD.*
I THOUGHT THAT WAS THE LAST WE'D SEE OF IT ONCE DOCTOR STRANGE BANISHED IT TO ANOTHER DIMENSION--

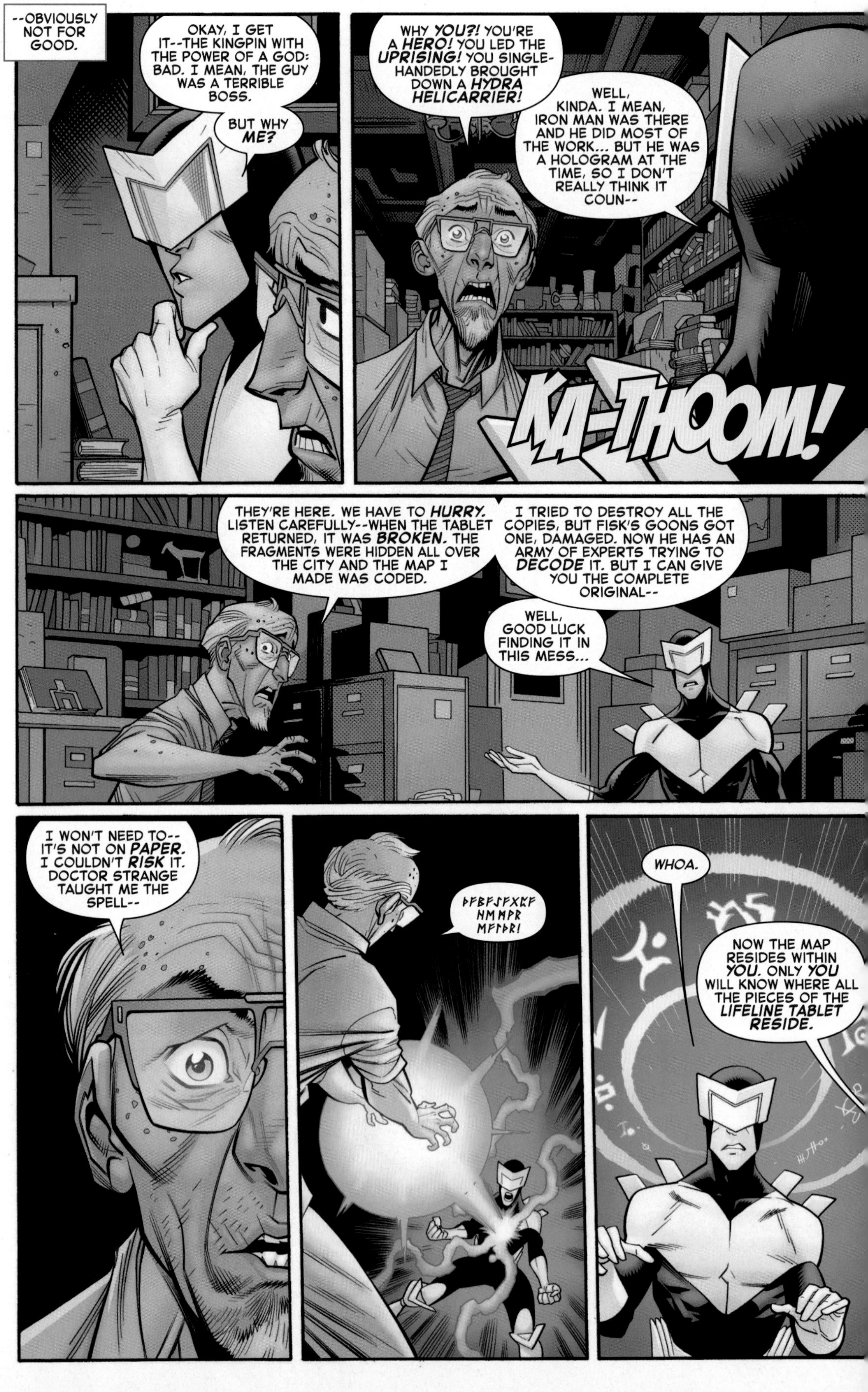
--OBVIOUSLY NOT FOR GOOD.
OKAY, I GET IT--THE KINGPIN WITH THE POWER OF A GOD: BAD. I MEAN, THE GUY WAS A TERRIBLE BOSS.
BUT WHY ME?
WHY YOU?! YOU'RE A HERO! YOU LED THE UPRISING! YOU SINGLE-HANDEDLY BROUGHT DOWN A HYDRA HELICARRIER!
WELL, KINDA. I MEAN, IRON MAN WAS THERE AND HE DID MOST OF THE WORK... BUT HE WAS A HOLOGRAM AT THE TIME, SO I DON'T REALLY THINK IT COUN--
KA-THOOM!
THEY'RE HERE. WE HAVE TO HURRY. LISTEN CAREFULLY--WHEN THE TABLET RETURNED, IT WAS BROKEN. THE FRAGMENTS WERE HIDDEN ALL OVER THE CITY AND THE MAP I MADE WAS CODED.
I TRIED TO DESTROY ALL THE COPIES, BUT FISK'S GOONS GOT ONE, DAMAGED. NOW HE HAS AN ARMY OF EXPERTS TRYING TO DECODE IT. BUT I CAN GIVE YOU THE COMPLETE ORIGINAL--
WELL, GOOD LUCK FINDING IT IN THIS MESS...
I WON'T NEED TO--IT'S NOT ON PAPER. I COULDN'T RISK IT. DOCTOR STRANGE TAUGHT ME THE SPELL--
WHOA.
NOW THE MAP RESIDES WITHIN YOU. ONLY YOU WILL KNOW WHERE ALL THE PIECES OF THE LIFELINE TABLET RESIDE.

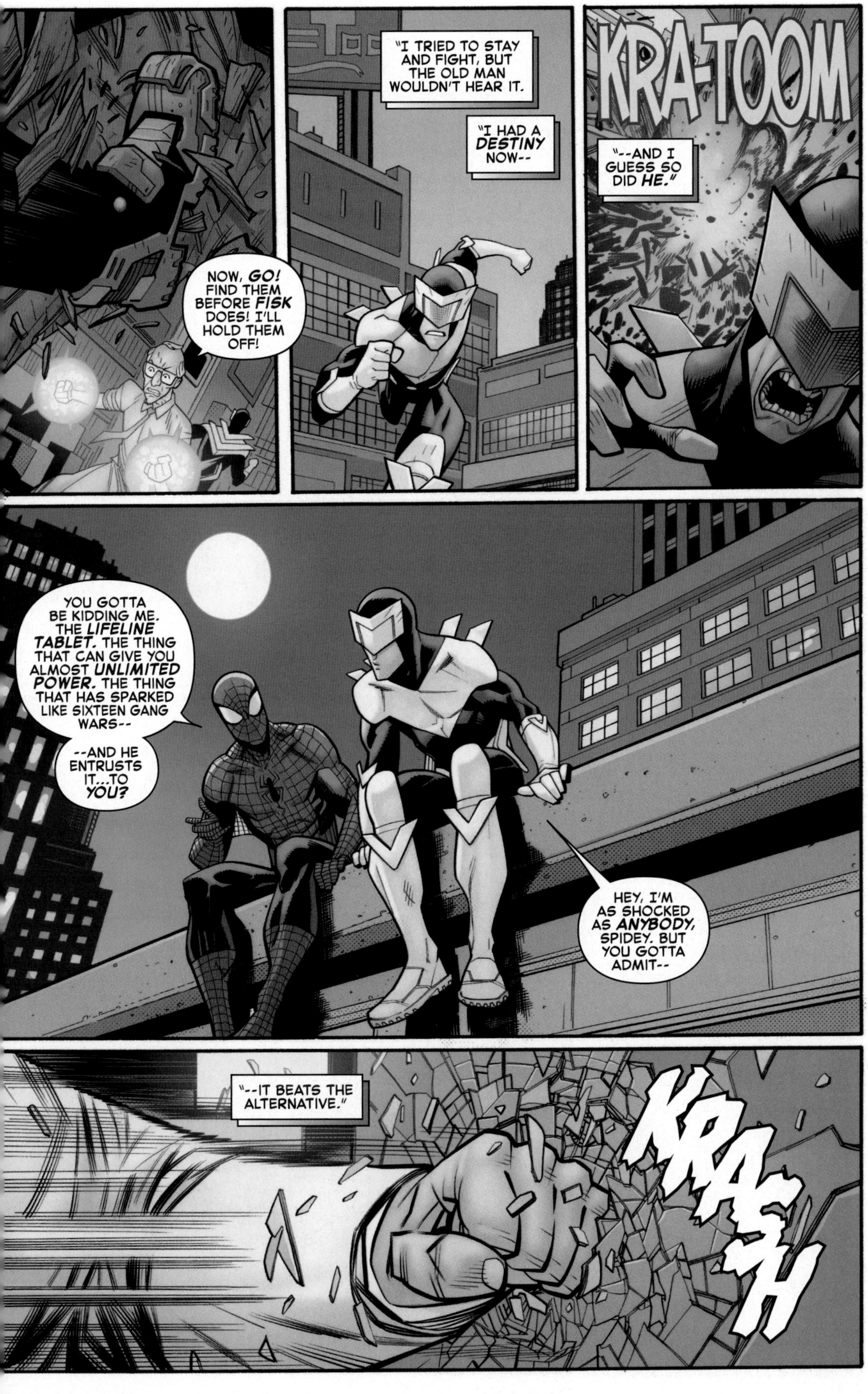
NOW, GO! FIND THEM BEFORE FISK DOES! I'LL HOLD THEM OFF!
"I TRIED TO STAY AND FIGHT, BUT THE OLD MAN WOULDN'T HEAR IT.
"I HAD A DESTINY NOW--
KRA-TOOM
"--AND I GUESS SO DID HE."
YOU GOTTA BE KIDDING ME. THE LIFELINE TABLET. THE THING THAT CAN GIVE YOU ALMOST UNLIMITED POWER. THE THING THAT HAS SPARKED LIKE SIXTEEN GANG WARS--
--AND HE ENTRUSTS IT...TO YOU?
HEY, I'M AS SHOCKED AS ANYBODY, SPIDEY. BUT YOU GOTTA ADMIT--
"--IT BEATS THE ALTERNATIVE."
KRASH

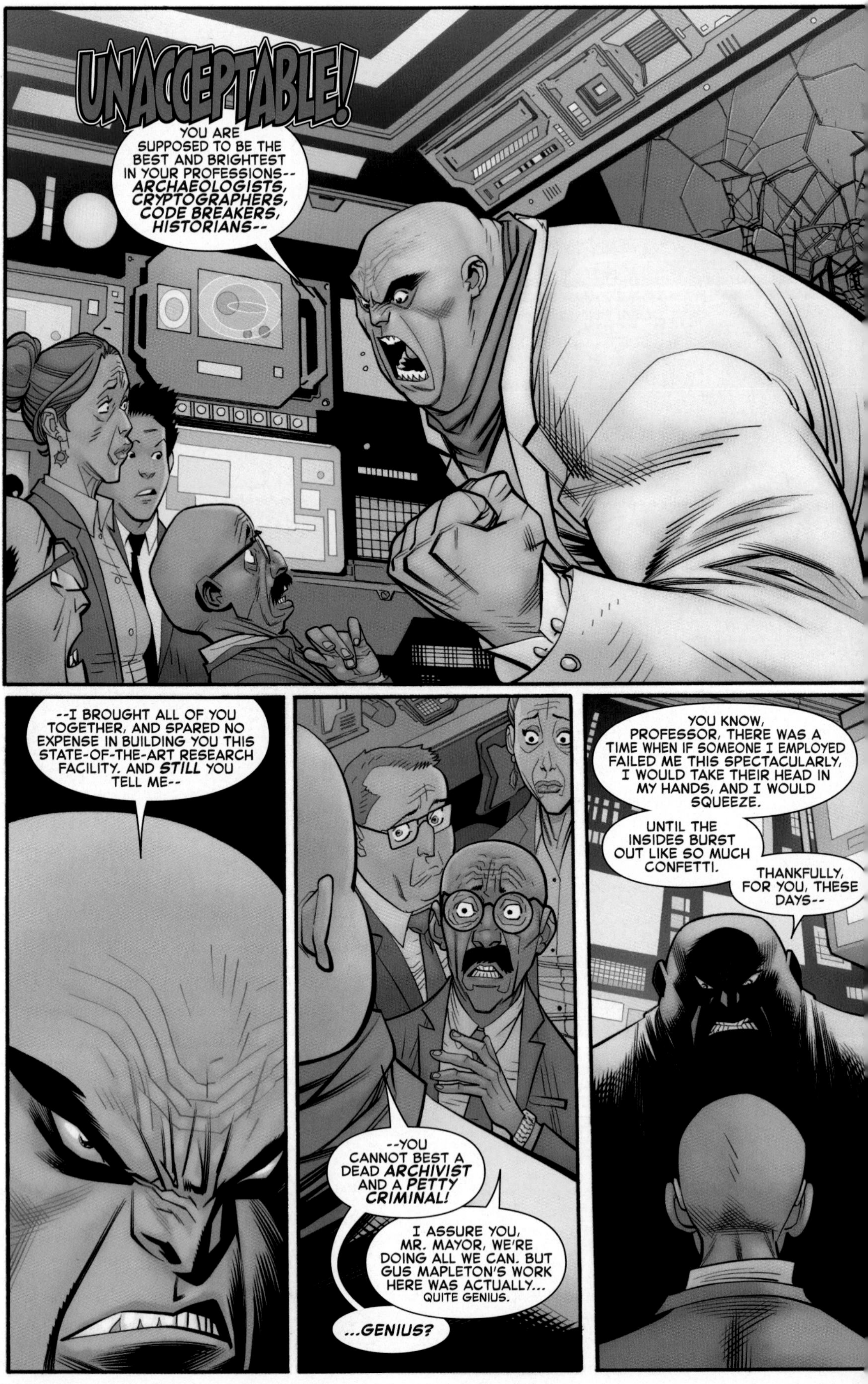

UNACCEPTABLE!
YOU ARE SUPPOSED TO BE THE BEST AND BRIGHTEST IN YOUR PROFESSIONS-- ARCHAEOLOGISTS, CRYPTOGRAPHERS, CODE BREAKERS, HISTORIANS--
--I BROUGHT ALL OF YOU TOGETHER, AND SPARED NO EXPENSE IN BUILDING YOU THIS STATE-OF-THE-ART RESEARCH FACILITY. AND STILL YOU TELL ME--
--YOU CANNOT BEST A DEAD ARCHIVIST AND A PETTY CRIMINAL!
I ASSURE YOU, MR. MAYOR, WE'RE DOING ALL WE CAN. BUT GUS MAPLETON'S WORK HERE WAS ACTUALLY... QUITE GENIUS.
...GENIUS?
YOU KNOW, PROFESSOR, THERE WAS A TIME WHEN IF SOMEONE I EMPLOYED FAILED ME THIS SPECTACULARLY, I WOULD TAKE THEIR HEAD IN MY HANDS, AND I WOULD SQUEEZE.
UNTIL THE INSIDES BURST OUT LIKE SO MUCH CONFETTI.
THANKFULLY, FOR YOU, THESE DAYS--

--I HAVE *OTHER* MEANS AT MY DISPOSAL.

W-WAIT... WHAT IS THIS?

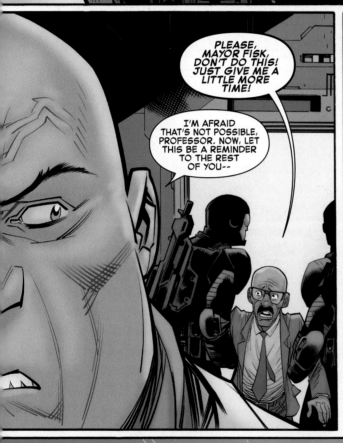

PLEASE, MAYOR FISK, DON'T DO THIS! JUST GIVE ME A LITTLE MORE TIME!

I'M AFRAID THAT'S NOT POSSIBLE, PROFESSOR. NOW, LET THIS BE A REMINDER TO THE REST OF YOU--

--ALWAYS PAY YOUR PARKING TICKETS.

SO, YEAH, OKAY, LET'S NOT GIVE *THAT* GUY THE POWER OF A GOD, RIGHT?

ME AND BOOMERANG, WE HAD A DEAL.

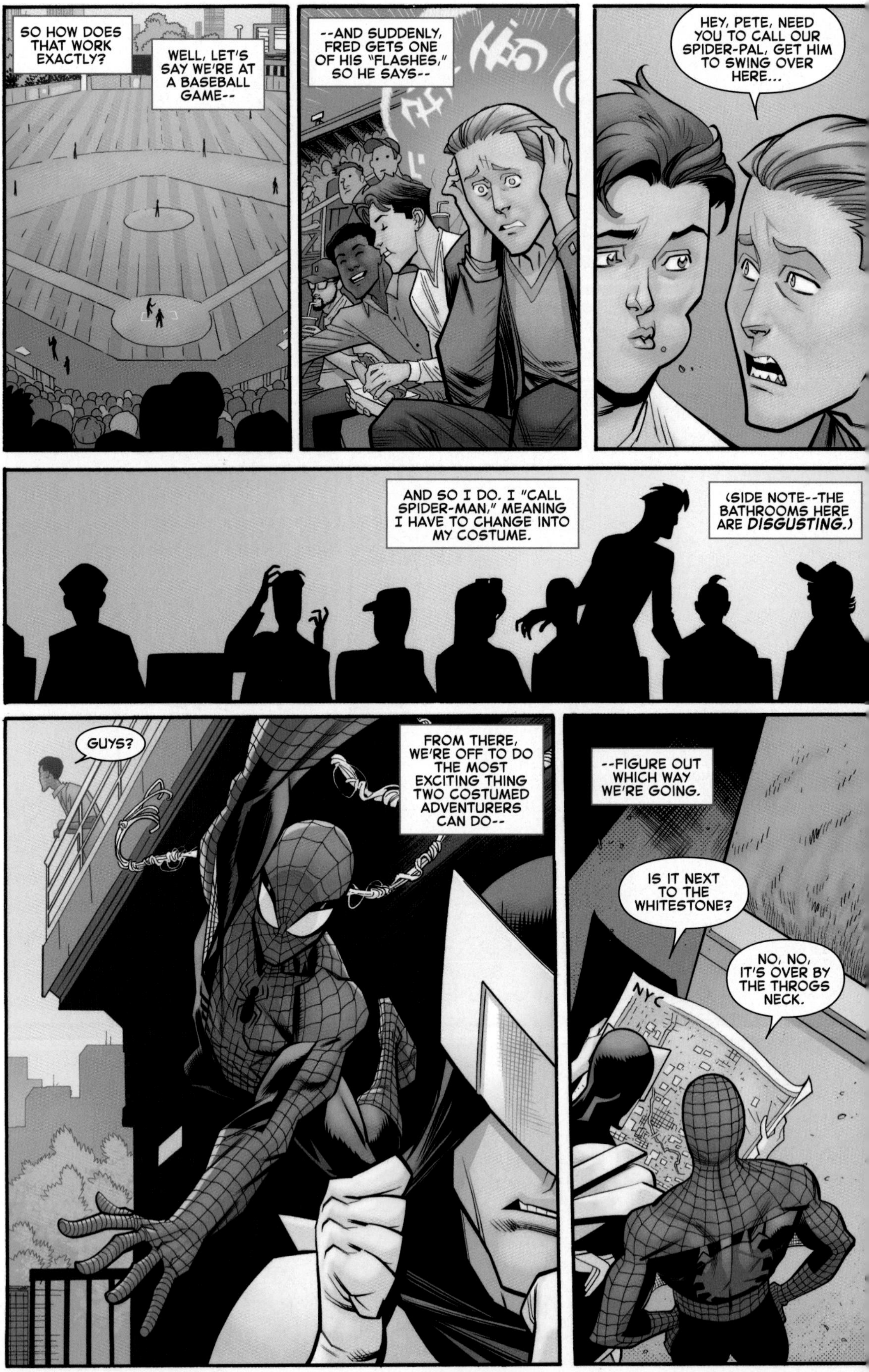

SO HOW DOES THAT WORK EXACTLY?
WELL, LET'S SAY WE'RE AT A BASEBALL GAME--
--AND SUDDENLY, FRED GETS ONE OF HIS "FLASHES," SO HE SAYS--
HEY, PETE, NEED YOU TO CALL OUR SPIDER-PAL, GET HIM TO SWING OVER HERE...
AND SO I DO. I "CALL SPIDER-MAN," MEANING I HAVE TO CHANGE INTO MY COSTUME.
(SIDE NOTE--THE BATHROOMS HERE ARE *DISGUSTING.*)
GUYS?
FROM THERE, WE'RE OFF TO DO THE MOST EXCITING THING TWO COSTUMED ADVENTURERS CAN DO--
--FIGURE OUT WHICH WAY WE'RE GOING.
IS IT NEXT TO THE WHITESTONE?
NO, NO, IT'S OVER BY THE THROGS NECK.
NYC

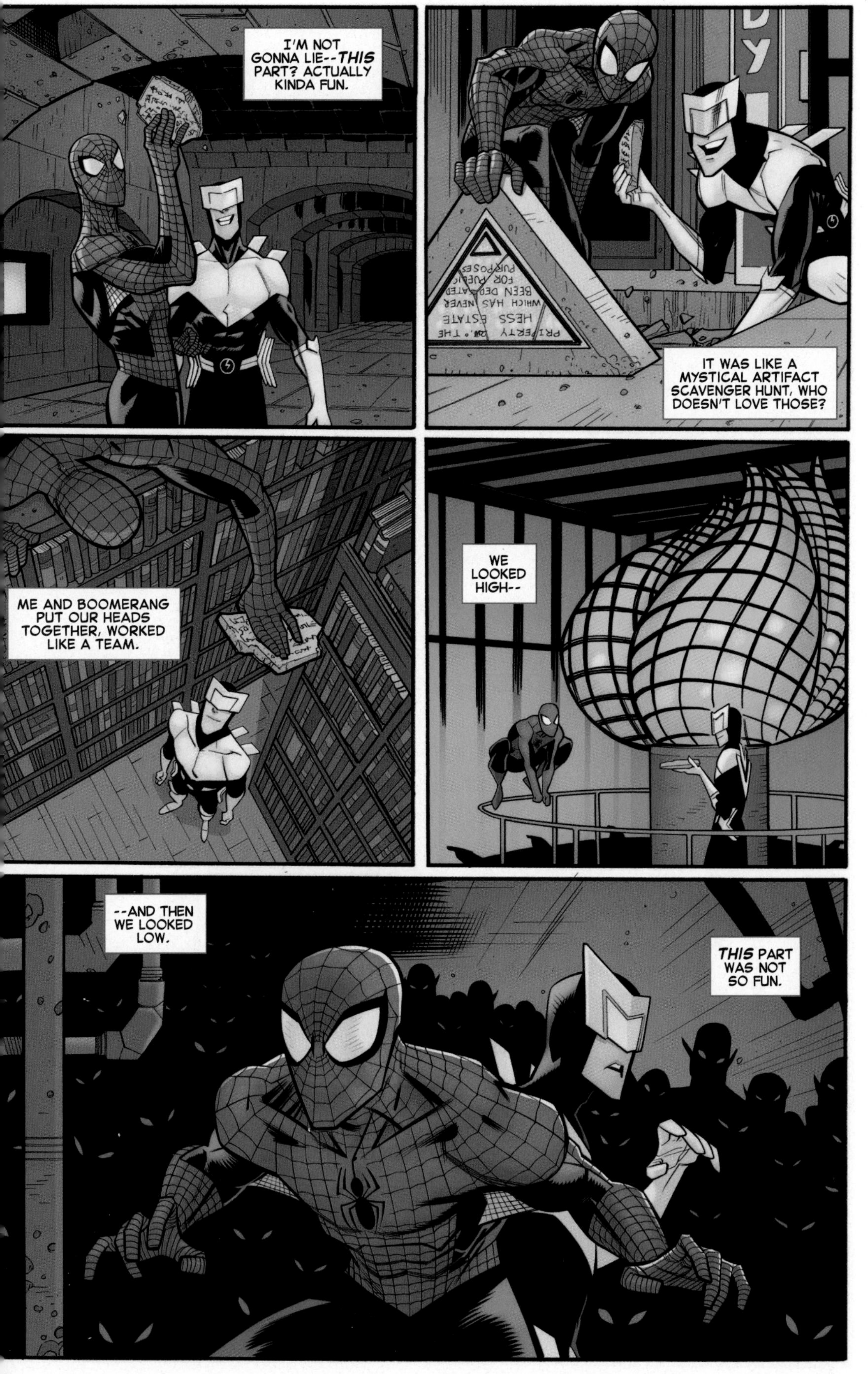
I'M NOT GONNA LIE--*THIS* PART? ACTUALLY KINDA FUN.
IT WAS LIKE A MYSTICAL ARTIFACT SCAVENGER HUNT, WHO DOESN'T LOVE THOSE?
ME AND BOOMERANG PUT OUR HEADS TOGETHER, WORKED LIKE A TEAM.
WE LOOKED HIGH--
--AND THEN WE LOOKED LOW.
THIS PART WAS NOT SO FUN.

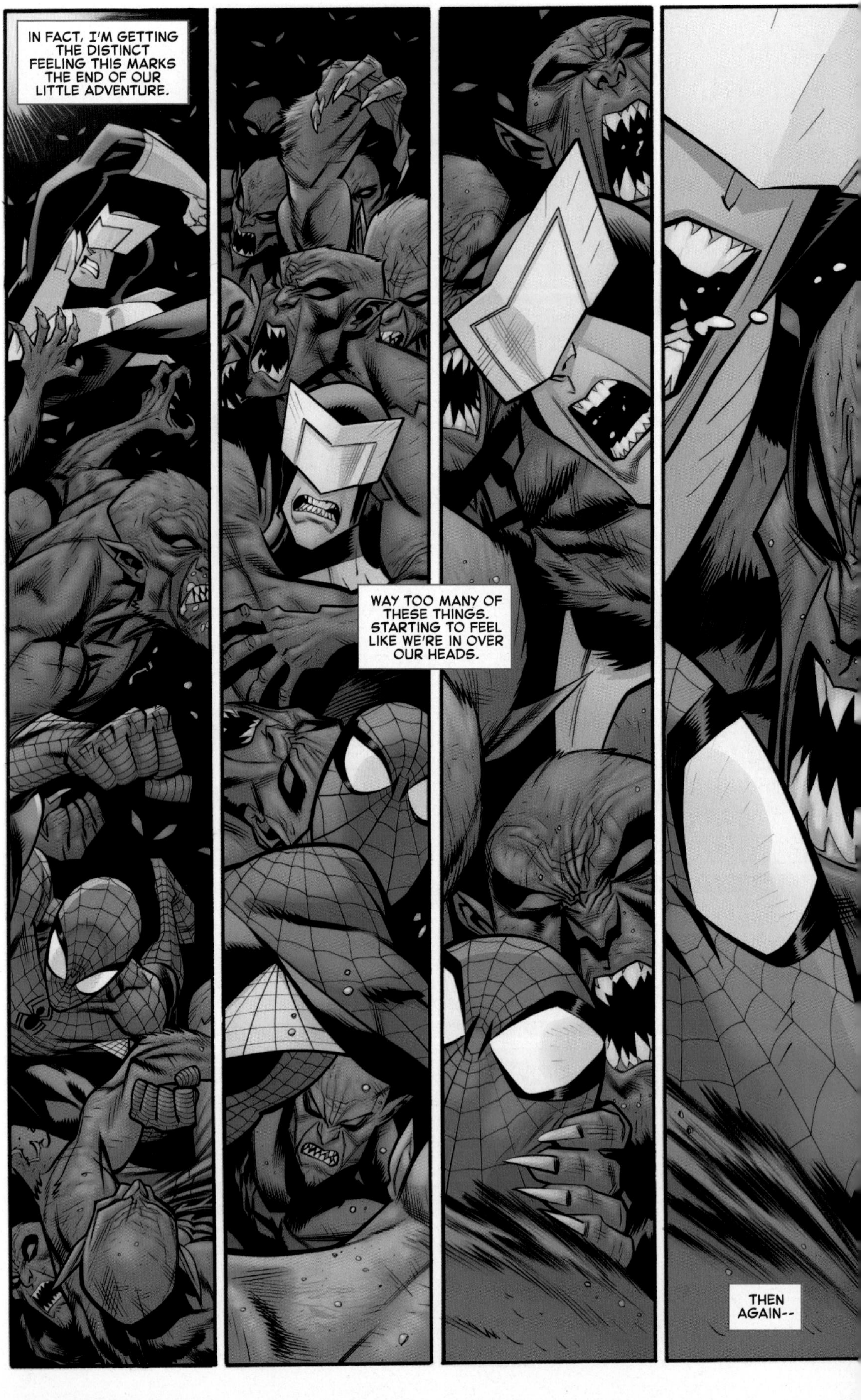
IN FACT, I'M GETTING THE DISTINCT FEELING THIS MARKS THE END OF OUR LITTLE ADVENTURE.
WAY TOO MANY OF THESE THINGS. STARTING TO FEEL LIKE WE'RE IN OVER OUR HEADS.
THEN AGAIN--

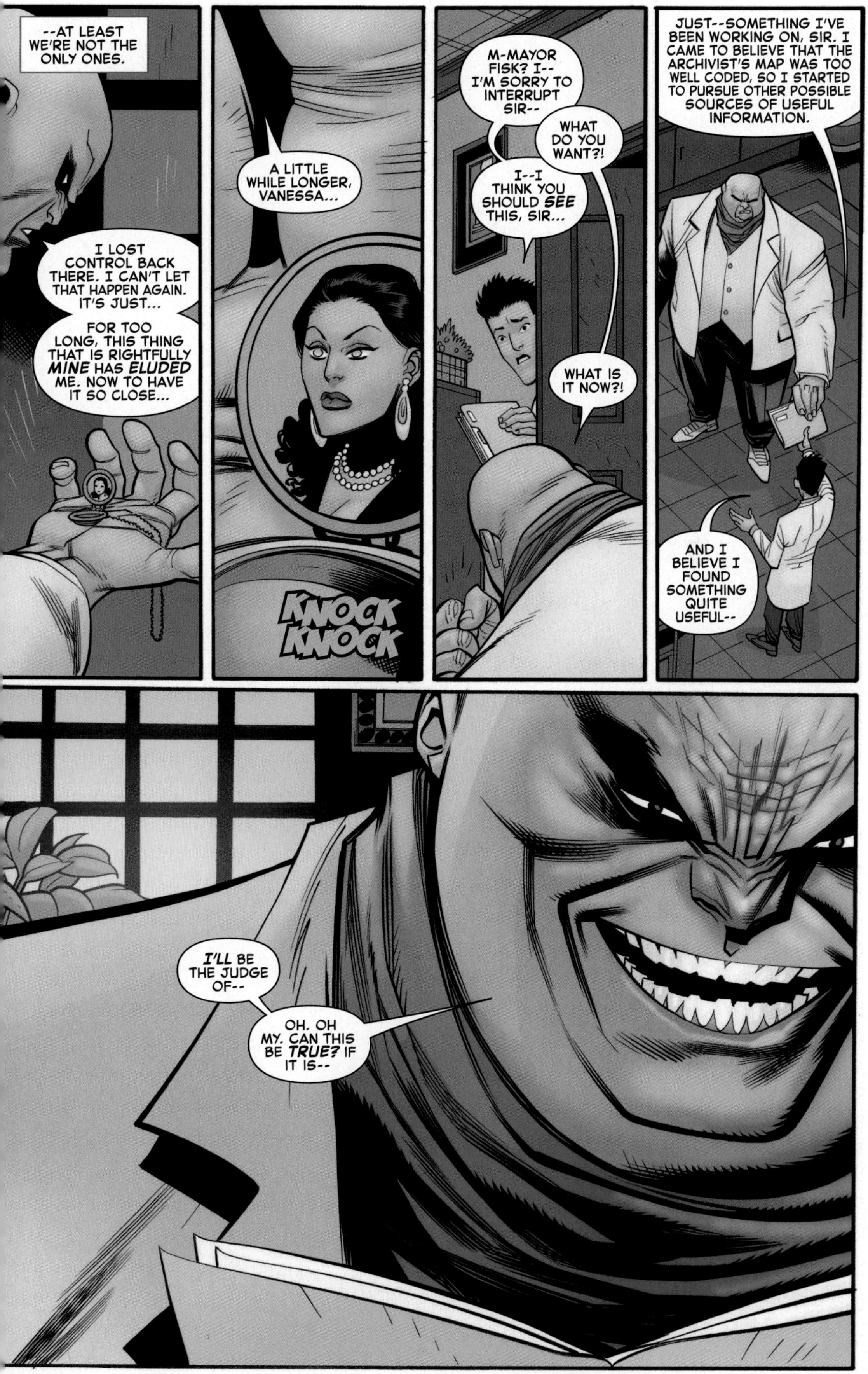
--AT LEAST WE'RE NOT THE ONLY ONES.
I LOST CONTROL BACK THERE. I CAN'T LET THAT HAPPEN AGAIN. IT'S JUST...
FOR TOO LONG, THIS THING THAT IS RIGHTFULLY MINE HAS ELUDED ME. NOW TO HAVE IT SO CLOSE...
A LITTLE WHILE LONGER, VANESSA...
KNOCK KNOCK
M-MAYOR FISK? I-- I'M SORRY TO INTERRUPT SIR--
WHAT DO YOU WANT?!
I--I THINK YOU SHOULD SEE THIS, SIR...
WHAT IS IT NOW?!
JUST--SOMETHING I'VE BEEN WORKING ON, SIR. I CAME TO BELIEVE THAT THE ARCHIVIST'S MAP WAS TOO WELL CODED, SO I STARTED TO PURSUE OTHER POSSIBLE SOURCES OF USEFUL INFORMATION.
AND I BELIEVE I FOUND SOMETHING QUITE USEFUL--
I'LL BE THE JUDGE OF--
OH. OH MY. CAN THIS BE TRUE? IF IT IS--

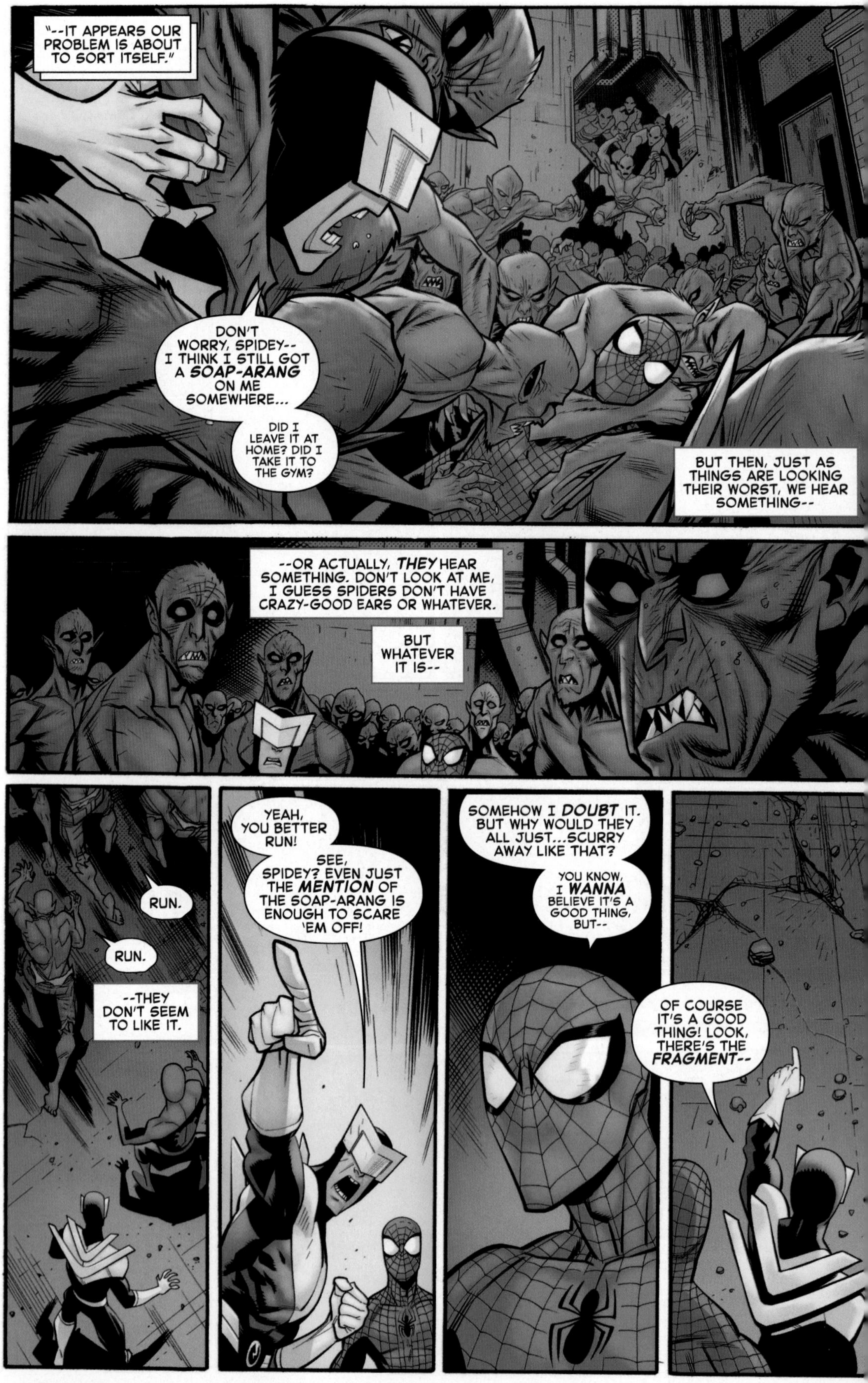
"--IT APPEARS OUR PROBLEM IS ABOUT TO SORT ITSELF."
DON'T WORRY, SPIDEY-- I THINK I STILL GOT A SOAP-ARANG ON ME SOMEWHERE...
DID I LEAVE IT AT HOME? DID I TAKE IT TO THE GYM?
BUT THEN, JUST AS THINGS ARE LOOKING THEIR WORST, WE HEAR SOMETHING--
--OR ACTUALLY, THEY HEAR SOMETHING. DON'T LOOK AT ME, I GUESS SPIDERS DON'T HAVE CRAZY-GOOD EARS OR WHATEVER.
BUT WHATEVER IT IS--
RUN.
RUN.
--THEY DON'T SEEM TO LIKE IT.
YEAH, YOU BETTER RUN!
SEE, SPIDEY? EVEN JUST THE MENTION OF THE SOAP-ARANG IS ENOUGH TO SCARE 'EM OFF!
SOMEHOW I DOUBT IT. BUT WHY WOULD THEY ALL JUST...SCURRY AWAY LIKE THAT?
YOU KNOW, I WANNA BELIEVE IT'S A GOOD THING, BUT--
OF COURSE IT'S A GOOD THING! LOOK, THERE'S THE FRAGMENT--

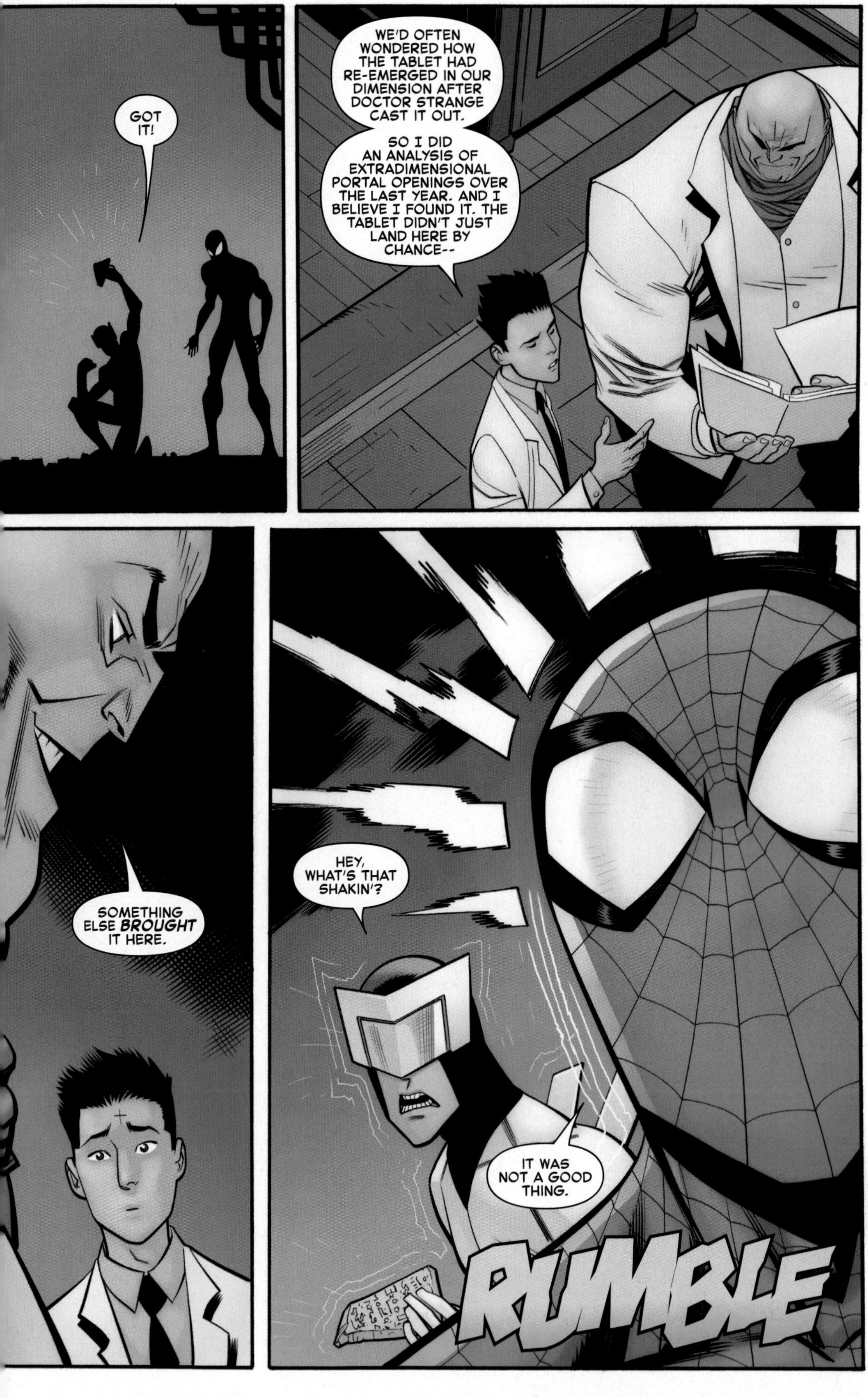
GOT IT!
WE'D OFTEN WONDERED HOW THE TABLET HAD RE-EMERGED IN OUR DIMENSION AFTER DOCTOR STRANGE CAST IT OUT.
SO I DID AN ANALYSIS OF EXTRADIMENSIONAL PORTAL OPENINGS OVER THE LAST YEAR. AND I BELIEVE I FOUND IT. THE TABLET DIDN'T JUST LAND HERE BY CHANCE--
SOMETHING ELSE **BROUGHT** IT HERE.
HEY, WHAT'S THAT SHAKIN'?
IT WAS NOT A GOOD THING.
RUMBLE

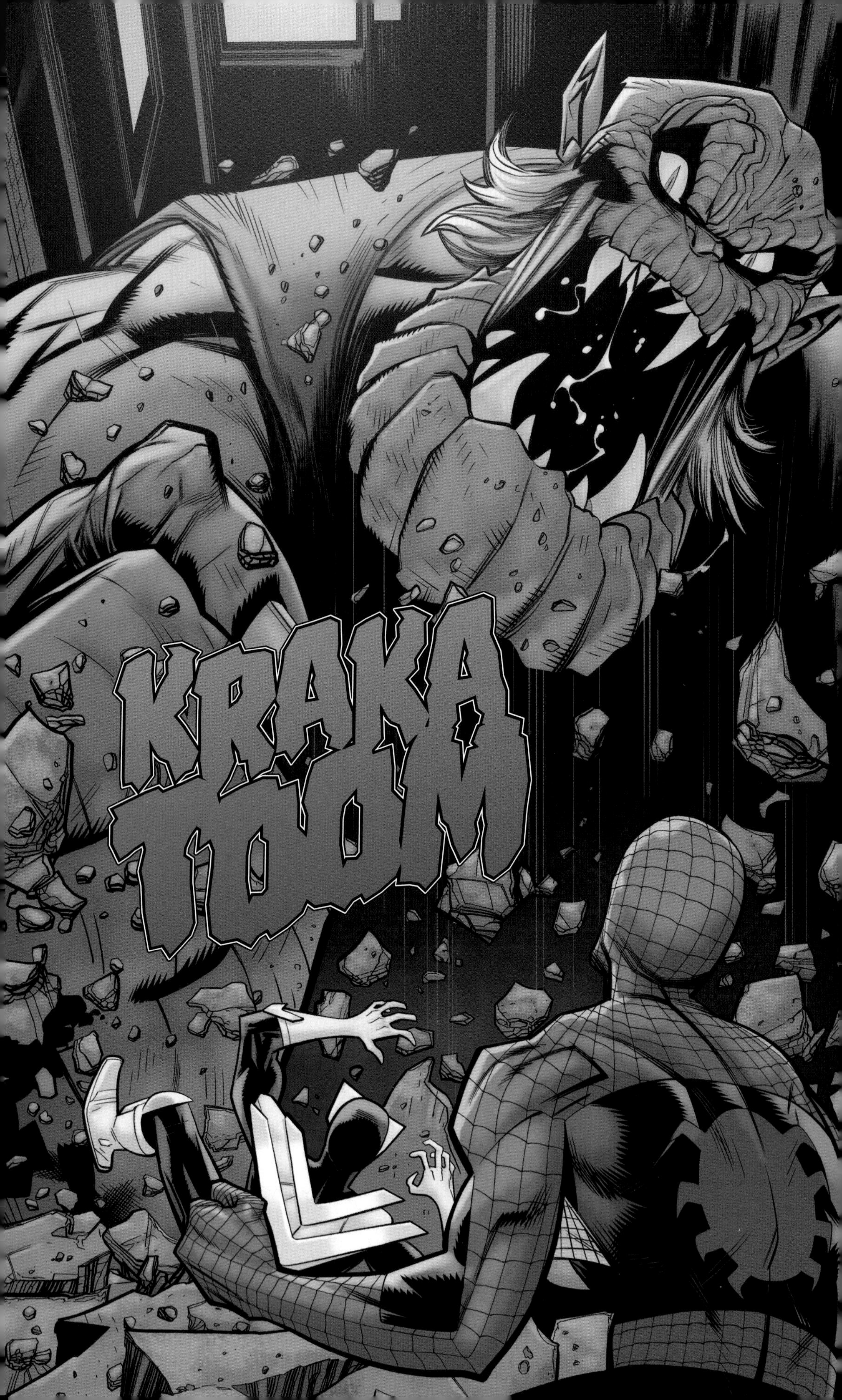
KRAKA
TOOM

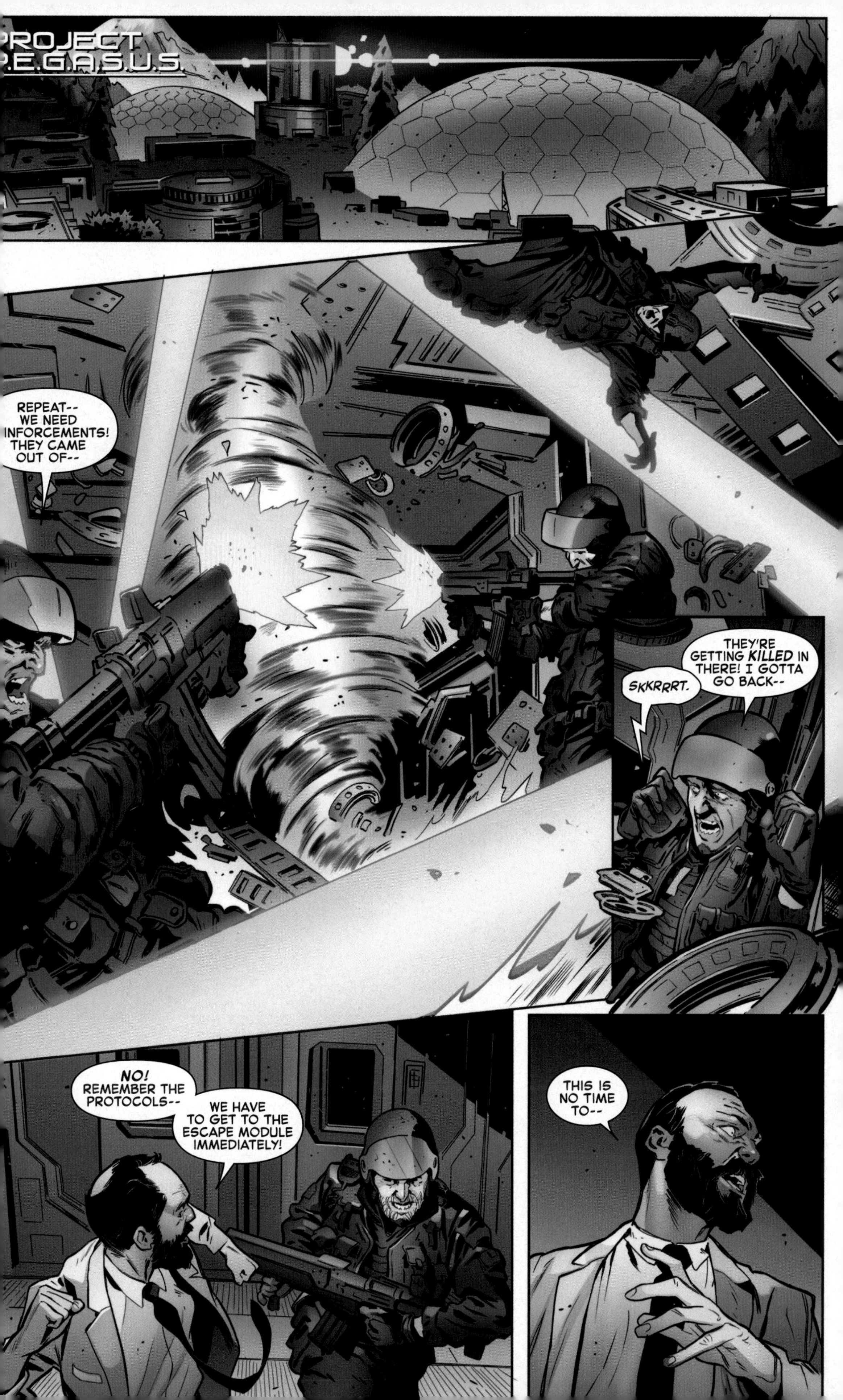
PROJECT P.E.G.A.S.U.S.
REPEAT-- WE NEED INFORCEMENTS! THEY CAME OUT OF--
SKKRRRT.
THEY'RE GETTING KILLED IN THERE! I GOTTA GO BACK--
NO! REMEMBER THE PROTOCOLS--
WE HAVE TO GET TO THE ESCAPE MODULE IMMEDIATELY!
THIS IS NO TIME TO--

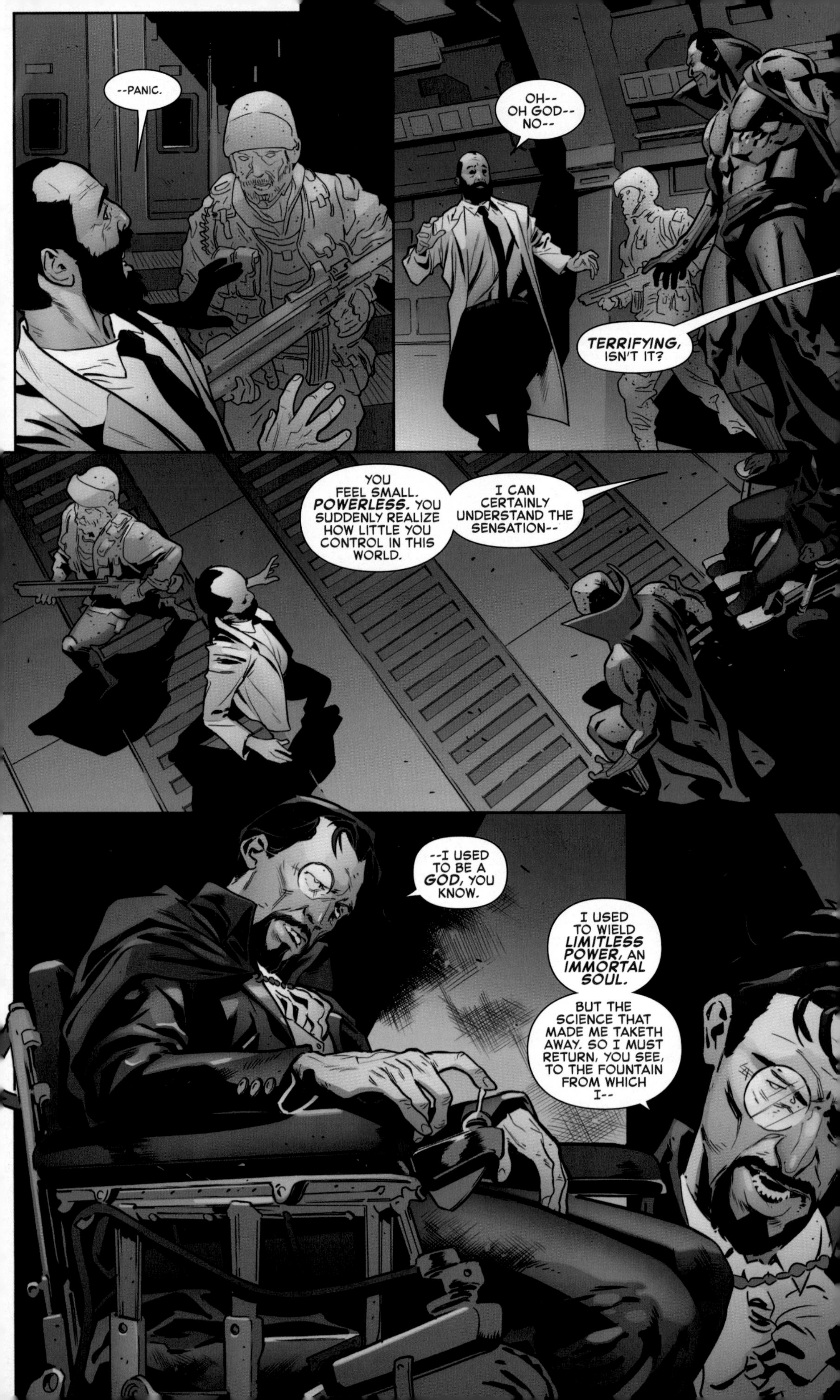

--PANIC.
OH-- OH GOD-- NO--
TERRIFYING, ISN'T IT?
YOU FEEL SMALL. POWERLESS. YOU SUDDENLY REALIZE HOW LITTLE YOU CONTROL IN THIS WORLD.
I CAN CERTAINLY UNDERSTAND THE SENSATION--
--I USED TO BE A GOD, YOU KNOW.
I USED TO WIELD LIMITLESS POWER, AN IMMORTAL SOUL.
BUT THE SCIENCE THAT MADE ME TAKETH AWAY. SO I MUST RETURN, YOU SEE, TO THE FOUNTAIN FROM WHICH I--

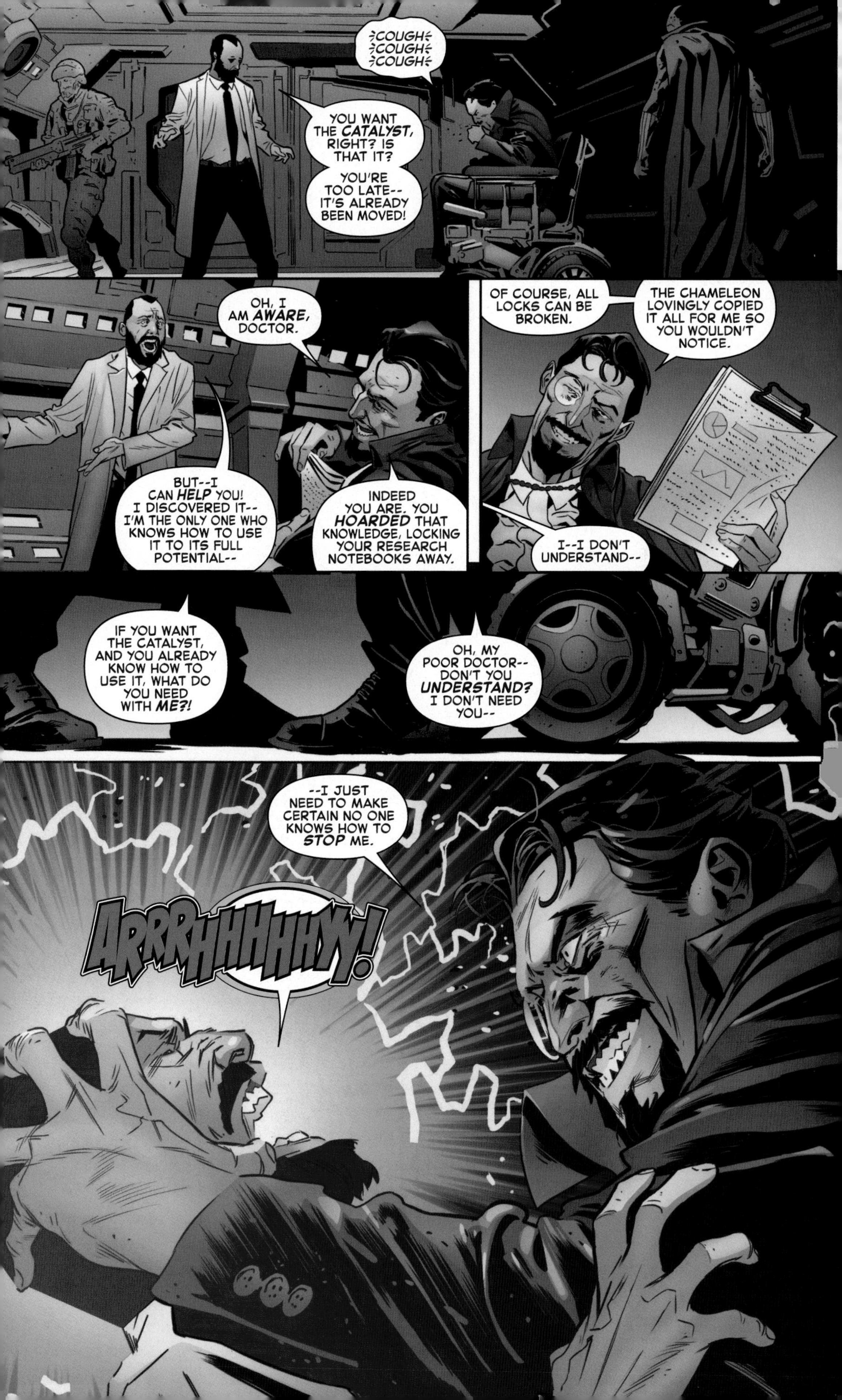
COUGH COUGH COUGH
YOU WANT THE CATALYST, RIGHT? IS THAT IT?
YOU'RE TOO LATE-- IT'S ALREADY BEEN MOVED!
OH, I AM AWARE, DOCTOR.
BUT--I CAN HELP YOU! I DISCOVERED IT-- I'M THE ONLY ONE WHO KNOWS HOW TO USE IT TO ITS FULL POTENTIAL--
INDEED YOU ARE. YOU HOARDED THAT KNOWLEDGE, LOCKING YOUR RESEARCH NOTEBOOKS AWAY.
OF COURSE, ALL LOCKS CAN BE BROKEN.
THE CHAMELEON LOVINGLY COPIED IT ALL FOR ME SO YOU WOULDN'T NOTICE.
I--I DON'T UNDERSTAND--
IF YOU WANT THE CATALYST, AND YOU ALREADY KNOW HOW TO USE IT, WHAT DO YOU NEED WITH ME?!
OH, MY POOR DOCTOR-- DON'T YOU UNDERSTAND? I DON'T NEED YOU--
--I JUST NEED TO MAKE CERTAIN NO ONE KNOWS HOW TO STOP ME.
ARRRHHHHHYY!

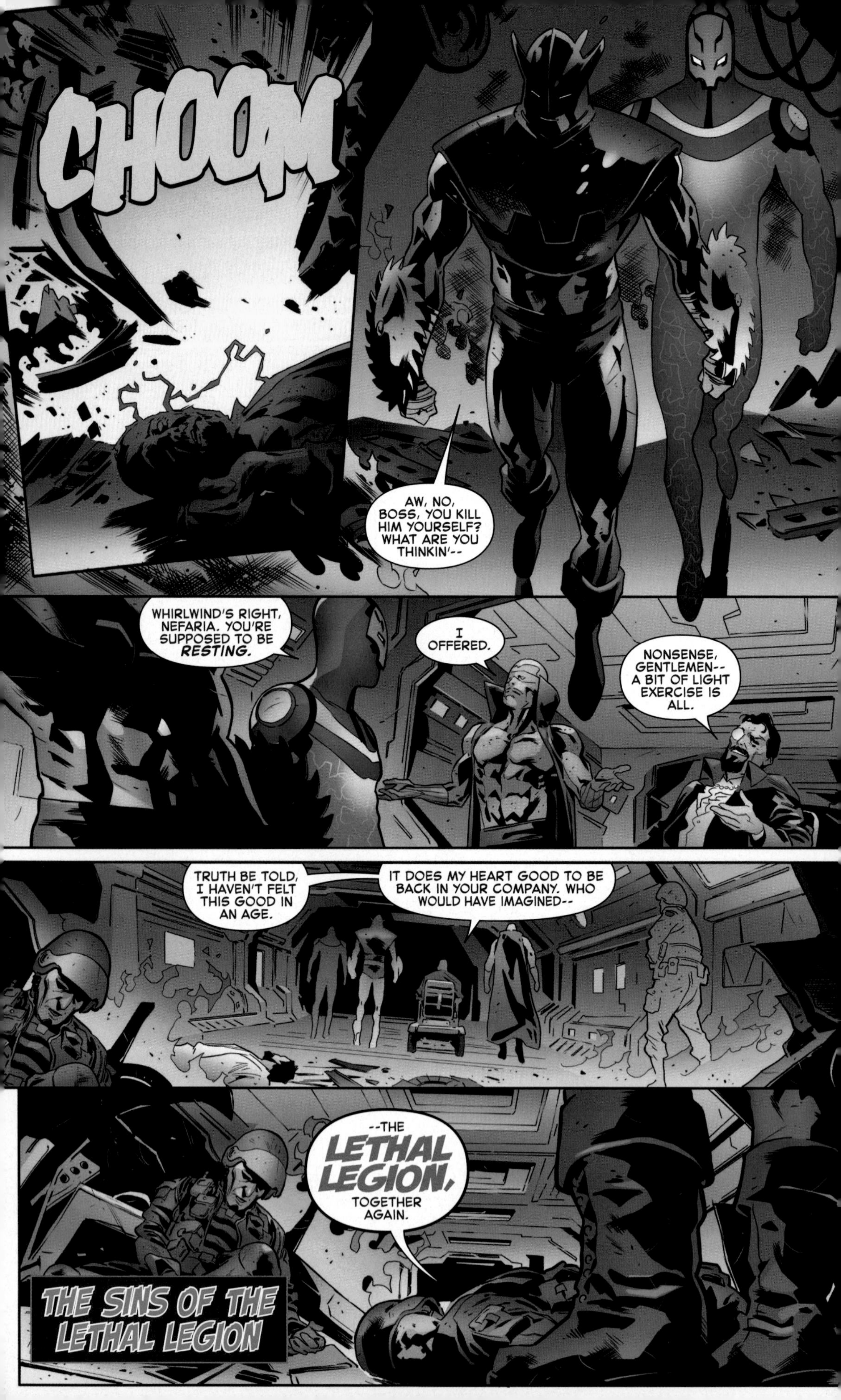
CHOOM
AW, NO, BOSS, YOU KILL HIM YOURSELF? WHAT ARE YOU THINKIN'--
WHIRLWIND'S RIGHT, NEFARIA. YOU'RE SUPPOSED TO BE RESTING.
I OFFERED.
NONSENSE, GENTLEMEN-- A BIT OF LIGHT EXERCISE IS ALL.
TRUTH BE TOLD, I HAVEN'T FELT THIS GOOD IN AN AGE.
IT DOES MY HEART GOOD TO BE BACK IN YOUR COMPANY. WHO WOULD HAVE IMAGINED--
--THE LETHAL LEGION, TOGETHER AGAIN.
THE SINS OF THE LETHAL LEGION

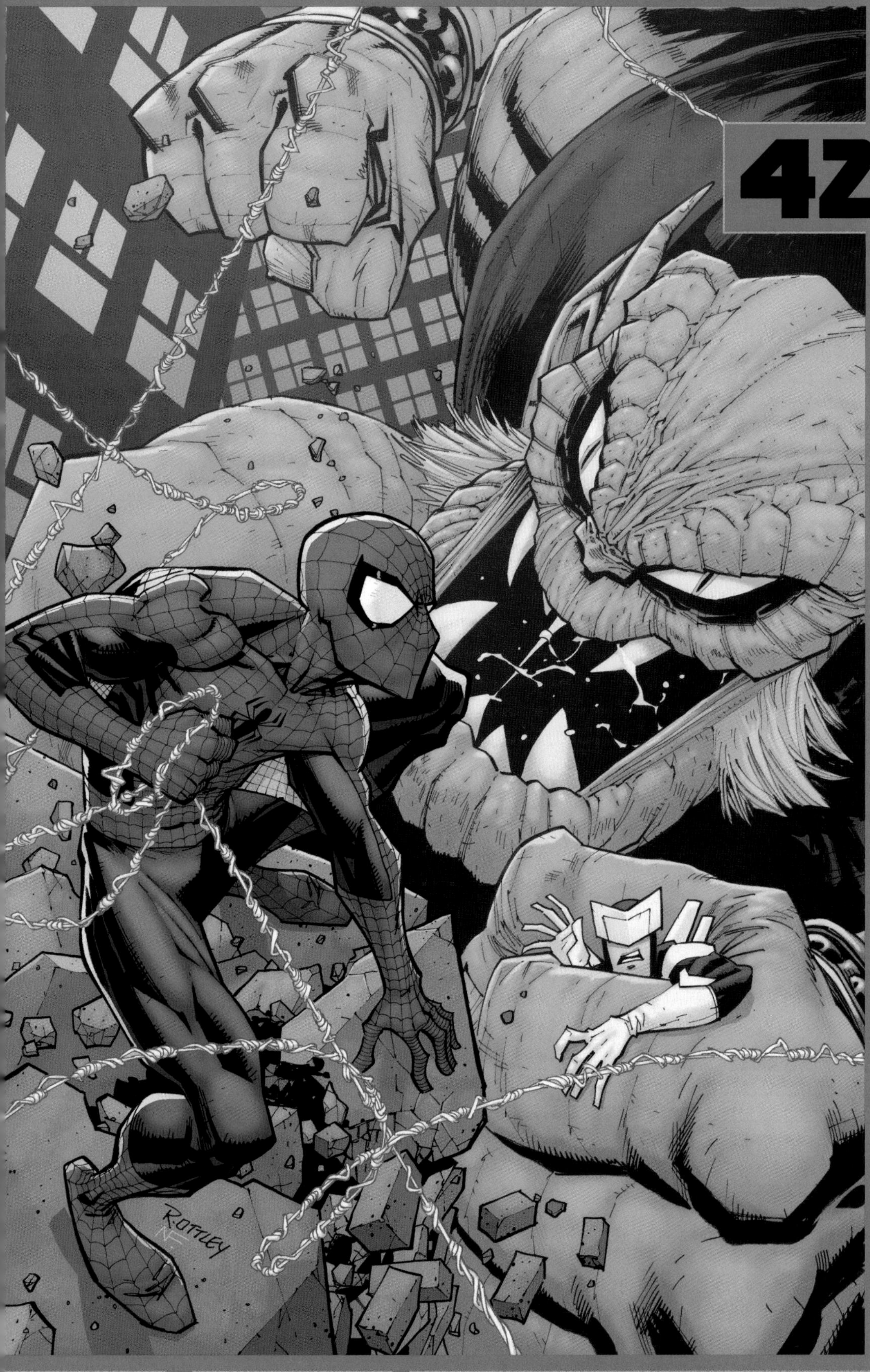

42
R.OTTLEY

TRUE COMPANIONS PART 2

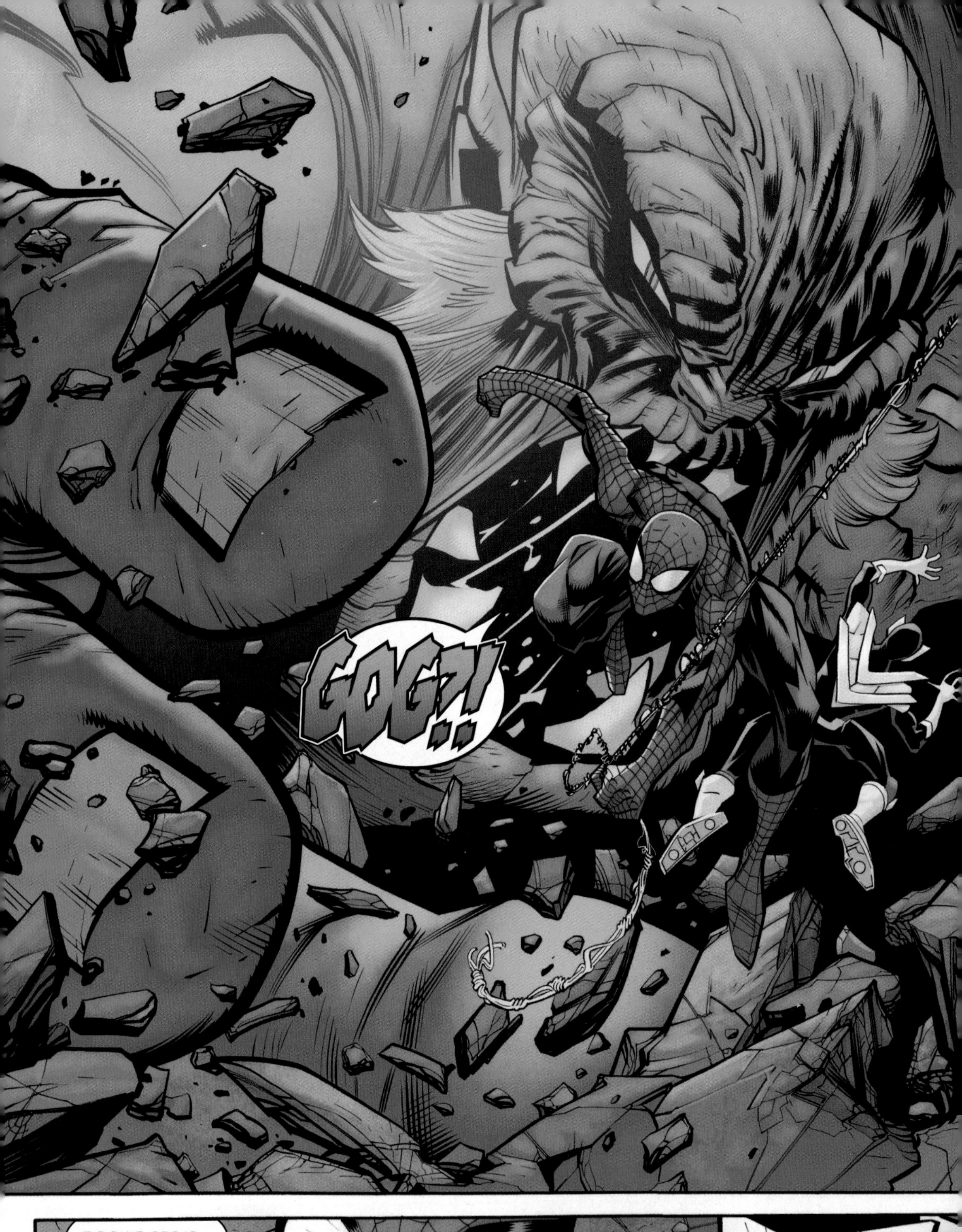
GOG?!

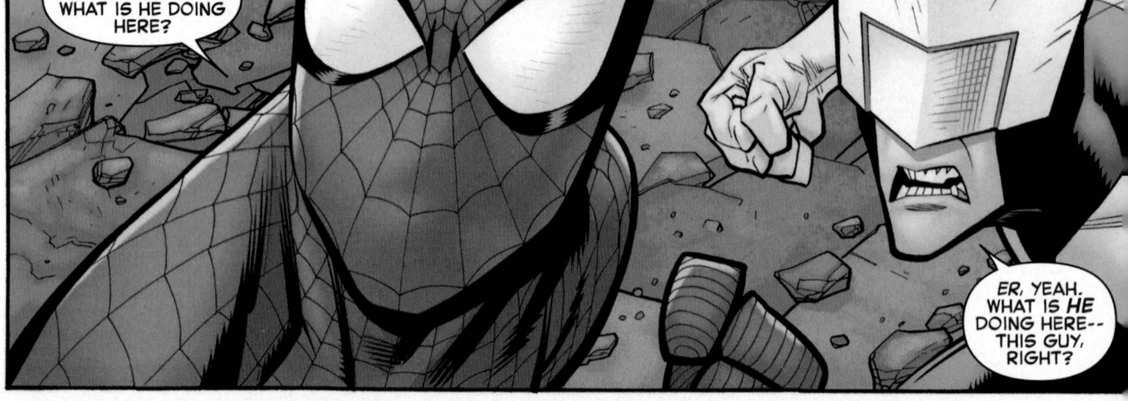
I DON'T GET IT--
WHAT IS HE DOING HERE?
ER, YEAH. WHAT IS HE DOING HERE--
THIS GUY, RIGHT?

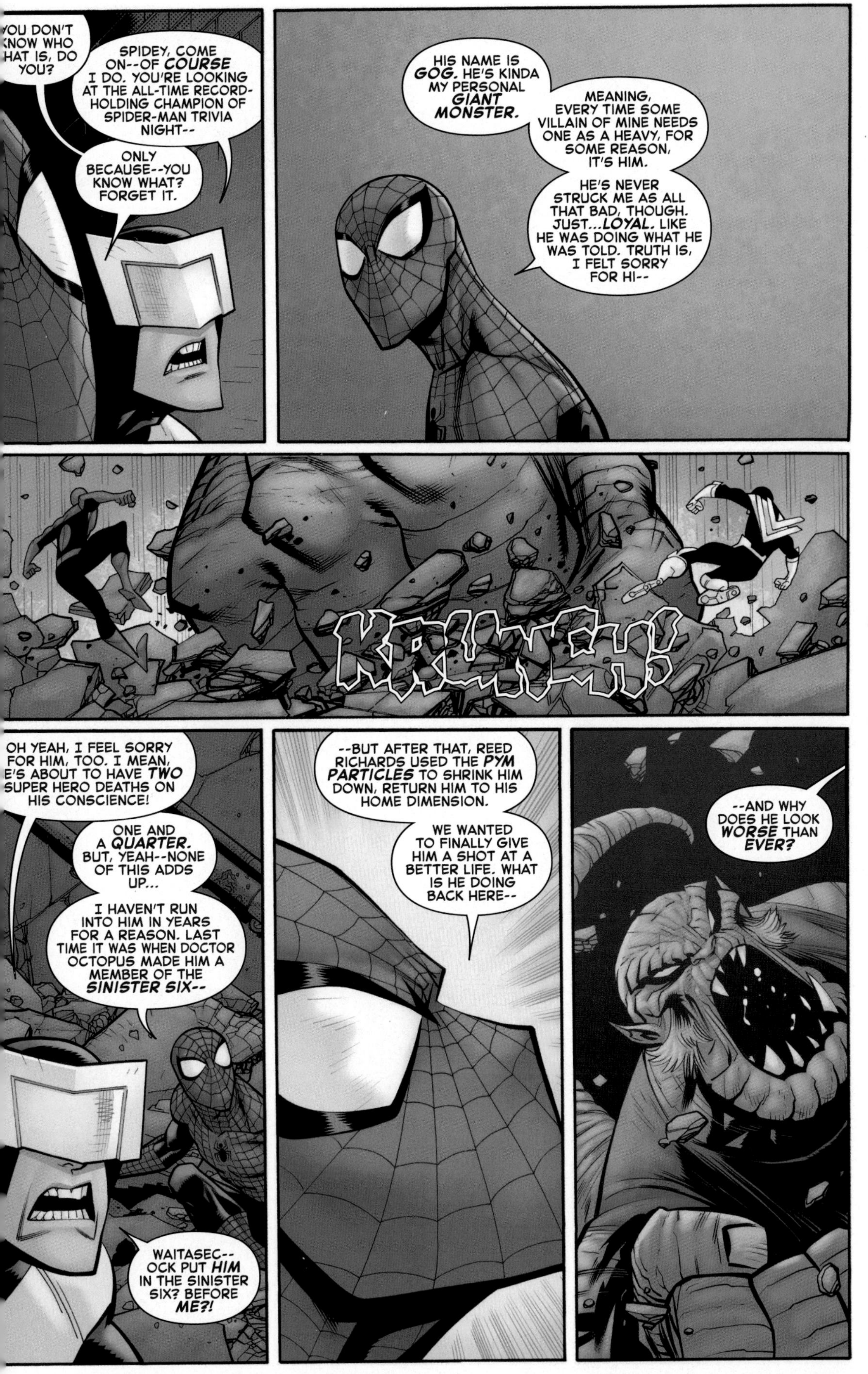

YOU DON'T KNOW WHO THAT IS, DO YOU?
SPIDEY, COME ON--OF COURSE I DO. YOU'RE LOOKING AT THE ALL-TIME RECORD-HOLDING CHAMPION OF SPIDER-MAN TRIVIA NIGHT--
ONLY BECAUSE--YOU KNOW WHAT? FORGET IT.
HIS NAME IS GOG. HE'S KINDA MY PERSONAL GIANT MONSTER.
MEANING, EVERY TIME SOME VILLAIN OF MINE NEEDS ONE AS A HEAVY, FOR SOME REASON, IT'S HIM.
HE'S NEVER STRUCK ME AS ALL THAT BAD, THOUGH. JUST...LOYAL. LIKE HE WAS DOING WHAT HE WAS TOLD. TRUTH IS, I FELT SORRY FOR HI--
KRUNCH!
OH YEAH, I FEEL SORRY FOR HIM, TOO. I MEAN, HE'S ABOUT TO HAVE TWO SUPER HERO DEATHS ON HIS CONSCIENCE!
ONE AND A QUARTER. BUT, YEAH--NONE OF THIS ADDS UP...
I HAVEN'T RUN INTO HIM IN YEARS FOR A REASON. LAST TIME IT WAS WHEN DOCTOR OCTOPUS MADE HIM A MEMBER OF THE SINISTER SIX--
WAITASEC--OCK PUT HIM IN THE SINISTER SIX? BEFORE ME?!
--BUT AFTER THAT, REED RICHARDS USED THE PYM PARTICLES TO SHRINK HIM DOWN, RETURN HIM TO HIS HOME DIMENSION.
WE WANTED TO FINALLY GIVE HIM A SHOT AT A BETTER LIFE. WHAT IS HE DOING BACK HERE--
--AND WHY DOES HE LOOK WORSE THAN EVER?

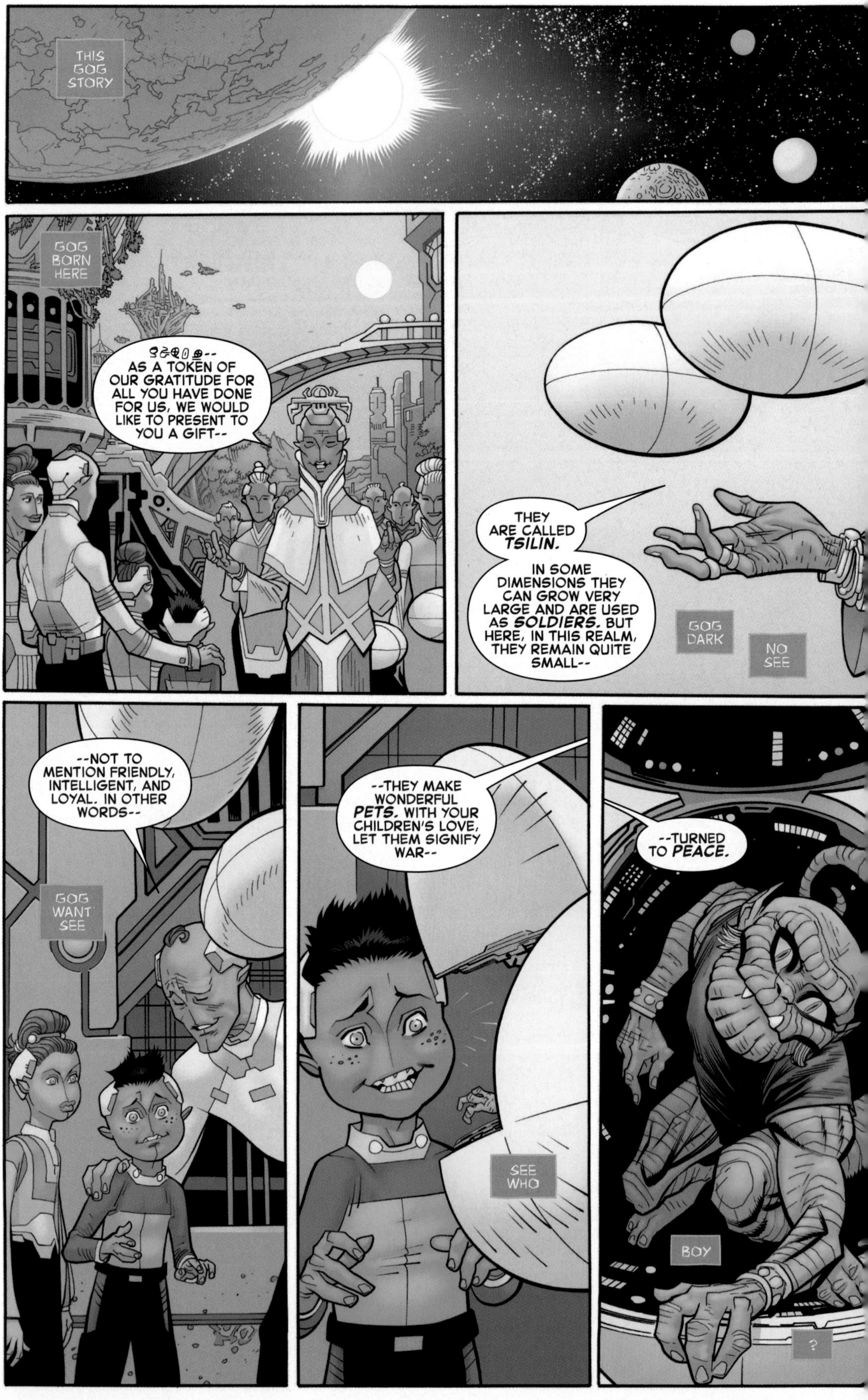
THIS GOG STORY
GOG BORN HERE
--AS A TOKEN OF OUR GRATITUDE FOR ALL YOU HAVE DONE FOR US, WE WOULD LIKE TO PRESENT TO YOU A GIFT--
THEY ARE CALLED TSILIN.
IN SOME DIMENSIONS THEY CAN GROW VERY LARGE AND ARE USED AS SOLDIERS. BUT HERE, IN THIS REALM, THEY REMAIN QUITE SMALL--
GOG DARK
NO SEE
--NOT TO MENTION FRIENDLY, INTELLIGENT, AND LOYAL. IN OTHER WORDS--
GOG WANT SEE
--THEY MAKE WONDERFUL PETS. WITH YOUR CHILDREN'S LOVE, LET THEM SIGNIFY WAR--
SEE WHO
--TURNED TO PEACE.
BOY
?

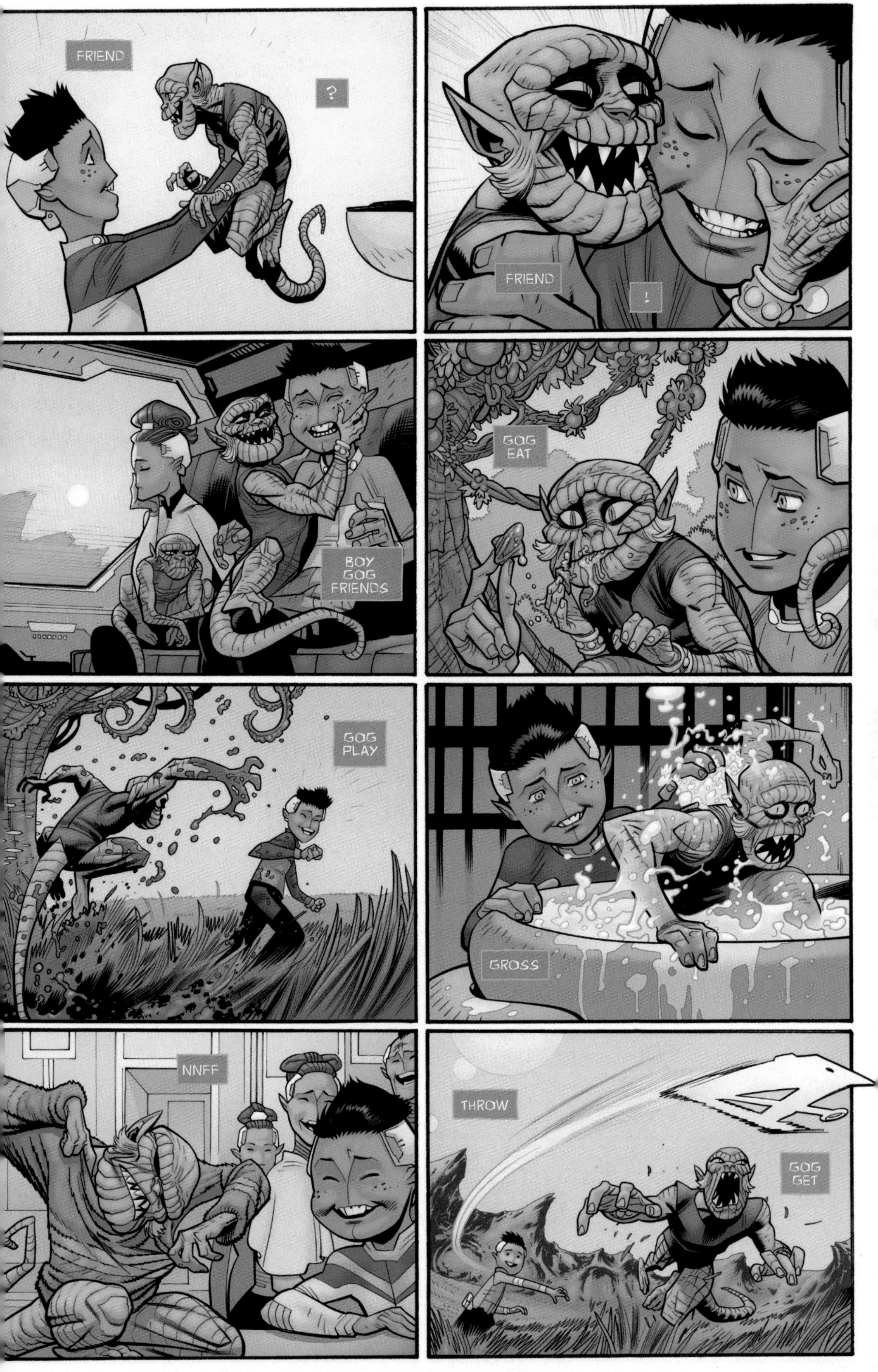
FRIEND
?
FRIEND
!
BOY GOG FRIENDS
GOG EAT
GOG PLAY
GROSS
NNFF
THROW
GOG GET

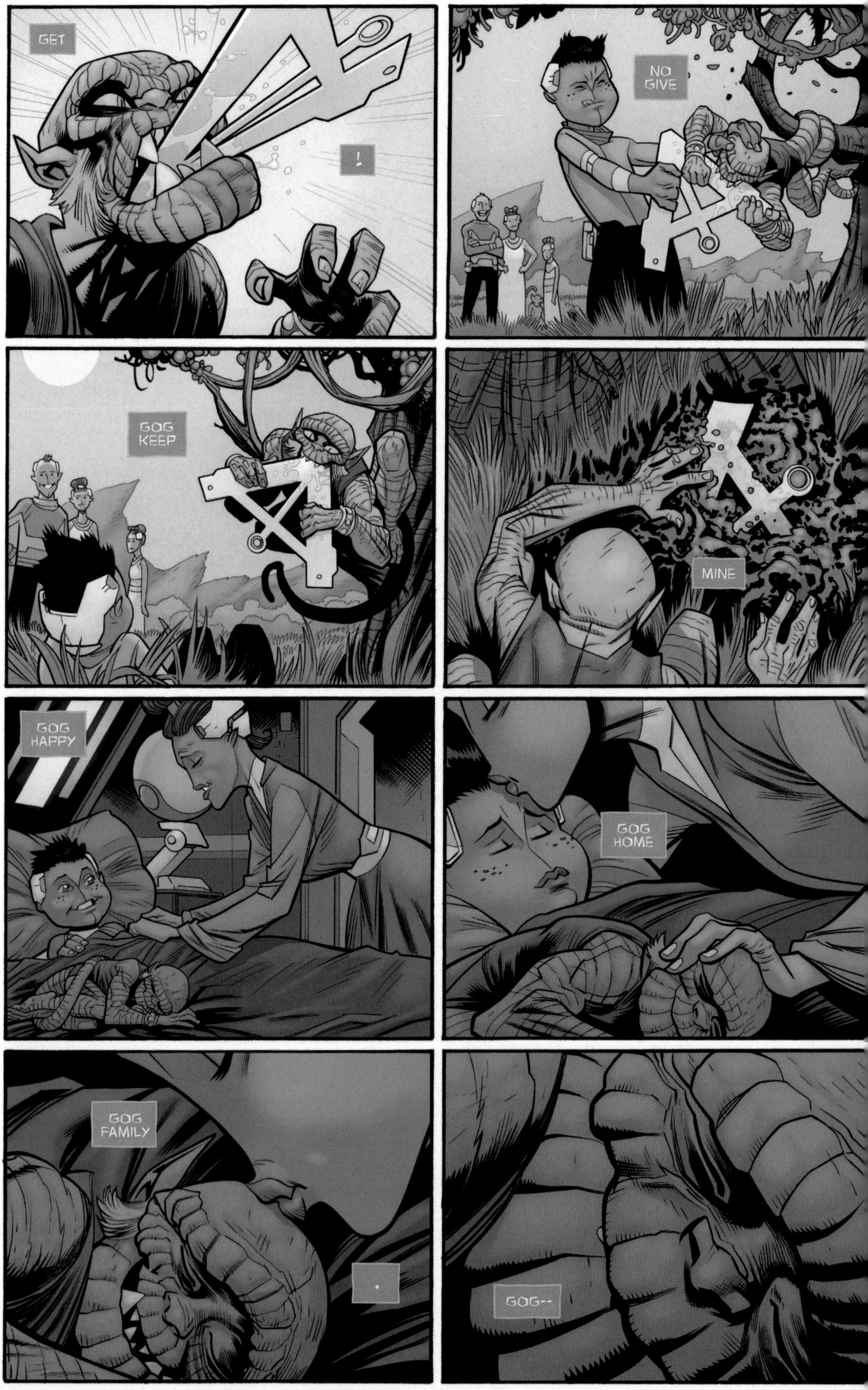
GET
!
NO GIVE
GOG KEEP
MINE
GOG HAPPY
GOG HOME
GOG FAMILY
.
GOG--

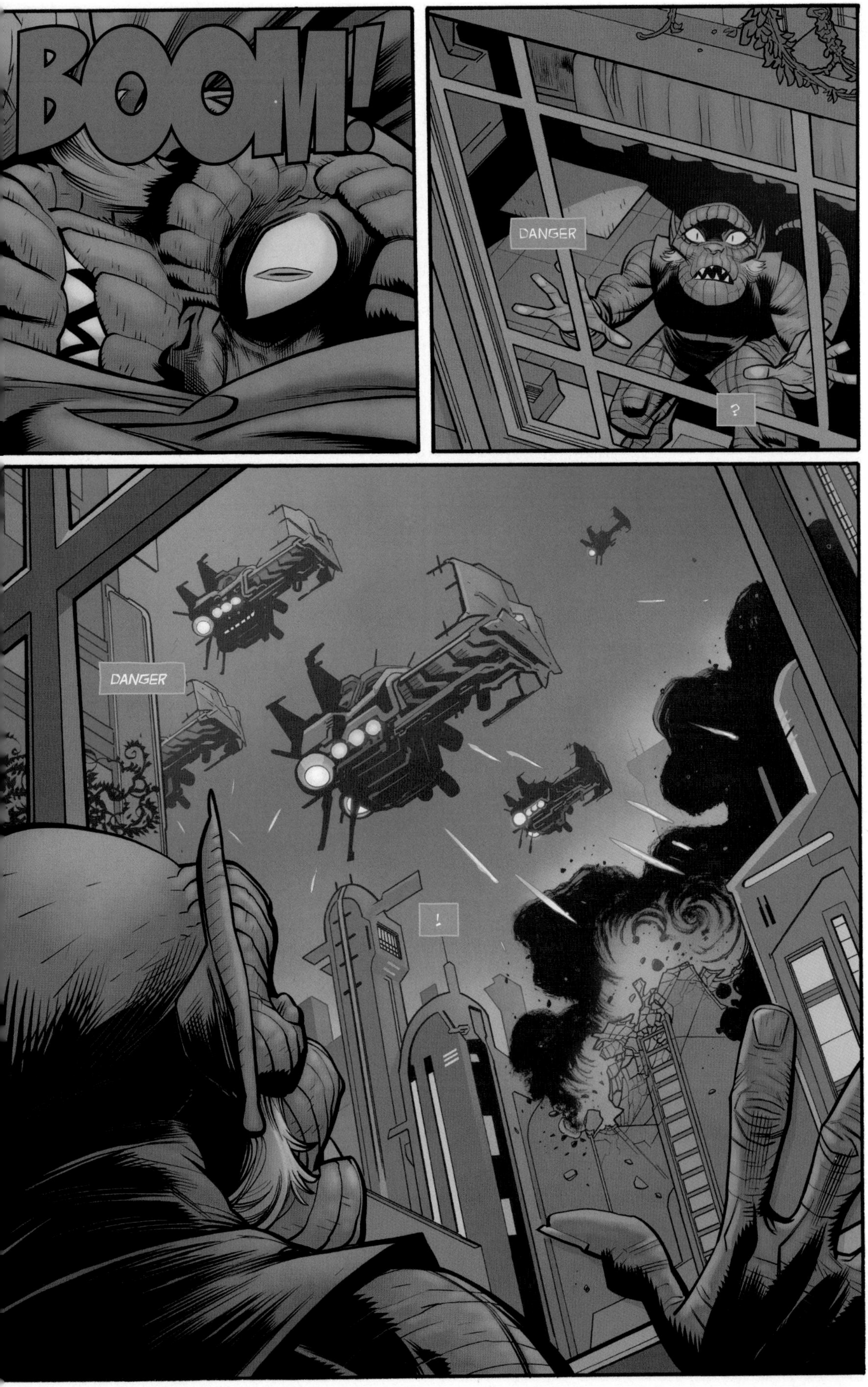
BOOM!
DANGER
?
DANGER
!

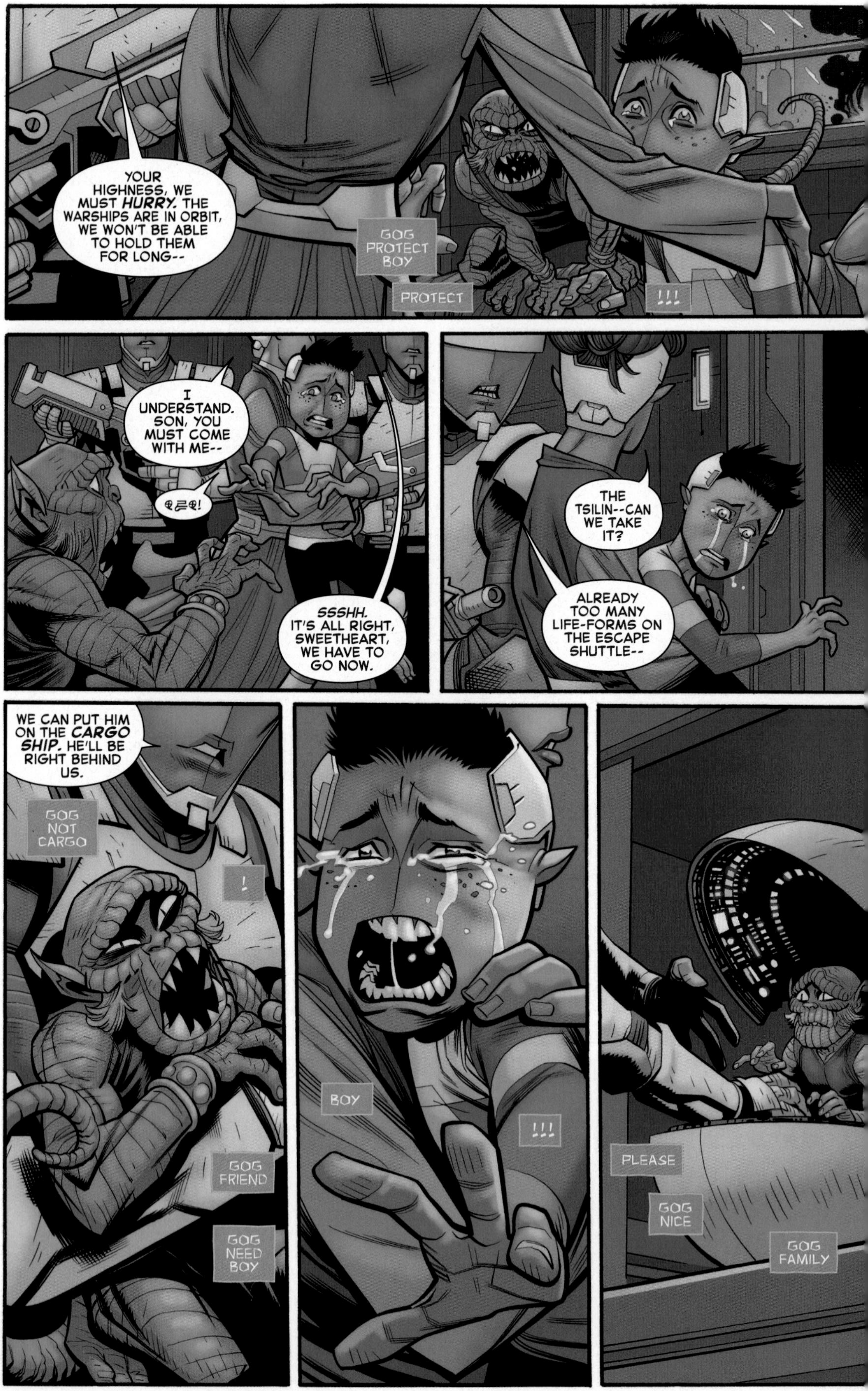
YOUR HIGHNESS, WE MUST *HURRY.* THE WARSHIPS ARE IN ORBIT, WE WON'T BE ABLE TO HOLD THEM FOR LONG--
GOG PROTECT BOY
PROTECT
!!!
I UNDERSTAND. SON, YOU MUST COME WITH ME--
SSSHH. IT'S ALL RIGHT, SWEETHEART, WE HAVE TO GO NOW.
THE TSILIN--CAN WE TAKE IT?
ALREADY TOO MANY LIFE-FORMS ON THE ESCAPE SHUTTLE--
WE CAN PUT HIM ON THE *CARGO SHIP.* HE'LL BE RIGHT BEHIND US.
GOG NOT CARGO
!
GOG FRIEND
GOG NEED BOY
BOY
!!!
PLEASE
GOG NICE
GOG FAMILY

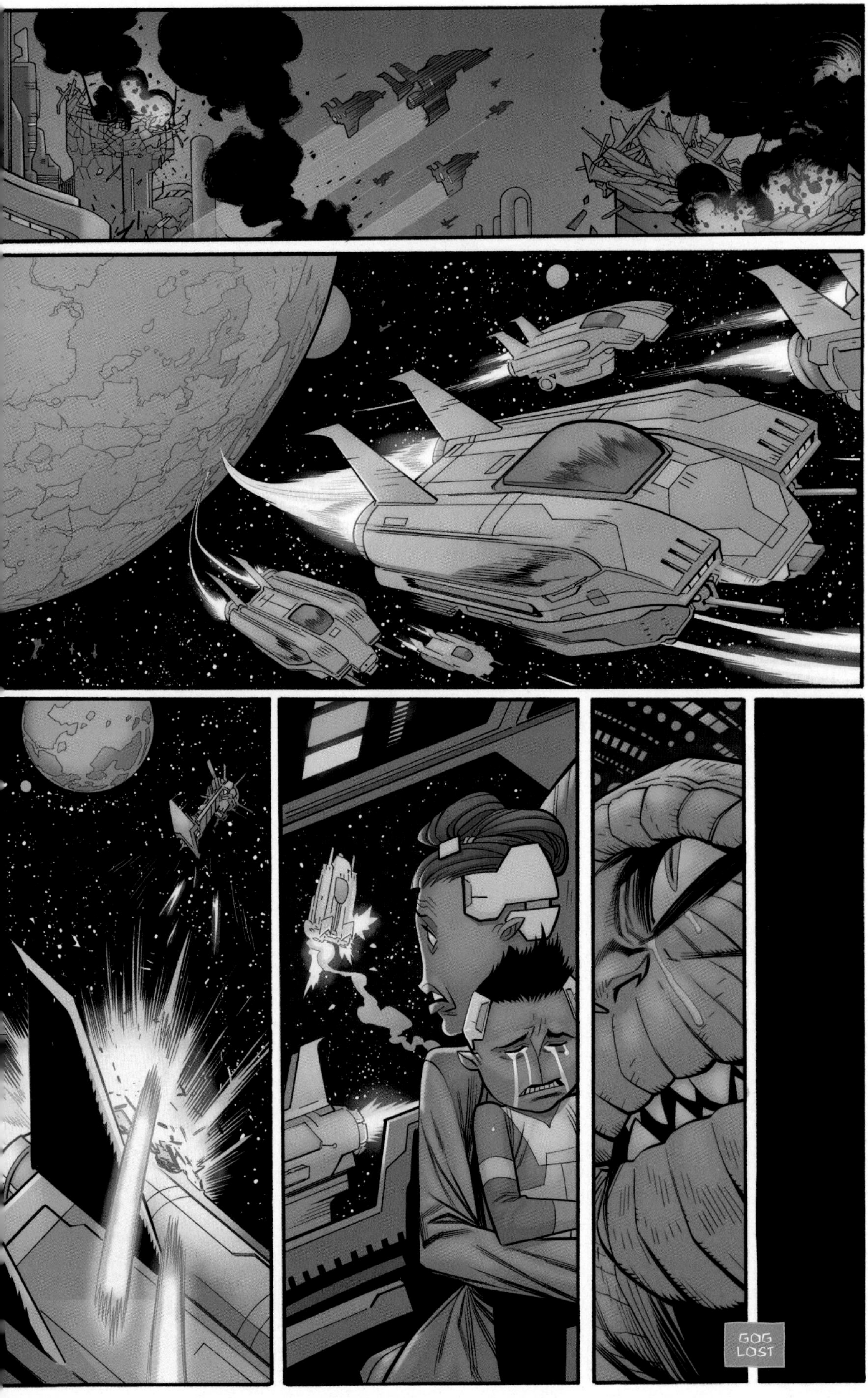
GOG
LOST

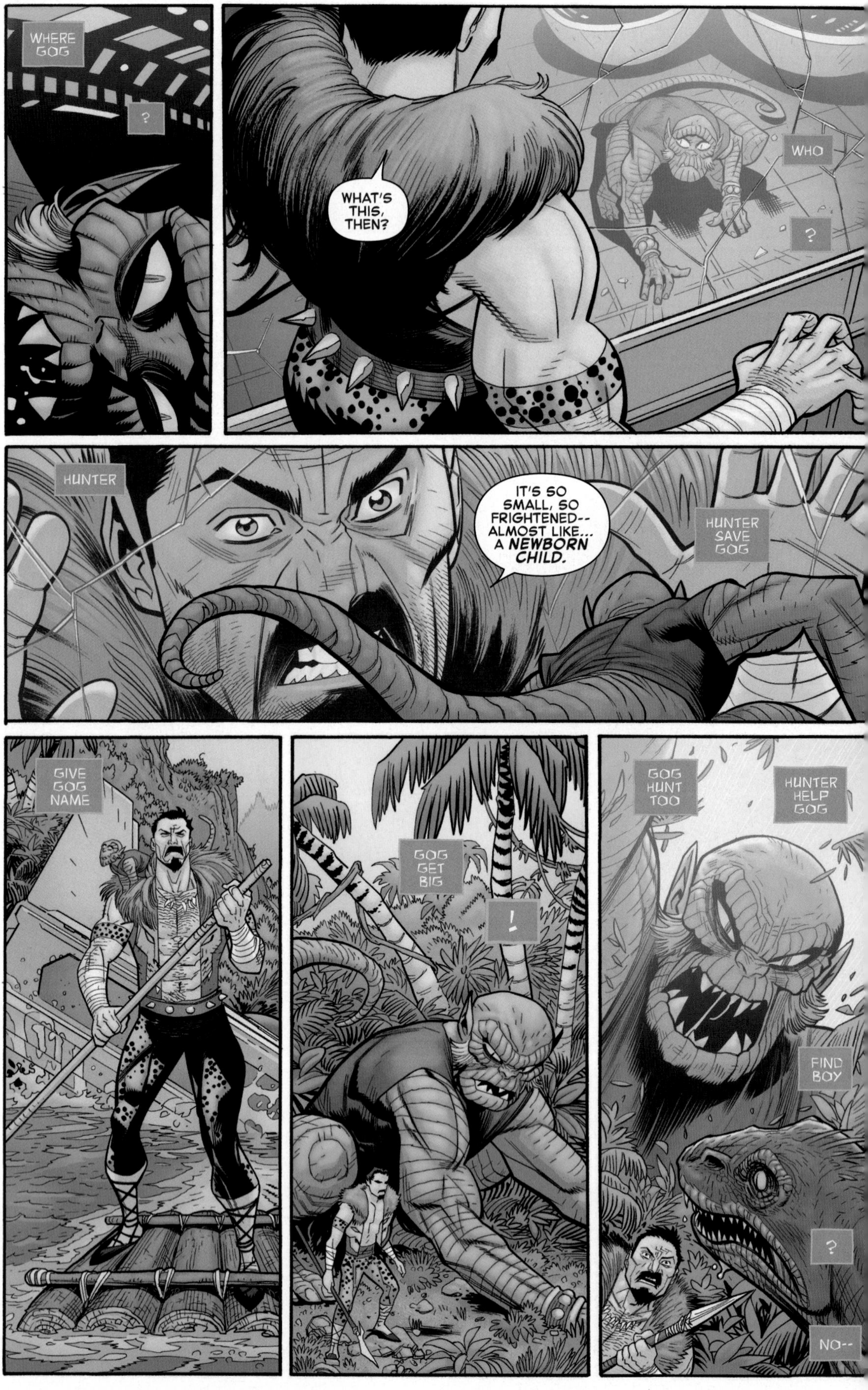

WHERE GOG
?
WHAT'S THIS, THEN?
WHO
?
HUNTER
IT'S SO SMALL, SO FRIGHTENED-- ALMOST LIKE... A NEWBORN CHILD.
HUNTER SAVE GOG
GIVE GOG NAME
GOG GET BIG
!
GOG HUNT TOO
HUNTER HELP GOG
FIND BOY
?
NO--

SPIDER

.

SPIDER HURT GOG

!

GOG TRAPPED

HUNTER HELP

?

HUNTER HURT

GOG ALONE AGAIN

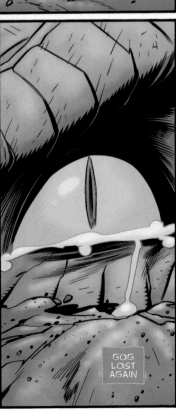

GOG LOST AGAIN

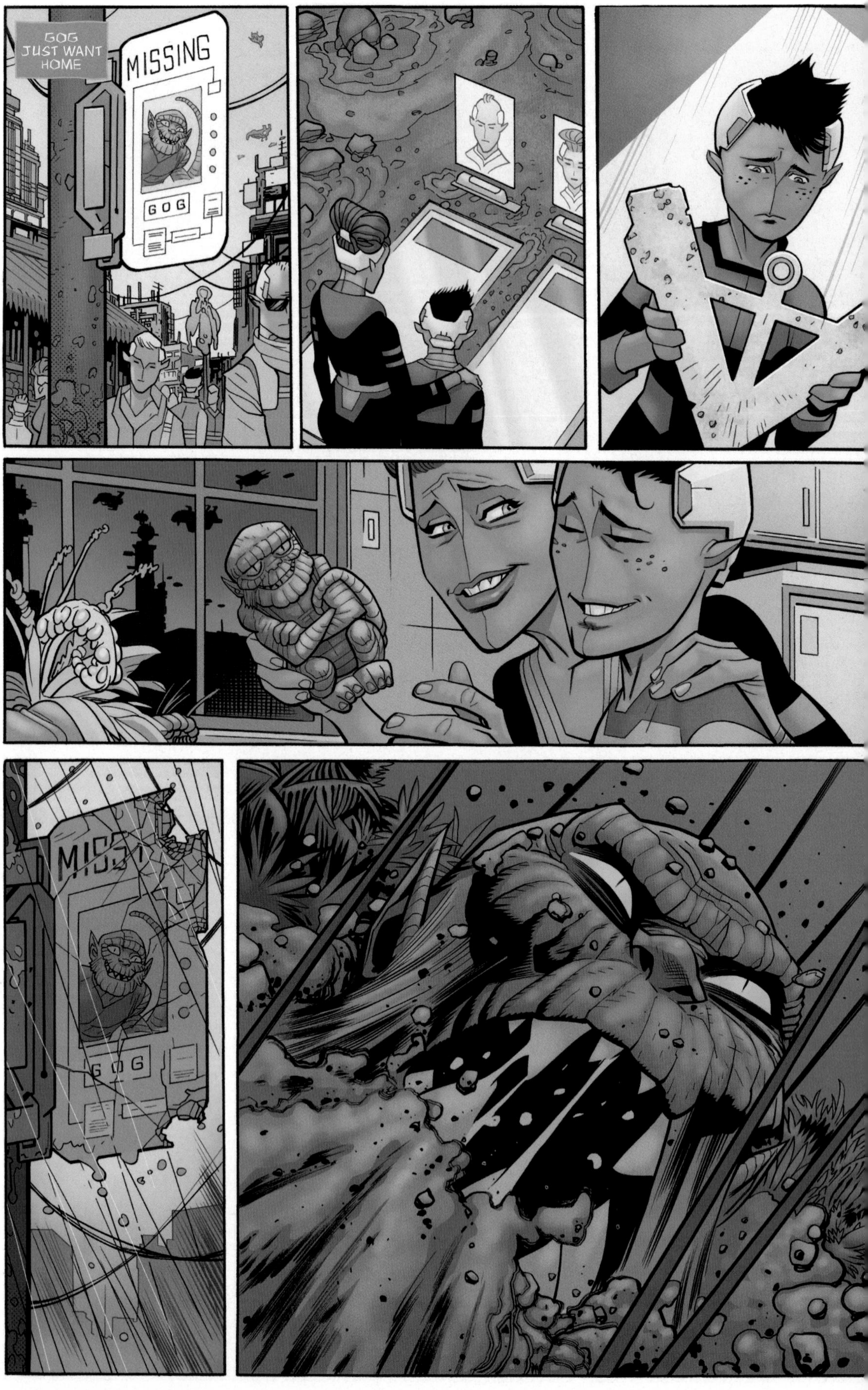
GOG
JUST WANT
HOME
MISSING
GOG
MISS
GOG

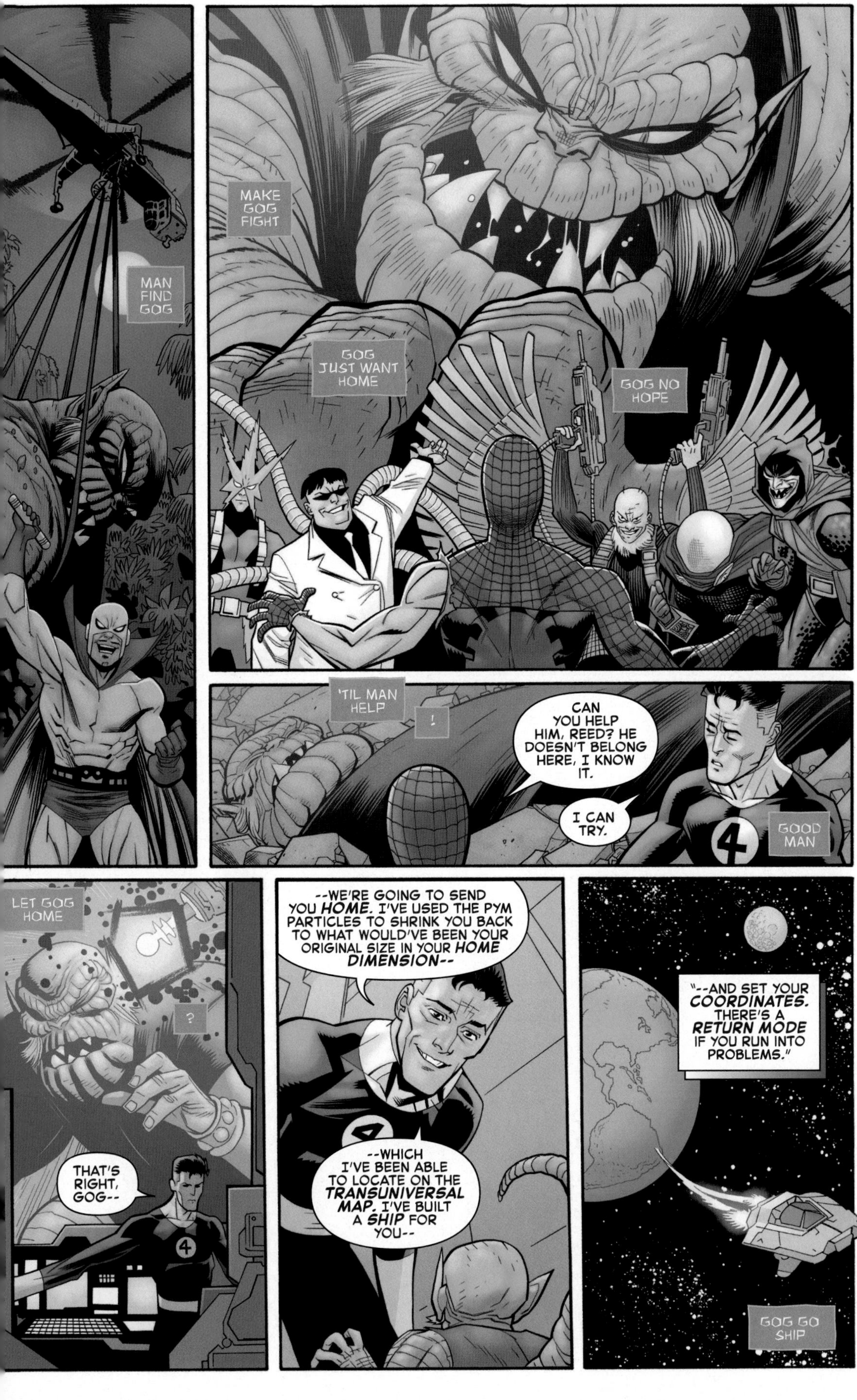
MAN FIND GOG
MAKE GOG FIGHT
GOG JUST WANT HOME
GOG NO HOPE
'TIL MAN HELP
!
CAN YOU HELP HIM, REED? HE DOESN'T BELONG HERE, I KNOW IT.
I CAN TRY.
GOOD MAN
LET GOG HOME
?
THAT'S RIGHT, GOG--
--WE'RE GOING TO SEND YOU HOME. I'VE USED THE PYM PARTICLES TO SHRINK YOU BACK TO WHAT WOULD'VE BEEN YOUR ORIGINAL SIZE IN YOUR HOME DIMENSION--
--WHICH I'VE BEEN ABLE TO LOCATE ON THE TRANSUNIVERSAL MAP. I'VE BUILT A SHIP FOR YOU--
"--AND SET YOUR COORDINATES. THERE'S A RETURN MODE IF YOU RUN INTO PROBLEMS."
GOG GO SHIP

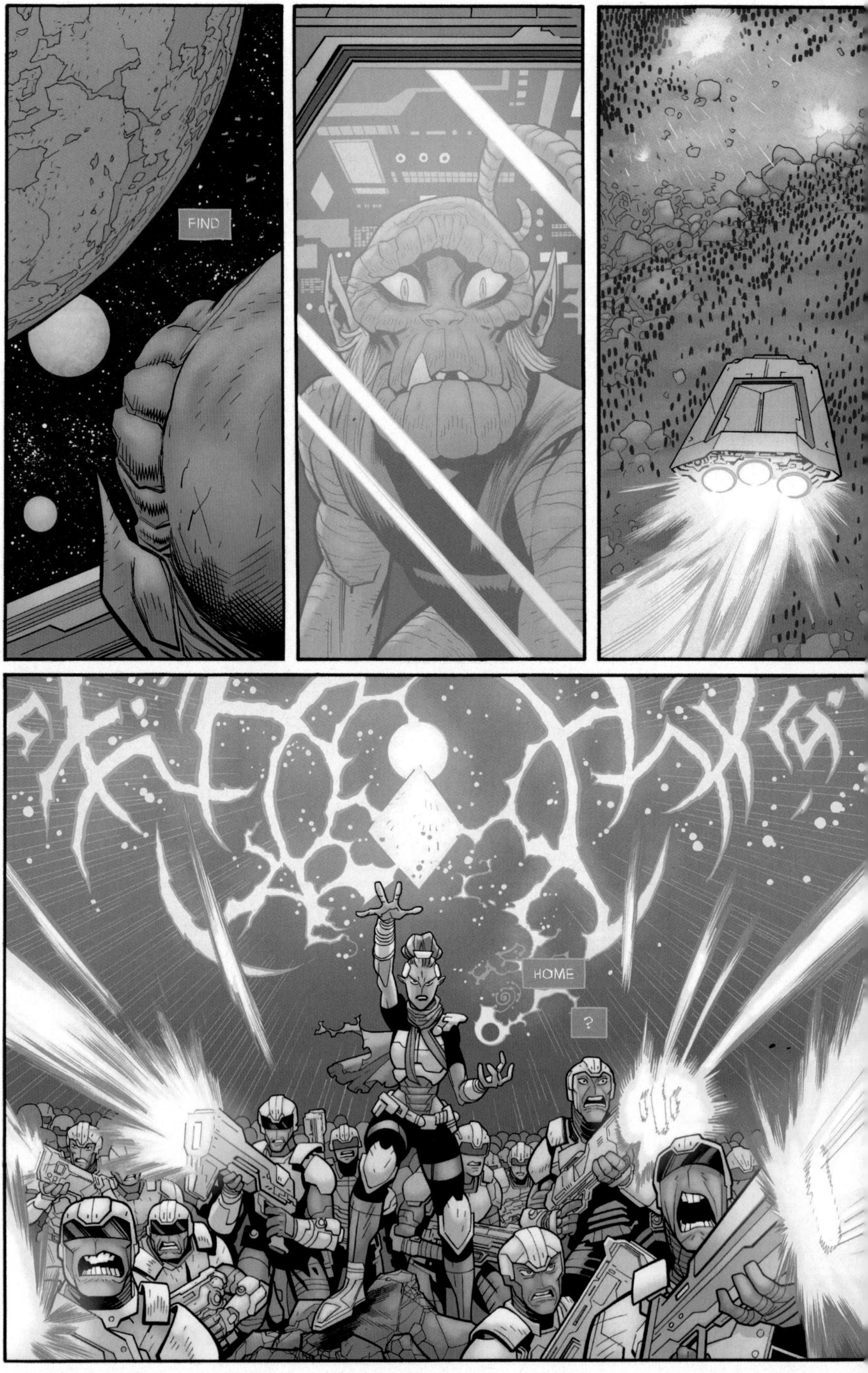
FIND
HOME
?

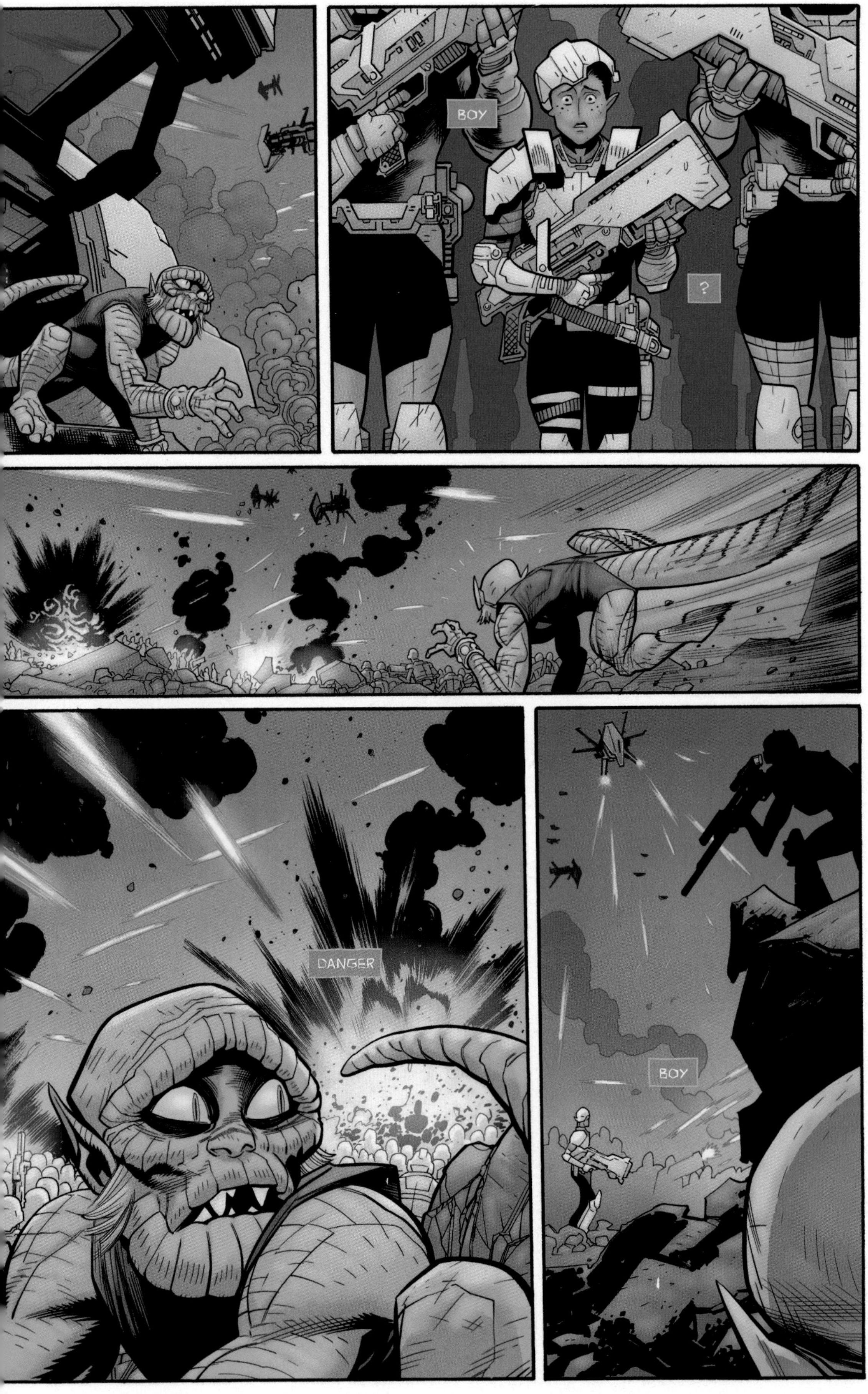
BOY
?
DANGER
BOY

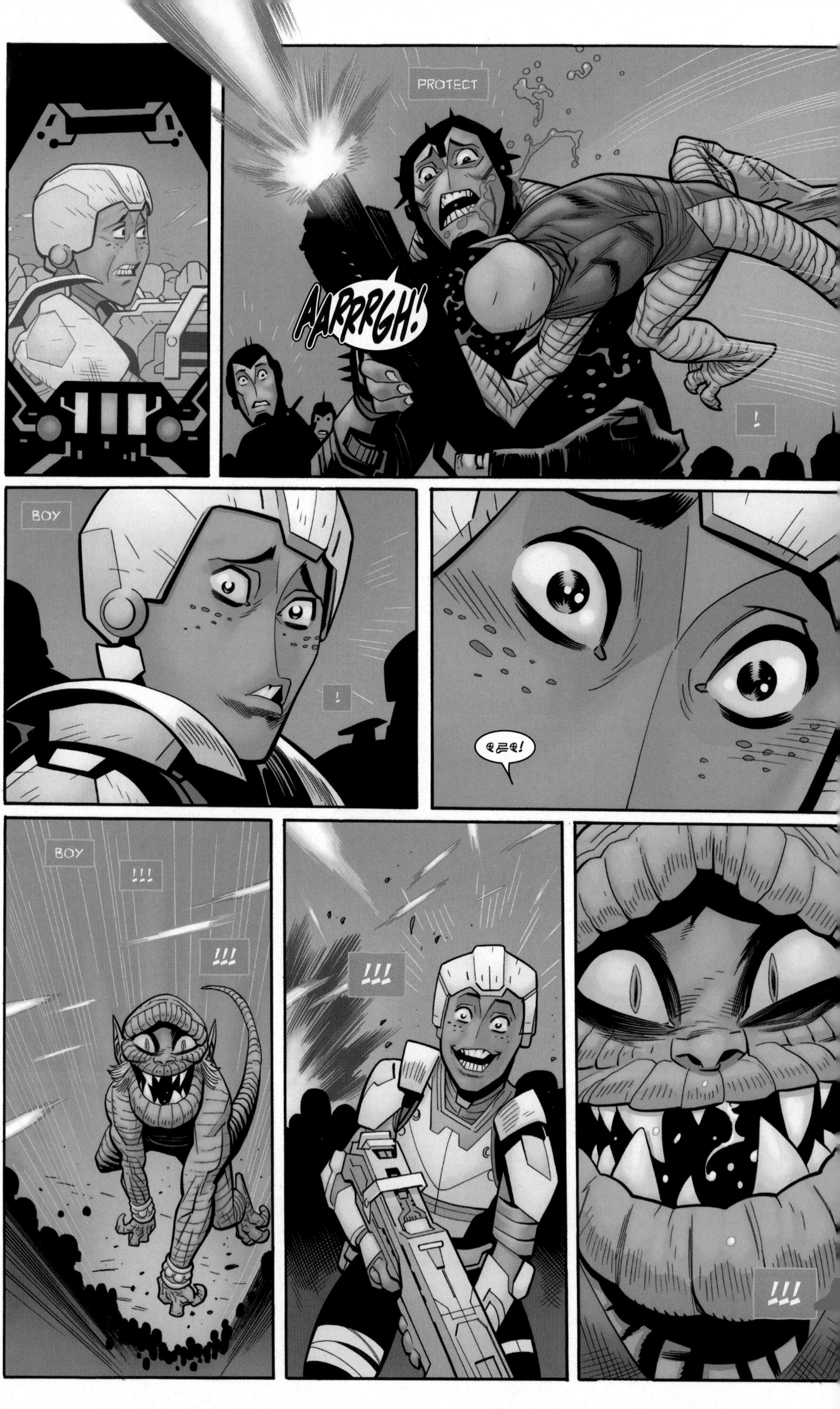
PROTECT
AARRRGH!
!
BOY
!
BOY
!!!
!!!
!!!
!!!

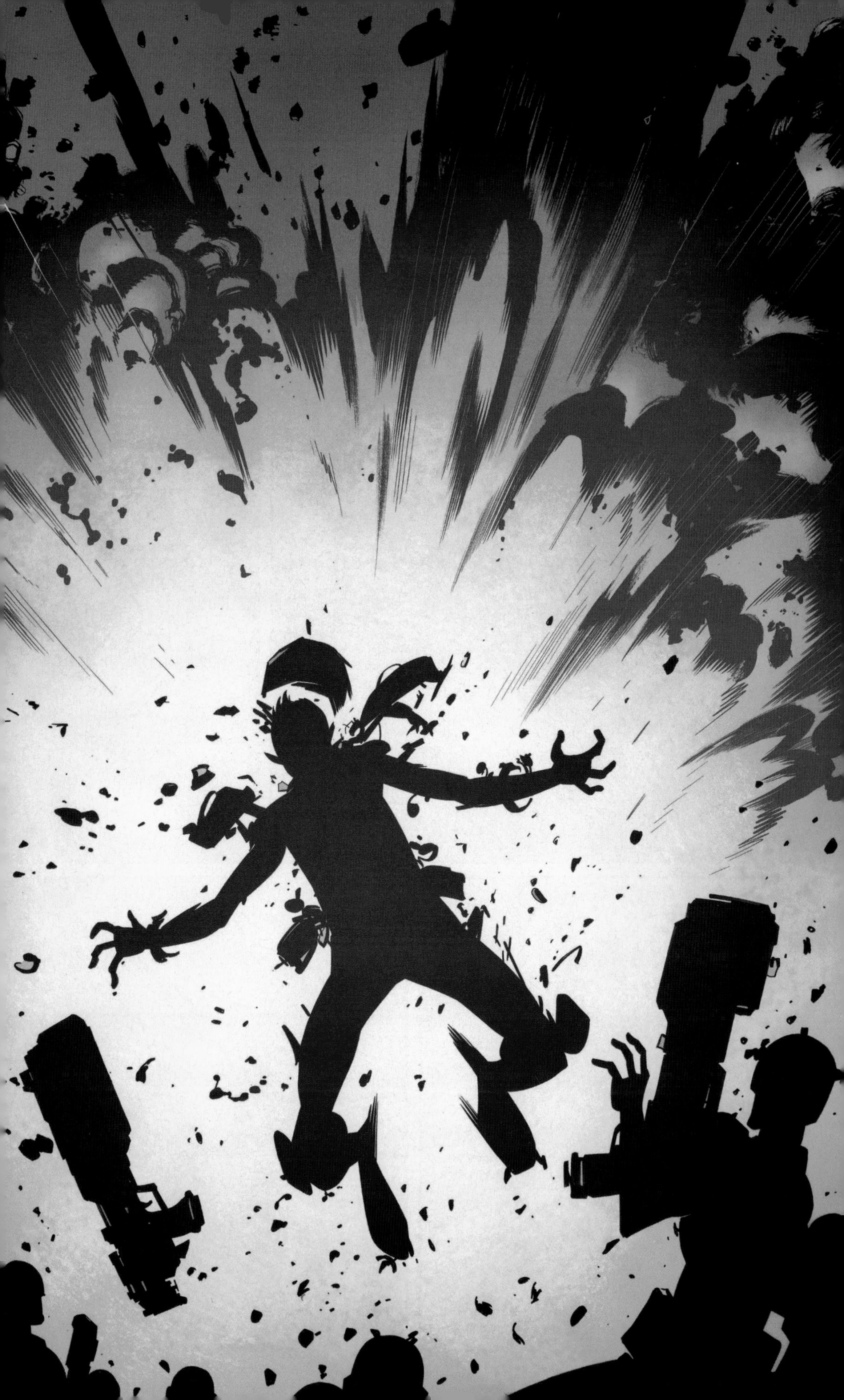

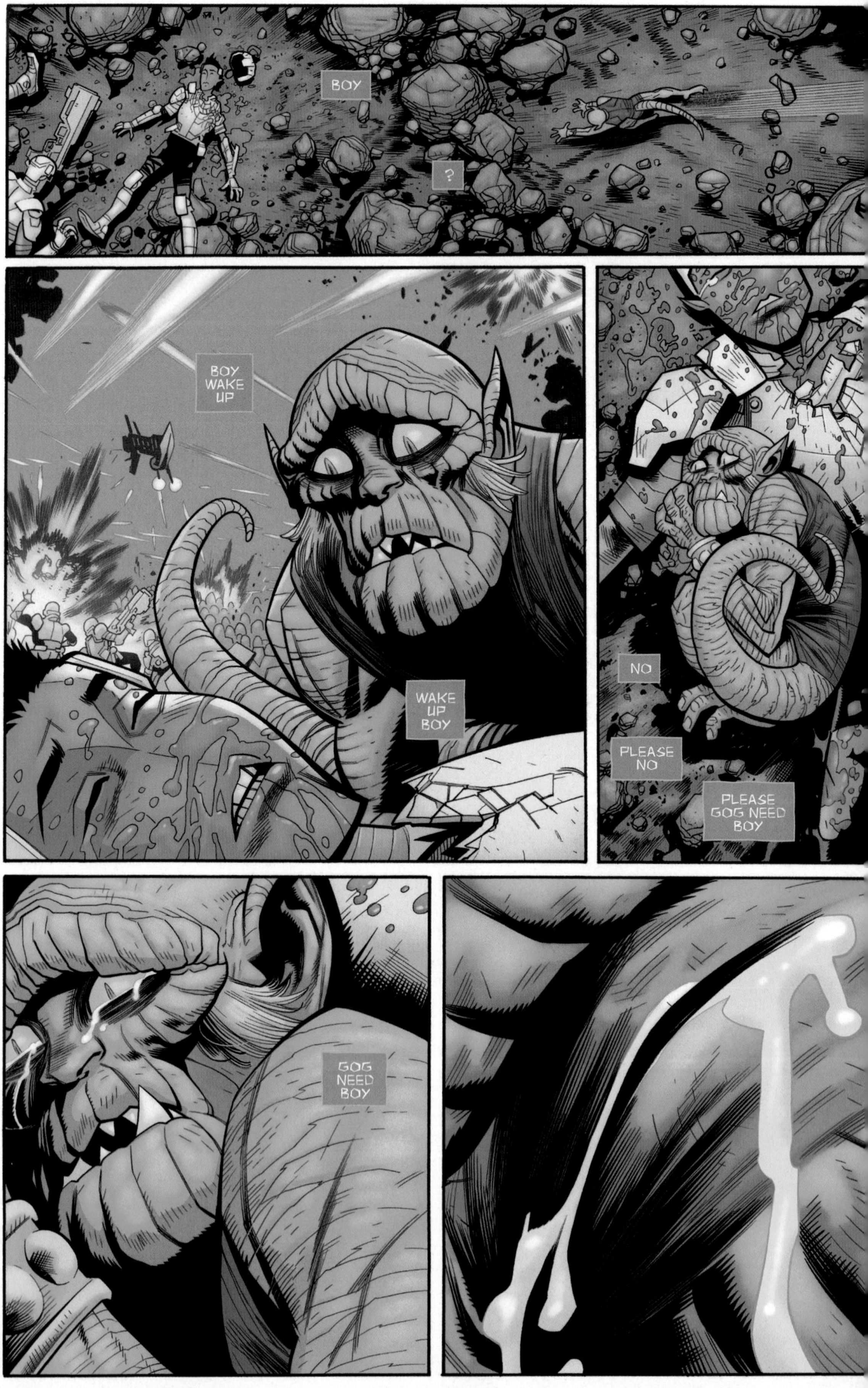
BOY
?
BOY WAKE UP
WAKE UP BOY
NO
PLEASE NO
PLEASE GOG NEED BOY
GOG NEED BOY

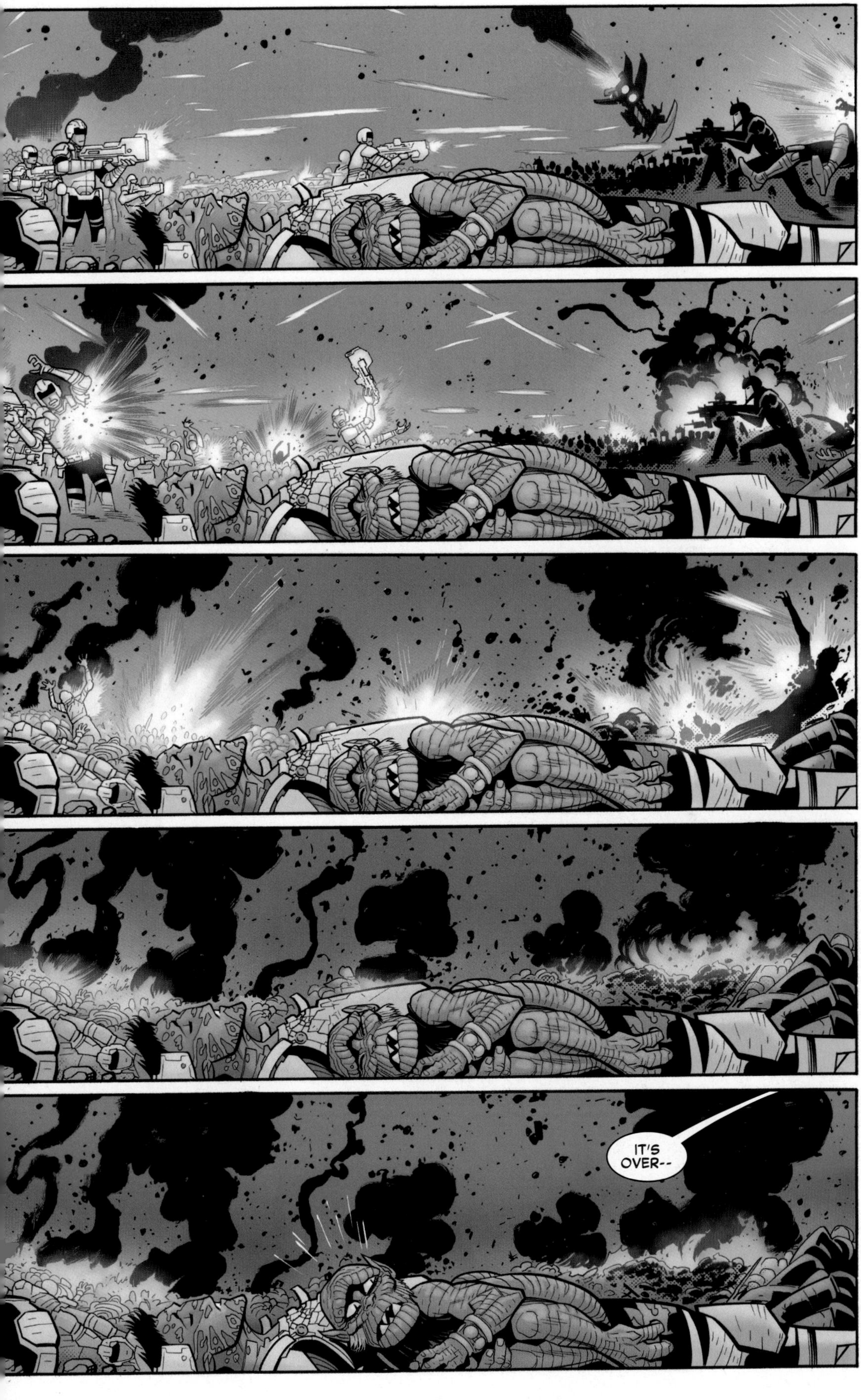
IT'S
OVER--

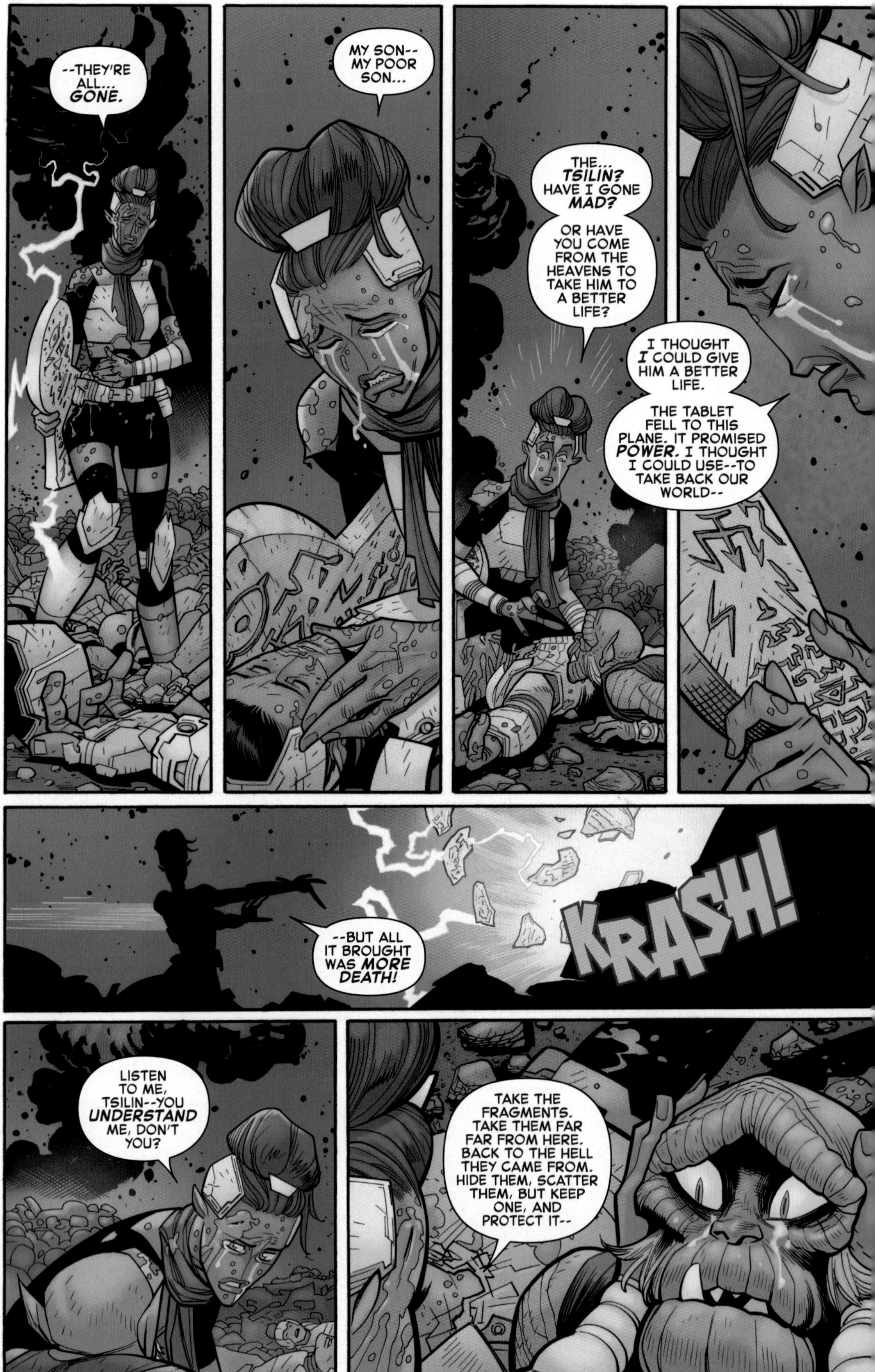
--THEY'RE ALL... GONE.
MY SON-- MY POOR SON...
THE... TSILIN? HAVE I GONE MAD?
OR HAVE YOU COME FROM THE HEAVENS TO TAKE HIM TO A BETTER LIFE?
I THOUGHT I COULD GIVE HIM A BETTER LIFE.
THE TABLET FELL TO THIS PLANE. IT PROMISED POWER. I THOUGHT I COULD USE--TO TAKE BACK OUR WORLD--
--BUT ALL IT BROUGHT WAS MORE DEATH!
KRASH!
LISTEN TO ME, TSILIN--YOU UNDERSTAND ME, DON'T YOU?
TAKE THE FRAGMENTS. TAKE THEM FAR FAR FROM HERE. BACK TO THE HELL THEY CAME FROM. HIDE THEM, SCATTER THEM, BUT KEEP ONE, AND PROTECT IT--

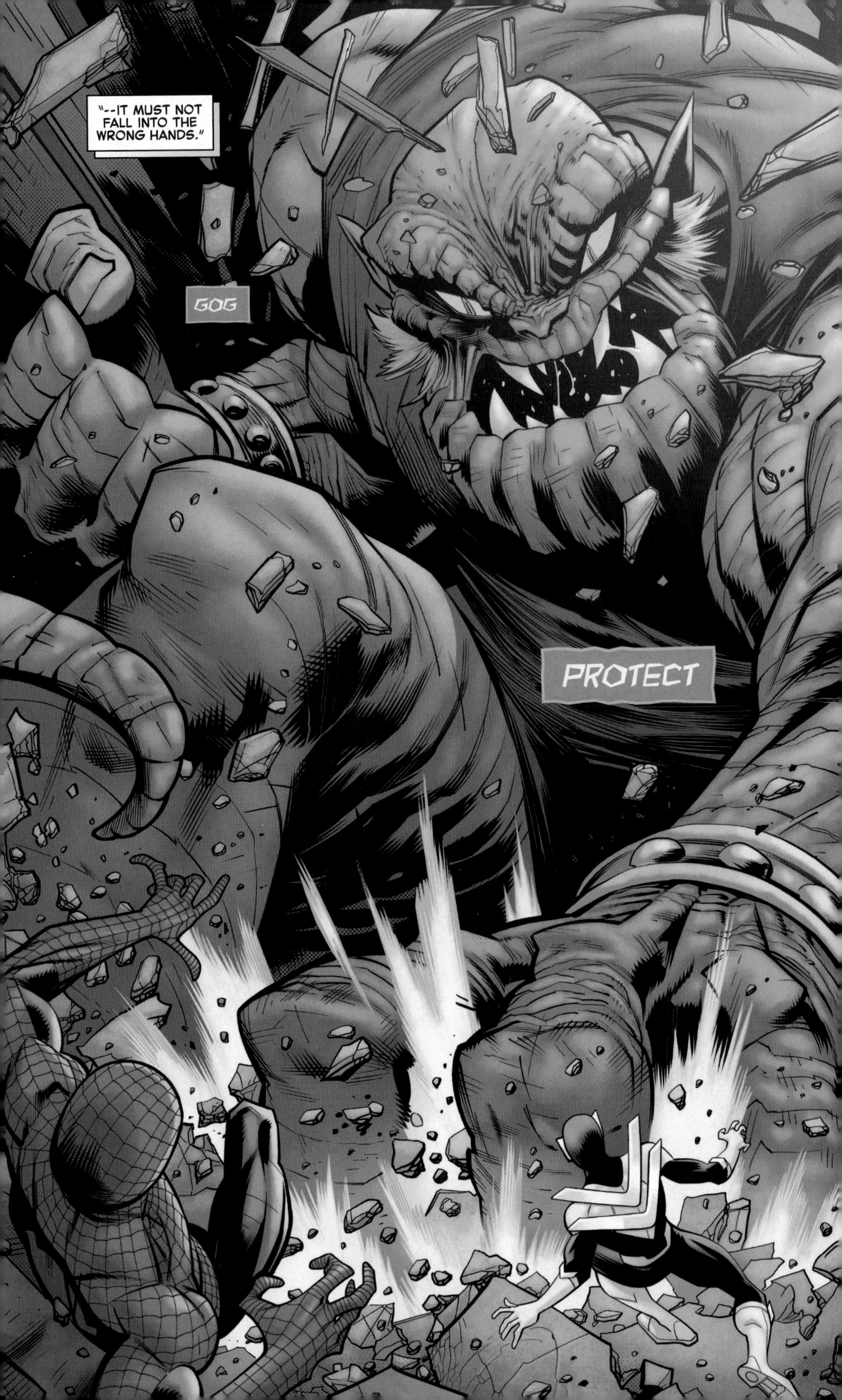
"--IT MUST NOT FALL INTO THE WRONG HANDS."
GOG
PROTECT

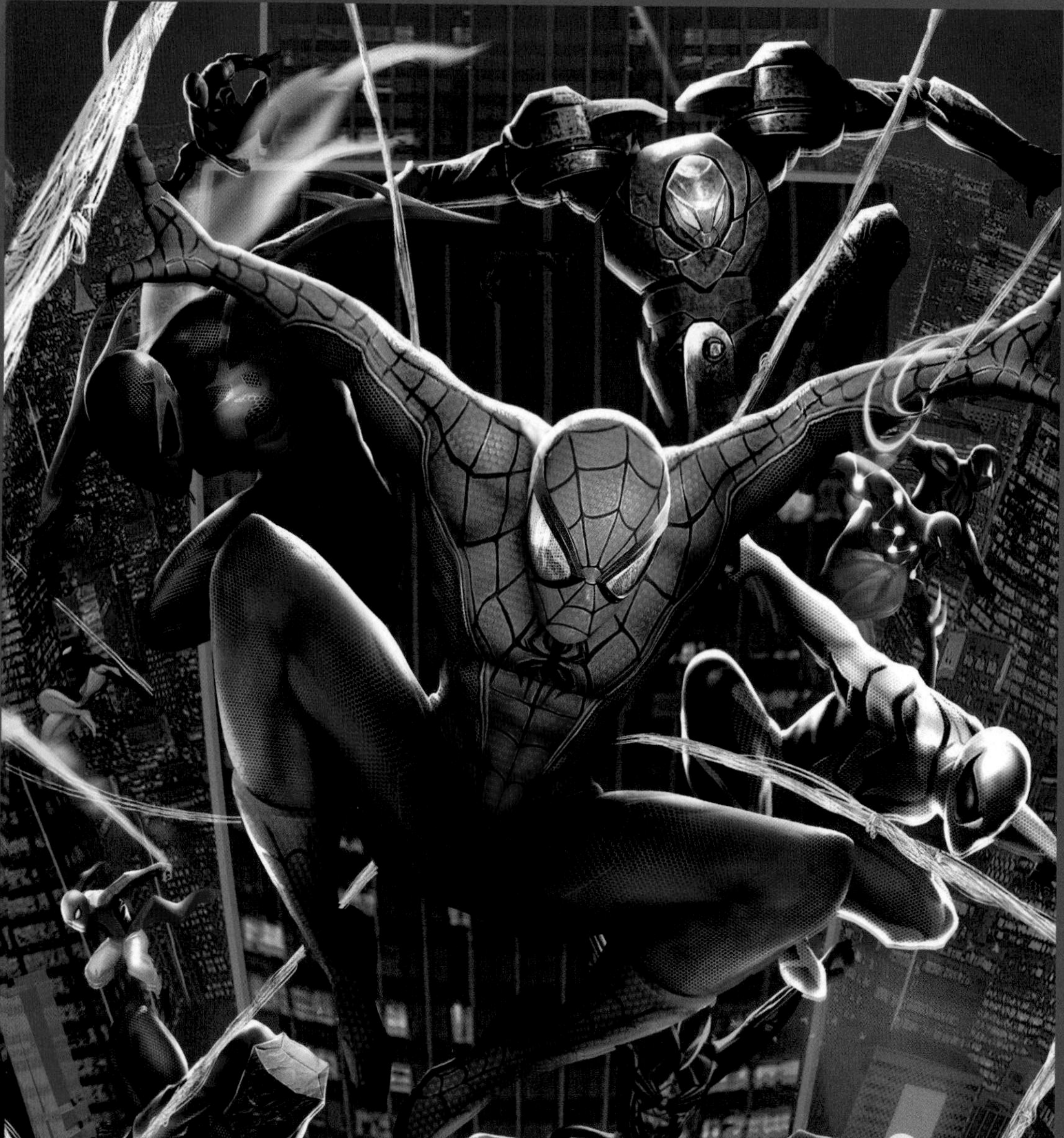

#39 CHINESE NEW YEAR CONNECTING VARIANT BY JIE YUAN

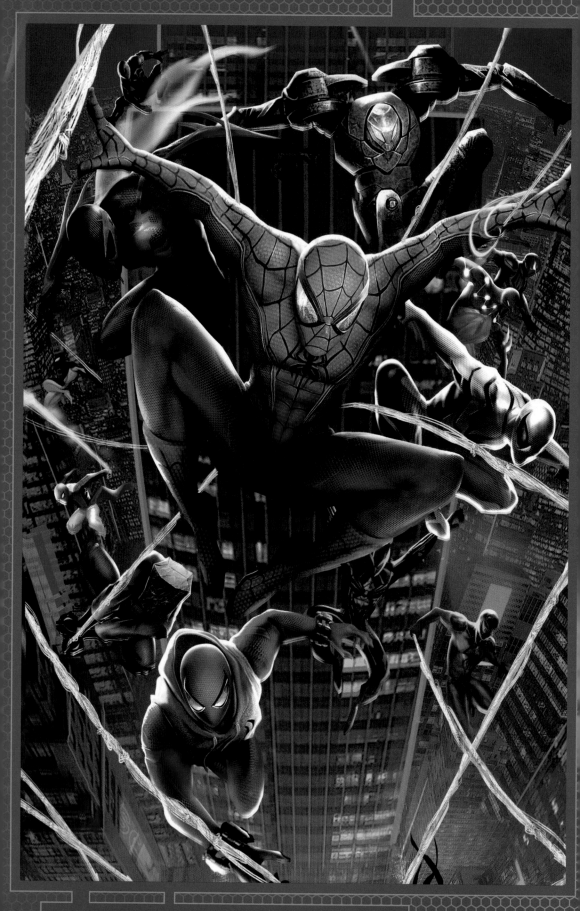

43

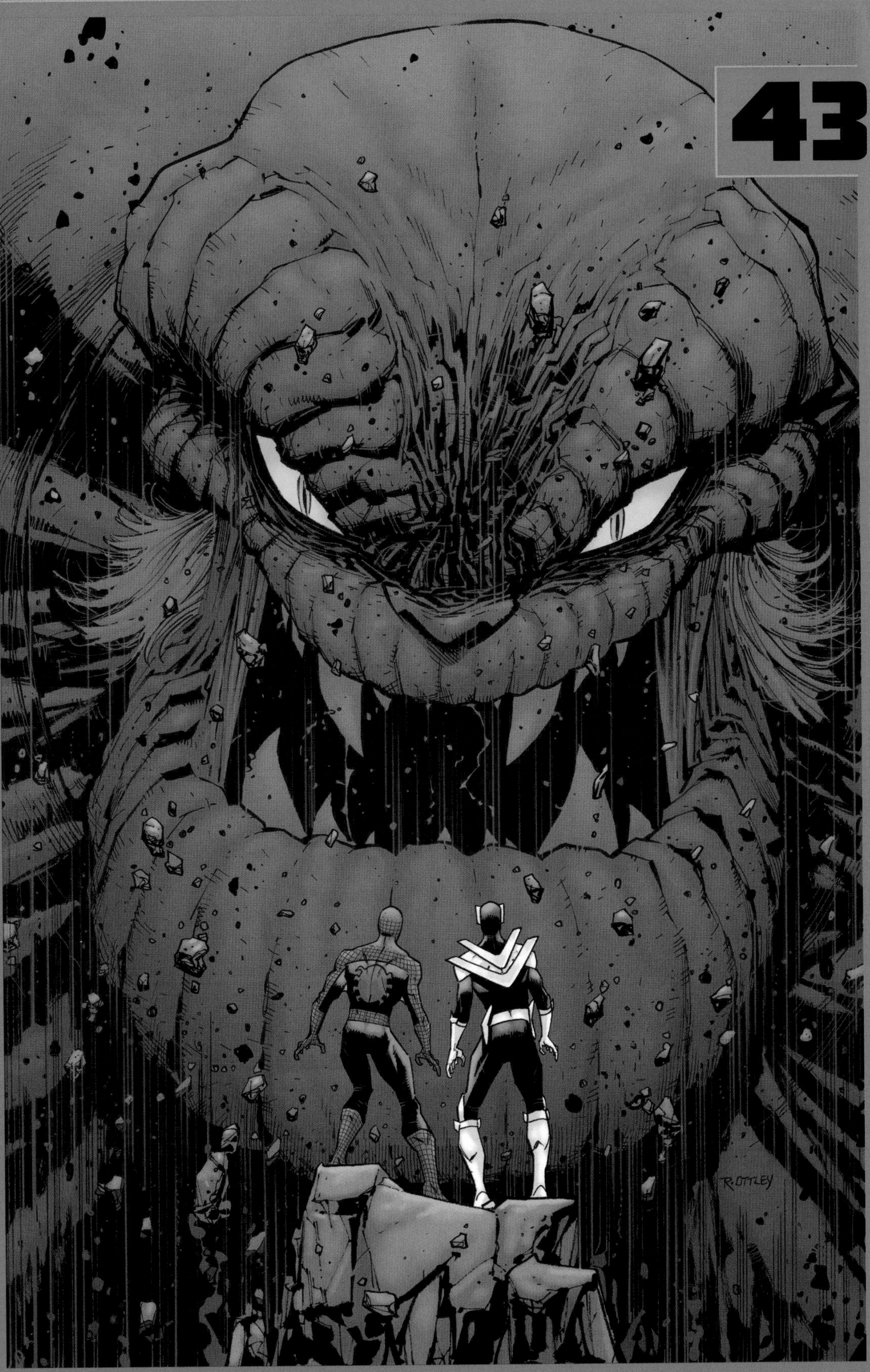
R. OTTLEY

TRUE COMPANIONS PART 3

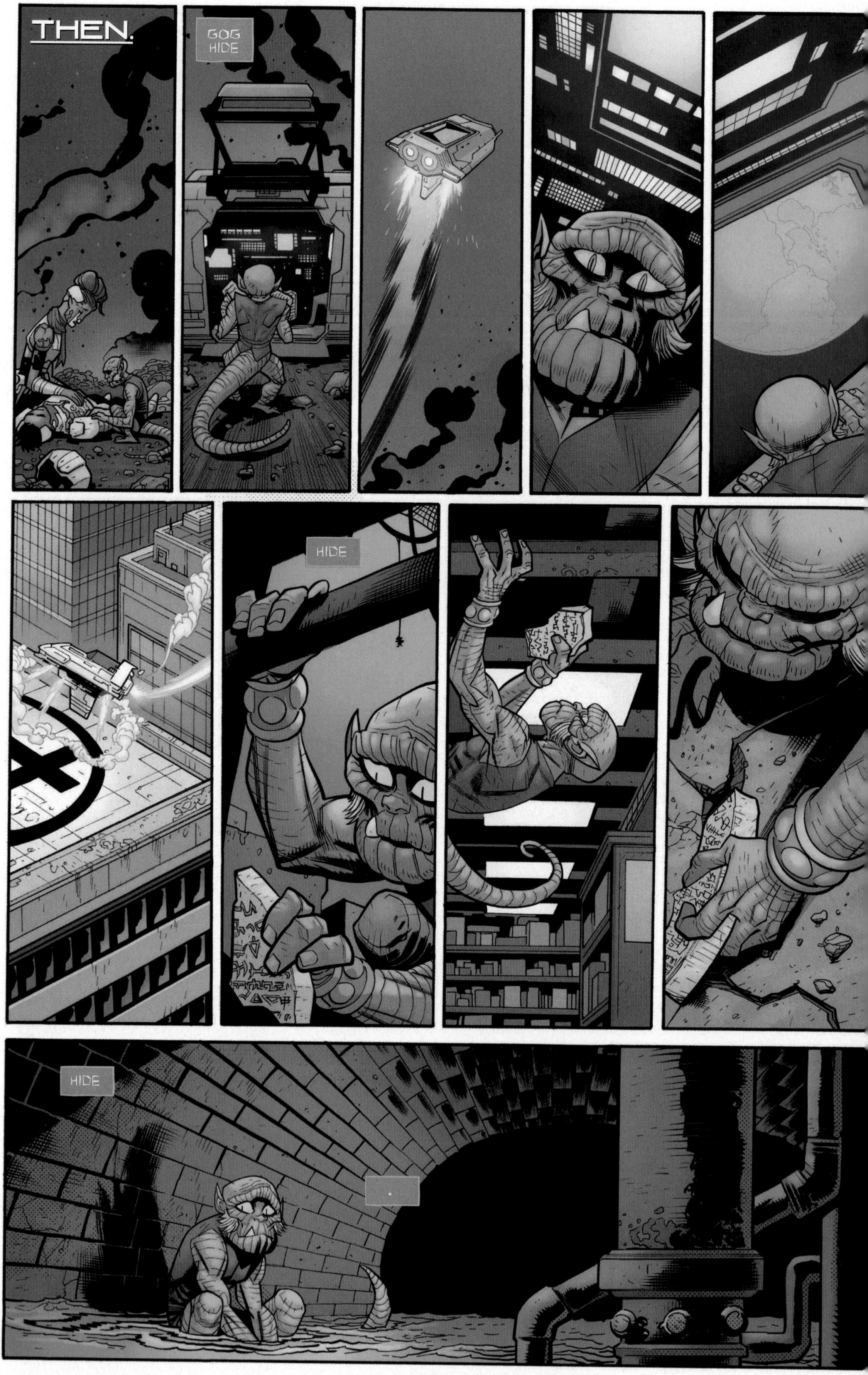
THEN.
GOG
HIDE
HIDE
HIDE
.

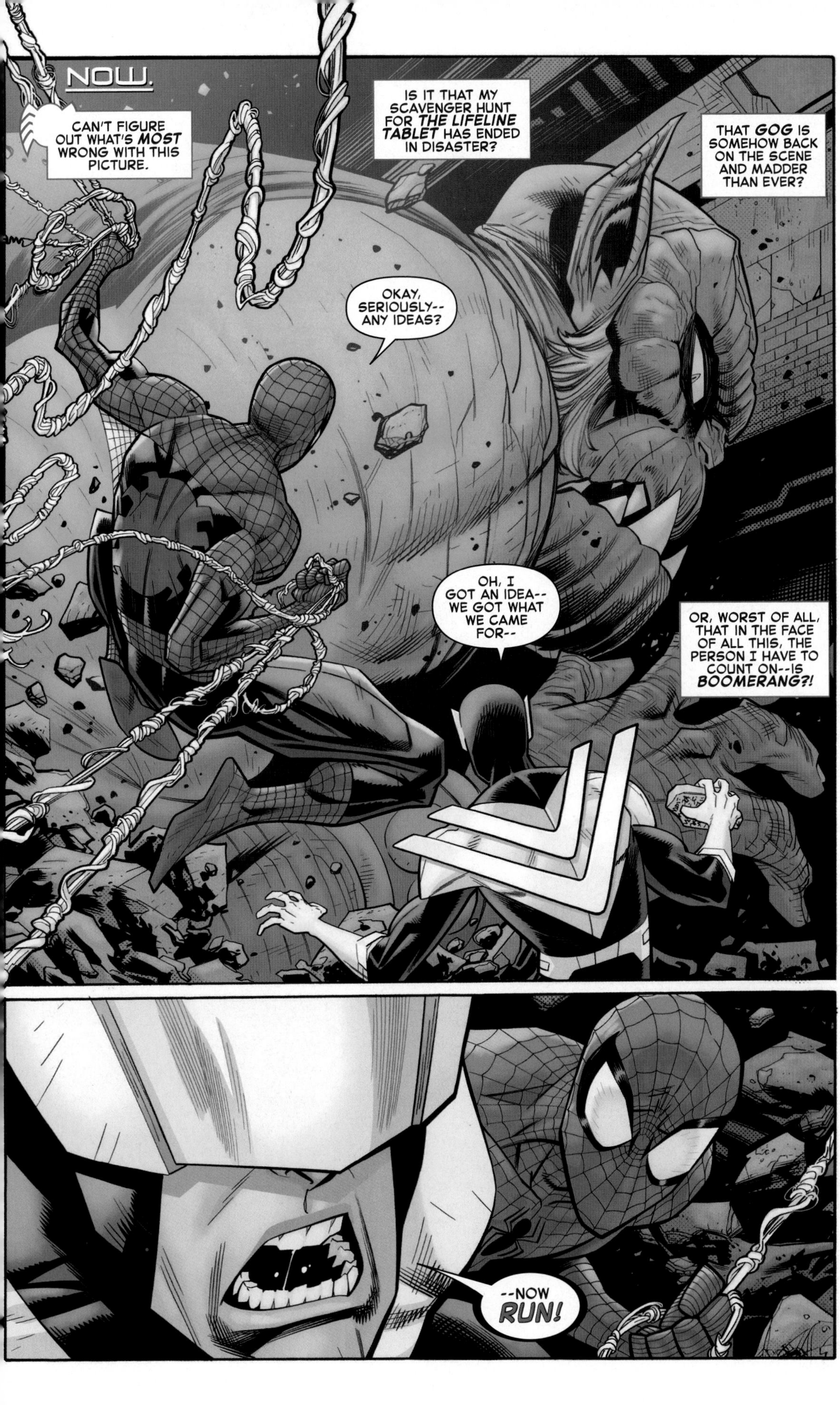
NOW.
CAN'T FIGURE OUT WHAT'S MOST WRONG WITH THIS PICTURE.
IS IT THAT MY SCAVENGER HUNT FOR THE LIFELINE TABLET HAS ENDED IN DISASTER?
THAT GOG IS SOMEHOW BACK ON THE SCENE AND MADDER THAN EVER?
OKAY, SERIOUSLY-- ANY IDEAS?
OH, I GOT AN IDEA-- WE GOT WHAT WE CAME FOR--
OR, WORST OF ALL, THAT IN THE FACE OF ALL THIS, THE PERSON I HAVE TO COUNT ON--IS BOOMERANG?!
--NOW RUN!

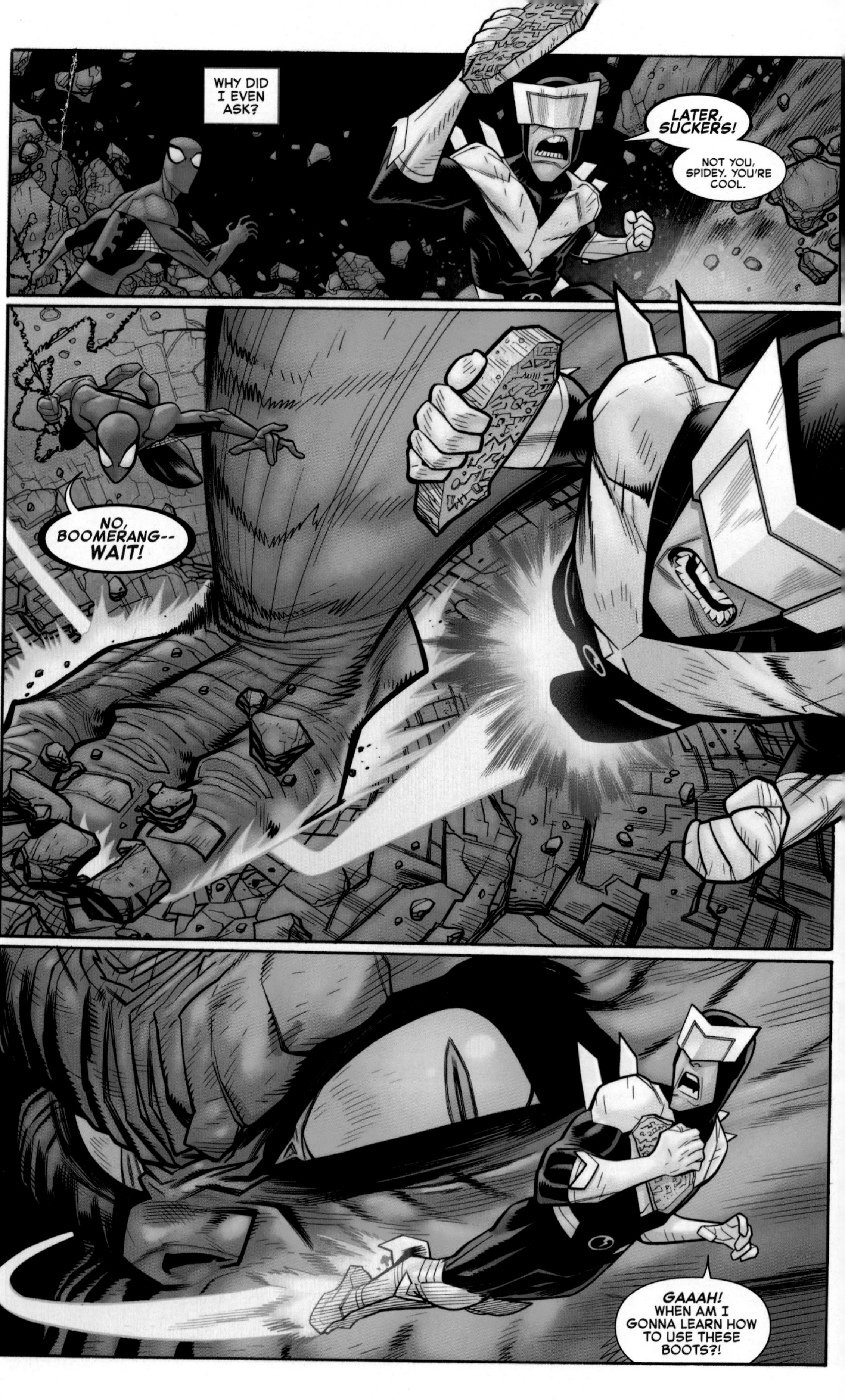
WHY DID I EVEN ASK?
LATER, SUCKERS!
NOT YOU, SPIDEY. YOU'RE COOL.
NO, BOOMERANG-- WAIT!
GAAAH! WHEN AM I GONNA LEARN HOW TO USE THESE BOOTS?!

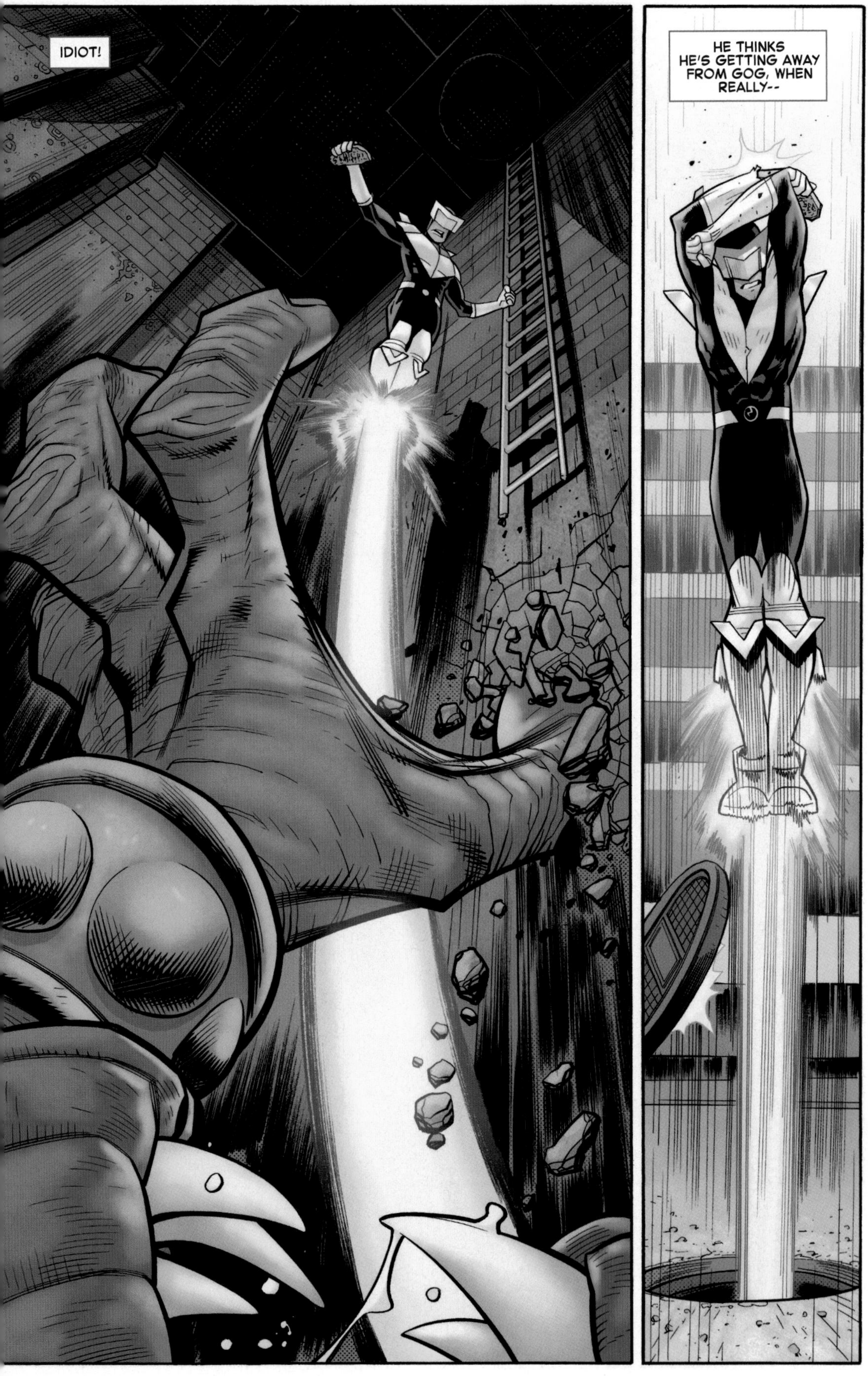
IDIOT!
HE THINKS HE'S GETTING AWAY FROM GOG, WHEN REALLY--

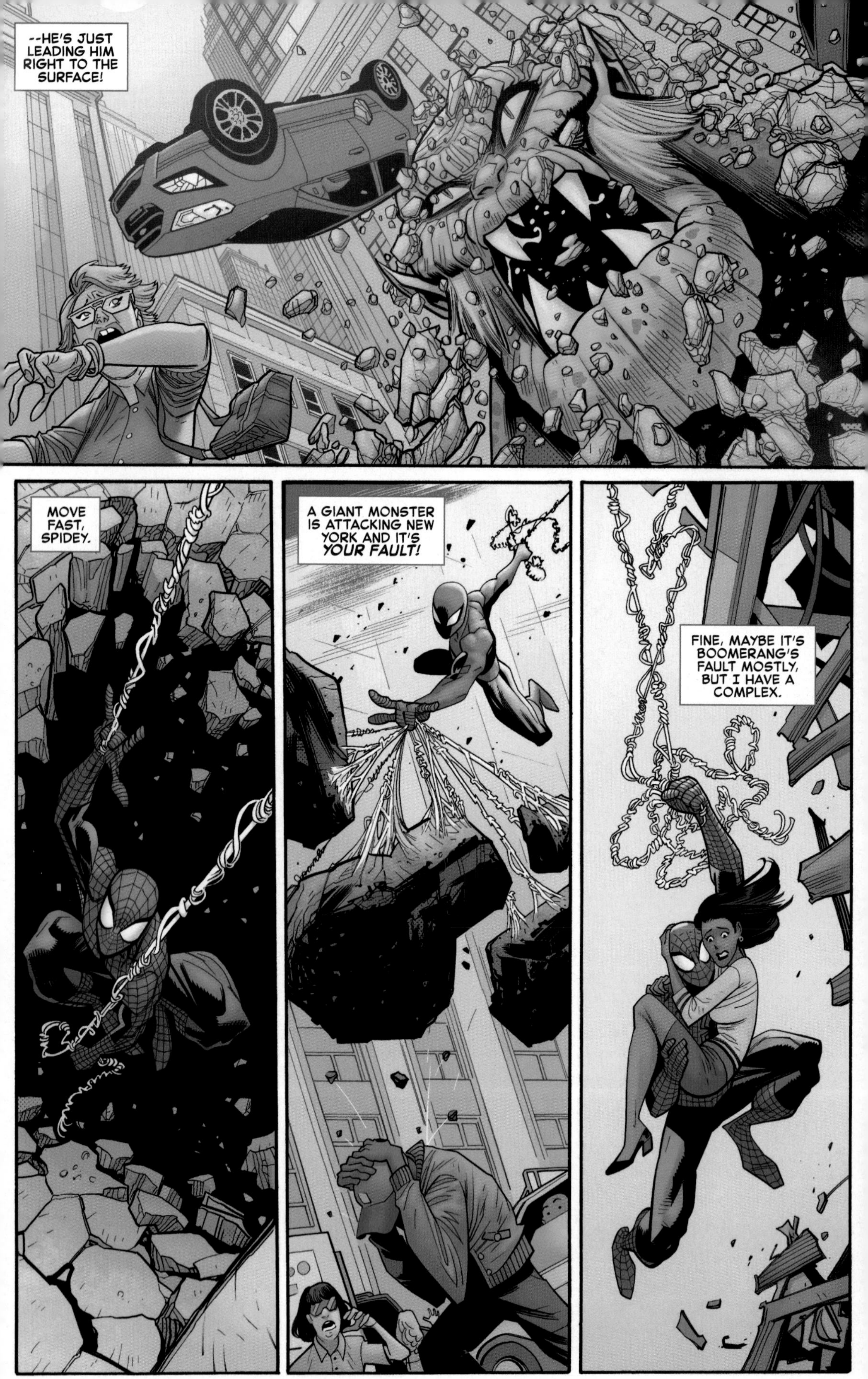
--HE'S JUST LEADING HIM RIGHT TO THE SURFACE!
MOVE FAST, SPIDEY.
A GIANT MONSTER IS ATTACKING NEW YORK AND IT'S *YOUR FAULT!*
FINE, MAYBE IT'S BOOMERANG'S FAULT MOSTLY, BUT I HAVE A COMPLEX.

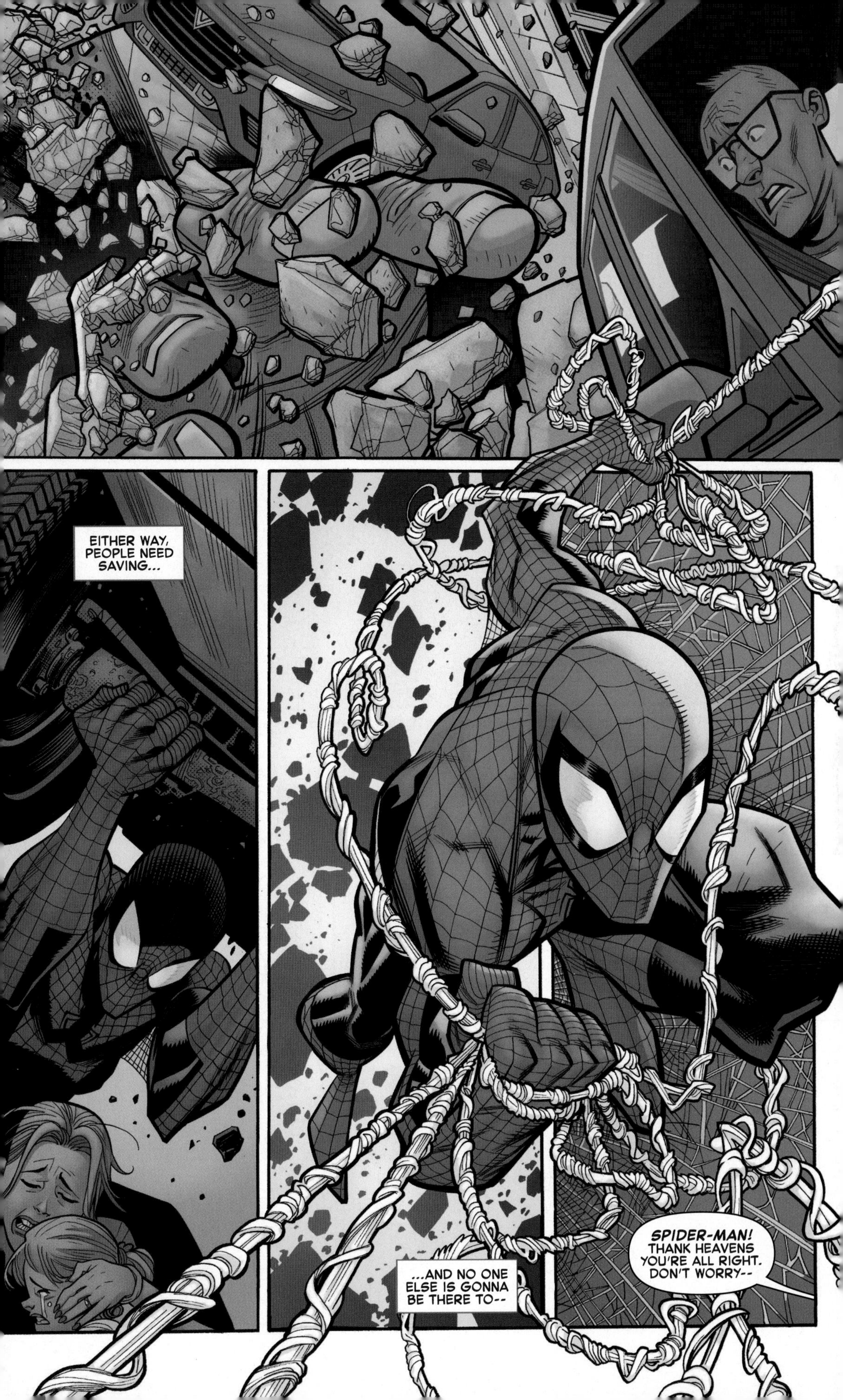
EITHER WAY, PEOPLE NEED SAVING...
...AND NO ONE ELSE IS GONNA BE THERE TO--
SPIDER-MAN! THANK HEAVENS YOU'RE ALL RIGHT. DON'T WORRY--

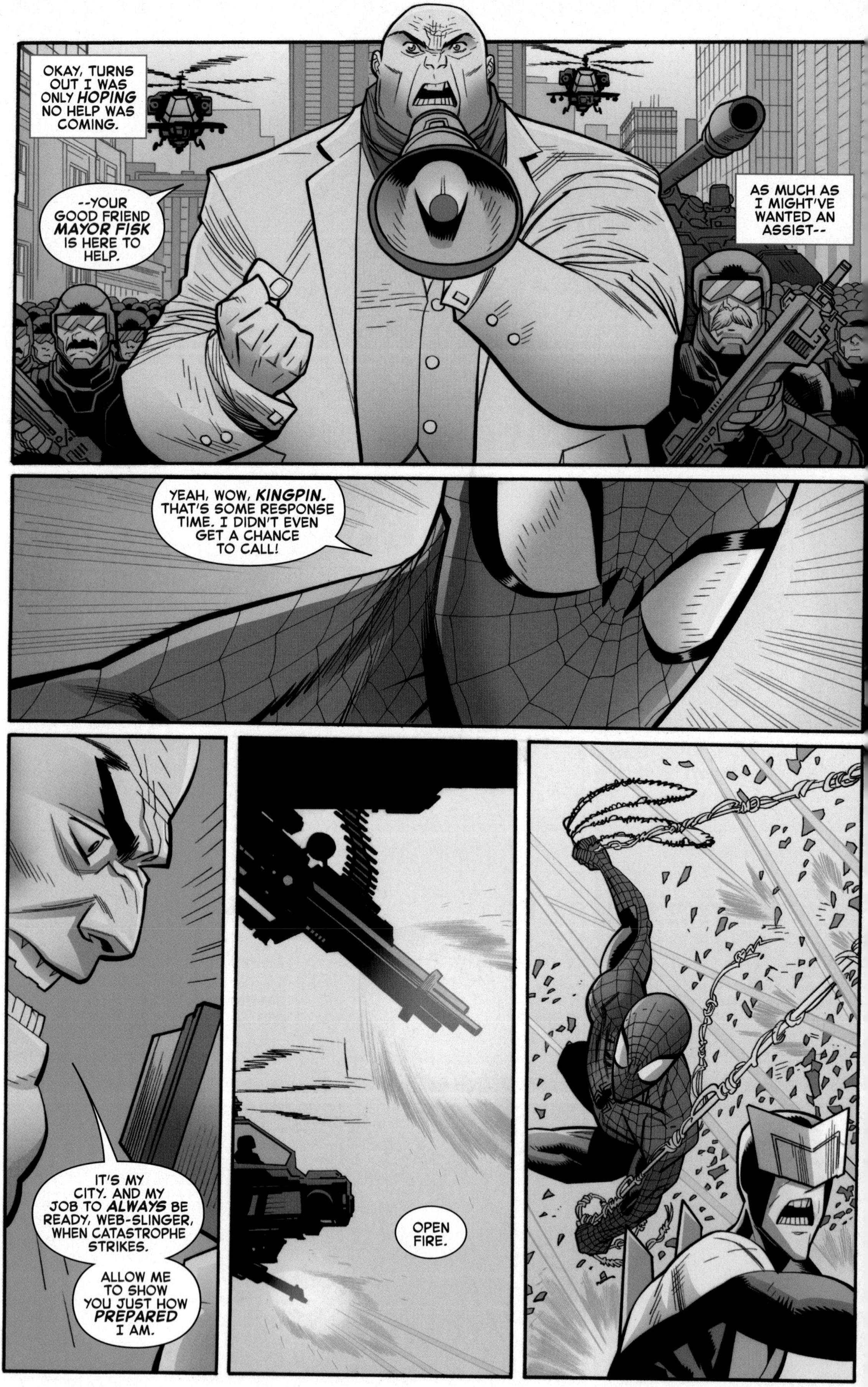

OKAY, TURNS OUT I WAS ONLY *HOPING* NO HELP WAS COMING.
--YOUR GOOD FRIEND *MAYOR FISK* IS HERE TO HELP.
AS MUCH AS I MIGHT'VE WANTED AN ASSIST--
YEAH, WOW, *KINGPIN.* THAT'S SOME RESPONSE TIME. I DIDN'T EVEN GET A CHANCE TO CALL!
IT'S MY CITY. AND MY JOB TO *ALWAYS* BE READY, WEB-SLINGER, WHEN CATASTROPHE STRIKES.
ALLOW ME TO SHOW YOU JUST HOW *PREPARED* I AM.
OPEN FIRE.

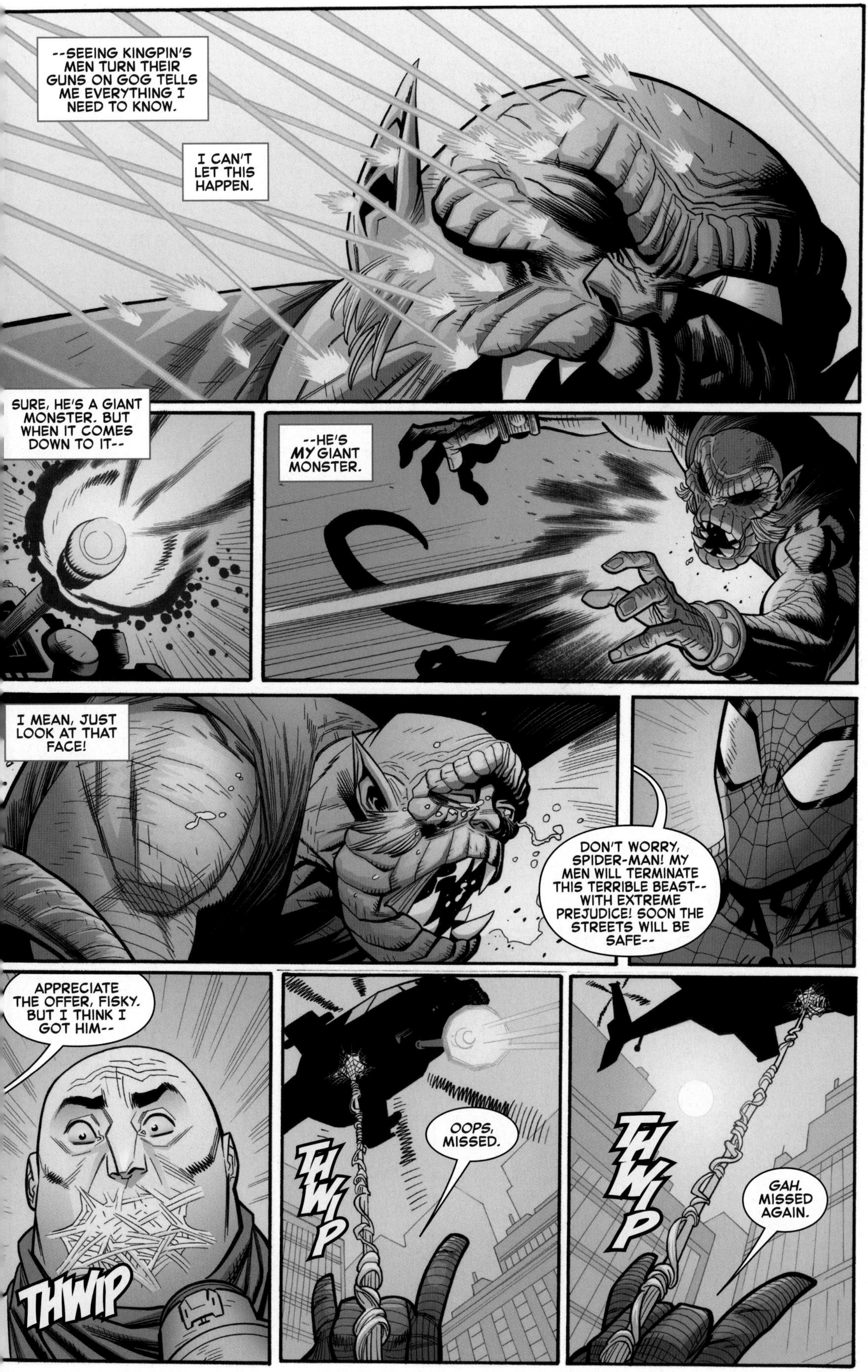

--SEEING KINGPIN'S MEN TURN THEIR GUNS ON GOG TELLS ME EVERYTHING I NEED TO KNOW.
I CAN'T LET THIS HAPPEN.
SURE, HE'S A GIANT MONSTER. BUT WHEN IT COMES DOWN TO IT--
--HE'S MY GIANT MONSTER.
I MEAN, JUST LOOK AT THAT FACE!
DON'T WORRY, SPIDER-MAN! MY MEN WILL TERMINATE THIS TERRIBLE BEAST--WITH EXTREME PREJUDICE! SOON THE STREETS WILL BE SAFE--
APPRECIATE THE OFFER, FISKY. BUT I THINK I GOT HIM--
THWIP
THWIP
OOPS, MISSED.
THWIP
GAH. MISSED AGAIN.

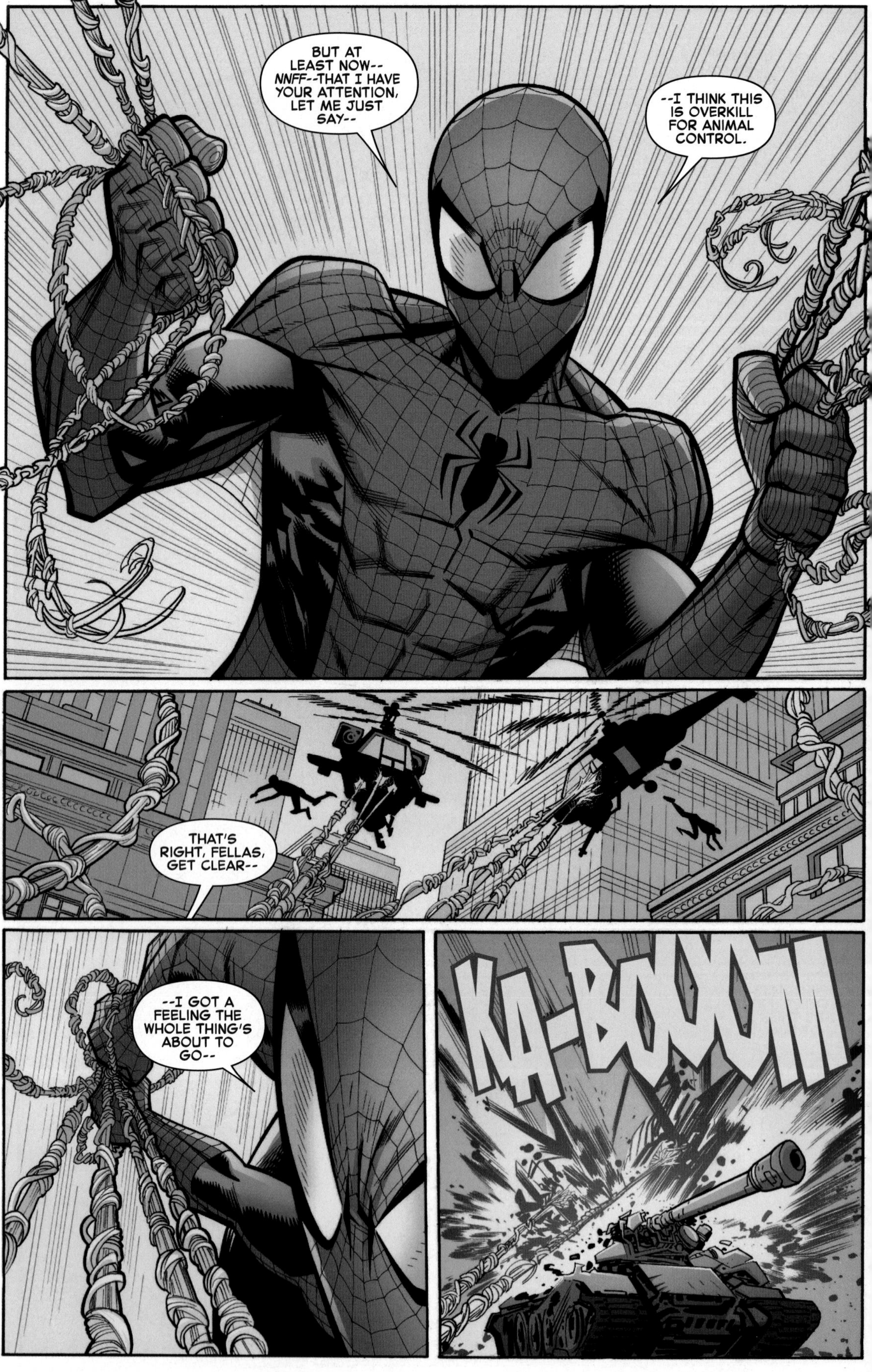
BUT AT LEAST NOW-- *NNFF*--THAT I HAVE YOUR ATTENTION, LET ME JUST SAY--
--I THINK THIS IS OVERKILL FOR ANIMAL CONTROL.
THAT'S RIGHT, FELLAS, GET CLEAR--
--I GOT A FEELING THE WHOLE THING'S ABOUT TO GO--
KA-BOOOM

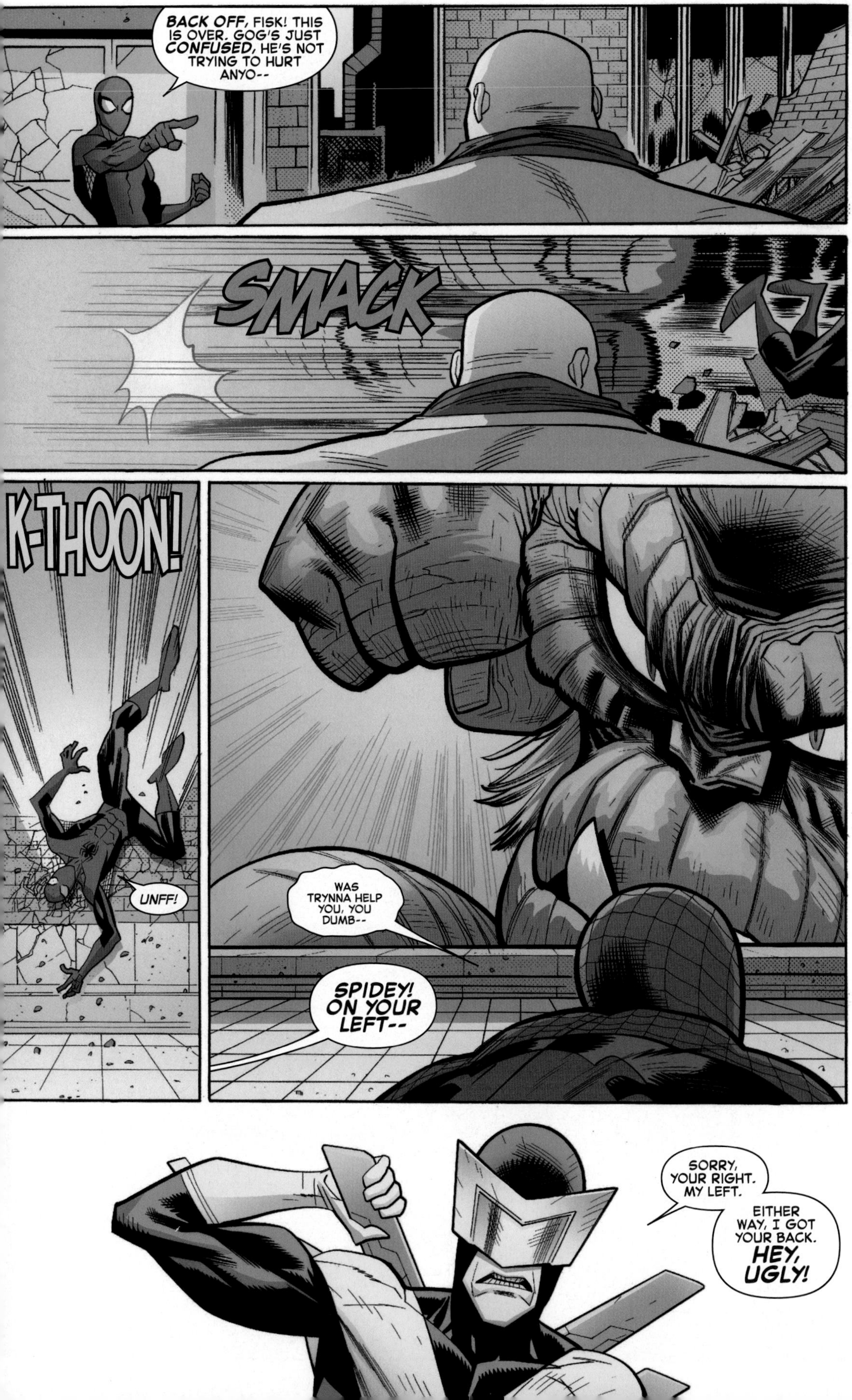
BACK OFF, FISK! THIS IS OVER. GOG'S JUST CONFUSED, HE'S NOT TRYING TO HURT ANYO--
SMACK
K-THOON!
UNFF!
WAS TRYNNA HELP YOU, YOU DUMB--
SPIDEY! ON YOUR LEFT--
SORRY, YOUR RIGHT. MY LEFT.
EITHER WAY, I GOT YOUR BACK. HEY, UGLY!

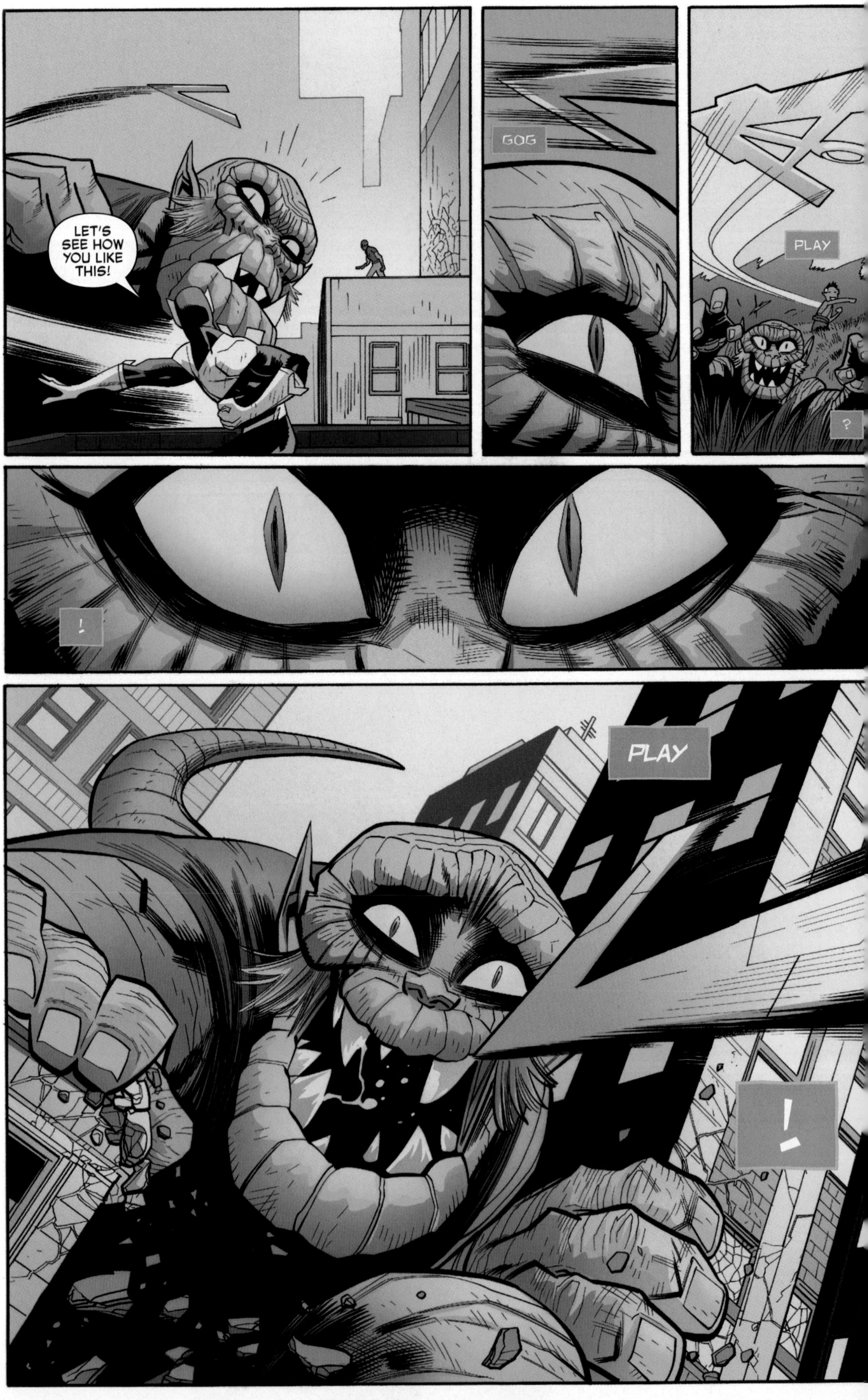
LET'S SEE HOW YOU LIKE THIS!
GOG
PLAY
?
!
PLAY
!

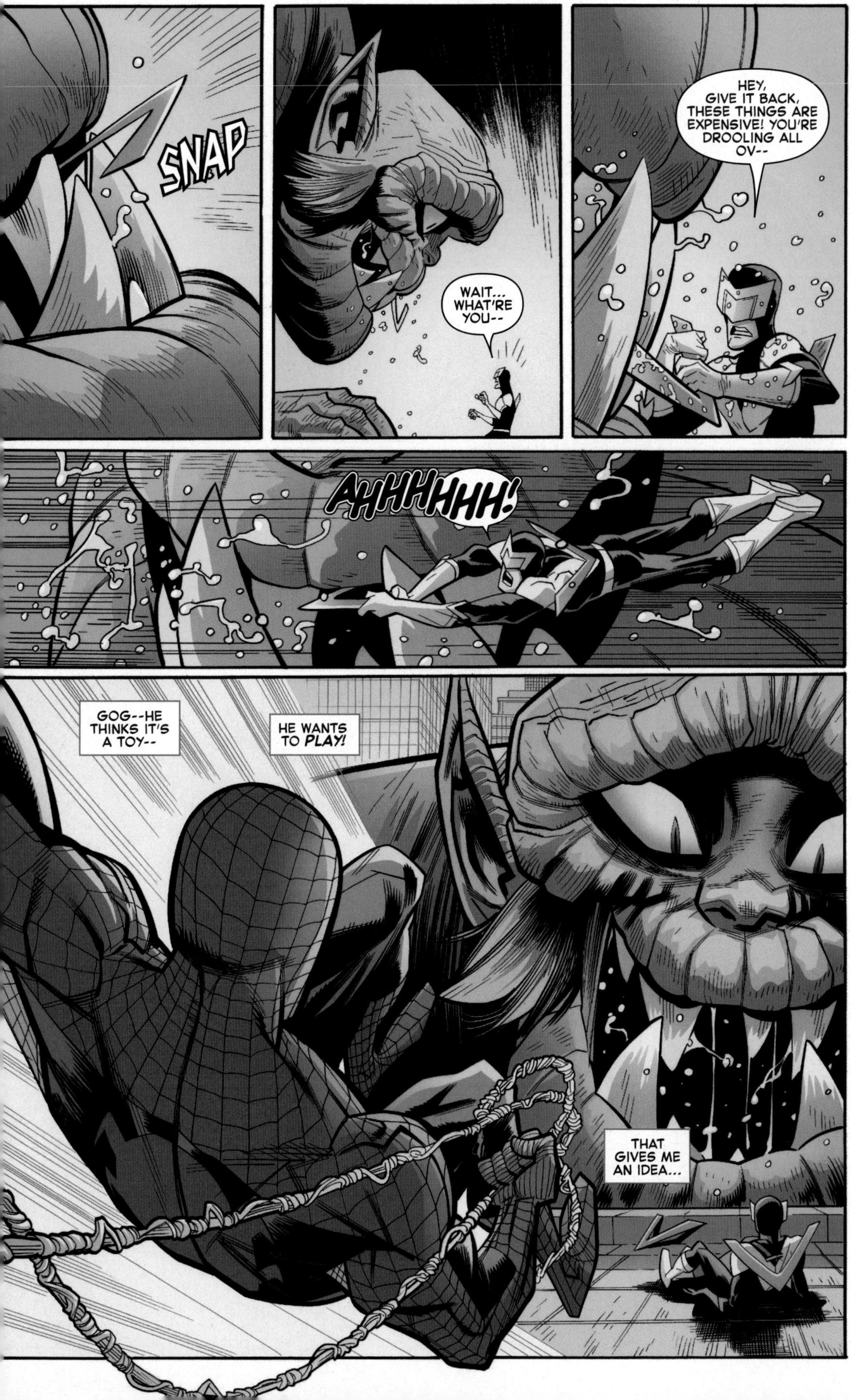
SNAP
WAIT... WHAT'RE YOU--
HEY, GIVE IT BACK, THESE THINGS ARE EXPENSIVE! YOU'RE DROOLING ALL OV--
AHHHHHHH!
GOG--HE THINKS IT'S A TOY--
HE WANTS TO *PLAY!*
THAT GIVES ME AN IDEA...

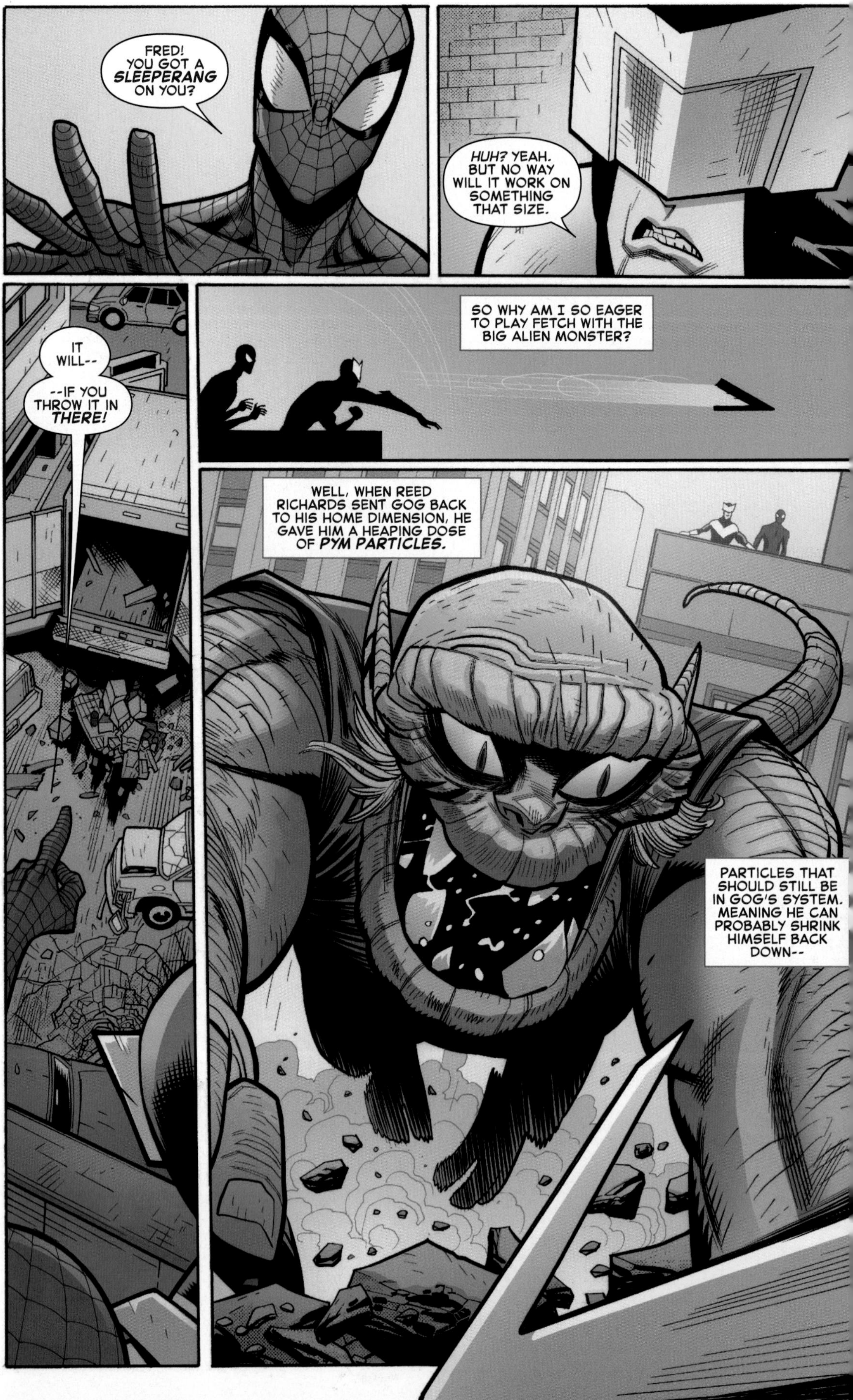
FRED! YOU GOT A SLEEPERANG ON YOU?
HUH? YEAH. BUT NO WAY WILL IT WORK ON SOMETHING THAT SIZE.
IT WILL--
--IF YOU THROW IT IN THERE!
SO WHY AM I SO EAGER TO PLAY FETCH WITH THE BIG ALIEN MONSTER?
WELL, WHEN REED RICHARDS SENT GOG BACK TO HIS HOME DIMENSION, HE GAVE HIM A HEAPING DOSE OF PYM PARTICLES.
PARTICLES THAT SHOULD STILL BE IN GOG'S SYSTEM. MEANING HE CAN PROBABLY SHRINK HIMSELF BACK DOWN--

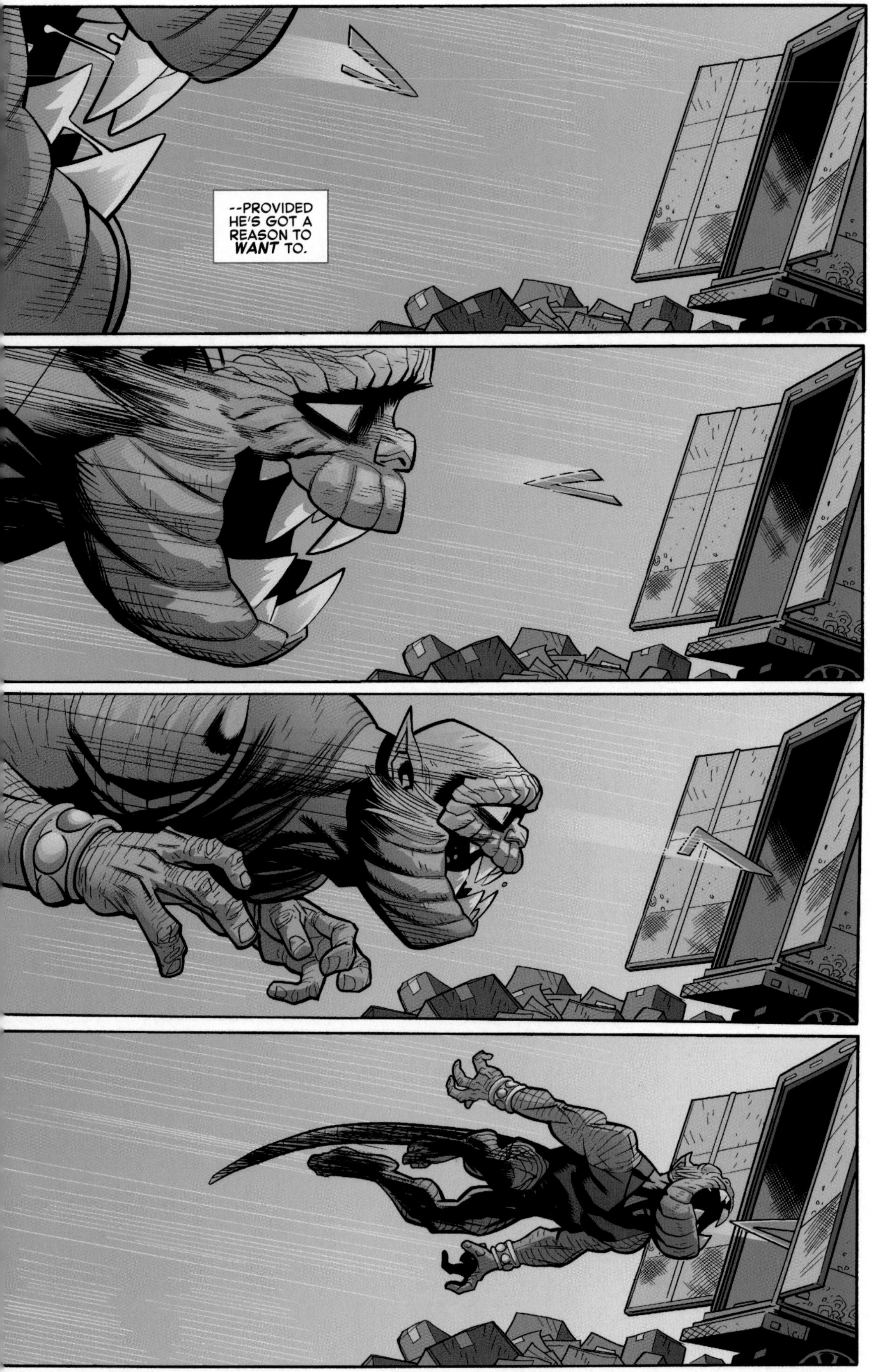
--PROVIDED HE'S GOT A REASON TO *WANT* TO.

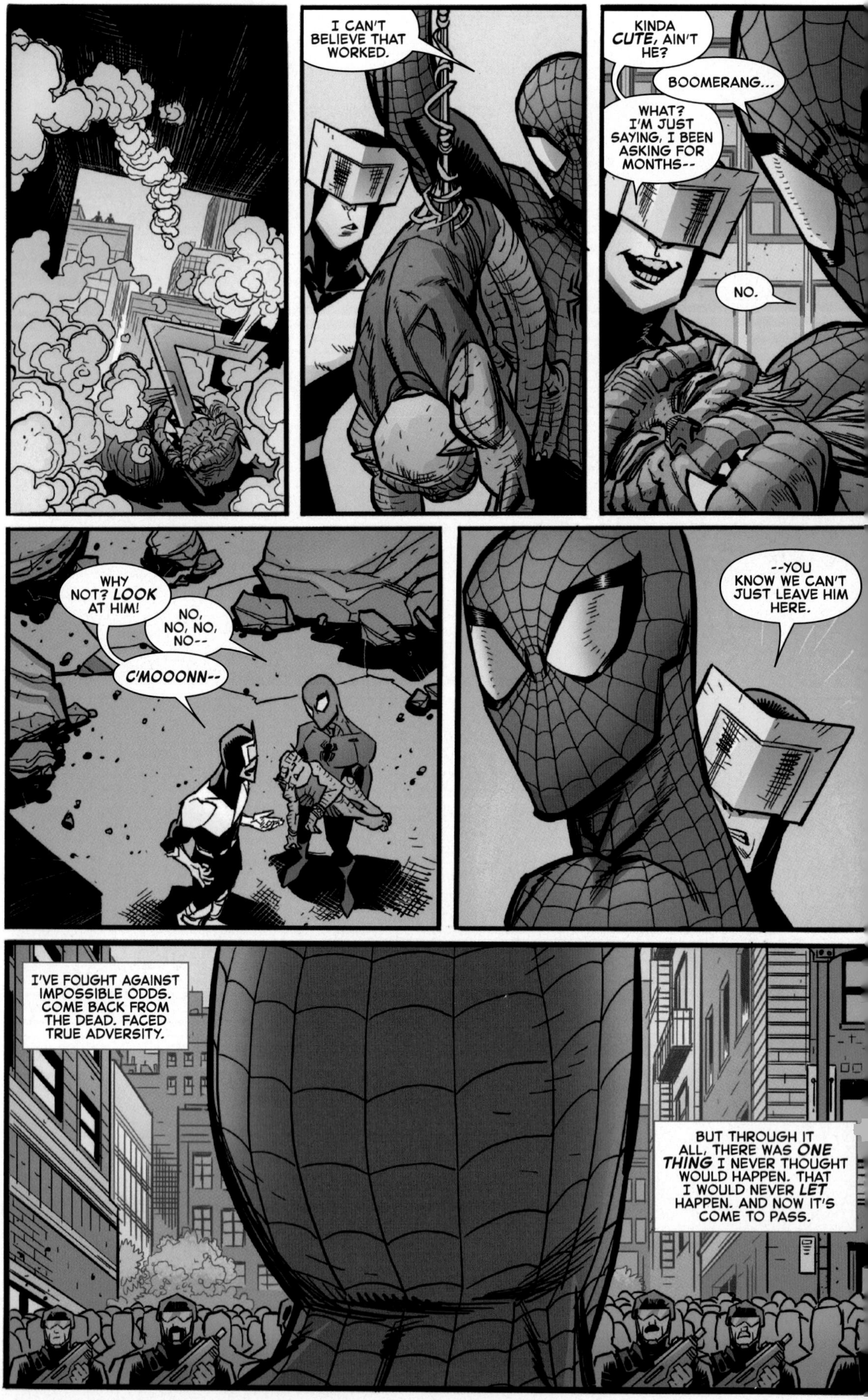
I CAN'T BELIEVE THAT WORKED.
KINDA *CUTE,* AIN'T HE?
BOOMERANG...
WHAT? I'M JUST SAYING, I BEEN ASKING FOR MONTHS--
NO.
WHY NOT? *LOOK* AT HIM!
NO, NO, NO, NO--
C'MOOONN--
--YOU KNOW WE CAN'T JUST LEAVE HIM HERE.
I'VE FOUGHT AGAINST IMPOSSIBLE ODDS. COME BACK FROM THE DEAD. FACED TRUE ADVERSITY.
BUT THROUGH IT ALL, THERE WAS *ONE THING* I NEVER THOUGHT WOULD HAPPEN. THAT I WOULD NEVER *LET* HAPPEN. AND NOW IT'S COME TO PASS.

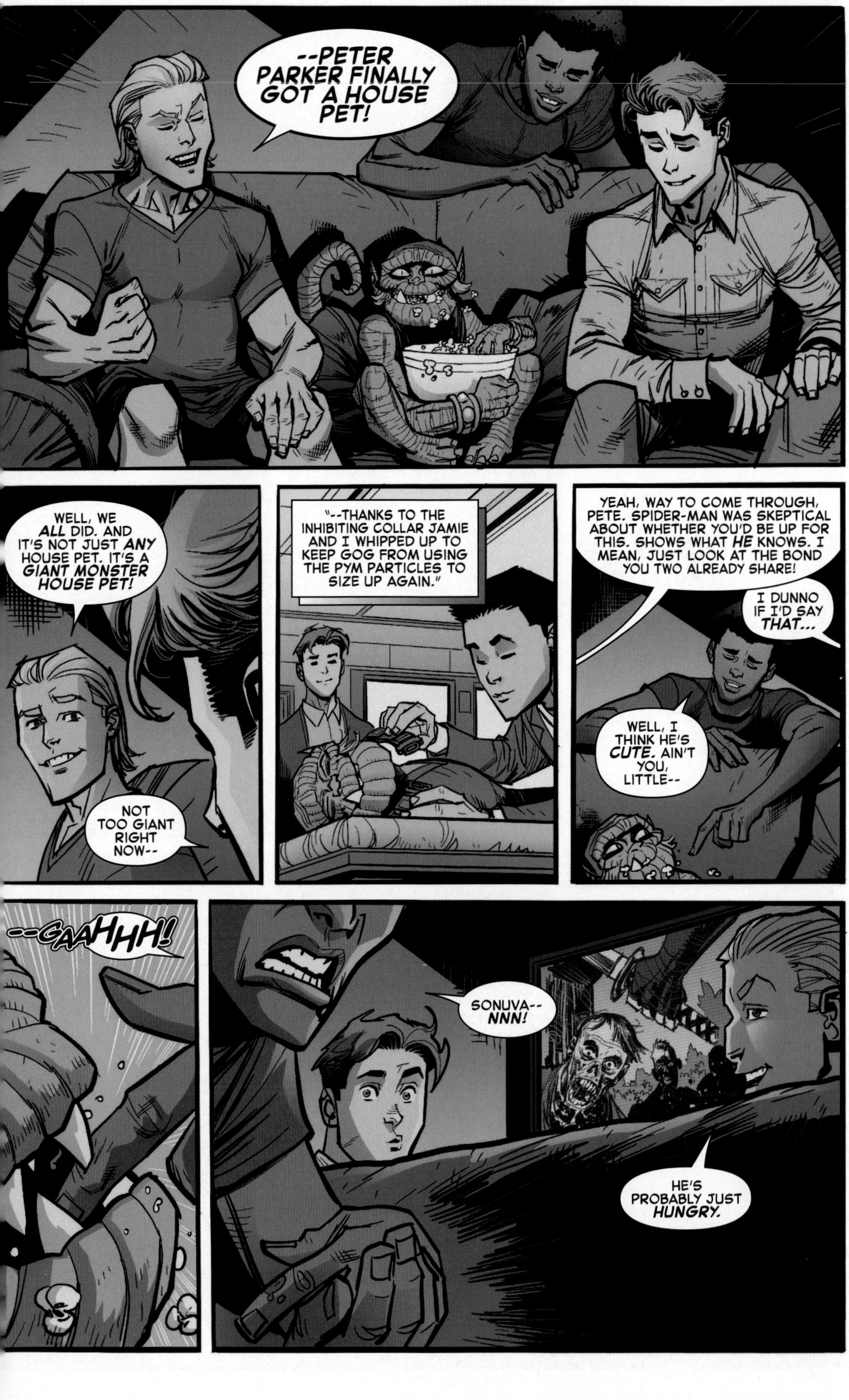
--PETER PARKER FINALLY GOT A HOUSE PET!
WELL, WE ALL DID. AND IT'S NOT JUST ANY HOUSE PET. IT'S A GIANT MONSTER HOUSE PET!
NOT TOO GIANT RIGHT NOW--
"--THANKS TO THE INHIBITING COLLAR JAMIE AND I WHIPPED UP TO KEEP GOG FROM USING THE PYM PARTICLES TO SIZE UP AGAIN."
YEAH, WAY TO COME THROUGH, PETE. SPIDER-MAN WAS SKEPTICAL ABOUT WHETHER YOU'D BE UP FOR THIS. SHOWS WHAT HE KNOWS. I MEAN, JUST LOOK AT THE BOND YOU TWO ALREADY SHARE!
I DUNNO IF I'D SAY THAT...
WELL, I THINK HE'S CUTE. AIN'T YOU, LITTLE--
--GAAHHH!
SONUVA-- NNN!
HE'S PROBABLY JUST HUNGRY.

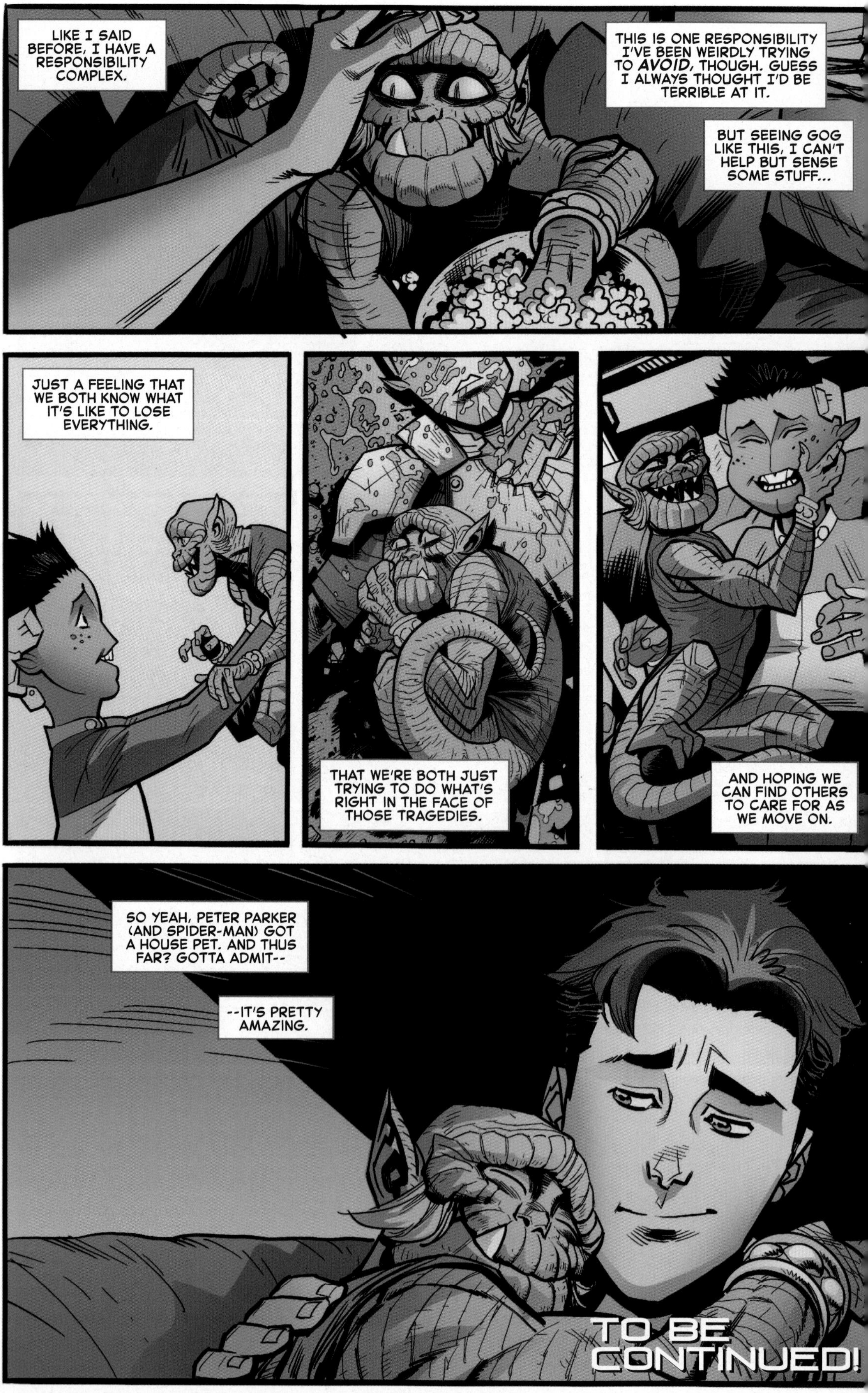
LIKE I SAID BEFORE, I HAVE A RESPONSIBILITY COMPLEX.
THIS IS ONE RESPONSIBILITY I'VE BEEN WEIRDLY TRYING TO *AVOID*, THOUGH. GUESS I ALWAYS THOUGHT I'D BE TERRIBLE AT IT.
BUT SEEING GOG LIKE THIS, I CAN'T HELP BUT SENSE SOME STUFF...
JUST A FEELING THAT WE BOTH KNOW WHAT IT'S LIKE TO LOSE EVERYTHING.
THAT WE'RE BOTH JUST TRYING TO DO WHAT'S RIGHT IN THE FACE OF THOSE TRAGEDIES.
AND HOPING WE CAN FIND OTHERS TO CARE FOR AS WE MOVE ON.
SO YEAH, PETER PARKER (AND SPIDER-MAN) GOT A HOUSE PET. AND THUS FAR? GOTTA ADMIT--
--IT'S PRETTY AMAZING.
TO BE CONTINUED!

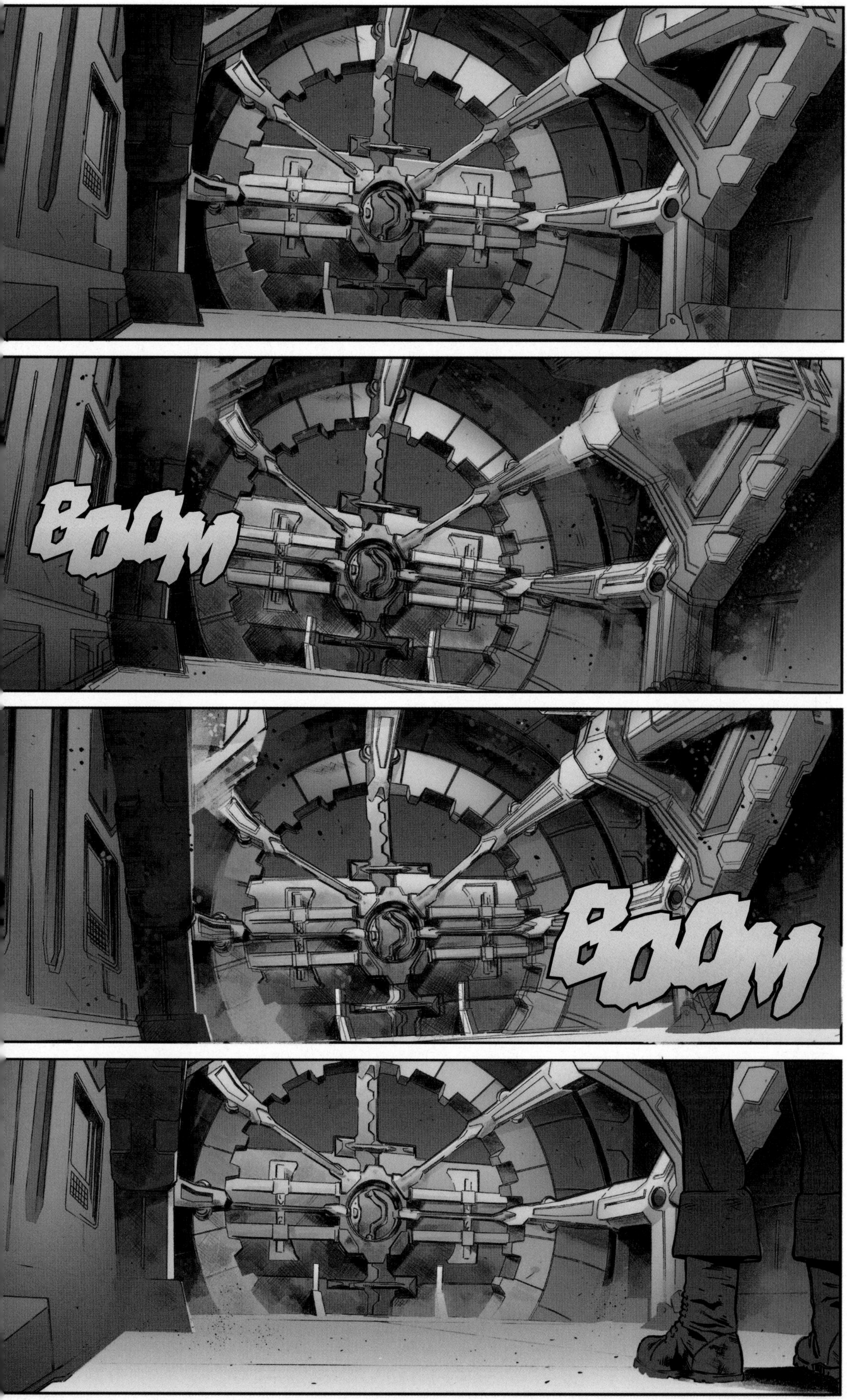
BOOM
BOOM

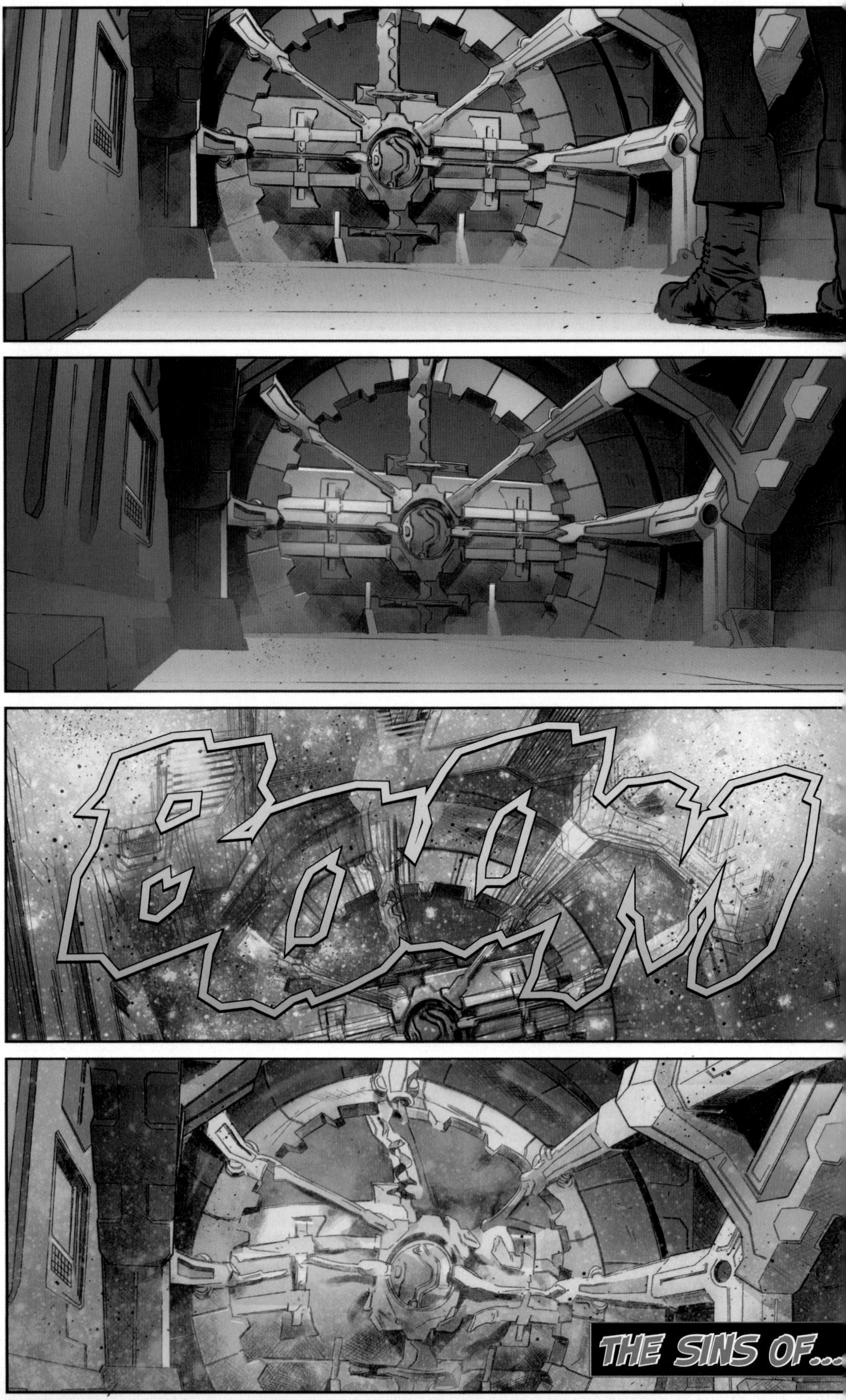
BOOM
THE SINS OF...

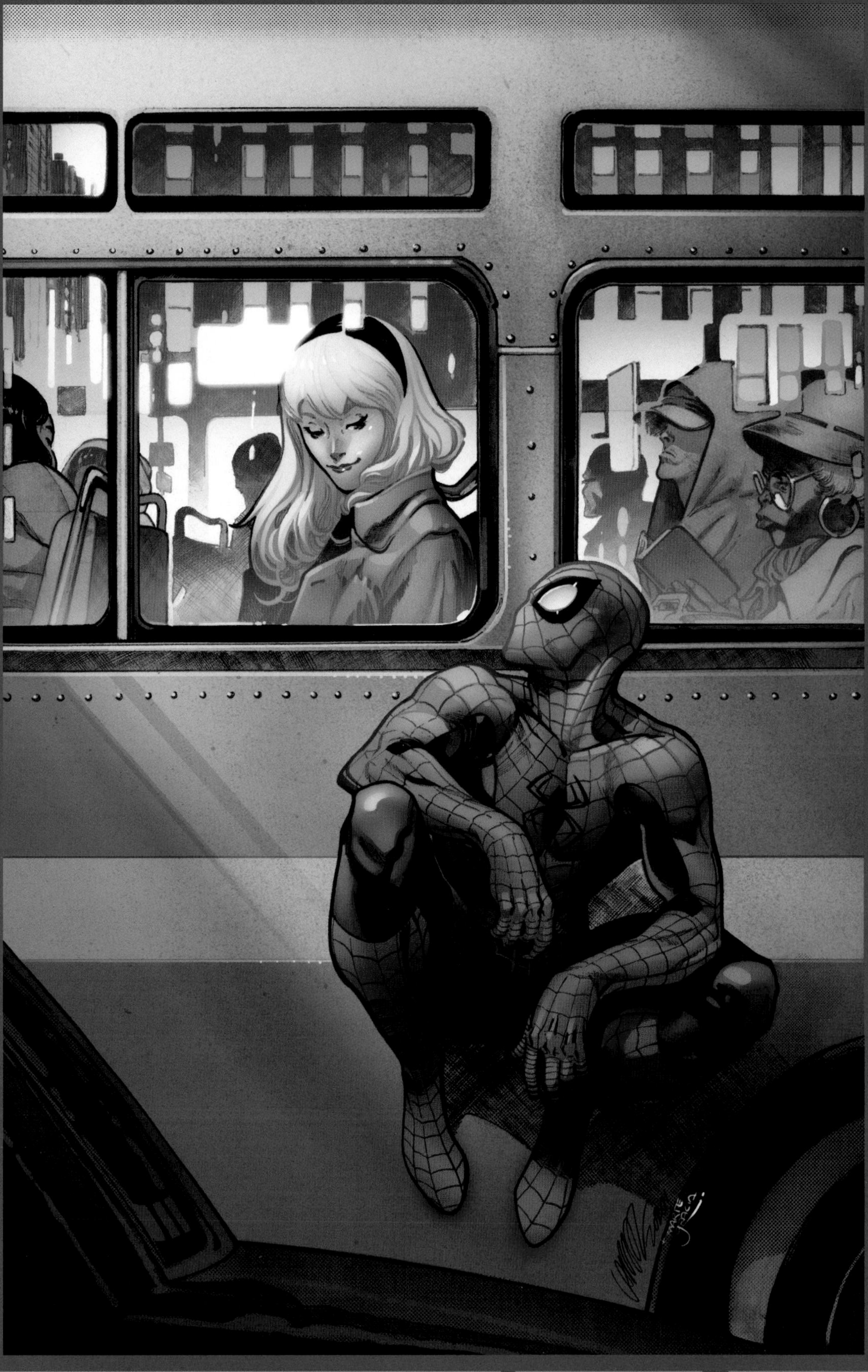

#39 GWEN STACY VARIANT BY PEPE LARRAZ & MARTE GRACIA

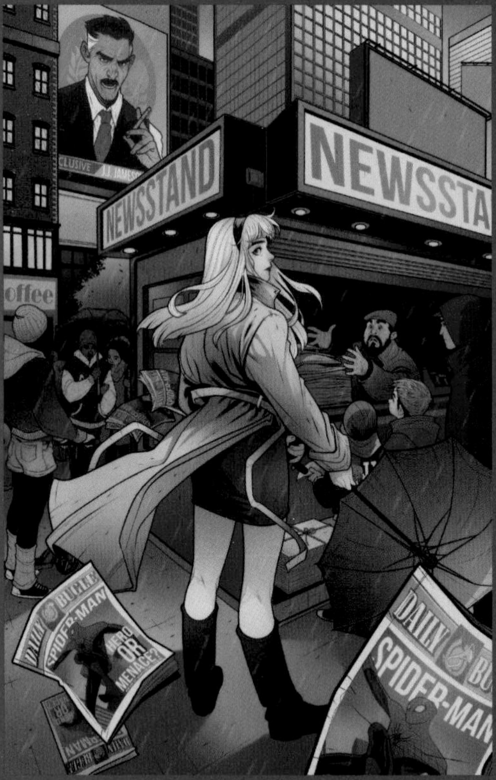
NEWSSTAND
SPIDER-MAN
HERO OR MENACE?

#40 GWEN STACY VARIANT BY
ELIZABETH TORQUE

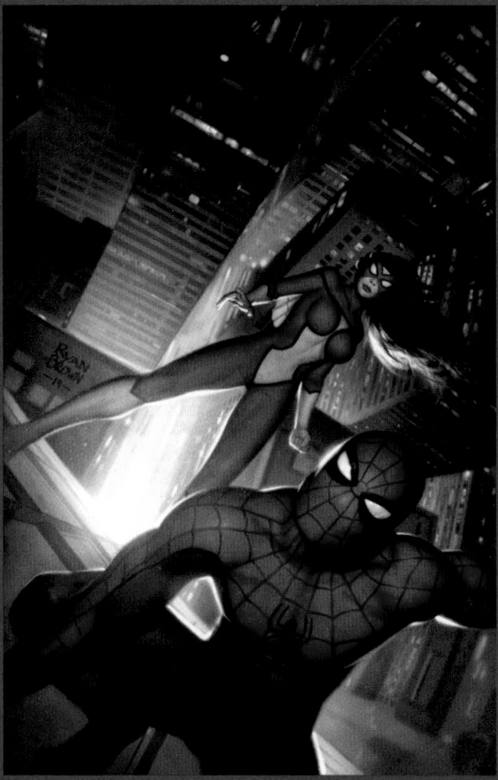

#41 SPIDER-WOMAN VARIANT BY
RYAN BROWN

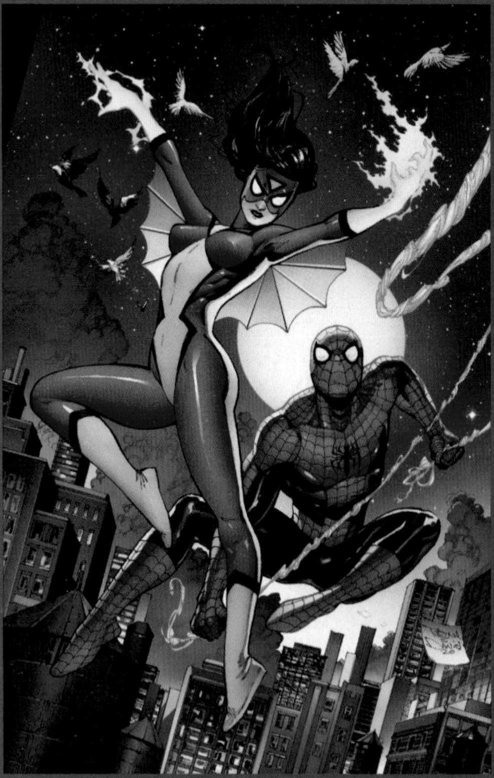

#42 SPIDER-WOMAN VARIANT BY
TONY DANIEL & DAVID CURIEL

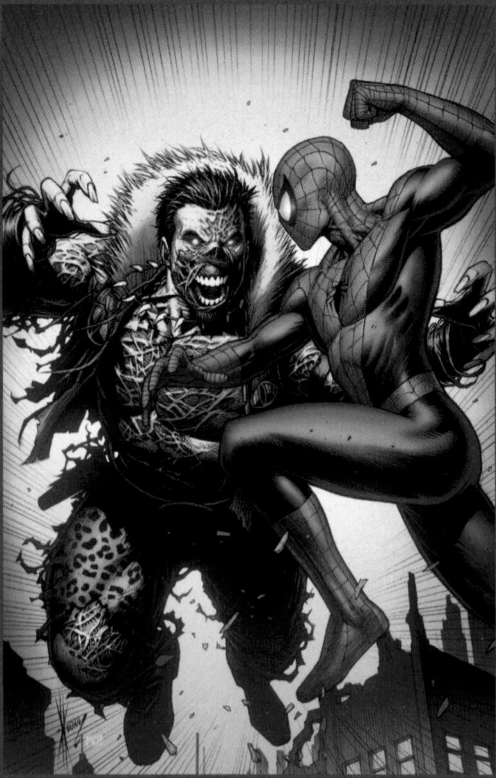

#43 MARVEL ZOMBIES VARIANT BY
DALE KEOWN & MORRY HOLLOWELL